FLORIDA'S BIRDS

Second Edition

A FIELD GUIDE AND REFERENCE

David S. Maehr
and Herbert W. Kale II

Illustrated by Karl Karalus

PINEAPPLE PRESS, INC. SARASOTA, FLORIDA

Inquiries should be addressed to:

Pineapple Press, Inc.
P.O. Box 3889
Sarasota, Florida 34230

www.pineapplepress.com

Library of Congress Cataloging-in-Publication Data

Maehr, David S., 1955-
   Florida's Birds : a field guide and reference / by David S. Maehr and Herbert W. Kale
II; illustrated by Karl Karalus.— 2nd ed.
        p. cm.
   Rev. ed. of: Florida's birds / H.W. Kale. 1st ed. c1990.
   Includes bibliographical references and index.
   ISBN 1-56164-335-1 (pbk.)
   1.   Birds—Florida—Identification. 2. Birds—Florida. I. Kale, H.W. II. Kale, H.W.
        Florida's birds. III. Title.
QL684.F6K35 2005
598'.09759—dc22

                                                                                2005012184

Second Edition
10 9 8 7

Design by Shé Hicks
Printed and bound in China

CONTENTS

PREFACE

This new edition of *Florida's Birds,* like the first one, was written for the average citizen or visitor to Florida who wants to identify the birds she or he is likely to see—for instance, the birds that frequent a backyard feeder, the gulls or sandpipers standing on the beach, the birds at a park or refuge, or the waders in a roadside ditch. The first edition of this book, published in 1990, was well-accepted, going into over a dozen printings. In this new edition we have attempted to keep the many popular elements of the first book and build on them with an easier-to-use format, many revised paintings and updated accounts, and the addition of thirty-five new species, including pelagic birds such as the jaegers and shearwaters, a new plate of parrots, and additional blackbirds. This edition includes accounts of nearly all of the native species that occur in Florida, and it has been expanded to include species that are sought by birders and that have increasingly been seen in the state or over its waters. We think it is helpful to have similar birds all together on a plate, as they were in the first edition, but this time we have also separated out the illustration of each species to join the main text about that species. We think this provides the best of both approaches. Careful readers who used the previous edition for years will notice a number of other additions and changes, including range maps for seventy-three birds that have unusual distributions—all to make the Florida birding experience easier and more pleasurable.

This edition keeps the useful chapters on beginning bird watching, bird study, bird finding, bird conservation, attracting and feeding birds, care and rehabilitation of sick, injured, or orphaned birds, and human/bird "problems" and suggested solutions. These, we believe, are the portions of the book that help separate it from continental guides and other Florida bird guides. A checklist of the birds of Florida is included in the back of the book, before the illustrated index of common names.

We must note here with great sorrow and respect that since the first edition was published Dr. Herb Kale passed away. He was a leading light in Florida birding and conservation and is missed by so many. We keep all of his contributions to this text. We have relied on the considerable knowledge of Florida bird expert William Pranty in revising our new edition and acknowledge his valuable help and insights.

We continue to hope this book will be of interest to all who have a love for Florida's birds and that it will help foster an appreciation and concern for these birds and their natural habitats.

—David S. Maehr

How to Use This Book

This book can be used in a variety of ways. It can serve as a field guide that can be consulted while using binoculars or other optical aids such as a spotting scope. In this case, a birder familiar with the phylogenetic order of species can quickly flip to the appropriate color plate where a suspected bird is illustrated—since the plates illustrate similar birds side by side. This will allow for easy comparison between similar species. The plates then direct the birder to the detailed written account that includes a description of the life history, key identification features, a range map, and other information. Less experienced birders will find the illustrated index of common names a helpful starting point for narrowing down the search for a bird in question. Most birders will find that using the index in this way will not only lead to a more proficient use of the book, but to a better understanding of Florida's diverse bird life.

We recommend that the range maps be used to reinforce a correct identification, or to eliminate a species from possible identification if the location of the sighting is far from its known boundaries. On the other hand, knowing the limits of a species' distribution in Florida may be helpful in revealing an unusual deviation from the norm or in identifying a possible range expansion (the landscape of Florida bird distribution is in constant flux for several species).

Each bird that appears on a plate is actually illustrated three times in the book: first, in the individual species accounts that provide detailed information on the bird's ecology and habits in Florida; second, on the large color plates that present each species with similar or related birds; and third, in the illustrated common name index. Birds that are illustrated with line drawings appear twice—first, in the illustrated species accounts; and second, in the illustrated common name index. The subject index includes not only topics, but also bird names when they appear on any page other than the species accounts or plates. We have also included an index of scientific names and a checklist that can be maintained as a Florida life list. This list can also be photocopied, stuffed in a pocket, and used to record the species seen on birding trips to various parts of Florida (it would also be useful for this purpose in other Southeastern states that are home to many species that occur outside the boundaries of the Sunshine State).

Florida's Birds is also a reference that goes beyond its usefulness as a field guide. Sections on bird study and bird feeding provide practical advice for enjoying Florida's birds; and sections on bird habitats, threatened and endangered species, exotic species, and bird conservation will assist the reader in understanding the ecological and cultural landscapes that have created one of the world's unique avifaunas. Thus, this is the kind of book that is not only useful in the field, but as an often-consulted bookshelf or coffee table reference, and as an informative lexicon of all things related to birds in Florida.

LISTING ORDER

Some readers may wonder about the sequence of the birds presented herein. It follows the order of the American Ornithologists' Union Check-list (with all the latest supplements). Go to www.aou.org and click on check-lists.This list places species in the sequence of what is considered to be their natural relationship, known as the phylogenetic order. Each species is assigned a two-word scientific name in Latin—a genus and a species. Related genera (plural of genus) are grouped into a family; and related families into an order. All the orders of birds comprise the class Aves, one of the five classes of the Vertebrata. The other vertebrate classes are mammals, reptiles (including snakes, lizards, turtles, and crocodiles), amphibians (including frogs, toads, salamanders), and fishes.

Several of the larger bird families are subdivided into subfamilies. For example, the large family *Emberizidae* includes the subfamilies *Parulinae* (wood-warblers), *Thraupinae* (tangers), *Cardinalinae* (cardinals, grosbeaks), *Emberizinae* (towhees, sparrows), and *Icterinae* (blackbirds, orioles). A population of birds that differs from other populations of the same species may be described as a subspecies or race of that species. For example, the Seaside Sparrow in Florida is represented by at least five distinctive subspecies (including the recently extinct Dusky Seaside Sparrow).

The species accounts are in phylogenetic order, but anyone desiring to look up the account or illustration of a particular species will also find it listed in alphabetical order (both by common name and by Latin name) in the indices.

RANGE MAPS

Some species include individualized range maps, especially for those that are not widespread or that have interesting distributions. For example, some birds such as the RED-COCKADED WOODPECKER and SWALLOW-TAILED KITE have patchy, restricted distributions that are the result of habitat loss—primarily deforestation. Others, such as the MISSISSIPPI KITE and WHITE-CROWNED PIGEON, reach their North American range limits in Florida and are found only in the north or extreme south, respectively. The specialized habitat requirements of the SNAIL KITE explain its unique wetland distribution, while many of Florida's exotic parrots and the HOUSE FINCH exhibit expanding ranges. Some, such as the YELLOW-THROATED VIREO, breed in central and north Florida, then winter in extreme south Florida. The PURPLE GALLINULE, on the other hand, breeds throughout the state but winters only south of Orlando. A few of the maps illustrate where distinct races of a particular species occur, such as the PRAIRIE WARBLER and EASTERN TOWHEE. Finally, some species that mostly migrate to South America in the fall remain all winter in extreme south Florida. These include the AMERICAN REDSTART and WORM-EATING WARBLER. Such maps, when combined with the month-bars (indicating when species are present), are intended to help birders know what to expect at a particular place and time, or if an observation is unusual. The absence of a map for a particular species means that it is extremely widespread, such as the year-round resident CAROLINA WREN and the wintering YELLOW-RUMPED WARBLER, or that it passes through the state during migration without a remarkable affinity for a particular place. In these cases, the presence/absence month bars will be the most helpful aid in knowing what to expect.

BIRD IDENTIFICATION

In each account we briefly list the most distinctive field marks of the species and explain in more detail, if necessary, in the text. In order to understand our descriptions it will be necessary to know the body parts and terms describing them, as illustrated below.

PARTS OF A BIRD

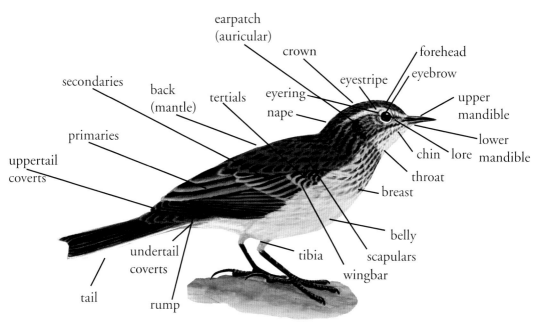

Note: The space between the bill and the eye is called the lore. The scapulars are feather tracts along each side of the back above the wings, and they may partly cover the wings (a sleeping bird tucks its head under the scapulars, not under the wing). The speculum (not shown) is a rectangular patch of color—usually white, blue, purple, or green—on the trailing edge of the secondaries (the inner flight feathers) of the wings of many duck species.

FIELD MARKS

To identify birds one needs to look for certain identifying characteristics or patterns, called field marks. Sometimes it is a simple task—the all-red bird with a top knot or crest is, of course, without question, a male NORTHERN CARDINAL. Some species of birds look very similar to other species, and more subtle marks need to be looked for. A few closely related species are so similar in appearance that they can be identified in the field only by their call notes. The illustrated index of common names can be used as a very rough initial template for narrowing down the list of potential species when one is unsure of a bird that has just been seen.

One way to identify a bird is simply to look at pictures in a guide until you find the bird. If the species is distinctive and unlike any other species then you will probably make a correct identification. In many cases it will not be that easy. Therefore, you should make an effort to remember or record several bits of information as you observe the bird:

Size Is it sparrow-size (about 5–6 in or 13–15 cm), robin-size (about 10–12 in or 25–30 cm), crow-size (about 20 in or 51 cm), or larger? What size is it in relation to a nearby species that you have already correctly identified?

Colors, patterns Note all colors and patterns (stripes, contrasts, wingbars, eyering, etc.). In many cases, the colors and patterns will allow you to differentiate the age and gender of the bird. For example, the female EASTERN TOWHEE is brown above, where the male is black.

Shape Wings may be long and pointed or short and rounded, etc. The bill may be stout, finchlike (sparrows, grosbeaks); thin, pointed (wrens, warblers); hooked (hawks, owls); long, decurved (ibis, curlews); etc. You may also note the shape of legs and feet: long legs and toes, webbed, hooked talons, small, weak, etc.

Season The avifauna of Florida includes species that are permanent residents, i.e., year-round occurrence; summer-only residents; winter-only residents; and transients, i.e. migrants that pass through the state only during spring and fall migrations to and from their northern breeding grounds and southern wintering grounds in Central and South America. The month bar in each entry indicates when the species is in the state, if it breeds in Florida, and the months it is most likely to do so.

Habitat Forest? Field? Marsh? Beach? You would not expect to see, deep in the woods, a species whose habitat is a marsh or open field. For each species depicted in this guide we have indicated the habitat (described in detail in the habitat chapter) in which that species is expected to occur.

Behavior Walking? Hopping? Soaring? Wading? Climbing a tree trunk? For example, BROWN CREEPERS climb head-first, whereas WHITE-BREASTED NUTHATCHES are often upside down and descending. Even subtle behaviors such as tail-bobbing are characteristic for some species (e.g., SOLITARY SANDPIPER, EASTERN PHOEBE, and PALM WARBLER), and are all one needs to correctly separate the bird in question from another species of similar shape and size.

Song Many birds are rarely seen because they live in dense vegetation, stay high in the treetops, or are active at night. But some birds tend to be very vocal and make their presence known despite being invisible. For these it is helpful to be familiar with bird songs. Most species have distinctive voices that can be easily learned with practice, and some have catchy mnemonics (e.g., the CAROLINA WREN's *tea-kettle, tea-kettle, tea-kettle*; the EASTERN TOWHEE's *drink-your-tea*; the BARRED OWL's *who-cooks-for-you?*). Even the Northern MOCKINGBIRD, which does not have a true song of its own, gives itself away by repeating the songs of other species in series of three. So, if the bird you are listening to is singing, try to describe the song, or better yet, record it. A recording presenting the songs of 100 species of Florida birds has been prepared by Dr. John W. Hardy, Curator Emeritus in Ornithology and Bioacoustics at the Florida Museum of Natural History in Gainesville, and is most helpful in identifying a singing bird. Bird sound clips are available for downloading at the museum's website, www.flmnh.ufl.edu. Contact the FMNH's Division of Ornithology at the University of Florida, Gainesville, Florida 32611-7800, for further information. Also check out *Bird Songs of Florida* by Geoffrey A. Keller, a commercially available audio guide published by the Cornell Laboratory of Ornithology.

HABITATS

Florida lacks the topographic variation typical of many other states. However, the patterns created by subtle changes in elevation, water drainage, and climate are apparent in the dizzying variety and combinations of vegetation. A drop or rise in elevation of only inches can explain the sudden occurrence of a cypress pond within a pine flatwoods or a longleaf pine sandhill within a live oak hammock. Water drainage is a major influence on the development of soils, which in turn determine the distribution of plant species and plant associations on a site. These patterns have helped ecologists recognize Florida's ecoregions (see the map on the next page), and are a useful first step in understanding why a particular habitat is found where we see it today.

In this book, we recognize fourteen habitat categories that are helpful in understanding what bird species should be expected in a particular place. Many of these habitats are closely linked to a particular ecoregion, whereas others are more widespread or are the result of human activity. Florida's bird habitats are often widely distributed throughout the state, such as coastal beaches and hardwood swamps. However, some are fairly restricted. For example, xeric scrub is mostly associated with the ecoregion known as "Central Florida ridges and uplands" a system of ancient coastal dunes that represent some of the oldest landscapes in the state. This habitat can be found elsewhere throughout the peninsula and in other ecoregions in relatively smaller patches. Salt marshes are found along both coasts and mostly in the upper portion of the state in the "Gulf coast flatwoods," "Eastern Florida flatwoods," and "Sea island flatwoods." Mangroves may be common along both coasts in the southern third of the peninsula, but these forests attain their best development and most extensive distribution in the "Southern coast and islands" ecoregion. Pine flatwoods and other pine-dominated habitats are found to some degree in every ecoregion, but they are nearly absent in the "Everglades" ecoregion. Florida's bird habitats are described in greater detail below.

Very often, vegetation is useful in predicting the resident bird species to be found in an area. One would not expect to find a BROWN PELICAN at the edge of a hardwood swamp; however; during spring it would be unusual not to find the cavity-nesting PROTHONOTARY WARBLER and nocturnal BARRED OWL there. During winter the Prothonotary's absence is more than compensated for by the influx of AMERICAN ROBINS, CEDAR WAXWINGS, AMERICAN GOLDFINCHES, RUBY-CROWNED KINGLETS, and other northern migrants. Most Florida bird habitats display a seasonal variation in species occurrence. It is this constant turnover of breeding, wintering, and migratory birds that makes Florida such an exciting place for bird watching at all times of the year.

11

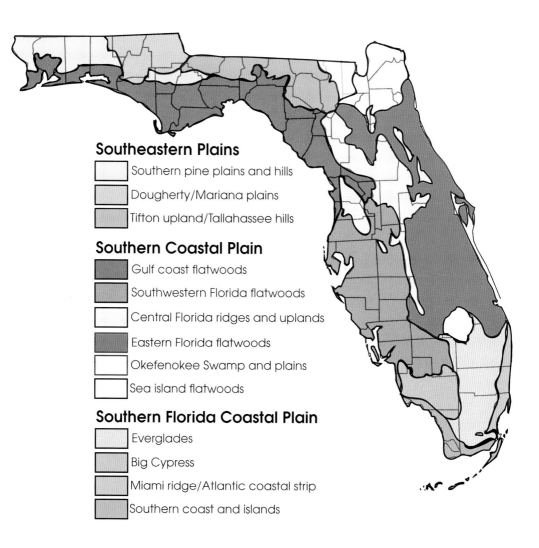

Southeastern Plains

Southern pine plains and hills

Dougherty/Mariana plains

Tifton upland/Tallahassee hills

Southern Coastal Plain

Gulf coast flatwoods

Southwestern Florida flatwoods

Central Florida ridges and uplands

Eastern Florida flatwoods

Okefenokee Swamp and plains

Sea island flatwoods

Southern Florida Coastal Plain

Everglades

Big Cypress

Miami ridge/Atlantic coastal strip

Southern coast and islands

Coastal Beaches

The coastal region of Florida supports the densest human populations of any habitat in the state. As a consequence, Florida's coastline also has experienced the most development and habitat alteration. It is, perhaps, as much a statement about human aesthetics as it is about the tenacity of birds that a large proportion of bird watching occurs before an endless backdrop of resorts and condominiums.

Those few undisturbed stretches of coastal beach remaining in Florida reflect the natural molding forces of wind and surf. Vegetation is often sparse and short and is specialized to withstand the stresses imparted by a salty, sandy environment. A series of dunes is characteristic of beach habitats, and these support a characteristic array of plant species. Annuals such as sea oats, morning glory, railroad vine, and dune panic grass are found closest to the shoreline, while more woody vegetation tends to dominate the back dunes. Scrub live oak, cabbage palm, saw palmetto, wax myrtle, cocoplum, and sea grape may be found in these more protected dunes. Life on Florida's beaches and dunes is well suited to this harsh and ever-changing environment. The persistence of these plant species following a hurricane's wind, rain, and sea surge attests to their tenacity.

Bird species to be looked for on open beaches and inlets are GULLS, TERNS, PLOVERS, SANDPIPERS, LOONS, SEADUCKS, PELICANS, and CORMORANTS. On the vegetated dunes, especially when these are interspersed with shallow pools of water, look for PUDDLE DUCKS, EGRETS, and SAVANNAH SPARROWS in winter, and WILSON'S PLOVERS and WILLETS in spring and summer.

A number of Florida birds can be seen flying over and feeding in the open water offshore from our many beaches. Many of these pelagic species are winter visitors such as the GANNET, or are wanderers over open ocean such as AUDUBON'S SHEARWATER.

SALT MARSHES

Salt marshes are highly productive marine systems and are found on the east coast behind barrier islands from Daytona Beach northward into Georgia, and on the Gulf coast from Tarpon Springs to Apalachee Bay, where they extend out into the Gulf of Mexico because of the shallow water and relatively insignificant wave action. Along the Panhandle westward to Alabama, salt marshes occur only in protected bays behind barrier islands.

Salt marsh plants have adapted to several environmental stresses, including wide tidal fluctuations, low soil oxygen levels, and drought conditions induced by the salty environment. Vegetation is usually found in a zoned arrangement. Beginning from open water one encounters bands of cord grass and needle rush interspersed with salt flats or pannes containing saltwort, glasswort, and torpedograss. Salt marshes provide essential nursery habitat for a variety of fish and invertebrates, many of which are important bird foods.

Birds to be looked for in salt marshes are CLAPPER RAIL, MARSH WREN, SEASIDE and SHARP-TAILED SPARROWS, HERONS, EGRETS, IBISES, NORTHERN HARRIER, and, in the numerous creek distributaries and oyster bars, RED-BREASTED MERGANSER, OYSTERCATCHERS, TERNS, and various SHOREBIRD SPECIES.

MANGROVE

Florida is one of the few places in the world where a transition zone between salt marsh and mangrove habitat occurs. Generally, mangroves range from St. Johns County on the east and Levy County on the west southward into the Caribbean. Red mangrove is per-

haps the most conspicuous of the four tree species that are found in Florida's mangrove zone. It is unique in preferring edges of tidal creeks and canals, in its bizarre arrangement of stiltlike prop roots, and in its habit of producing large, fleshy seeds that germinate while still on the parent plant. Black mangrove can often be found growing in a zone behind red mangrove and can be distinguished by its emergent, pencil-like root extensions known as pneumatophores. It is more cold-tolerant than the other mangrove species and is the tree that pioneers north of the subtropical zone. White mangrove and buttonwood are less conspicuous than the other two mangrove species and are restricted to areas of less significant tidal action. Dwarf mangroves may occur when tidal influence is infrequent and salt concentrations are high or substrates are shallow. Periodic hard freezes kill back mangroves along the central Florida coasts.

High nutrient levels in waters supporting mangroves make these forests an important starting point for many estuarine and marine organisms. Mangroves also are important in stabilizing marine sediments and shoreline soils. Retaining mangrove systems near human developments should be encouraged to maintain this natural sea-land buffer zone.

Birds associated with mangrove include most WADING BIRDS—HERONS, EGRETS, IBISES, SPOONBILLS, and STORKS—as well as CLAPPER RAILS, BROWN PELICANS, CORMORANTS, and, in winter, several species of DUCKS and SHOREBIRDS. In summer, the MANGROVE CUCKOO, GRAY KINGBIRD, BLACK-WHISKERED VIREO, and PRAIRIE WARBLER breed in mangroves.

WET PRAIRIES AND FRESHWATER MARSHES

Wet prairies and freshwater marshes are treeless expanses of herbaceous (non-woody) vegetation. They are unusual in requiring both the regular influence of changing water levels and fire to maintain their unique structure and species composition. Marshes and wet prairies include a number of varieties such as the much reduced but still extensive sawgrass Everglades of south Florida to highly variable cattail marshes throughout the state. Other types include pickerel weed ponds, alligator flag and duck potato marshes, and needle rush, maidencane, and sedge grass prairies. The exclusion of fire or a permanent drop in water level allows the invasion of woody species such as persimmon, slash pine, and wax myrtle. Good examples of a variety of these vegetation types can be found in Payne's Prairie Preserve State Park near Gainesville.

Highly fertile soils are often associated with these wetland habitats, and abundant invertebrate populations may support a number of wildlife species from crayfish and leopard frogs to SANDHILL CRANES and round-tailed muskrats. Like other wetland habitats, wet prairies and freshwater marshes are threatened by drainage and agricultural expansion. Typical bird species found here include most of the LONG-LEGGED WADERS—HERONS, EGRETS, IBISES, RAILS, WOOD STORKS—as well as DUCKS, LIMPKINS, SNAIL KITES, RED-SHOULDERED HAWKS, SANDHILL CRANES, and ANHINGAS.

DRY PRAIRIE

Much of the grassland and cattle pasture surrounding the north and west sides of Lake Okeechobee today was once an extensive band of dry prairies. Commonly found between pine flatwoods or other wooded habitats and permanently wet sites, dry prairies depend upon fire to maintain their simple treeless structure. Saw palmetto often dominates a blanket of wiregrass and broomsedge, while gallberry, fetterbush, and wax myrtle are occasionally abundant.

A number of bird species, including the BURROWING OWL, CRESTED CARACARA, and

GRASSHOPPER SPARROW, find their greatest abundance in this habitat type. These are populations of birds native to the prairie region of the western United States. This prairie once extended around the edge of the Gulf of Mexico when sea level was much lower during glacial times. Hence, these "Western" species, now isolated by distance and time, are considered "relict" populations. The conversion of dry prairie vegetation to improved pasture or citrus groves may threaten the existence of a number of wildlife species.

XERIC SCRUB

One of the better known and more widely distributed habitats in Florida is xeric (very

dry, well-drained, and nutrient poor) scrub, which occurs abundantly in the Ocala National Forest of central Florida. White, sandy soils often support a thick canopy made up entirely of sand pine. Understory plants (i.e., those living under the sand pine canopy) include several scrub oaks, scrub hickory, saw palmetto, rosemary, staggerbush, and scrub holly. Unlike in most Florida pine communities, fires are infrequent yet still essential in maintaining the structure and species composition typical of this habitat. Although the infrequent fires burn hot and devastate standing vegetation, this prepares the site for vigorous reproduction which ultimately returns to a sand pine-dominated community. A variety of xeric oak species are typical in this habitat. These are important producers of food and nest sites for bird species that are resident in this habitat type. Interestingly, as sand pines recolonize and mature following a fire, many of the scrub-dwelling bird species decline. The FLORIDA SCRUB-JAY is a Florida specialty typical of the early successional stages of xeric scrub. Other birds found here include a variety of WOODPECKERS, the WHITE-EYED VIREO, GNATCATCHERS, WRENS, and the PINE WARBLER. During spring and fall a variety of migrant WARBLERS and other SONGBIRDS travels through scrub habitats.

LONGLEAF PINE/TURKEY OAK SANDHILL

Florida's sandhill vegetation, like many upland vegetation communities, is much reduced in its present statewide distribution. The well-drained soils and often scenic landscapes have made these habitats a prime target for development. Like xeric scrub vegetation, sandhills depend upon fire to maintain their structure and species composition. Sandhill fires occur more frequently, however, and the structure of vegetation reflects this increased disturbance. The dominant species, longleaf pine and turkey oak, are thick-barked trees that can withstand ground fires occurring once every four or five years. Other species such as bluejack oak, post oak, wiregrass, and gopher apple also are adapted to withstand the influence of periodic burning. In sandhills where burning still occurs on a regular basis, vegetation is patchy and the understory is typically open and easily walked through. The burrows of gopher tortoises and pocket gophers are often conspicuous, and may also provide shelter from heat, cold, and fire for numerous other sandhill residents such as diamondback rattlesnakes, opossums, indigo snakes, and gopher frogs. The TUFTED TITMOUSE, CAROLINA CHICKADEE, EASTERN SCREECH-OWL, MOURNING DOVE, BACHMAN'S SPARROW, and a number of other SONGBIRDS reside in sandhills.

MESIC HAMMOCKS

Mixed broadleaf forests or mesic (moist, but not wet or flooded) hammocks exhibit the highest diversity and most complex structure of any vegetation community in Florida. Fire is much less an influence in this high-moisture habitat, resulting in the dominance of fire-intolerant trees such as southern magnolia, laurel oak, swamp chestnut oak, basswood, musclewood, and flowering dogwood. Vines and epiphytes, such as resurrection fern and green fly orchid, also may be conspicuous. A few coniferous species are typical in some areas and may include Atlantic white cedar, red cedar, loblolly pine, and spruce pine.

An important characteristic of hardwood-dominated hammocks is an abundance of hollow trees and limbs. Cavities caused by decay of old branches, lightning, and wind damage provide nesting and roosting habitat for a variety of wildlife species from flying squirrels to CAROLINA CHICKADEES and BARRED OWLS.

Mesic hammocks include live oak/cabbage palm/red cedar forests in coastal, island, and lake margin situations. Plant species diversity is typically lower here than in mixed broadleaf forests. A unique hardwood community is the tropical hammock of south Florida. The Caribbean influence in this extreme southeastern extension of the North American continent is evident in the predominance of a variety of tropical plant species. Trees such as wild tamarind, poisonwood, pigeon plum, Spanish stopper, mahogany, gumbo limbo, and strangler fig create a landscape more typical of the tropics.

Warmer temperatures also allow a profusion of tree-blanketing orchids and bromeliads (air plants). The colorful and variable tree snail, *Liguus,* is an eye-catching jewel in these verdant jungles. Unfortunately, the vast majority of tropical communities has disappeared in south Florida. Expanding urbanization, increasingly intensive agriculture, and rampant plant- and snail-collecting have taken their toll on the distribution and diversity of these Florida habitats.

Bird species to be expected in mesic hammocks include the BLUE JAY, TUFTED TITMOUSE, RED-BELLIED WOODPECKER, DOWNY WOODPECKER, BLUE-GRAY GNATCATCHER, CAROLINA CHICKADEE, and RED-EYED VIREO. Typical species in subtropical hammocks include the WHITE-CROWNED PIGEON, MANGROVE CUCKOO, BLACK-WHISKERED VIREO, and NORTHERN CARDINAL.

MIXED PINE/HARDWOOD FORESTS

In Florida, many typically northern plant species find their southern range limit in the high clay soils of northwest Florida. Higher levels of soil moisture and nutrients combine with a cooler climate to permit trees such as American beech, southern magnolia, mockernut hickory, tulip poplar, and a variety of oak species to thrive. A well-developed understory is usually present and may include musclewood, dogwood, redbud, and several azalea species. Shortleaf pine, spruce pine, and loblolly pine occur throughout this habitat type in varying amounts.

The feature that sets the mixed pine/hardwood community apart from all other Florida habitats is topographic diversity. While not comparable to mountainous terrain, the more rugged nature of northwest Florida provides many more life-style opportunities for plants and animals alike. The distribution of plants is particularly affected by percent slope and aspect (north- or south-facing); drier site species require higher, south-facing slopes, while species requiring greater moisture dominate lower, north-facing slopes. Typical birds include the NORTHERN CARDINAL, RED-EYED VIREO, NORTHERN PARULA, SUMMER TANAGER, INDIGO BUNTING, YELLOW-THROATED VIREO, and CHUCK-WILL'S-WIDOW.

CYPRESS FORESTS

Cypress-dominated habitats provide some of the most picturesque scenery in all of the South. The old sentinel trees festooned with Spanish moss and bromeliads seem to be an unofficial symbol of interior Florida.

Cypress swamps are not often extensive and may be interspersed within larger systems such as pine flatwoods and freshwater marshes. Subtle changes in drainage patterns and topography may explain the distribution of this plant community. Cypress is a deciduous conifer, losing its leaves in autumn. Other unique characteristics include trunk buttressing and the development of "knees." Knees are knoblike extensions of the root system that protrude above the water surface. It has been suggested that these structures aid the plant in respiration and stability in waterlogged soils. Cypress can be found bordering lakes and streams, in meandering strands, or in isolated depressions where they form "domes"—a result of the older, taller trees growing in the center surrounded by younger or smaller trees. Cypress also may grow with a variety of other water-tolerant tree species such as swamp tupelo and laurel oak. Wherever it occurs, though, naturally growing cypress is a sure sign of at least poorly drained if not frequently flooded sites.

Most of the large cypress trees in Florida were logged out during the last century. The disappearance of these often hollow giants meant the disappearance of denning and feeding habitat for a number of swamp-dwelling, cavity-nesting species including the black bear, and the now-extinct CAROLINA PARAKEET. Today, expect to see BARRED OWLS, SWALLOW-TAILED KITES, PROTHONOTARY WARBLERS, WOOD DUCKS, and WHITE-EYED VIREOS among other SONGBIRDS.

HARDWOOD SWAMPS

With the exception of the Fakahatchee strand in Collier County, Florida's hardwood swamps are only found north of Lake Okeechobee. The deciduous trees characteristic of this habitat are restricted to lake margins and river basins that experience floods or other significant water level fluctuations.

Hardwood swamps contain some of the tallest and largest diameter trees (on the average) of any forested landscape in Florida. Other characteristics include a high tree density, a very open understory, and fewer tree species than occur in other hardwood habitats. Some of the typical tree species include bald cypress, cabbage palm, water oak, red maple, Florida elm, sweet bay, loblolly bay, red bay, and sweetgum. Swamp tupelo, another common swamp tree, may develop an above-ground convoluted root system that resembles the knees of cypress and may also aid the tree in gas exchange and stability.

The Fakahatchee Strand, east of Naples, represents an extensive south Florida example of hardwood swamp. The tropical influence in this habitat is evident in trees festooned with epiphytic bromeliads, ferns, and a myriad of orchids with Caribbean and South American origins. Scattered pond apple sloughs in this swamp system are home to the spectacular and bizarre leafless ghost orchid and also are part of the last stronghold of the endangered Florida panther.

The annual fluctuations in water level permit the existence of these intriguing plant communities. Rising and falling water levels are essential in maintaining soil nutrients and oxygen levels to which these plants are adapted. Channelization and drainage operations pose a serious threat to swamp vegetation and associated wildlife. Typical bird species include the PILEATED WOODPECKER, WOOD DUCK, BLUE-GRAY GNATCATCHER, WHITE IBIS, YELLOW-THROATED WARBLER, and CAROLINA WREN.

PINE FLATWOODS

Half of Florida is virtually covered with pine flatwoods, and, as would be expected in such a vast area, much variation occurs within this habitat type. Flatwoods are characterized by relatively level sandy soils underlain by an impermeable layer (hardpan) that maintains a "perched" water table during the rainy season. Flatwoods may be dominated by pond pine, longleaf pine, or most commonly today, slash pine. Pond and longleaf pine flatwoods probably accounted for most of this extensive habitat type before the advent of modern timber practices. With the recognition that slash pine provided higher economic returns in planted situations, most of the other pine flatwoods were converted to this species—often to the detriment of native wildlife species.

Fire played an important role in the original distribution of these three pine species. Longleaf is most fire-tolerant, prefers drier flatwoods, and was probably the most abundant of the three. Pond pine tolerates wet conditions best, and is least fire-tolerant, yet needs fire to open its cones. Slash pine is intermediate between the other two species, and was probably restricted to swamp margins and sites intermediate in drainage characteristics. The south Florida variety of slash pine is commonly found in extensive open flatwoods south of Lake Okeechobee. Here, the understory shrub species are commonly of tropical origin.

Naturally occurring summer fires kept pine flatwoods appearing rather open and parklike. Scattered understory species include saw palmetto, gallberry, low bush blueberry, wax myrtle, runner oak, and fetterbush. Cypress-gum swamps, bayheads, and titi swamps (in north Florida) are often interspersed within the extensive flatwoods landscape. Intensively managed sites tend to have dense tree canopies and poorly developed understories. As a consequence, the value to wildlife is much reduced in many commercial pine flatwoods today. Good examples of old-fashioned (natural) flatwoods can still be found in the Apalachicola and Osceola National Forests. Management of pine flatwoods for shorter rotation harvests has reduced considerably the habitat for the endangered RED-COCKADED WOODPECKER. The decline in numbers of older pines infected with heart-rot has reduced the availability of nest sites to the point that the RED-COCKADED WOODPECKER now is in serious trouble throughout its range. Other species commonly found in pine flatwoods are the EASTERN TOWHEE, BACHMAN'S SPARROW, BROWN-HEADED NUTHATCH, CAROLINA WREN, NORTHERN CARDINAL, PINE WARBLER, RED-BELLIED WOODPECKER, and GREAT HORNED OWL. The variety and number of bird species depend on the openness of the flatwoods, the presence or absence of hardwood trees and shrubs in the understory, and the size of the forest patch. Larger patches of forest tend to have more species than smaller patches.

URBAN ENVIRONMENTS

Florida's growing cities and suburbs are making significant impacts on the state's birdlife. The continued influx of new residents from other states and abroad is expected to increase Florida's population to 24.4 million by 2030. Most of these new residents will be located in large urban and mostly coastal counties including Broward, Miami-Dade, Palm Beach, Orange, and Hillsborough.

To the naturalist, the most obvious impact of urban sprawl is the loss of natural plant and animal communities. This is especially true in coastal counties that will experience nearly 80% of Florida's growth and will be home for nearly 80% of the state's human population. Most native birds cannot survive in these highly altered asphalt and concrete environments.

It seems incredible, then, that some of the most interesting bird watching can be enjoyed in megalopolized Florida. South Florida's large urban areas have become home for nearly 30 species of breeding exotic (nonnative) birds. Numerous other exotic species, though they may not yet breed in south Florida, survive as the result of the warm climate and food obtained at feeders and from introduced fruit-producing plants. Most of these birds are released cage birds or escapees from private bird collections and wildlife exhibits.

In the less altered and more vegetated suburbs, a number of native species—NORTHERN MOCKINGBIRD, BLUE JAY, NORTHERN CARDINAL, MOURNING DOVE, and COMMON GRACKLE—do quite well. In some areas even the BALD EAGLE is tolerant of living a suburban life. This becomes apparent in winter when a variety of migrants and residents make regular use of backyard feeders.

Few generalizations can be made about Florida's urban birdlife because these areas are influenced by variation in climate, vegetation, rainfall, and urban characteristics such as architecture, human population size, landscaping (greenspace), and building density. Many urban birds, however, share one characteristic: they are habitat generalists capable of tolerating or taking advantage of a wide variety of habitats and food. In most cases this also includes a tolerance of, if not dependence upon, people. For example, MOCKINGBIRDS, MOURNING DOVES, BLUE JAYS, NORTHERN CARDINALS, and CAROLINA WRENS occur both in wild areas and in close proximity to people, while ROCK PIGEONS (feral pigeons), EUROPEAN STARLINGS, HOUSE SPARROWS, and BUDGERIGARS are exotics largely dependent upon humans and human-made structures for food and nesting sites. Birds such as BALD EAGLES, WILD TURKEYS, RED-COCKADED WOODPECKERS, PROTHONOTARY WARBLERS, and many other species all are essentially wilderness species and are not expected to live or nest close to human developments. The preservation of many of Florida's unique native bird species is in no small part related to the control of urban sprawl.

In addition to the species already mentioned above, numerous others occur in our cities where trees, shrubs, and lawns abound. Some of these are the EASTERN SCREECH-OWL, TUFTED TITMOUSE, CAROLINA CHICKADEE, and BROWN THRASHER.

AGRICULTURAL ENVIRONMENTS

Agriculture is another intensive land use that has had significant impacts on Florida's birdlife. Our warm climate has permitted the establishment of a diverse array of crops, most of which are destined for produce departments in northern supermarkets. Beef production on extensive cattle ranches is also an important Florida industry. These land uses have damaging impacts on many Florida birds, but at the same time have created new habitats for others.

Our once extensive scrublands have been much reduced due to the spread of the citrus industry. Muck farms, major producers of winter vegetables in central and south Florida, have eliminated large tracts of productive wetlands. Other large farming operations have eliminated tropical hammocks in south Florida and other forest lands throughout the state. Improved pasture associated with cattle ranching is a dominant land use in parts of central and south Florida and has been created by draining and clearing large forests and prairies.

Florida's agricultural areas are similar in that they have greatly reduced plant diversity (i.e., reduced number of species). Indeed, many of these land uses can be considered monocultures (dominated by a single plant or crop). Such habitats are usually unproductive for birds and other wildlife. Because of this, citrus groves are seldom visited by bird watchers though a few NORTHERN MOCKINGBIRDS or CATTLE EGRETS may make regular visits there.

On the other hand, where crop lands are seasonally flooded and then drained, spectacular gatherings of migrant SHOREBIRDS and resident WATERFOWL occur. Fertile soils and fluctuating water levels stimulate the growth and increase of aquatic invertebrates such as snails, worms, and copepods. The muckland farming areas in south and central Florida, especially near Lake Okeechobee, are good examples of this phenomenon.

Finally, some habitats associated with phosphate mining in north and central Florida are extremely attractive to many birds. Nearly 200 species of birds have been found in or around these highly altered mined lands. Large freshwater impoundments, spoil piles, sand dunes, and willow swamps are characteristic of phosphate mines and provide nesting and feeding habitat for a variety of residents and migrants. A number of unusual birds, primarily WATERFOWL and other wetland species, have turned up in these unnatural landscapes. Unfortunately, many of these habitats are only temporary while the losses of natural habitats are permanent. Old mines reclaimed to pasture or housing subdivisions are unsatisfactory.

SPECIES ACCOUNTS

ORDERS

KEY TO SPECIES ACCOUNTS

The **page number** in an account refers to the plate on which the painting of the bird can be found. Similar birds are grouped together on a plate so that you can compare them.

Some of the birds are illustrated with **black-and-white line drawings** because they are rare and/or not often seen in Florida and do not appear on a plate.

The color-coded **month bar** in each account indicates the months during which each species is present and/or breeding in Florida. *Yellow-orange* means breeding and *purple* means present but not breeding.

Some species have **range maps** in addition to the range indication in the text. These maps indicate the breeding range (*orange*) or the winter range (*green*). The absence of a map for a particular species means that it is extremely widespread or that it passes through the state during migration without a remarkable affinity for a particular place.

Where indicated, **status** applies to an imperiled species based on the list of the Florida Fish and Wildlife Conservation Commission. **SSC** stands for Species of Special Concern, a species that is facing a high risk of extinction in the wild. **T** stands for Threatened, which means that the species is facing a very high risk of extinction in the wild. **E** stands for Endangered, meaning the species faces an extremely high risk of extinction in the wild.

Species Accounts

Order *Gaviiformes: Loons*

These are large-bodied water birds with webbed front toes and straight pointed bills. Their legs are located far back on the body, making them excellent at diving and underwater swimming, but awkward at walking.

Family *Gaviidae: Loons*

RED-THROATED LOON (*Gavia stellata*)

Length 24–27 in (61–69 cm)   Weight 3.4 lb (1.54 kg)

Description Long, pointed, straight, slightly upturned bill
Habitat Open saltwater; occasionally open freshwater
Range Statewide, coastal

Jan	Feb	Mar	Apr	May	June	July	Aug	Sep	Oct	Nov	Dec

This rare wintering loon is smaller than the Common Loon, with a thinner, straight, slightly upturned bill, and in winter plumage it shows a more defined line between the dark head and the white of face and neck. It generally inhabits inlets along the Atlantic and Gulf coasts off the northern half of the state between November and April. Only a handful of records derive from the Florida Keys. Its diet consists primarily of fish.

Family *Gaviidae: Loons*

COMMON LOON (*Gavia immer*)   p. 214

Length 14 in (36 cm)   Weight 9.1 lb (4.12 kg)

Description Large, thick, straight bill
Habitat Open saltwater; open freshwater
Range Statewide, mostly coastal

Jan	Feb	Mar	Apr	May	June	July	Aug	Sep	Oct	Nov	Dec

Floridians seldom see this large diving bird in its distinctive black and white breeding plumage, nor do they hear its distinctive call of the summer north woods. Wintering Common Loons have a light-colored, heavy, sharply pointed bill, are white underneath and drab gray-brown above. In Florida, Common Loons chiefly inhabit the Atlantic Ocean and Gulf of Mexico, but can also be found in large bays and lagoons. They are less commonly seen on inland lakes and ponds. A nighttime migrant, the Common Loon rarely is seen flying but occasionally may alight on land after mistaking slick pavement for water. In such cases, the loon is helpless without human assistance. Because their feet are located so far back on their bodies, loons and grebes cannot walk on land, or take flight from land, but require a water surface to become airborne. In January and February when loons molt their flight feathers they are unable to fly.

Generally, Common Loons reside in Florida from November through March and occasionally into summer when, rarely, a bird may be seen in full breeding plumage. Foods consist chiefly of small fish, but invertebrates and other aquatic life also are taken.

ORDER *Podicipediformes: Grebes*
Small diving birds with lobed toes, pointed bills, and legs
placed far back on the body.

FAMILY *Podicipedidae: Grebes*   p. 214
PIED-BILLED GREBE (*Podilymbus podiceps*)
LENGTH 13.5 in (34 cm)   WEIGHT 15.6 oz (0.44 kg)

Other names Didapper

Description Short, stout, ringed bill and black throat (breeding) or white throat and plain bill (nonbreeding)

Habitat Open freshwater; wet prairies and marshes

Range Statewide

Jan	Feb	Mar	Apr	May	June	July	Aug	Sep	Oct	Nov	Dec

This resident of Florida's freshwater lakes and ponds is one of our most widespread water birds. In the breeding season, the Pied-billed Grebe sports a white bill with a central, vertical black band and a black chin and throat. The rest of the year the bill is a single pale hue and the throat is white. Its plumage is a drab brown-gray. Three to ten light brown eggs are laid in a floating nest. Pied-bills occasionally utter an unusual chortling call that has a ventriloquial quality; this call is reminiscent of the Yellow-billed Cuckoo. This bird may be seen floating buoyantly, swimming partly submerged, or actively diving and resurfacing while feeding on aquatic invertebrates and small fish. In Florida it has a long breeding season that extends from March to December. Pied-bills become much more numerous in winter with an influx of northern migrants.

FAMILY *Podicipedidae: Grebes*
HORNED GREBE (*Podiceps auritus*)
LENGTH 12–15 in (30–38 cm)   WEIGHT 1 lb (0.45 kg)   p. 214

Description White cheeks and throat (winter)

Habitat Open saltwater; open freshwater

Range Statewide

Jan	Feb	Mar	Apr	May	June	July	Aug	Sep	Oct	Nov	Dec

Horned Grebes can be found in very small numbers along the Gulf coast, in protected bays and inlets of the east coast, and occasionally on large inland lakes and ponds from October through April. It is most often encountered in the northern reaches of the state. This small grebe has a rather drab winter plumage that is white below and gray-brown above. A good field mark is a white cheek patch that extends behind the head. It shows more white and has a more slender bill than does the Pied-billed Grebe.

ORDER *Procellariiformes: Petrels, Shearwaters, Storm-Petrels*

This group of birds is seen primarily well off the coast in the Atlantic Ocean. These are generally large, long-winged seabirds with tubular nostrils. They fly with stiff wings and frequently glide.

FAMILY *Procellariidae: Petrels, Shearwaters*

BLACK-CAPPED PETREL (*Pterodroma hasitata*)

LENGTH 16 in (41 cm)   WEIGHT 9.8 oz (0.27 kg)

Other names Diablotin

Description Long, pointed wings; stout bill; white upper tail coverts

Habitat Open saltwater

Range Atlantic coast

Jan	Feb	Mar	Apr	May	June	July	Aug	Sep	Oct	Nov	Dec

The Black-capped Petrel is about the size of a Peregrine Falcon. It is mostly gray above with pointed wings and bright white upper tail coverts. It is mostly white underneath with a distinctive black bar on each wing. The Black-capped Petrel feeds in the Gulf Stream usually no closer than about 15 miles from shore. It can be seen mostly from spring through fall and primarily from Brevard County southward. It is seen infrequently in the Gulf of Mexico. Black-capped Petrels often swim to feed on squids and other invertebrates on the water surface.

FAMILY *Procellariidae: Petrels, Shearwaters*

CORY'S SHEARWATER (*Calonectris diomedea*)   p. 215

LENGTH 18 in (46 cm)   WEIGHT 1.2 lb (0.54 kg)

Description Brown above, white wing-linings, mostly yellow bill

Habitat Open saltwater

Range Primarily Atlantic coast

Jan	Feb	Mar	Apr	May	June	July	Aug	Sep	Oct	Nov	Dec

This shearwater is a fairly predictable summer visitor in Florida, and is seen almost anywhere off of the Atlantic coast, but occasionally in the Gulf of Mexico. Cory's Shearwater is larger than the Black-capped Petrel. It can occasionally be seen soaring, and often forms huge flocks. It sits on the water to feed or snatches small fish and invertebrates from the water's surface while in flight. It occasionally swims under water to capture prey.

FAMILY *Procellariidae: Petrels, Shearwaters*
GREATER SHEARWATER (*Puffinus gravis*)
p. 215
LENGTH 18 in (46 cm)   WEIGHT 1.9 lb (0.86 kg)

Description Dark head, partial gray band around neck, dark inner wing markings, dark bill
Habitat Open saltwater
Range Primarily Atlantic coast

The Greater Shearwater is slightly smaller than the Cory's Shearwater, but is still large and powerful. A dark area on the belly and pink feet can identify it when seen from below. Its flocks of 50–100 are seen unpredictably in the Atlantic Ocean and Gulf of Mexico from spring through fall. It feeds like other shearwaters for squids, crustaceans, and other invertebrates that live near the water's surface. It also scavenges for the wastes that are discarded by fishing vessels. The **Sooty Shearwater** (*Puffinus griseus*) is slightly smaller than the Greater Shearwater and appears much browner overall with white wing linings and dark primaries. It is sometimes seen in groups with other shearwaters during summer in both the Gulf of Mexico and Atlantic Ocean. Some individuals are occasionally seen from shore.

FAMILY *Procellariidae: Petrels, Shearwaters*
AUDUBON'S SHEARWATER (*Puffinus lherminieri*)
p. 215
LENGTH 12 in (30 cm)   WEIGHT 5.9 oz (0.16 kg)

Description Dark above, white below, dark edgings around the wings, dark tail
Habitat Open saltwater
Range Primarily Atlantic coast

This smallest Florida shearwater is about the size of a Common Tern, stocky, with broad wings. It beats its wings more rapidly than other Atlantic Shearwaters. It is a common visitor to the east coast during summer and less so in the Gulf of Mexico and the Keys. It eats fish and squids in typical shearwater fashion. The slightly larger **Manx Shearwater** (*Puffinus puffinus*) has more pointed wings, is whiter underneath, and flies with slower wing beats. It is seen off the Atlantic coast and in the Florida Straits during warmer months. Its habits are similar to other shearwaters.

FAMILY *Hydrobatidae: Storm-Petrels*
WILSON'S STORM-PETREL (*Oceanites oceanicus*) p. 215
LENGTH 7.25 in (18 cm)   WEIGHT 1.1 oz (0.03 kg)

Description Dark above, pointed wings, squared-off tail, white rump patch
Habitat Open saltwater
Range Coastal, statewide

| Jan | Feb | Mar | Apr | May | June | July | Aug | Sep | Oct | Nov | Dec |

The Wilson's Storm-Petrel is smaller than the Least Tern. With a nearly worldwide distribution this species is considered by some to be the most globally abundant bird. It can be identified by its short square tail and long legs extending past the tail. It is found mostly offshore in the Atlantic Ocean during summer (between April and November), but occasionally in the Gulf of Mexico. Wilson's Storm-Petrels often follow ships in search of prey churned up by commercial fishermen. Its flight is graceful and reminiscent of a swallow. It feeds on plankton, small fish, crustaceans, and other small invertebrates, and often appears to walk on water while flapping its wings in pursuit of prey. The **Leach's Storm-Petrel** (*Oceanodroma leucorhoa*) is slightly larger than Wilson's and is all dark with buff, diagonal bars on the upper wing surfaces. The **Band-rumped Storm-Petrel** (*Oceanodroma castro*) is very similar to the Wilson's but its feet do not extend beyond the tail when in flight. Both of these species are occasionally encountered during warmer months primarily off the Atlantic Coast.

ORDER *Pelicaniformes: Tropicbirds, Boobies, Pelicans, Cormorants, Anhinga, Frigatebirds*
Large fish-eating birds with short legs and large wings.
All members have all four toes joined in a web.

FAMILY *Phaethontidae: Tropicbirds*
WHITE-TAILED TROPICBIRD (*Phaethon lepturus*) p. 216
LENGTH 30 in (76 cm)   WEIGHT 15.3 oz (0.43 kg)

Other names Yellow-billed Tropicbird, Bos'un Bird, Longtail
Description All white, black stripes on wing, yellow or orange bill, long white tail
Habitat Open saltwater
Range Atlantic coast, Dry Tortugas

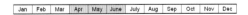

| Jan | Feb | Mar | Apr | May | June | July | Aug | Sep | Oct | Nov | Dec |

Considered one of Florida's most spectacular specialties, the White-tailed Tropicbird is seldom seen anywhere else in North America. This graceful relative of the pelican nests in the nearby Bahamas and Greater Antilles, but also on scattered islands in the Pacific and Indian oceans. It lays a single egg in a cave or crevice along limestone cliffs. Occasionally swept to south Florida waters following tropical storms, White-tailed Tropicbirds were once seen with relative regularity from April to June only in the Dry Tortugas (Ft. Jefferson at Dry Tortugas National Park), which can be accessed by boat or float plane. Tropicbirds seem to frequent the old military garrison in the early morning, providing an eye-catching contrast to the Civil War–era brick fort.

This tropicbird is mostly white with a yellow bill, black eyestripe, black primary feathers, black streaking on the back, and a white tail with two long streaming tail feathers. Immature birds lack the long tail feathers. A similar species, the **Red-billed Tropicbird** (*Phaethon aethereus*), is rarely seen along Florida's east coast. It can be told from the White-tailed by its thick red bill, all black primaries and mottled back in adult plumages. Tropicbirds feed on marine invertebrates and fish.

FAMILY *Sulidae: Boobies and Gannets*
MASKED BOOBY (*Sula dactylatra*)   p. 216
LENGTH 32 in (81 cm)   WEIGHT 3.2 lb (1.45 kg)

Other names Atlantic Blue-faced Booby
Description White body, black tail, wingtips, and trailing edge of wing (adult) or brown upperparts with white patches, white below (immature)
Habitat Open saltwater; coastal beaches
Range Statewide, coastal

Jan	Feb	Mar	Apr	May	June	July	Aug	Sep	Oct	Nov	Dec

At first glance the Masked Booby can be mistaken for the closely related Northern Gannet, but the yellowish bill and feet, and black tail, secondaries, and facial mask set this large seabird apart. Immatures are whiter underneath than are gannets or Brown Boobies while having similar brown upperparts. Nesting colonies of Masked Boobies are as near as the West Indies, but the Masked Booby occurs regularly in Florida only in the Dry Tortugas, where it can be seen loafing on buoys and shifting sand bars, and offshore in the Gulf of Mexico and Atlantic Ocean. Masked Boobies began nesting on Middle Key near Ft. Jefferson in 1984 and have continued to do so. The nest is simply a scrape where one or two eggs are laid, usually during spring. Like its relatives, the Masked Booby feeds mostly on fish. It can plunge straight down from high in the air to catch fish deep underwater.

FAMILY *Sulidae: Boobies and Gannets*
BROWN BOOBY (*Sula leucogaster*) p. 216
LENGTH 30 in (76 cm) WEIGHT 2.4 lb (1.09 kg)

Other names White-bellied Booby

Description Dark brown head, breast, and back, white belly (adult)or all brown (immature)

Habitat Open saltwater; mangrove

Range Coastal, statewide

Jan	Feb	Mar	Apr	May	June	July	Aug	Sep	Oct	Nov	Dec

According to John James Audubon, the Brown Booby once nested in the Dry Tortugas, but this 1832 record and another from the nineteenth century are in doubt. Although they are not known to breed in Florida, Brown Boobies still can be seen in spring and summer in the vicinity of these distant islands. They occasionally are seen along Florida's east coast and in the Gulf of Mexico far from shore, where they like to perch on buoys and channel markers. Brown Boobies are dark brown above with contrasting white underbelly and wing linings. Immatures have light brown underparts. This bird's feeding methods are similar to those of the Northern Gannet, relying on fish taken from dives. Its primary prey are flying fish and mullet. The **Red-footed Booby** (*Sula sula*) is smaller than other Florida boobies and has been seen occasionally in and around the Dry Tortugas in its brown morph plumage. It apparently feeds under low light conditions for squids and other nocturnal prey.

FAMILY *Sulidae: Boobies and Gannets*
NORTHERN GANNET (*Morus bassanus*) p. 216
LENGTH 37 in (94 cm) WEIGHT 6.5 lb (2.95 kg)

Description White body, long, black-tipped wings (adult) or gray with or without white underparts (immature)

Habitat Open saltwater

Range Coastal, statewide

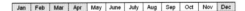

Jan	Feb	Mar	Apr	May	June	July	Aug	Sep	Oct	Nov	Dec

The Northern Gannet is an impressive winter visitor from its northern breeding grounds. These large white seabirds have wingspans reaching 6 feet, and can be observed from shore skimming wave tops and making spectacular dives for fish, sometimes even chasing them underwater. Adult wingtips and elegant facial highlights are black and the head is washed with a creamy buff. Immature gannets are mostly gray-brown; the second-year birds display increasing amounts of white on wings and head. They require four years to reach sexual maturity. Gannets nest in huge colonies on islands in the northern Atlantic Ocean. They are seen individually, in small groups, or large flocks most often offshore along Florida's east coast and occasionally off the Gulf coast from December to April or May.

FAMILY *Pelecanidae: Pelicans*

AMERICAN WHITE PELICAN (*Pelecanus erythrorhynchos*) p. 214

LENGTH 62 in (158 cm)　　WEIGHT 15.4 lb (7 kg)

Description Large white body, black on wings

Habitat Open saltwater; open freshwater; wet prairies and marshes; mangroves

Range Statewide

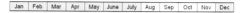

Jan	Feb	Mar	Apr	May	June	July	Aug	Sep	Oct	Nov	Dec

With a wingspread of nearly 3 meters (10 feet), distinctive black wingtips, and white plumage, the American White Pelican is one of Florida's most spectacular winter visitors. It is seen occasionally in north Florida freshwater lakes and coastal areas, but is more common in central and south Florida localities such as lakes of the upper St. Johns River, Merritt Island National Wildlife Refuge, Lake Okeechobee, and Florida Bay. Flying birds are usually seen in V-formation. In fall and spring huge migrating flocks may be seen circling high overhead along the Gulf coast. The American White Pelican is a cooperative feeder, forming groups on the water surface and "herding" fish into a concentrated mass. Finding refuge from their north central U.S. and central Canada breeding grounds, American White Pelicans are regularly seen in Florida from December to March. In recent years, a few hundred nonbreeding birds have remained on some lakes and marshes during summer. The American White Pelican breeds in western North America from southwestern Minnesota to southern British Columbia.

FAMILY *Pelecanidae: Pelicans*

BROWN PELICAN (*Pelecanus occidentalis*) p. 214

LENGTH 48 in (122 cm)　　WEIGHT 8.2 lb (4 kg)　　STATUS **SSC**

Description Grayish-brown body, white head and neck (adult) or all brown or with whitish underparts (immature)

Habitat Coastal beaches; open saltwater; mangrove

Range Coastal, statewide

Jan	Feb	Mar	Apr	May	June	July	Aug	Sep	Oct	Nov	Dec

The Brown Pelican is, perhaps, Florida's most distinctive and widely recognized bird. Captured in photographs, paintings, sculpture, and poetry (not to mention fisherman's lines), its image shows up everywhere from license plates to bank lobbies. Brown Pelicans dive (the only pelican species to do so) 20 to 30 feet for fish, and can be seen flying to and from feeding grounds in loose V-formations. Breeding pairs build bulky, flimsy-looking nests where usually three white eggs are laid. Colonies, most often on coastal mangrove islands, usually contain several hundred birds. In the past as many as 3,000 pairs nested on Pelican Island in the Indian River opposite Sebastian. Four plumages are typically seen: the drab first-year juvenile plumage, which is dark above with white underparts; the second-year plumage, which has a dark breast and belly, with head and neck a dull brown; the breeding adult, which has dark body feathers, dark reddish-brown on sides and back of neck, and white and yellow on the top of the head; and the post-nuptial adult, where white feathers replace the rich brown neck feathers of courting birds. Adults are silent; only the young of the year make any sounds. Brown Pelicans are common along Florida's coastline (less so along the Panhandle) and did not suffer the same magnitude of insecticide-related population declines experienced in other southeastern states and California. In recent years a few birds have been seen using central Florida lakes and phosphate mines.

FAMILY *Phalacrocoracidae: Cormorants*
DOUBLE-CRESTED CORMORANT (*Phalacrocorax auritus*) p. 217
LENGTH 32 in (81 cm)   WEIGHT 4 lb (1.81 kg)

Other names Shag

Description All dark with orange throat patch, hooked bill (adult) or brown above, pale white below (immature)

Habitat Open saltwater; open freshwater; mangrove; cypress swamps; agricultural environments

Range Statewide

Jan	Feb	Mar	Apr	May	June	July	Aug	Sep	Oct	Nov	Dec

Florida supports a resident breeding population of Doubled-crested Cormorants and, in winter, numerous individuals from northern climes. This heavy-bodied relative of the pelican is an inhabitant of large bodies of open water, both fresh and salt, where it procures its diet of fish. Double-crested Cormorants are dark overall with an orange throat patch. First-year birds appear tawny underneath and dark brown above. Cormorants often swim with neck and head above water, but can be distinguished from Anhingas by their heavier, hooked bills. Three to four powder blue to whitish eggs are laid in a flimsy stick nest, often in the company of hundreds of other nesting cormorants and herons. Colonies appear in stands of cypress, mangrove, Australian pine, or other large trees along the coast as well as in the interior of the peninsula. Large colonies also occur in some phosphate mine impoundments where dead trees remain standing. Nesting may occur year-round, but is concentrated from March through August. A larger species, the **Great Cormorant** (*Phalacrocorax carbo*), is occasionally seen during winter near east coast inlets. It is distinguishable from the Double-crested Cormorant by its heavier bill, larger size, yellow throat patch, and the bright white belly of the immature.

FAMILY *Anhingidae: Anhingas*

ANHINGA (*Anhinga anhinga*)   p. 217

LENGTH 35 in (89 cm)   WEIGHT 2.7 lb (1.22 kg)

Other names Snakebird, Water Turkey, Darter

Description Long, snakelike neck, straight bill, long tail

Habitat Open freshwater; cypress swamps; wet prairies and marshes

Range Statewide

Jan	Feb	Mar	Apr	May	June	July	Aug	Sep	Oct	Nov	Dec

The Anhinga symbolizes the mysterious Spanish moss–draped interior wetlands of the Deep South and Florida. As if standing sentinel over swampland haunts, these graceful birds perch with wings outspread over tannin-stained waters. Because their feathers become waterlogged to facilitate diving and swimming under water, Anhingas must spread their wings to dry when they emerge from the water. They skewer fish with sharp, needle-like bills and will occasionally eat young alligators. The head and neck of the male is black, females exhibit a tan neck, and immatures appear mostly brown. The primary nesting season is March to June, when three to five white to light bluish eggs are laid in colonies of other nesting Anhingas, herons, or ibises. Two clutches may be raised in a single breeding season. Equally at home in water and air, the Anhinga is an extremely strong flier, and is often seen soaring vulturelike high over lakes and swamps. The very long neck and turkeylike tail distinguish this bird in flight.

FAMILY *Fregatidae: Frigatebirds*

MAGNIFICENT FRIGATEBIRD (*Fregata magnificens*)   p. 216

LENGTH 40 in (102 cm)   WEIGHT 2.8 lb (1.27 kg)

Other names Man-o'-war Bird, Hurricane Bird

Description Long forked tail, long hooked bill

Habitat Open saltwater; mangrove

Range Coastal, statewide

Jan	Feb	Mar	Apr	May	June	July	Aug	Sep	Oct	Nov	Dec

Frigatebirds are distinctive coastal residents with huge wingspans (7–8 feet) and deeply forked tails. These elegant scavengers glean food scraps from the water's surface, catch young birds and sea turtle hatchlings on the ground, or harass other seabirds to give up their catch (they are even known to rob the baskets of South American fishermen). Primarily an inhabitant of tropical seas, the only known breeding site in North America occurs in mangroves, on Long Key in the Dry Tortugas. Magnificent Frigatebirds are seldom seen inland, unless blown by storms, but show up regularly along both coasts of Florida's mainland. Adult males are completely black with a bright red inflatable throat pouch. Females also are black with a white breast patch, while juvenile birds possess white heads and underparts. Breeding pairs lay one egg per nesting cycle, and young may not fledge until six months of age. The status of the Magnificent Frigatebirds may become imperiled because they nest in such a limited area.

ORDER *Ciconiiformes: Bitterns, Herons, Ibises, Spoonbills, Storks, American Vultures*

Long-legged and usually long-necked wading birds. American Vultures have a highly developed sense of smell, are essentially voiceless, and feed on carrion.

FAMILY *Ardeidae: Bitterns and Herons*
AMERICAN BITTERN (*Botaurus lentiginosus*)   p. 218
LENGTH 28 in (71 cm)   WEIGHT 1.6 lb (0.73 kg)

Other names Stake Driver, Thunder Pump, Sun-gazer, Indian Hen
Description Brown with black neck stripes
Habitat Salt marshes; wet prairies and marshes
Range Statewide

Jan	Feb	Mar	Apr	May	June	July	Aug	Sep	Oct	Nov	Dec

The American Bittern probably nests throughout Florida (no verified records in the state), but it becomes noticeably more abundant during winter after northern birds arrive. An inhabitant of freshwater and saltwater marshes, this large bittern uses its concealing plumage and behavior to stay hidden in tall marsh grass. Shades of tawny-brown above, dark-tipped wings, creamy below with brown flecking, black stripe below each eye, greenish legs, and a habit of standing erect with head pointed upward combine to create an effective camouflage for this secretive marsh bird. It may also sway with wind-blown vegetation. Its deep resonant cry, *oonk-a-lunk,* which resembles a variety of hydraulic machines, gave rise to some of this bird's local names. Nests are usually flattened tangles of marsh grass in which about four eggs are laid during spring and summer. Food items include frogs, fish, and a variety of invertebrates.

FAMILY *Ardeidae: Bitterns and Herons*
LEAST BITTERN (*Ixobrychus exilis*)   p. 218
LENGTH 13 in (33 cm)   WEIGHT 3 oz (0.09 kg)

Description Black crown and back (brown in female), buffy wing patches, dark wingtips
Habitat Wet prairies and marshes; agricultural environments
Range Statewide

Jan	Feb	Mar	Apr	May	June	July	Aug	Sep	Oct	Nov	Dec

Our smallest heron, the Least Bittern is a denizen of Florida's freshwater and saltwater marshes and mangrove swamps. It also is our only heron in which the sexes have noticeably different plumages. Mostly brown above and light below, males exhibit a greenish-black top of head, tail, and back. In females the back and wings are mostly a rusty-brown. Immatures appear browner overall, and more streaked below. A low, monotonous, ventriloquial *cluck,* and a song like that of the Black-billed Cuckoo are often the only evidence of this secretive bird's presence. Least Bitterns are so inconspicuous that little is known of their life history. Apparently preferring freshwater marshes for breeding, they construct nests of twigs or marsh grass placed over water, usually in cattails. About four eggs are laid during spring or summer, and the young leave the nest in six to ten days. Food consists of frogs, fish, insects, and other invertebrates. Wherever clumps of cattails occur on Florida lakes, whether in urban centers or in open country, one may expect to find this species. Although they are frequently struck by airboats and highway vehicles, the greatest threat to the species' existence is wetlands loss.

FAMILY *Ardeidae: Bitterns and Herons*

GREAT BLUE HERON (*Ardea herodias*) p. 219

LENGTH 46 in (117 cm)   WEIGHT 5.7 lb (2.59 kg)

Other names Blue Crane, Poor Joe, Ward's Heron, Pond Scoggin, Gray Gaulin, Arsnicker, Great White Heron

Description Gray-blue with heavy yellow bill (adult) or all white with light yellow bill and legs (white morph)

Habitat Coastal beaches, salt marshes; open freshwater; mangrove; hardwood swamps; cypress swamps; wet prairies and marshes; urban environments; agricultural environments

Range Statewide

Jan	Feb	Mar	Apr	May	June	July	Aug	Sep	Oct	Nov	Dec

The Great Blue Heron is one of Florida's most widely distributed and easily observed species of long-legged waders. It also is a heron that readily loses its fear of people and may be seen in wetlands along busy highways as well as in suburban backyards. Florida birds are somewhat paler than their northern relatives, and a white color phase, or morph, is common in south Florida throughout the Keys. Formerly considered a separate species from the Great Blue Heron, the **Great White Heron** (*Ardea (herodias) occidentalis*) may again enjoy this status in the future, but for now it is considered the same species. The breeding range of the white morph is indicated on the range map. The Great Blue Heron's large size distinguishes it from all other herons in Florida. Adult birds are blue-gray, with yellow bill, white head, black stripe above each eye, and neck streaked with black. Immature birds have black crowns, and appear less resplendent than adults. White morphs possess large yellow bills and yellow legs. Occasionally a dark-bodied heron with a white head and neck—a "hybrid" form (**Würdemann's Heron**)—is seen in the Keys. Great Blues usually nest in trees, and may form large, single-species colonies. Less commonly, they may nest as single pairs. The breeding season may last from November through July or August, and up to four light blue eggs are laid in a large, loosely constructed stick nest. Food is obtained by "still-hunting" (waiting for prey to swim or slither within striking range) and includes many fish as well as frogs, lizards, snakes, small mammals, and, occasionally, other birds. Foraging occurs at night, especially under bright moonlight, as well as during the day.

FAMILY *Ardeidae: Bitterns and Herons*
GREAT EGRET (*Ardea alba*)
p. 219
LENGTH 39 in (99 cm)   WEIGHT 2 lb (0.91 kg)

Other names American Egret, Common Egret, White Crane, Longwhite, Plume Bird

Description All white with black legs and feet, bright yellow bill

Habitat Coastal beaches; salt marshes; open freshwater; mangrove; hardwood swamps; cypress swamps; wet prairies and marshes; urban environments; agricultural environments

Range Statewide

Jan	Feb	Mar	Apr	May	June	July	Aug	Sep	Oct	Nov	Dec

This white heron is a methodical, stalking hunter that seeks its prey in shallow wetlands such as salt marshes and shallow lake margins. Great Egrets have long black legs and a yellow bill. Breeding birds possess striking green flesh parts around the eyes, and long flowing plumes called aigrettes. Great Egrets usually nest with large numbers of other wading birds in thick swamps dominated by low bushes and/or large trees and on mangrove-covered coastal islands. The breeding season extends from January through June, when three to four light blue eggs usually are laid in a shallow stick nest. Early in the twentieth century, the Great Egret was hunted nearly to extinction to supply the high-fashion millinery trade with this bird's elegant plumes. An ounce of aigrettes sold for as much as thirty-two dollars. Through intensive conservation efforts, and a fortunate change in fashions, this stately bird is once again abundant and widespread in Florida. Now the chief threat to this species, and all other wading birds, is continued drainage of wetlands.

FAMILY *Ardeidae: Bitterns and Herons*
SNOWY EGRET (*Egretta thula*)
p. 219
LENGTH 24 in (61 cm)   WEIGHT 13.1 oz (0.37 kg)   STATUS **SSC**

Other names Snowy Heron, Little Plume Bird, Little Snowy, Short White

Description All white with thin black bill, black legs, yellow feet

Habitat Coastal beaches; salt marshes; mangrove; hardwood swamps; cypress swamps; wet prairies and marshes; urban environments; agricultural environments

Range Statewide

Jan	Feb	Mar	Apr	May	June	July	Aug	Sep	Oct	Nov	Dec

The Snowy Egret is another of Florida's stately white herons that was nearly wiped out at the beginning of the twentieth century. The prominent head, neck, and back plumes of breeding adults made it a prime target for plume hunters. Like its larger cousin, the Great Egret, the Snowy has made a remarkable comeback from drastically low numbers. All-white plumage, black legs with yellow feet, black bill, and yellow around the eyes distinguish this active wader. It is about half the size of the Great Egret. Snowy Egrets stride quickly through shallow wetlands while in pursuit of frogs, fish, worms, shrimp, crayfish, aquatic insects, and even small snakes. Snowies nest in multi-species colonies located in shrub-covered wetlands or islands in lakes and coastal lagoons. Nesting begins in March or April and continues until August. Two to five light blue eggs are laid in a loosely constructed stick nest.

FAMILY *Ardeidae: Bitterns and Herons*
LITTLE BLUE HERON (*Egretta caerulea*) p. 220
LENGTH 24 in (61 cm)   WEIGHT 12.9 oz (0.37 kg)   STATUS **SSC**

Other names Calico Crane, Blue Crane

Description Slate blue (reddish head and neck when breeding), greenish legs, gray bill (adult) or white with dusky wingtips, greenish yellow legs, whitish bill (immature)

Habitat Coastal beaches; salt marshes; mangrove; hardwood swamps; cypress swamps; wet prairies and marshes; agricultural environments

Range Statewide

Jan	Feb	Mar	Apr	May	June	July	Aug	Sep	Oct	Nov	Dec

This medium-size heron is widely distributed in Florida and utilizes a variety of nesting and feeding habitats. Although many nesting colonies may occur on saltwater sites, Little Blues seem to prefer fresh water for feeding. Foods consist of small fish, frogs, and invertebrates obtained by slow stalking. Adults are slate-blue overall, with a somewhat darker head.

Breeding individuals develop long back plumes, purplish feathers, and plumes on the head, black legs, and cobalt bill with black tip. Little Blues are unusual in exhibiting white plumage in juvenile birds and a calico blue-and-white pattern during their first winter as blue feathers replace white feathers. All nonbreeding birds have lime green to blue-green legs. Little Blue Herons nest throughout Florida between late February and August in single-species or mixed colonies. Usually three light blue eggs are laid on a stick platform. Infrequently, calico birds are seen as breeding individuals. The general population trend of this interesting species is downward. While certainly related to wetlands losses, some have speculated that competition with Cattle Egrets for nest sites also may contribute to this decline.

FAMILY *Ardeidae: Bitterns and Herons*
TRICOLORED HERON (*Egretta tricolor*) p. 220
LENGTH 26 in (66 cm)   WEIGHT 14.6 oz (0.45 kg)   STATUS **SSC**

Other names Louisiana Heron, Blue Crane

Description Blue-gray upperparts, white neck and belly

Habitat Coastal beaches; salt marshes; mangrove; wet prairies and marshes; agricultural environments

Range Statewide

Jan	Feb	Mar	Apr	May	June	July	Aug	Sep	Oct	Nov	Dec

This medium-size heron is still abundant through much of peninsular Florida. However, as with other herons, Tricoloreds have declined due to wetlands habitat loss. It was once considered the most abundant heron in the state. White underparts contrast with dark dorsal plumage in adults and immatures. Adults have bluish head, neck and wings, maroon at base of neck, and buff feathers on lower back. Immature birds exhibit rufous-brown patches on wings and on sides and back of neck. Primarily a bird of salt marshes, tidal flats, and estuaries, the Tricolored Heron is most abundant coastally in the peninsula; however, it occurs in inland freshwater marshes also. Tricolored Herons use a variety of methods—from "still-hunting" (waiting for prey to swim or slither within striking range) to rapidly running—to procure their primarily fish diet. A shallow platform nest is placed in a mangrove or other dense-growing aquatic shrub. Blue eggs, usually three or four, are laid between late February and July.

FAMILY *Ardeidae: Bitterns and Herons*
REDDISH EGRET (*Egretta rufescens*) STATUS SSC
LENGTH 30 in (76 cm) WEIGHT 15.9 oz (0.45 kg)

p. 220

Description Rufous head and neck, blue-gray body (dark phase) or all white (white phase); both phases have pink bill with black anterior half.
Habitat Coastal beaches; mangrove
Range Coastal, statewide

Jan	Feb	Mar	Apr	May	June	July	Aug	Sep	Oct	Nov	Dec

Apparently still suffering the effects of the late nineteenth- and early twentieth-century plume hunting that nearly wiped out several species of Florida heron, the Reddish Egret is Florida's least common heron. The rate of recovery following protection has been much slower than for other species. Primarily a Gulf coast bird, Reddish Egrets nest from Florida Bay north to Tampa Bay. In the mid-1970s nesting Reddish Egrets were found near Vero Beach in the Indian River and Merritt Island National Wildlife Refuge, both of which are on the east coast. Specific locations are indicated on the breeding range map. Often associated with mangroves, this colorful heron is strictly a coastal species. Nonbreeding individuals have been seen as far north as Fernandina Beach on the east coast and St. Marks National Wildlife Refuge on the Gulf coast. Appearing either in all-white plumage or blue-gray with reddish-brown head and neck, both phases have similar soft part (skin) coloration. Breeding adults develop flowing back plumes, a maned appearance on head and neck, bright pink bill with black tip, purple around eyes, and cobalt legs. Immature dark morph birds are gray-brown overall without the two-toned bill. Reddish Egrets employ an erratic but active feeding style that includes spread wings and rapid steps to secure their marine prey. Breeding can occur from December in south Florida through June in northern locations. Red mangrove appears to be a favored nest site, where two to five eggs are laid on a loosely constructed platform of sticks.

FAMILY *Ardeidae: Bitters and Herons*

CATTLE EGRET (*Bubulcus ibis*)

p. 219

LENGTH 20 in (51 cm)　　WEIGHT 11.9 oz (0.34 kg)

Other names Buff-backed Heron, Cowbird

Description White with buff on head, neck, breast and back (breeding) or all white with short yellow bill, yellowish legs (nonbreeding)

Habitat Dry prairies; wet prairies and marshes; agricultural environments

Range Statewide

Jan	Feb	Mar	Apr	May	June	July	Aug	Sep	Oct	Nov	Dec

The Cattle Egret represents an amazing feat in avian natural history. Originally an Old World species, often associated with large ungulates on the East African plains, the Cattle Egret now is perhaps the most common heron in Florida. It apparently reached South America on its own by the 1880s, and breeding individuals were found in Florida in 1953. The Cattle Egret now occupies most of the Western Hemisphere and continues its range expansion. A relatively short-legged heron, the Cattle Egret appears white most of the year. During courtship, adult birds lose the yellowish coloration on bill and the dark legs, and acquire orange-to-red flesh parts and red irises. Buff feathers on the back, head, and chest complete the courtship color changes. The breeding season lasts throughout the spring, when they are found in the company of other native colonial nesting herons. Cattle Egrets frequently are observed near livestock and farm equipment waiting for grazing animals or tractors to flush insects. These highly social herons even have been observed perched on the backs of cattle, horses, and deer. They also forage along roadside swales. Food items include grasshoppers, flies, butterflies, caterpillars, damselflies, spiders, frogs, lizards, snakes, and small rodents. Only occasionally do Cattle Egrets feed in or near water; they prefer to nest in shrubs or trees over water, or on tree-covered islands surrounded by water. Usually four light blue eggs are laid in a simple stick nest. Because of their open-feeding habits, Cattle Egrets are occasionally preyed on by Red-tailed Hawks, Crested Caracaras, Bald Eagles, and red foxes.

FAMILY *Ardeidae: Bitters and Herons*

GREEN HERON (*Butorides virescens*)

p. 220

LENGTH 18 in (46 cm)　　WEIGHT 7.5 oz (0.21 kg)

Other names Green-backed Heron, Skeow, Shietpoke, Little Green Heron

Description Small with dark crown, green-gray back, chestnut neck, yellow legs

Habitat Salt marshes; mangrove; hardwood swamps; cypress swamps; wet prairies and marshes; urban environments; agricultural environments

Range Statewide

Jan	Feb	Mar	Apr	May	June	July	Aug	Sep	Oct	Nov	Dec

The Green is a small, cryptically colored heron. Normally seen perched in a frozen repose near a pond or stream edge, this bird prefers the seclusion of a wooded canopy. Adults have a greenish-black crown, and white undersides that are streaked with brown. The upper wing surfaces, tail, and back appear slate-gray. Immatures are browner overall with heavy brown streaking on white undersides. Flesh parts are grayish-yellow except during breeding, when males exhibit bright orange legs. Green Herons are typically solitary birds, but may nest in large colonies with other Green Herons and, occasionally, in mixed-species colonies. Three to four pale blue eggs are laid in a frail stick platform between March and June. Primarily a predator of small fish, Greens also take crustaceans, mollusks, and a variety of insects. Some Green Herons have learned to fish with bait, dropping pieces of bread and insects in water to attract minnows. An explosive *skeow* call is given when disturbed.

FAMILY *Ardeidae: Bitterns and Herons*
BLACK-CROWNED NIGHT-HERON (*Nycticorax nycticorax*)   p. 218
LENGTH 25 in (64 cm)   WEIGHT 1.9 lb (0.86 kg)

Other names Quock, Indian Pullet

Description Stocky; black crown, back; white underparts (adult) or brown with white spotting (immature)

Habitat Salt marshes; mangrove; hardwood swamps; cypress swamps; wet prairies and marshes; agricultural environments

Range Statewide

Jan	Feb	Mar	Apr	May	June	July	Aug	Sep	Oct	Nov	Dec

This aptly named medium-size heron is widely distributed throughout the United States as well as in Florida. Solid black crown and back, gray on sides of neck and wings, white undersides, and short yellowish legs distinguish the Black-crowned Night-Heron. Immatures are brown above with tawny-streaked undersides, and are distinguishable from Yellow-crowned Night-Herons by yellow eyes, longer, narrower bill, and shorter legs. Black-crowned Night-Herons frequent shrub-bordered lakes and stream margins in search of fish, amphibians, crustaceans, snakes, and insects, as well as small birds and mammals, usually at night. Occasionally they will eat nestlings of other heron species in the colony. In flight, these nocturnal herons utter a deep-pitched *quawk*, which gave rise to one of its local names. In Florida, Black-crowns often are found nesting in multi-species heron colonies throughout the state. Nesting can begin as early as December in south Florida and last until June or July in the north. Two to five pale blue eggs are laid in a bulky nest of sticks.

FAMILY *Ardeidae: Bitterns and Herons*
YELLOW-CROWNED NIGHT-HERON (*Nyctanassa violacea*)   p. 218
LENGTH 24 in (61 cm)   WEIGHT 1.6 lb (0.73 kg)

> **Other names** Crab-eater, Crabier, Grosbec, Gauldin, Arsenicker, Quock, Indian Pullet, Skwok
>
> **Description** All gray, black head with buffy white crown, white ear patch (adult) or gray-brown with narrow white spots (immature)
>
> **Habitat** Salt marshes; wet prairies and marshes
>
> **Range** Statewide

Jan	Feb	Mar	Apr	May	June	July	Aug	Sep	Oct	Nov	Dec

Longer-legged than their black-crowned relative, Yellow-crowned Night-Herons also are less nocturnal. Adults are gray above and below, and the black head is crowned with white and marked with white cheek patches. During the breeding season a brilliant yellow patch highlights the forehead. Immature birds resemble young Black-crowned Night-Herons, but have longer legs, shorter and thicker all-black bills, and orange eyes. Yellow-crowns can be found in a variety of habitats from coastal mangroves (such as Tampa Bay) to interior hardwood swamps (such as Osceola National Forest), and can be seen feeding in surf. Food consists primarily of crustaceans such as fiddler crabs and crayfish, although a variety of other wetland prey is taken. Yellow-crowned Night-Herons may nest singly, with other Yellow-crowns, or in large mixed-species colonies. Nest sites range from mangroves to Australian pines and live oaks. Loosely constructed stick nests may be found with three to four pale blue eggs from March through June.

FAMILY *Threskiornithidae: Ibises and Spoonbills*
WHITE IBIS (*Eudocimus albus*)   p. 221
LENGTH 25 in (64 cm)   WEIGHT 2.3 lb (1.04 kg)   STATUS **SSC**

> **Other names** White Curlew, Brown Curlew, Spanish Curlew, Stone Curlew, Chokoloskee Chicken, Florida Curlew
>
> **Description** All white, black wingtips, red decurved bill and legs (adult) or brown with white underparts (immature)
>
> **Habitat** Hardwood swamps; cypress swamps; wet prairies and marshes; agricultural environments
>
> **Range** Statewide

Jan	Feb	Mar	Apr	May	June	July	Aug	Sep	Oct	Nov	Dec

Although distributed throughout the state, the White Ibis is characteristic of south Florida's wild wetlands. Striking white plumage, black wingtips, and bright red flesh parts distinguish adults. Females are somewhat smaller and have shorter, less down-curved bills. Immatures are mostly brown above with white underparts. The White Ibis nests in large colonies throughout the state from March through May. Well-constructed stick nests usually contain three to four white or light green eggs splotched with brown, tan, and purple. Interbreeding with the **Scarlet Ibis** (*Eudocimus ruber*), introduced in Greynold's Park, Miami, from South America in the 1960s, resulted in pink-colored hybrids. Such individuals have been seen infrequently as far north as Gainesville. White Ibises may be seen singly or in large impressive flocks on their way to or from feeding areas. Preferred habitats are freshwater marshes, shallow lakes, and estuaries, where crayfish, aquatic insects, grasshoppers, crabs, grass shrimp, and small snakes are consumed. The Florida population of this species has experienced drastic declines and fluctuations since the early 1900s, but the White Ibis is probably still the most abundant wading bird south of Lake Okeechobee. Human development and disturbance are apparently responsible for the decline of the White Ibis.

FAMILY *Threskiornithidae: Ibises and Spoonbills*
GLOSSY IBIS (*Plegadis falcinellus*)   p. 221
LENGTH 23 in (58 cm)   WEIGHT 1.1–1.76 lb (0.5–0.8 kg)

Other names Black Curlew, Bronze Curlew

Description Dark plumage, chestnut-bronze in some light, decurved brownish bill

Habitat Wet prairies and marshes; agricultural environments

Range Statewide

Jan	Feb	Mar	Apr	May	June	July	Aug	Sep	Oct	Nov	Dec

Until recently, the Glossy Ibis was not an abundant Florida resident. Over the last half of the twentieth century, this ibis greatly increased its range, which now extends throughout Florida, through coastal Louisiana, and on the east coast to Maine. It is less common in the Florida Panhandle. The long, decurved bill distinguishes this bird as an ibis. Appearing mostly dark overall, Glossies exhibit a reddish plumage with a green and purple iridescence when seen in good light. Immature birds appear browner, especially on the head and neck. Glossy Ibises nest colonially with other wading birds. Colonies have been found in wooded wetlands from the Everglades through north Florida. Spring and summer constitute the breeding season, when three or four eggs are laid in a stick platform nest or on the ground. Glossy Ibises seem to prefer fresh water, where crayfish are an important food. Other foods include fish, snakes, grasshoppers, and other insects.

FAMILY *Threskiornithidae: Ibises and Spoonbills*
ROSEATE SPOONBILL (*Platalea ajaja*)
LENGTH 32 in (81 cm)   WEIGHT 2.65–3.97 lb (1.2–1.8 kg)   STATUS **SSC**   p. 221

Other names Pink Curlew, Pink

Description Pink body with spatulate bill, bare greenish head, orange tail (adult) or paler, more white (immature)

Habitat Salt marshes; mangrove; wet prairies and marshes; agricultural environments

Range Central and south Florida

Jan	Feb	Mar	Apr	May	June	July	Aug	Sep	Oct	Nov	Dec

An unmistakable bird of south Florida's mangroves and freshwater estuaries, the Roseate Spoonbill is on the increase after drastic declines caused by plume- and egg-hunters. Nearly extirpated by the start of the twentieth century, Spoonbills now nest in several large Florida Bay colonies and recently have returned as a breeding species to Tampa Bay and Merritt Island, as indicated on the breeding range map. The light pink wings and backs of immature birds deepen gradually over three years, when adults take on a much brighter pink, highlighted by an orange tail, bright red rump, shoulders, and chest patch, and black skin on sides and back of neck. The broad, flattened bill is distinctive in all ages. Spoonbills build deep, well-constructed stick nests usually in association with heron and ibis colonies located in mangroves. In Florida Bay three eggs are usually laid during November or December. Farther northward breeding occurs in April. Feeding is accomplished by moving the bill side to side underwater or through shallow mud in search of small fish, insects, and crustaceans. Although population trends of this attractive wader are up, feeding habitat for spoonbills is being lost at an increasing rate. The survival of this species depends upon maintaining its shallow feeding grounds.

Family *Ciconiidae: Storks*
WOOD STORK (*Mycteria americana*) p. 221
Length 40 in (102 cm)　　Weight 6 lb (2.72 kg)　　Status **E**

Other names Flinthead, Gourdhead, Ironhead, Gannet, Preacher, Spanish Buzzard, Wood Ibis

Description White with black primaries and tail, blackish head (naked in adult), heavy bill, pink feet

Habitat Salt marshes; cypress swamps; wet prairies and marshes; agricultural environments

Range Statewide

| Jan | Feb | Mar | Apr | May | June | July | Aug | Sep | Oct | Nov | Dec |

The Wood Stork is an inhabitant of some of Florida's most pristine swamplands, often nesting in the thousands. A large, white-bodied wader, the Wood Stork exhibits a black tail, black on wingtips and trailing edges, black legs with pink feet, and a dark, featherless head capped with a lighter horny plate. Immatures have a more completely feathered neck and yellowish bill. Wood Storks are apparently much reduced in numbers, totaling less than 20% of their estimated 1930s population of 75,000, and are now on federal and state endangered lists. Degradation of nesting and feeding habitat certainly has contributed to this decline, yet Wood Stork colonies are still scattered widely throughout Florida, though they are less common in the Panhandle. The largest colonies are in southwest Florida, at National Audubon's Corkscrew Swamp Sanctuary. Wood Storks require concentrations of fish in shallow water where they "grope-feed" with bill partly open until prey contact is made. High water or extended droughts in feeding areas may reduce nesting success. Two to four white eggs are laid in bulky stick nests in cypress trees or mangroves from November in the south to April or May in north Florida. Successful nesting requires extensive areas of 6–10 inch (15–20 centimeter) deep, and dropping water. Typically in south Florida, dropping water levels occur from winter through spring after the cessation of summer afternoon thunderstorms. Lower water levels concentrate fish and invertebrate prey and allow Wood Storks to obtain more prey with less work. Ideal conditions result in successful reproduction.

FAMILY *Cathartidae: American Vultures*
BLACK VULTURE (*Coragyps atratus*)
p. 227
LENGTH 25 in (64 cm)   WEIGHT 4.8 lb (2.18 kg)

Other names Black Buzzard

Description Black head, white at base of primaries, short tail

Habitat Coastal beaches; salt marshes; xeric scrub; mangrove; hardwood swamps; dry prairies; cypress swamps; mesic hammocks; mixed pine and hardwood forests; wet prairies and marshes; urban environments; pine flatwoods; sandhills; agricultural environments

Range Statewide

Jan	Feb	Mar	Apr	May	June	July	Aug	Sep	Oct	Nov	Dec

Black Vultures differ from Turkey Vultures in several subtle ways. Shorter wings and tail, black head, and white outer primaries distinguish this vulture. In flight, Black Vultures hold their wings flat, they flap more often than Turkey Vultures, and their feet usually extend beyond the tail. Feeding habits are similar to those of Turkey Vultures but Black Vultures are more aggressive around carcasses, often dominating the kill. Black Vultures are less adept at locating carrion due to their less sensitive sense of smell, and often take advantage of food found by Turkey Vultures. They will occasionally take live prey, including nestlings in heron colonies. Nesting habits also are similar to those of Turkey Vultures, but the breeding season extends from January to August. A preferred nest site is often a bare patch of ground in a dense saw palmetto thicket. The Black Vulture is most commonly encountered away from coastlines, and is a frequent visitor to some urban areas.

FAMILY *Cathartidae: American Vultures*
TURKEY VULTURE (*Cathartes aura*)
p. 227
LENGTH 27 in (69 cm)   WEIGHT 3.2 lb (1.45 kg)

Other names Turkey Buzzard

Description Red head (black in immatures), long tail, underside of wings dark anteriorly, lighter posteriorly

Habitat Coastal beaches; salt marshes; xeric scrub; mangrove; hardwood swamps; dry prairies; cypress swamps; mesic hammocks; mixed pine and hardwood forests; wet prairies and marshes; urban environments; pine flatwoods; sandhills; agricultural environments

Range Statewide

Jan	Feb	Mar	Apr	May	June	July	Aug	Sep	Oct	Nov	Dec

Turkey Vultures can scarcely be overlooked on warm summer afternoons, soaring effortlessly on thermal updrafts in search of fresh "road kills" or other carrion. There is virtually no place in Florida where this species cannot be observed. Bare red head, light primaries and secondaries when seen from underneath, relatively long tail, and wings held in a nearly flat "V" (dihedral)—all are characteristic of this most widespread of Florida's vultures. Immatures lack the red head of the adult. Turkey Vultures nest on the ground in the protection of dense vegetation, hollow logs, or other cavities. The nesting season extends from March through July, when usually two eggs are laid. During winter there is an influx of vultures from northern states. Occasionally vulture roosts containing several thousand individuals have been observed in south Florida. An extremely sensitive sense of smell allows this bird to detect rotting flesh from great distances.

ORDER *Phoenicopteriformes: Flamingos*
These are large waders with long legs and bent bills.

FAMILY *Phoenicopteridae: Flamingos*
GREATER FLAMINGO (*Phoenicopterus ruber*)   p. 221
LENGTH 46 in (117 cm)   WEIGHT 7.8 lb (3.54 kg)

Description Large; pink body, black primaries, short heavy bill (adult) or grayish white, with some pink (immature)
Habitat Salt marshes; wet prairies and marshes
Range Coastal, south and central Florida

Jan	Feb	Mar	Apr	May	June	July	Aug	Sep	Oct	Nov	Dec

Perhaps one of the world's most elegant animals, flamingos primarily are associated with the tropics. Apparently once common in extreme south Florida and occasionally north to Tampa Bay and Indian River, Greater Flamingos are now most often seen near Snake Bight in Everglades National Park. Individuals observed in the Miami area may be the result of escaped zoo animals, although birds visiting in Florida Bay may be wild birds from the Bahamas, Cuba, or the Yucatan. Most observations were of birds present during winter. Birds that regularly occur in southeast Florida (and occasionally elsewhere in the state) are likely from the captive flock in Hialeah, and occasional migrants from the Bahamas or Cuba. It seems that breeding of wild flamingos in Florida has not occurred in about 100 years. Except for black primaries and bill tip, adult Greater Flamingos are entirely pink (juvenile birds usually have no pink, but are mostly white in plumage). Extremely long legs and neck, extended in flight, further characterize this bird. This species may have once nested in the Everglades, but no evidence supports this belief. Food consists primarily of crustaceans, algae, diatoms, and mollusks that are obtained by sucking and filtering their prey from marl and mud flats.

ORDER *Anseriformes: Swans, Geese, Ducks*
Waterbirds with short legs, webbed front toes, and a nail-like
hook at the tip of the bill.

FAMILY *Anatidae: Swans, Geese, Ducks*

FULVOUS WHISTLING-DUCK (*Dendrocygna bicolor*)

LENGTH 20 in (51 cm)   WEIGHT 1.6 lb (0.74 kg)

Other names Fulvous Tree Duck, Mexican Squealer

p. 222

Description Tawny color with dark back, long
neck and legs, white rump

Habitat Wet prairies and marshes, agricultural environments

Range Statewide

| Jan | Feb | Mar | Apr | May | June | July | Aug | Sep | Oct | Nov | Dec |

Despite its name, the Fulvous Whistling-Duck is probably a closer relative of
swans and geese than of typical ducks. Considered an accidental through the
middle of the twentieth century, it is now an established breeder in south
Florida with a statewide population of over 20,000. Long legs extending beyond the black tail in
flight, long neck, rufous-brown undersides, black back barred with brown, white band on rump,
and black wings distinguish this species. A high-pitched whistle may be given in flight. This bird is
most evident in and around agricultural land in central and south Florida where it breeds over
water in tall grasses and rice fields. The expansion of large-scale vegetable farms where they find
abundant food may explain the establishment of Fulvous Whistling-Ducks in Florida. Its rapid
increase may be partly due to large clutch sizes—12 to 17 eggs on average.

FAMILY *Anatidae: Swans, Geese, Ducks*

BLACK-BELLIED WHISTLING-DUCK

(*Dendrocygna autumnalis*)

p. 222

LENGTH 21 in (53 cm)   WEIGHT 1.8 lb (0.81 kg)

Description Distinctive white wing stripe, red bill, black under
wings, gray head

Habitat Ponds and lakes, nests in hollow trees

Range Central and south Florida

| Jan | Feb | Mar | Apr | May | June | July | Aug | Sep | Oct | Nov | Dec |

The Black-bellied Whistling-Duck has dramatically increased its range in Florida
since a flock was found near Sarasota in the early 1980s. Small groups may be
seen throughout the peninsula, and several pairs have bred near Gainesville and
in Hardee County in recent years. Its present breeding range is shown on the range
map, and further expansion is likely. Red-orange bill, pink feet, brown back, and large white
wing patches separate this cavity-nesting whistling-duck from the Fulvous. Clutches consist of
8–12 eggs laid from spring through summer. The call is a six-syllable whistle. Until recent
decades, the closest breeding populations occurred in Mexico and south Texas.

FAMILY *Anatidae: Swans, Geese, Ducks*
SNOW GOOSE (*Chen caerulescens*)   p. 222
LENGTH 28 in (71 cm)   WEIGHT 3.53–7.28 lb (1.6–3.30 kg)
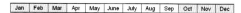

Other names Blue Goose

Description White with black primaries (white morph) or gray with white head and neck (blue morph)

Habitat Salt marshes; open freshwater; wet prairies and marshes; agricultural environments

Range Statewide

Jan	Feb	Mar	Apr	May	June	July	Aug	Sep	Oct	Nov	Dec

This large goose appears in two color phases: an all-white morph with black primaries, and a dark, or blue, morph with a white head. The bill of adults is pink; the grayish (white morph) or brown (dark morph) immatures have a black bill. It is an uncommon wintering bird, found chiefly in north Florida and most often seen at St. Marks National Wildlife Refuge, but several occasionally winter in south Florida. Food is primarily vegetation.

FAMILY *Anatidae: Swans, Geese, Ducks*
CANADA GOOSE (*Branta canadensis*)   p. 222
LENGTH 40 in (102 cm)   WEIGHT 8.4 lb (3.81 kg)

Other Names Honker

Description Black head and neck, white chin strap

Habitat Salt marshes, open freshwater, wet prairies and marshes; agricultural environments

Range North Florida

Jan	Feb	Mar	Apr	May	June	July	Aug	Sep	Oct	Nov	Dec

With flocks numbering over 30,000 birds through the 1950s, the Canada Goose was one of Florida's most conspicuous wintering waterbirds. An expanding Midwestern corn and grain belt has "short-stopped" these southward migrants, eliminating the need to travel to the unfrozen south. Nonetheless, Canada Geese still are regularly observed in north Florida, albeit in greatly reduced numbers. Efforts to establish a nonmigratory flock have been mostly unsuccessful, although some nesting occurs locally throughout the peninsula. The large size, white cheek patches, black head and neck, and grayish bodies make the Canada Goose unmistakable. Nests are usually on the ground near water and contain four to eight eggs. Flocks of Canada Geese fly in long lines or V-formations and can be heard overhead uttering their characteristic *honk*.

FAMILY *Anatidae: Swans, Geese, Ducks*
BRANT (*Branta bernicla*)
LENGTH 25 in (64 cm)   WEIGHT 3 lb (1.36 kg)

Description A small, dark goose with dark head and white necklace

Habitat Coastal marine waters with eelgrass

Range Coastal, statewide

Jan	Feb	Mar	Apr	May	June	July	Aug	Sep	Oct	Nov	Dec

The Brant bears a superficial resemblance to the Canada Goose but is generally smaller, darker, and has a daintier bill. Its head is entirely black and adults have a partial white necklace near the top of the neck. Juvenile birds are similar to adults but lack the necklace. Its voice is variable and includes a gurgling *cronk* and a low murmur when flocked. Flocks migrate in irregular "V" formations. In Florida, these coastal-living geese are rarely seen during winter along both sides of the peninsula from the Keys to Jacksonville and the Big Bend. The Brant is seldom seen in interior lakes and rivers. It feeds mainly in marine habitats on eelgrass by tipping up like a dabbling duck.

FAMILY *Anatidae: Swans, Geese, Ducks*
TUNDRA SWAN (*Cygnus columbianus*)   p. 222
LENGTH 52 in (132 cm)   WEIGHT 8.38–23.5 lb (3.8–10.66 kg)

Other names Whistling Swan

Description Large white body, long neck (adult) or brownish or tan (immature)

Habitat Open freshwater; wet prairies and marshes; agricultural environments

Range North Florida

Jan	Feb	Mar	Apr	May	June	July	Aug	Sep	Oct	Nov	Dec

One of the largest but most unpredictable winter visitors to Florida is the Arctic-nesting Tundra Swan. These graceful white birds with black bills are seen only rarely in north Florida wetlands. Immature birds appear buff-gray overall. They occur in Florida primarily from November through March. Foods consist of a variety of grains, seeds, tubers, and submerged invertebrates. A similar bird, the **Mute Swan** (*Cygnus olor*), native to the Old World, is becoming increasingly common in residential areas although it is not yet established as a feral breeding species in Florida. The Mute Swan differs from the Tundra Swan in that it has a bright orange bill with a black knob at its base, and it holds its neck in an "S" shape versus the straight neck of the Tundra Swan. Wings may be held in an arch over the back.

Family *Anatidae: Swans, Geese, Ducks*
Muscovy Duck (*Cairina moschata*)
p. 222
Length 28 in (71 cm)   Weight 5–15 lbs (2.27–6.8 kg)

Other names Royal Duck

Description Both sexes variable—all black, black and white, or all white; male has red warty face

Habitat Urban environments; agricultural environments

Range Statewide

Jan	Feb	Mar	Apr	May	June	July	Aug	Sep	Oct	Nov	Dec

The wild form of this widely distributed exotic occurs in Central and South America. About the size of a large domesticated Mallard, Muscovies are commonly seen in urban parks where they can be quite prolific. Nests often are made in root tangles at the bases of trees, under yard shrubbery, and sometimes on condominium balconies. Trees also provide night roosts. A wide variety of color patterns are encountered in Florida, ranging from all-white to a dark, lustrous green-black (similar to the wild form), with intermediate pied forms. Large patches of bumpy flesh encircle the eyes and base of the bill, especially in males. This large, aggressive duck is often considered a pest. It is reputed to harbor diseases and parasites that may adversely affect native waterfowl in common habitats. The continued release and feeding of this exotic should be discouraged, although all known populations depend to some degree on human protection.

Family *Anatidae: Swans, Geese, Ducks*
Wood Duck (*Aix sponsa*)
p. 223
Length 18 in (46 cm)   Weight 1.5 lb (0.68 kg)

Other names Summer Duck, Woodie, Squealer, Swamp Duck, Acorn Duck

Description Crested green head, white neck, red breast, red eye and base of bill (male) or dull brown, white teardrop eye patch (female)

Habitat Hardwood swamps; cypress swamps; wet prairies and marshes; agricultural environments

Range Statewide

Jan	Feb	Mar	Apr	May	June	July	Aug	Sep	Oct	Nov	Dec

A characteristic bird of Florida's wooded wetlands, the Wood Duck once was on the verge of extinction due to over-hunting. With stricter hunting regulations, Wood Ducks today are found wherever large tracts of swamplands and adjacent woodlands provide adequate cavities for nest sites and acorns, their principal fall food. It is least common in southeastern Florida. Certainly our most colorful duck, males exhibit iridescent back and head plumage, red eye and base of bill, tan sides, white throat, and white-spotted maroon chest. Both sexes exhibit head crests. Females are less resplendent with grayish plumage above, white undersides, white eye ring and eye line, and a light blue speculum (wing patch). During the fall, Wood Ducks may form large flocks in areas with abundant food. Shallow, flooded oak woods are favored feeding grounds. Florida's breeding population of Wood Ducks is resident and nonmigratory, but interacts with a large number of northern Wood Ducks during fall and winter. The nest cavity may be located as high as 50 feet up in a tree and far from water. The female lays up to 20 eggs, one each day until her clutch is complete, then incubates them for 30 days. Within a day after hatching, she leaves the cavity and calls the nestlings from the ground, and they come tumbling out, dropping many feet to the ground, unhurt, and follow their mother to the nearest pond or river. Wood Ducks readily use artificial nest boxes and will even nest in highly urban locations, as long as both lakes and trees are abundant nearby.

FAMILY *Anatidae: Swans, Geese, Ducks*
GADWALL (*Anas strepera*) p. 224
LENGTH 20 in (51 cm)   WEIGHT 2.2 lb (1 kg)

Other names Gray Duck, Gray Mallard

Description Gray with white belly, black undertail coverts (male) or mottled brown body, lighter head, white belly (female)

Habitat Open freshwater; wet prairies and marshes; agricultural environments

Range North and central Florida

Jan	Feb	Mar	Apr	May	June	July	Aug	Sep	Oct	Nov	Dec

The Gadwall is a rather nondescript medium-size duck that occurs in modest numbers throughout north and central Florida during winter. Males have light gray vermiculated sides, gray mottled chest, white belly, and brown head and back. Females are mottled brown above, with buff head and neck and white underparts. Both sexes have a white speculum (smaller in the female), and show a white patch of inner secondaries while swimming or at rest. Gadwalls usually arrive in Florida during late October and remain through early March, when they may be observed on large freshwater impoundments, lakes, and marshes. Their predominantly vegetable diet consists of stems of pondweeds as well as filamentous algae and other succulent plant growth. The Gadwall has experienced a sharp decline in recent decades.

FAMILY *Anatidae: Swans, Geese, Ducks*
AMERICAN WIGEON (*Anas americana*) p. 224
LENGTH 19 in (48 cm)   WEIGHT 1.7 lb (0.77 kg)

Other names Baldpate, Gray Duck

Description White forehead and cap, green ear patch (male) or grayish head (female)

Habitat Salt marshes; open freshwater; wet prairies and marshes; agricultural environments

Range Statewide

Jan	Feb	Mar	Apr	May	June	July	Aug	Sep	Oct	Nov	Dec

A distinctive white crown and metallic green eyestripe sets the male American Wigeon apart from other waterfowl species. The female has a grayish head and a brown mottled body. In flight a white wing patch is evident in front of a black/green speculum in the male and a dark speculum in the female. Many thousands of Wigeons winter each year throughout Florida, although their numbers have declined since the 1950s. Migrants arrive here in early October and may remain until mid-April. These handsome ducks may be seen in coastal estuaries and interior lakes or ponds feeding on leaves and stems of succulent vegetation. Occasionally Wigeons are observed robbing Coots, Redheads, and other diving ducks of their food. Vegetation accounts for over 90% of their fare. One of the best places to see this species close-up is Wakulla Springs State Park, south of Tallahassee. Each winter one or more **Eurasian Wigeons** (*Anas penelope*) occur in Florida, usually in a flock of American Wigeons. The male has gray sides and back, a rusty red head, and a cream-colored hood stripe. The female is very similar to American Wigeon females but may exhibit a rusty head.

FAMILY *Anatidae: Swans, Geese, Ducks*
AMERICAN BLACK DUCK (*Anas rubripes*)
LENGTH 23 in (58 cm)   WEIGHT 3.1 lb (1.4 kg)   p. 223

Other names Black Mallard, Red Leg

Description Black-brown body, pale face and neck, yellow bill, violet spectrum

Habitat Salt marshes; wet prairies and marshes; agricultural environments

Range North Florida

| Jan | Feb | Mar | Apr | May | June | July | Aug | Sep | Oct | Nov | Dec |

Resembling the hen Mallard in size and coloration, the American Black Duck is somewhat darker, exhibits a contrast between buff-colored head and darker body, and lacks a white border on speculum and tail feathers. Once a common wintering bird in Florida's freshwater and coastal marshes, American Black Ducks are seen infrequently today. Small groups and individuals can be seen occasionally from early October to April throughout north Florida. They are very rare in central and south Florida. Previously a very abundant duck in northern and eastern North America, it has been hunted heavily. It also seems that it is being displaced by Mallards. American Black Ducks are habitat generalists and have a diverse diet. Important foods include a variety of wetlands grasses and sedges as well as snails, insects, and mussels.

Family *Anatidae: Swans, Geese, Ducks*
MALLARD (*Anas platyrhynchos*)
p. 223
LENGTH 23 in (58 cm)   WEIGHT 2.4 lb (1.09 kg)

Other names Greenhead (drake), Gray Mallard (hen), Susie (hen)

Description Green head, chestnut breast, grayish white back and sides (male) or mottled brown body; orange bill with black markings (female)

Habitat Wet prairies and marshes; agricultural environments

Range North and central Florida

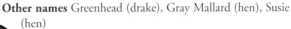

Because of the drake's brilliant coloration and its popularity as a domestic, Mallards are probably the most widely recognized duck. Males have a metallic green head with white collar, yellow bill, chestnut breast, and curled tail feathers. Females are a lighter brown color than Mottled Ducks and have an orange bill marked with black. Both sexes exhibit a metallic blue speculum bordered front and back with white. Mallards are the most vocal of our ducks and are heard frequently during fall when other species are silent. Mallards are fairly common winter visitors from late September to early March in north Florida, where they can be seen feeding ("tipping up") in shallow fresh water. Aquatic vegetation makes up the bulk of its food. Although not a significant part of the waterfowl harvest in Florida, Mallards are considered an important game duck in North America. True wild Mallards do not breed in Florida. The breeding Mallards, chiefly seen on urban lakes and ponds, are of semi-domesticated stock, and many more now breed in the wild throughout the peninsula.

Family *Anatidae: Swans, Geese, Ducks*
MOTTLED DUCK (*Anas fulvigula*)
LENGTH 22 in (56 cm)   WEIGHT 2.3 lb (1.04 kg)
p. 223

Other names Florida Duck, Summer Mallard, Summer Duck

Description Pale black-brown body, lighter head and neck, greenish speculum

Habitat Salt marshes; wet prairies and marshes; agricultural environments

Range Statewide

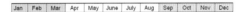

The Mottled Duck is a year-round resident throughout most of peninsular Florida. Both sexes exhibit fuscous-brown plumage that is lighter than the Black Duck yet darker than the hen Mallard. Females have dull olive bills, while males have bright yellow bills with a black spot at the base. The speculum is blue, often with a greenish cast. Primarily associated with freshwater and brackish marshes, more than half of Florida's Mottled Duck population occurs in Charlotte, Glades, Hendry, and Lee counties. A large population also occurs in the St. Johns River marshes and Merritt Island National Wildlife Refuge in Brevard County. Nests are constructed near water in dense grass and/or in the cover of dense shrubs. In agricultural lands, nests even have been found in tomato fields. Most nesting activity occurs between early March and mid-April but may extend into September, when about ten eggs are laid. The breeding range is indicated on the range map. Food habits vary geographically but Mottled Ducks primarily are vegetarian. Animal foods such as insects and snails account for one-third of the diet in summer. Mottled Ducks are an important game species in Florida with over 13,000 harvested each year.

FAMILY *Anatidae: Swans, Geese, Ducks*
BLUE-WINGED TEAL (*Anas discors*)   p. 224
LENGTH 16 in (41 cm)   WEIGHT 14.4 oz (0.41 kg)

Other names Bluewing, Summer Teal, White-faced Teal
Description Gray head with white crescent on face (male) or mottled brown with spotted undertail coverts (female)
Habitat Salt marshes, wet prairies and marshes; agricultural environments
Range Statewide

Jan	Feb	Mar	Apr	May	June	July	Aug	Sep	Oct	Nov	Dec

The Blue-winged Teal is our most abundant and widely distributed winter duck, arriving as early as late July and August, and remaining until April or May. This small duck is an irregular breeder in Florida, preferring shallow lakes and ponds and freshwater marshes for feeding and nesting activities. The breeding male has a gray head with a prominent white crescent in front of each eye. Through most of the fall, however, males resemble females, which are a mottled brown overall. Both sexes exhibit a green speculum (brighter in the male), and a large, light blue wing patch. Hen Blue-wings occasionally may be heard "quacking" like Mallards. Foods include a variety of insects, seeds, and other vegetation. Although it is a heavily harvested duck, its numbers appear to be on the increase. The closely related **Cinnamon Teal** (*Anas cyanoptera*) is an occasional winter visitor throughout Florida and is often seen in the company of the Blue-winged Teal. As its name implies, the adult male appears reddish in comparison to the Blue-winged Teal.

Family *Anatidae: Swans, Geese, Ducks*
NORTHERN SHOVELER (*Anas clypeata*)
LENGTH 19 in (48 cm)   WEIGHT 1.4 lb (0.64 kg)

p. 224

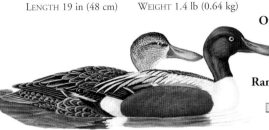

Other names Spoonbill, Spoon-billed Wigeon
Description Large spatulate bill
Habitat Open freshwater; wet prairies
and marshes; agricultural environments
Range Statewide

Jan	Feb	Mar	Apr	May	June	July	Aug	Sep	Oct	Nov	Dec

The large, spatulate bill is the most diagnostic feature of this wintering marsh bird. Males exhibit a green head, black bill, white chest, and brown sides. Females resemble Blue-winged Teal hens but are considerably larger, and possess the spatulate bill that is used like a strainer to filter foods that are stirred up by their feet from the bottom of shallow wetlands. Northern Shovelers arrive in Florida during late September and may remain through April. Large flocks may be encountered throughout the state, feeding with other dabblers in freshwater lakes and marshes. Shovelers feed on surface plankton, small clams, aquatic insects, and a variety of aquatic vegetation.

Family *Anatidae: Swans, Geese, Ducks*
NORTHERN PINTAIL (*Anas acuta*)
LENGTH 20–26 in (51–66 cm)   WEIGHT 2.3 lb (1.04 kg)

p. 223

Other names Sprig, Sprigtail, Spike, Spiketail
Description Brown head, long neck, white of chest
extends up side of neck, long central tail feathers (male) or
mottled brown body with pale head and neck (female)
Habitat Salt marshes; wet prairies and marshes; agricultural
environments
Range Statewide

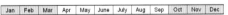

Jan	Feb	Mar	Apr	May	June	July	Aug	Sep	Oct	Nov	Dec

A large, distinctive duck, the Northern Pintail is a common winter resident, especially on north Florida marshes and lakes. White on chest extending up the side of the neck, vermiculated gray body, chocolate-brown head, and long central tail feathers distinguish the male. Females are mottled brown with bluish bill and long tail (although shorter than the male's). Both sexes have relatively long, slender necks, exhibit a greenish speculum bordered with white, and they appear to float very buoyantly on the water. Some birds pass through Florida on their way to Cuba and the Caribbean in winter, but some winter residents can be seen here from mid-October to late March. Large ponds, freshwater marshes, and grain fields seem attractive to this handsome duck. The Northern Pintail eats a variety of vegetation including rice, panicum grasses, and sedges.

FAMILY *Anatidae: Swans, Geese, Ducks*
Green-winged Teal (*Anas crecca*)   p. 223
LENGTH 14 in (36 cm)   WEIGHT 12.8 oz (0.36 kg)

Other names Greenwing, Common Teal

Description Chestnut head with green ear patch, gray flanks (male) or brown, white undertail coverts, small bill (female)

Habitat Salt marshes; mangrove; wet prairies and marshes; agricultural environments

Range Statewide

Jan	Feb	Mar	Apr	May	June	July	Aug	Sep	Oct	Nov	Dec

One of many migrant duck species, the Green-winged Teal is also our smallest dabbling duck. It is a common visitor after early fall, but is not as abundant as the Blue-winged Teal. Green-wings migrate in large flocks, usually at night. Males exhibit russet head and broad green eyestripe; back and sides are vermiculated gray, and a white stripe divides flanks and chest. Females are mottled brown, with a black line through the eye. In both sexes a green speculum is visible in flight. Green-wings are fond of shallow fresh water and often may be seen feeding on exposed mudflats where small seeds of marsh vegetation are eaten. Foraging birds also use flooded pastures and prairies.

FAMILY *Anatidae: Swans, Geese, Ducks*   p. 224
Canvasback (*Aythya valisineria*)
LENGTH 21 in (53 cm)   WEIGHT 2.8 lb (1.27 kg)

Other names Can

Description Chestnut head and neck, white back (male) or brown head and neck, gray back (female); both have long sloping forehead and bill

Habitat Salt marshes; open saltwater; open freshwater; wet prairies and marshes; agricultural environments

Range Statewide

Jan	Feb	Mar	Apr	May	June	July	Aug	Sep	Oct	Nov	Dec

One of our handsomest ducks, the Canvasback is distinguished from the Redhead by its "ski slope" head and bill, and white back and flanks. It is a diving duck that gives the appearance of riding low on the water. In the male, chestnut head and neck are sharply demarcated from the black chest, with sides and back a light gray (shows white from a distance). Females exhibit similar proportions but have brown heads and buff-gray backs and sides. Canvasbacks are not abundant in Florida, but can be seen regularly in small flocks from early November to early March on large Florida lakes and estuaries such as Tampa Bay and St. Marks National Wildlife Refuge. Their numbers declined considerably during the twentieth century due, in part, to a decline in their major food, wild celery. While vegetation accounts for at least 80% of the diet, animal foods such as mollusks and aquatic insects also are eaten.

Family *Anatidae: Swans, Geese, Ducks*
REDHEAD (*Aythya americana*)
LENGTH 19 in (48 cm)   WEIGHT 2.6 lb (1.18 kg)

p. 224

Other names Pochard

Description Rounded red head, gray bill with white ring (male) or brown head (female)

Habitat Salt marshes; open saltwater; open freshwater; wet prairies and marshes; agricultural environments

Range North and central Florida

Jan	Feb	Mar	Apr	May	June	July	Aug	Sep	Oct	Nov	Dec

A large diving duck, the Redhead is similar to the Canvasback in overall coloration. The male's bluish bill has a white-bordered black tip, and the back and flanks are grayish (in contrast to the white back and sides of the Canvasback). Like Canvasbacks, Redheads have declined in the last 30 years, but Florida remains an important wintering ground. From early November to early March, these birds can be seen in large numbers along the east coast, especially Merritt Island, and on the Gulf coast from Apalachicola Bay to Tampa Bay. Redheads are expert divers but also may be seen "tipping up" to feed in shallow water. Plants such as shoalgrass, coontail, and pondweeds account for about 90% of its diet.

Family *Anatidae: Swans, Geese, Ducks*
RING-NECKED DUCK (*Aythya collaris*)
LENGTH 17 in (43 cm)   WEIGHT 1.6 lb (0.73 kg)

p. 225

Other names Ringbill, Ring-billed Duck, Blackjack, Blackhead

Description Purplish head, white crescent between black breast and gray sides, white ring on bill (male) or brown (female)

Habitat Salt marshes; open saltwater; open freshwater; wet prairies and marshes; urban environments; agricultural environments

Range Statewide

Jan	Feb	Mar	Apr	May	June	July	Aug	Sep	Oct	Nov	Dec

The Ring-necked Duck is one of Florida's most abundant wintering waterfowl and a very rare breeder. Although found frequently on salt water, Ring-necks seem to prefer inland fresh water such as Lake Okeechobee and even phosphate mine settling impoundments, and are often the most abundant duck on urban lakes and ponds. These medium-size divers arrive in late October and may remain into early April, feeding in flocks on a variety of seeds, snails, clams, and aquatic insects. Although a brown necklace on breeding males is detectable at very close range, the first two alternate names probably are more descriptive for this bird. A gray bill ending with terminal bands of white and black are visible even from a distance. The purplish-black head is slightly peaked, and a white triangle in front of the wings and a black back distinguish it from the Lesser Scaup. Females are mostly brown, with dark crown, white eye ring, eyestripe, and facial mottling. This diving duck will occasionally tip up to feed and is primarily a vegetarian.

FAMILY *Anatidae: Swans, Geese, Ducks*
LESSER SCAUP *(Aythya affinis)*   p. 225
LENGTH 17 in (43 cm)   WEIGHT 1.9 lb (0.86 kg)

Other names Bluebill, Bullhead, Raft Duck, Little Bluebill, Blackhead

Description Peaked crown, purple gloss on head, dark back, white sides (male) or brown with white patch around base of bill (female)

Habitat Salt marshes; open saltwater; open freshwater; wet prairies and marshes; agricultural environments

Range Statewide

Jan	Feb	Mar	Apr	May	June	July	Aug	Sep	Oct	Nov	Dec

Similar in size and color to the Ring-necked Duck, Lesser Scaup males have a purplish "peaked" head, grayish-blue bill, and light gray back. Females are mostly brown but exhibit a distinct white facial crescent between bill and eye. Over 250,000 scaup winter throughout Florida using many types of open water from small lakes in urban settings to the Indian River Lagoon, Tampa Bay, and Lake Okeechobee where very large flocks are common. Lesser Scaups arrive here in late October and may linger through April. Occasionally, this species breeds in Florida. Lesser Scaup feed in relatively deep water (10–25 feet), primarily on aquatic invertebrates such as clams, snails, crabs, shrimp, and a variety of insects. The **Greater Scaup** (*Aythya marila*) is very similar to but much less common than the Lesser Scaup. Fewer than 10% of all scaup harvested by hunters in Florida are Greaters. A larger bird, the Greater Scaup exhibits a smoothly rounded, greenish-black head. Females are similar to Lesser Scaup but have larger bills and may have darker heads. Feeding habits are similar. In flight, (or whenever wings are outstretched), the Lesser shows a distinct white stripe on the secondary feathers only, while this stripe on the Greater extends well out onto the primaries.

FAMILY *Anatidae: Swans, Geese, Ducks*
SURF SCOTER *(Melanitta perspicillata)*   p. 226
LENGTH 20 in (51 cm)   WEIGHT 2.2 lb (1 kg)

Other names Skunkhead, Coot, Sea Coot

Description Black with white patches on forehead and nape; black, white, orange bill (male) or brown with two white patches on side of face (female)

Habitat Open saltwater; open freshwater

Range Coastal, statewide

Jan	Feb	Mar	Apr	May	June	July	Aug	Sep	Oct	Nov	Dec

The Surf Scoter is a rare but regular visitor to Florida, primarily reported along the east coast near Jacksonville and in the Gulf south of Tallahassee. They are seen infrequently inland. The male is black overall with white patches on the forehead and nape of neck. The bill is large and brightly patterned in orange, white, and black. Females are dull gray with a white patch behind the eyes and in front of and below the eye. The front white patch is more vertically oriented than in the female White-winged Scoter. As in the other scoter species, its diet is comprised chiefly of mollusks and crustaceans.

Family *Anatidae: Swans, Geese, Ducks*
WHITE-WINGED SCOTER (*Melanitta fusca*)
p. 226
Length 21 in (53 cm)   Weight 2–4 lb (0.91–1.81 kg)

Other names Whitewing, Coot, Sea Coot
Description Black with white crescent below eye, white in wings, black knob at base of orange bill (male) or brown with indistinct facial patches (female)
Habitat Open saltwater; open freshwater
Range Coastal, north and central Florida

Jan	Feb	Mar	Apr	May	June	July	Aug	Sep	Oct	Nov	Dec

Our largest scoter, the White-winged is another unusual winter visitor in Florida, and is the rarest of the scoters. White eye rings, white wing patches, and an orange bill with a basal knob distinguish the male. The dull gray female also exhibits a small white wing patch as well as white, elliptical patches in front of and behind the eyes. Because of the prominent white patches on this large sea duck, it is perhaps the easiest scoter to identify. It primarily is a bird of open salt water, and in Florida is seen very infrequently inland. White-winged Scoters feed mostly on mollusks, as well as crustaceans and insects.

Family *Anatidae: Swans, Geese, Ducks*
BLACK SCOTER (*Melanitta nigra*)
p. 226
Length 19 in (48 cm)   Weight 2.4 lb (1.09 kg)

Other names American Scoter, Common Scoter, Coot, Black Coot, Sea Coot, Black Duck
Description All black, orange knob at base of bill (male) or brown with pale face and throat (female)
Habitat Open saltwater
Range Coastal, statewide

Jan	Feb	Mar	Apr	May	June	July	Aug	Sep	Oct	Nov	Dec

Primarily a bird of cold coastal waters, the Black Scoter is occasionally seen along the extreme north of Florida's Atlantic coast, and, in recent years, the upper Gulf coast. It is the most frequently encountered scoter in Florida. Except for the yellow swelling at the base of the bill, males are entirely black, the only all-black duck in North America. Males sometimes spend winters farther north than females. Females are dark gray with a light facial patch extending from the base of the bill to the throat. Mollusks form the bulk of the Black Scoter's diet.

FAMILY *Anatidae: Swans, Geese, Ducks*
LONG-TAILED DUCK (*Clangula hyemalis*)
p. 226
LENGTH 22 in (56 cm)   WEIGHT 1.8–2.2 lbs (0.82–1 kg)

Other names Oldsquaw, Sea Pintail, Cocker-tail, Coween Kakawi, Oldwife

Description Mostly white, brown breast and back, long tail (winter male) or whitish head, dark wings (female)

Habitat Open saltwater; open freshwater; agricultural environments

Range Coastal, north and central Florida

Jan	Feb	Mar	Apr	May	June	July	Aug	Sep	Oct	Nov	Dec

This distinctive white sea duck is highlighted with dark on chest, cheeks, and back. Males exhibit a long upturned tail plume. Considered a rare winter visitor in Florida, a Long-tailed Duck may be seen occasionally along both coasts. Recently, inland-freshwater sightings have become more common in north central Florida. Food is obtained by diving up to 200 feet (61 meters), and consists of mollusks, shrimp, crustaceans, insects, seaweed, and small fishes.

FAMILY *Anatidae: Swans, Geese, Ducks*
BUFFLEHEAD (*Bucephala albeola*)
p. 226
LENGTH 13 in (33 cm)   WEIGHT 1 lb (0.45 kg)

Other names Butterball, Dipper, Spirit Duck

Description Black above, white below, large white head patch (male) or dark head and back, small white face patch (female)

Habitat Open saltwater; open freshwater; agricultural environments

Range North and central Florida

Jan	Feb	Mar	Apr	May	June	July	Aug	Sep	Oct	Nov	Dec

The Bufflehead is a small wintering duck that is most commonly encountered along the northern Gulf coast but also on inland streams and lakes in peninsular Florida. Approximately 1000 spend the winter in Florida. A metallic-green head distinguishes the male with a large white patch extending from behind the eye to the top of the head, and white chest and flanks. Females are grayish-brown with white chest and a smaller, horizontal white patch behind the eye. Buffleheads are diving ducks, subsisting on fish, insect larvae, and plant seeds. Unlike other diving ducks, the Bufflehead can take off from the water. It usually dives in groups, often leaving a "lookout" on the surface. These attractive birds may be seen from December through February.

FAMILY *Anatidae: Swans, Geese, Ducks*
COMMON GOLDENEYE (*Bucephala clangula*)
LENGTH 18 in (46 cm)   WEIGHT 2.2 lb (1 kg)

p. 226

Other names Whistler
Description Green head, white face spot, yellow eye
(male) or brown head, yellow eye (female)
Habitat Open saltwater; open freshwater
Range North and Central Florida

Jan	Feb	Mar	Apr	May	June	July	Aug	Sep	Oct	Nov	Dec

The Common Goldeneye is a regular but uncommon winter visitor in north Florida, especially along the northwest coast. A black, knobby head, with a white patch in front of the eye and a black back spotted with white distinguishes the male from mergansers and the Bufflehead. Females and immatures have more rounded brown heads that contrast with mottled-gray flanks and back. A visitor from mid-December through early March, Common Goldeneyes feed by diving for crabs, crayfish, insect larvae, mollusks, seeds, and tubers in large rivers, coastal bays and estuaries.

FAMILY *Anatidae: Swans, Geese, Ducks*
HOODED MERGANSER (*Lophodytes cucullatus*)
LENGTH 18 in (46 cm)   WEIGHT 1.5 lb (0.68 kg)

p. 225

Other names Sawbill, Fish Duck, Hairy-head
Description Black crested head with white patch
(male) or reddish-brown crest with no white
(female)
Habitat Salt marshes; open freshwater; hardwood
swamps; cypress swamps; wet prairies and marshes;
urban environments; agricultural environments
Range Statewide

Jan	Feb	Mar	Apr	May	June	July	Aug	Sep	Oct	Nov	Dec

The striking black and white crest of the male Hooded Merganser is a conspicuous field mark. White breast with a diagonal black bar, white wing stripe, and tawny-vermiculated flanks further characterize the male. The female is mostly light brown with a rufous crest and dark back. In both sexes the crest can be quickly erected and relaxed. Migrants arrive in late November and may remain through April. Primarily a winter resident in Florida, Hooded Mergansers increasingly have been found nesting, especially in the northern peninsula. These cavity-nesters are frequent residents in Wood Duck boxes where about ten white eggs are laid in late winter or early spring. Mixed-species clutches have been reported where Hoodeds have "dumped" eggs in Wood Duck nests. Hoodeds are inhabitants of lakes and ponds, wooded streams, hardwood swamps, and coastal salt marsh creeks. Small fish, crustaceans, and aquatic insects provide the bulk of their diet.

FAMILY *Anatidae: Swans, Geese, Ducks*
RED-BREASTED MERGANSER (*Mergus serrator*)   p. 225
LENGTH 23 in (58 cm)   WEIGHT 2.5 lb (1.13 kg)

Other names Sawbill, Fish Duck, Hairy-head

Description Green shaggy head, white collar, red-streaked breast (male) or brown shaggy head, pale throat and neck (female)

Habitat Salt marshes; open saltwater; open freshwater; agricultural environments

Range Mostly coastal, statewide

Jan	Feb	Mar	Apr	May	June	July	Aug	Sep	Oct	Nov	Dec

Our most abundant large merganser, the Red-breasted Merganser is a common winter visitor in Florida. The green, tufted head of the male and the shaggy-headed female give this species one of its other common names. Adult males (which are rarely seen in Florida) exhibit a white throat, brown chest band, black back, and gray, vermiculated flanks. Females and immatures are grayer overall with contrasting white and black showing on the folded wings. Both sexes have a long, narrow, serrated bill. Red-breasted Mergansers are particularly common along Florida's Atlantic and Gulf coasts, but are also seen regularly on large inland lakes and impoundments. Migrants arrive in Florida in late October and may remain throughout winter and spring. Red-breasted Mergansers are entirely carnivorous, feeding primarily on small fish as well as shrimp and crabs. The much less abundant **Common Merganser** (*Mergus merganser*) is a larger duck that prefers freshwater habitats. Males are untufted with more white on the flanks, while females have a distinct contrast between the slightly tufted head and throat. Each winter one or more Common Mergansers are reported in north Florida, rarely as far south as Tampa Bay or Cape Canaveral. However, it is likely that many of these sightings are cases of mistaken identity.

FAMILY *Anatidae: Swans, Geese, Ducks*
RUDDY DUCK (*Oxyura jamaicensis*)   p. 225
LENGTH 15 in (38 cm)   WEIGHT 1.3 lb (0.59 kg)

Other names Butterball, Bull-necked Teal, Spiketail, Winetail, Sleeper, Dip-tail Diver, Fool Duck, Broadbill Dipper, Dumb Bird, Bumblebee Coot, Hardhead

Description Dark cap, white cheeks, long cocked tail; cheek patch of females less distinct

Habitat Open saltwater; open freshwater; wet prairies and marshes; agricultural environments

Range Statewide

Jan	Feb	Mar	Apr	May	June	July	Aug	Sep	Oct	Nov	Dec

The Ruddy Duck has a stout appearance, with short wings, thick neck, and an erect, fan-shaped tail. Black on top of the head, white cheeks, blue bill, and rust-brown body and wings distinguish the male. Females and immatures are grayer overall with a light gray cheek patch and blue bill. Florida is an important wintering location for this widely nicknamed duck. Most birds arrive in October and remain through April. Recently, Ruddy Ducks have been found breeding in north Florida phosphate mine impoundments and other artificial wetlands near Tampa. Ruddies may be seen on both coasts, brackish estuaries, as well as in a variety of inland freshwater habitats. Ruddy Ducks primarily are vegetarians feeding on a variety of seeds, tubers, and grasses. Animal food consists of midge larvae and amphipods. A similar species, the **Masked Duck** (*Oxyura dominica*), is seen infrequently in Florida. This tropical bird exhibits white wing patches in flight, and during winter has distinct buff and dark brown stripes on the head. Breeding males have dark brown heads and reddish-brown mottled bodies. Nesting of the Masked Duck has been suspected to occur in Lake Okeechobee.

ORDER *Falconiformes: Birds of Prey*
Birds of prey, strong flyers with powerful talons and hooked bill.

FAMILY *Accipitridae: Kites, Eagles, Hawks*
OSPREY (*Pandion haliaetus*)   p. 228
LENGTH 24 in (61 cm)   WEIGHT 3.1 lb (1.41 kg)   STATUS **SSC**

Other names Fish Hawk
Description Dark brown above, white below; dark eye-stripe
Habitat Coastal beaches; salt marshes; open saltwater; open freshwater; mangrove; wet prairies and marshes
Range Statewide

| Jan | Feb | Mar | Apr | May | June | July | Aug | Sep | Oct | Nov | Dec |

The Osprey is widely distributed in Florida due to the abundance of productive open-water habitats. A fish-catching specialist, it can be observed over many of our inland lakes and coastlines hovering at great heights (50–200 feet) and plunging into the water feet first. At first glance these birds may be confused with the Bald Eagle, but a black streak behind the eye, light streaking on the white belly, barring on secondaries, primaries, and tail, and crooked wings in flight set them apart. The Osprey is a species of special concern in Florida due to habitat loss and environmental contaminants. These factors were responsible for the drastic declines in Osprey populations throughout the rest of North America in the 1950s and '60s. The banning of chlorinated hydrocarbon pesticides led to the recovery of the northern population. Three eggs are usually laid in large, bulky nests, built in dead or live trees near abundant food supplies. Females do all of the incubating. In particularly good areas, nests appear clustered, or colonial. They will nest on tall artificial platforms and other structures. The nesting season occurs from late spring through early summer. An influx of northern birds occurs in fall and early spring as birds travel to and from wintering grounds in tropical America.

FAMILY *Accipitridae: Kites, Eagles, Hawks*
SWALLOW-TAILED KITE (*Elanoides forficatus*)

LENGTH 23 in (58 cm)   WEIGHT 15.6 oz (0.44 kg)

p. 229

Description Deeply forked tail; dark above, white below
Habitat Xeric scrub; hardwood swamps; cypress swamps;
mesic hammocks; mixed pine and hardwood forests; pine flatwoods; sandhills; agricultural environments
Range Statewide

Jan	Feb	Mar	Apr	May	June	July	Aug	Sep	Oct	Nov	Dec

When seen in flight, the Swallow-tailed Kite is undoubtedly one of the world's most beautiful birds. A deeply forked tail, contrasting black and white plumage, and graceful, often acrobatic, flight set this bird apart from all others. In proper lighting conditions the upper wing and back reflect a metallic green-blue surface. Swallow-tailed Kites are still fairly abundant in peninsular Florida, nesting in bottomland hardwoods and pine flatwoods in tall pines or cypress trees. The nesting season extends from late March through June, when two eggs are laid in a substantial nest placed near the top of the tree. The breeding range is indicated on the range map. A variety of prey, from grasshoppers to lizards, is deftly snatched from leaves and branches, and occasionally a snake can be seen dangling from a kite's talons as it returns to its nest. They reside in Florida from early February through August and occasionally September. In late summer it forms flocks of hundreds of birds in preparation for migration to the tropics. The Swallow-tailed Kite is a symbol of the Deep South, although it once nested as far north as Minnesota. Protection of hardwood bottomlands from development and conversion to pine plantations is essential in maintaining healthy populations of this elegant raptor.

FAMILY *Accipitridae: Kites, Eagles, Hawks*
WHITE-TAILED KITE (*Elanus leucurus*)

LENGTH 15 in (38 cm)   WEIGHT 12 oz (0.34 kg)

Other names Black-shouldered Kite
Description Gray above, white below, black shoulders,
pointed wings
Habitat Open prairie, marshes, agricultural lands with scattered
trees and shrubs
Range Central and south Florida

Jan	Feb	Mar	Apr	May.	June	July	Aug	Sep	Oct	Nov	Dec

This gull-like kite returned to Florida as a breeding bird in 1986 after an absence of more than 50 years. Black shoulders, white underparts, and mostly white tail separate this kite from the similar Mississippi Kite. Immatures have a brown cinnamon wash on head and breast. Nests are built in tops of isolated trees in wet prairies or on dikes near marshes in south Florida. Three or four white eggs with brown blotches are laid in March or April. Young are usually fledged by June. The White-tailed Kite's breeding range is indicated on the range map. The diet is primarily made up of small mammals (especially cotton rats); however, insects, birds, and reptiles also are taken.

FAMILY *Accipitridae: Kites, Eagles, Hawks*
SNAIL KITE (*Rostrhamus sociabilis*)
LENGTH 17 in (43 cm)   WEIGHT 13.3 oz (0.38 kg)   STATUS **E**

p. 229

Other names Everglade Kite, Snail Hawk
Description White at base of tail, red or orange eyes and facial skin; slate blue (male) or brown (female and immature)
Habitat Wet prairies and marshes
Range Central and south Florida

Jan	Feb	Mar	Apr	May	June	July	Aug	Sep	Oct	Nov	Dec

Although common in the Neotropics, the Snail Kite's distribution in North America is restricted to the freshwater marshlands of central and south Florida. Drastic population declines through the 1960s resulted in the bird's endangered classification. Apparently, the population has rebounded somewhat and is in less danger of extinction today. Although large numbers may die and no production may occur during severe drought years in south Florida, high reproduction in other years compensates for these losses. Hence, the population experiences "boom or bust" cycles. Except for the sharply hooked bill, Snail Kites have a typical raptor form. Males are slate-gray, and darker on head, tail, secondaries, and primaries. Females are generally brown overall with a white and brown streaked breast. Immatures have brown eyes, while those of the adult are red. All ages and sexes exhibit a squared-off tail, white at the base with a light terminal band. This bird derives its name from its exclusive prey, the apple snail, *Pomacea paludosa*. Snail Kites snatch their prey on the wing, then extract the animal with hooked bill while perched. Three to five light blue, brown-spotted eggs are laid in a loosely constructed nest in emergent marsh vegetation. Nesting usually occurs from February to June, but may extend from January through November; breeding range is indicated on the range map. Wetlands drainage and the exotic weed, water hyacinth, must be controlled to ensure the continued existence of this unusual Florida specialty.

FAMILY *Accipitridae: Kites, Eagles, Hawks*
MISSISSIPPI KITE (*Ictinia mississippiensis*)
LENGTH 14 in (36 cm)   WEIGHT 12.6 oz (0.36 kg)

p. 229

Description Dark gray back, light gray head, long wings and tail
Habitat Mesic hammocks; mixed pine and hardwood forests; urban environments
Range Central and north Florida

Jan	Feb	Mar	Apr	May	June	July	Aug	Sep	Oct	Nov	Dec

The Mississippi Kite is a denizen of north Florida's moist hardwood forests. In the last 20 years it has expanded its range from a strictly Panhandle distribution to one that now extends south to Gainesville and Ocala, as indicated on the range map. This beautifully marked kite exhibits a light gray head and secondaries and a nearly black tail and wingtips. In flight, it appears dark overall and has been described as looking like a large swallow. Mississippi Kites are early spring nesters. After their two eggs hatch, adult birds become busy supplying insects and small vertebrates to their chicks. Nests are built in tall pines or hardwoods and often are near human habitations. It is not unusual to see a soaring kite above a busy urban intersection with nearby woods. Most Mississippi Kites leave Florida for the tropics during September and return by early April.

FAMILY *Accipitridae: Kites, Eagles, Hawks*

BALD EAGLE (*Haliaeetus leucocephalus*)

LENGTH 31–37 in (79–94 cm)   WEIGHT 9.1 lb (4.13 kg)   STATUS **T**

p. 227

Description White head and tail (adult) or all dark, with variable white streaking below (immature); thigh feathers do not cover legs

Habitat Coastal beaches; salt marshes; dry prairies; mixed pine and hardwood forests; wet prairies and marshes; pine flatwoods; sandhills; agricultural environments

Range Statewide

Jan	Feb	Mar	Apr	May	June	July	Aug	Sep	Oct	Nov	Dec

The Bald Eagle has experienced population declines throughout most of its range due to habitat destruction and environmental contamination. Despite the loss of many of Florida's wetlands, Bald Eagles are still abundant here, with the largest population in the lower 48 states. In part because of its secure status in Florida, it was downgraded from endangered to threatened in the southeastern United States by the U.S. Fish & Wildlife Service in 1995. Adults are unmistakable, with white head and tail visible from great distances. First- and second-year eagles appear lighter in color due to a scattering of white feathers at the base of the tail, secondaries, and wing linings. Bald Eagles soar with wings held rigidly flat. Nests are usually built in tall living pine trees near lakes, marshes, or coastlines. Paired eagles will use the same nest year after year, adding material each season until it becomes huge. Sometimes an alternate nest may be maintained and occasionally used not far from the primary nest tree. Two, and occasionally three, eggs are laid during late fall or winter. The breeding range is indicated on the range map. Young eagles are usually fed fish (which are sometimes pirated from Ospreys) by both parents. Large wetland birds such as the American Coot, Pied-billed Grebe, and Cattle Egret are also eaten. Despite Florida's large eagle population, our national symbol is under continuous pressure due to habitat loss and increased human disturbance. Only concerted efforts to protect wetlands and nest sites statewide will ensure the continued existence of this magnificent bird.

FAMILY *Accipitridae: Kites, Eagles, Hawks*
NORTHERN HARRIER (*Circus cyaneus*)   p. 227
LENGTH 20 in (51 cm)   WEIGHT 12.6 oz (0.39 kg)

Other names Marsh Hawk

Description Gray upperparts, white rump (male) or brown upperparts, white rump (female)

Habitat Salt marshes; dry prairies; wet prairies and marshes; agricultural environments

Range Statewide

Jan	Feb	Mar	Apr	May	June	July	Aug	Sep	Oct	Nov	Dec

This is an abundant but declining avian predator during winter in Florida and can be expected to arrive with the earliest fall cold fronts. Harriers are usually seen flying close to the ground, seldom flapping, while hunting for small vertebrate prey. Females and immatures are predominantly brown, while the smaller males are mostly light gray. A good field mark for both sexes is a distinctive white rump patch that can be seen from a distance. It prefers open, treeless habitats including old fields, pastures, wet prairies, and herbaceous marshes.

FAMILY *Accipitridae: Kites, Eagles, Hawks*
SHARP-SHINNED HAWK (*Accipiter striatus*)   p. 229
LENGTH 10–14 in (25–36 cm)   WEIGHT 3.6 oz (0.11 kg)

Other names Little Blue Darter

Description Short, square tail and small head

Habitat Xeric scrub; mesic hammocks; mixed pine and hardwood forests; wet prairies and marshes; pine flatwoods; sandhills; agricultural environments

Range Statewide

Jan	Feb	Mar	Apr	May	June	July	Aug	Sep	Oct	Nov	Dec

Like its larger relative the Cooper's Hawk, the Sharp-shinned Hawk is a bird-eating specialist, but will also eat a variety of small mammals and insects. In general it looks like a Cooper's Hawk, but is two-thirds the size and has a more squared-off tail. Males have less contrast between the back and crown and are smaller than females. Sharp-shinned Hawks do not nest in Florida but are common winter residents, following migrating passerine birds to and from their wintering grounds. They can be seen throughout Florida from late October through May.

FAMILY *Accipitridae: Kites, Eagles, Hawks*
COOPER'S HAWK *(Accipiter cooperii)*
p. 229
LENGTH 14–20 in (36–51 cm)   WEIGHT 12.3 oz (0.35 kg)

Other names Big Blue Darter, Chicken Hawk
Description Long rounded tail, large head
Habitat Xeric scrub; mesic hammocks; mixed pine and hardwood forests; pine flatwoods; sandhills; agricultural environments
Range Central and north Florida

Jan	Feb	Mar	Apr	May	June	July	Aug	Sep	Oct	Nov	Dec

The Cooper's Hawk is a medium-size raptor that preys primarily on small birds, but can take birds as large as a Rock Pigeon. Stout rounded wings and a relatively long tail suit this bird to a life in the forest, using its speed and maneuverability to pursue avian prey. Adults are grayish-blue above, with a black crown, banded tail, and a lightly barred red and white breast. Immatures are generally brown with white-streaked head and breast. All Cooper's Hawks exhibit a distinctly rounded tail in flight (in contrast to the more squared tail of the Sharp-shinned Hawk). In Florida, Cooper's Hawks nest from April to July, and may breed as far south as Miami. Three to four eggs are laid in a loosely constructed nest that can be found in a variety of woodlands, usually 20–50 feet (6–15 meters) high in a pine or hardwood tree.

FAMILY *Accipitridae: Kites, Eagles, Hawks*
RED-SHOULDERED HAWK *(Buteo lineatus)*
p. 230
LENGTH 19 in (48 cm)   WEIGHT 1.1 lb (0.5 kg)

Other names Chicken Hawk
Description Reddish shoulders, tail with narrow white bands, whitish crescent at base of primaries (adult) or browner, little or no red on shoulders (immature)
Habitat Xeric scrub; hardwood swamps; cypress swamps; mesic hammocks; mixed pine and hardwood forests; wet prairies and marshes; urban environments; pine flatwoods; sandhills; agricultural environments
Range Statewide

Jan	Feb	Mar	Apr	May	June	July	Aug	Sep	Oct	Nov	Dec

The Red-shouldered is a common woodland hawk with a permanent, resident population throughout the mainland and Florida Keys. Reddish-barred undersides and rufous shoulders characterize adults. A light wing "window" is visible from below in flying birds. Adults exhibit a black tail with white bands, and white highlights on dark upper plumage. Immatures are heavily streaked below and show little if any rufous coloring. A paler, smaller form is distinctive in south Florida, where they can be observed perched on signs and fence posts. Red-shouldered Hawks are inhabitants of moist hardwood forests and mixed pine/broadleaf woodlands. Their voice, a distinctive *kee-ah* (often imitated by Blue Jays), is frequently heard near their nest site, which is often in the fork of a well-foliaged forest tree. Two or three eggs are laid during late winter. Prey consists of small mammals, lizards, snakes, frogs, crayfish, and insects.

FAMILY *Accipitridae: Kites, Eagles, Hawks*
BROAD-WINGED HAWK (*Buteo platypterus*)
LENGTH 16 in (41 cm)   WEIGHT 14.8 oz (0.42 kg)

p. 230

Description Wide black and white bands on tail, light underwings with dark border

Habitat Mangrove; hardwood swamps; cypress swamps, mesic hammocks; mixed pine and hardwood forests; pine flatwoods; sandhills; agricultural environments

Range Statewide

| Jan | Feb | Mar | Apr | May | June | July | Aug | Sep | Oct | Nov | Dec |

While never an abundant breeder in Florida, the distribution of nesting Broad-winged Hawks may be less today than in the early twentieth century. Slightly smaller than the Red-shouldered Hawk, the adult has broad white and black tail bands, reddish-barred belly, and dark-outlined wings. Immatures have paler tails and streaked undersides. The call is often heard while in flight, and is similar to that of the Eastern Wood-Pewee. Breeding birds are most likely to be encountered in the Panhandle and south to Gainesville between March and June. Two to three eggs are placed in a nest that is usually at least 30 feet (9 meters) above the ground and positioned close to the trunk. Broad-wings are probably seen most often during migration when large flocks navigate the coastlines. Most birds are circum-Gulf migrants, although a few remain all winter in southern Florida. Occasionally, tremendous flocks of more than 1,000 have been observed on their way to the tropics. Nesting and feeding habits are similar to that of the Red-shouldered Hawk.

FAMILY *Accipitridae: Kites, Eagles, Hawks*
SHORT-TAILED HAWK (*Buteo brachyurus*)
LENGTH 16 in (41 cm)   WEIGHT 1 lb (0.45 kg)

p. 230

Description Black above, black underparts (dark morph) or black above, white underparts (light morph)

Habitat Hardwood swamps; dry prairies; mesic hammocks; mixed pine and hardwood forests; wet prairies and marshes

Range Statewide except Panhandle

| Jan | Feb | Mar | Apr | May | June | July | Aug | Sep | Oct | Nov | Dec |

This uncommon Florida specialty is a resident from central Florida south through the peninsula. A stocky-appearing bird, the Short-tailed Hawk displays black and white banding on the tail (which is not particularly short), secondaries, and primaries, and either white or dark undersides. Immatures have buff undersides in the light morph and dark mottling in the dark morph. In general, the dark morph is more common in Florida than the light morph. Short-tails utilize a variety of woodland types so long as open grasslands or marshes are adjacent. The mixed woodland-savannahs of Glades and Highlands counties and the upper St. Johns River provide good nesting and feeding habitat for this hawk. One or more pairs nest in Everglades National Park, and in winter as many as eight to ten individuals have been seen along the road to Flamingo. The

Short-tailed Hawk employs an active pursuit technique to capture small birds, especially mead-owlarks and Red-winged Blackbirds. While hunting, it will often soar to great heights, which may help make this species inconspicuous. Nests are located near the tops of tall woodland edge trees where two eggs are laid in early spring; breeding range is indicated on the range map.

FAMILY *Accipitridae: Kites, Eagles, Hawks*　　　　　　　　　　　　　　　p. 230
RED-TAILED HAWK (*Buteo jamaicensis*)
LENGTH 22 in (56 cm)　　WEIGHT 2.3 lb (1.04 kg)

Other names Buzzard

Description Chestnut tail, dark belly band (most adult birds) or finely banded brown tail (immature)

Habitat Xeric scrub; hardwood swamps; dry prairies; cypress swamps; mesic hammocks; mixed pine and hardwood forests; wet prairies and marshes; urban environments; pine flatwoods; sandhills; agricultural environments

Range Statewide

Jan	Feb	Mar	Apr	May	June	July	Aug	Sep	Oct	Nov	Dec

Although it may be our most visible, widely distributed, and largest hawk, the Red-tail is certainly not the most abundant. A propensity to perch on power lines bordering major highways makes this raptor conspicuous. When seen in flight the adult's red tail is diagnostic. A brownish band across the otherwise white belly is often visible. Immature birds have black and dark brown tail bands and are heavily streaked below. It is tolerant of many habitat types but prefers to hunt in open country. Nests containing two to three eggs can be found in late winter in cabbage palms, live oaks, pines, and other large trees. Red-tailed Hawks eat rodents, rabbits, snakes, and insects. Its call is the high-pitched descending scream that is often depicted in films of the "Wild West." The **Swainson's Hawk** (*Buteo swainsoni*) is a regular winter visitor in the southern peninsula. It is similar in size to the Red-tailed Hawk, but has a grayish, banded tail and darker flight feathers (primaries and secondaries). It breeds in the Great Plains of the western United States.

FAMILY *Accipitridae: Kites, Eagles, Hawks*　　　　　　　　　　　　　　　p. 227
GOLDEN EAGLE (*Aquila chrysaetos*)
LENGTH 30–40 in (76–102 cm)　　WEIGHT 3.5 lb (1.59 kg)

Description Brown with golden wash on head, neck (adult); leg feathers reach to toes

Habitat Salt marshes; wet prairies and marshes, agricultural environments

Range Statewide

Jan	Feb	Mar	Apr	May	June	July	Aug	Sep	Oct	Nov	Dec

Primarily a bird of the western United States, the Golden Eagle is a rarity in Florida. They are similar in overall proportions to the more common Bald Eagle, but are a much darker-appearing bird. White base of tail and white under wing patches distinguish the immature bird, while a slightly barred tail is the most recognizable adult field mark. Although unusual anywhere in Florida, stragglers are most likely to occur in the Panhandle near water during winter. Foods include snakes, small mammals, and occasionally carrion.

FAMILY *Falconidae: Caracaras and Falcons*
CRESTED CARACARA (*Caracara cheriway*)
LENGTH 23 in (58 cm)   WEIGHT 2.1 lb (0.95 kg)   STATUS **T**   p. 228

Other names Mexican Eagle, Mexican Buzzard, Audubon's Caracara
Description Dark overall with white throat, neck, and barring on tail and wings, red-orange facial skin
Habitat Dry prairies; agricultural environments
Range Central and south Florida

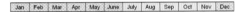

| Jan | Feb | Mar | Apr | May | June | July | Aug | Sep | Oct | Nov | Dec |

The open grasslands and palmetto country to the north and west of Lake Okeechobee makes up most of the Crested Caracara's range in eastern North America. It exhibits the appearance and behaviors of both falcons and vultures. It is often seen on the ground or perched along fence lines and posts in south Florida pasturelands. Caracaras have long legs, black crown and crest, red facial skin, white and black banded tail with a wide, dark terminal band, and have black and white barring at the base of the primaries. Immature birds are similar, but duller overall and with streaking instead of barring on the breast. Much of the ecology of this species has only recently been learned. Cabbage palms are the preferred nest site where two to three eggs are laid between September and March; incubation lasts 28 days. Foods include reptiles, birds, mammals, and carrion (it is often seen feeding with or harassing vultures at carcasses). It often runs down living prey. The spread of improved pastures and citrus as well as indiscriminant killing lead to a range-wide decline in Florida. With only about 250 pairs remaining, it was officially listed as threatened by the U.S. Fish & Wildlife Service in 1987.

FAMILY *Falconidae: Caracaras and Falcons*
AMERICAN KESTREL (*Falco sparverius*)
LENGTH 10 in (25 cm)   WEIGHT 3.9 oz (0.11 kg)   STATUS **T**   p. 228

Other names Sparrow Hawk, Killy Hawk
Description Small; russet back and tail, two black facial stripes
Habitat Xeric scrub; dry prairies; mixed pine and hardwood forests; urban environments; pine flatwoods; sandhills; agricultural environments
Range Statewide

| Jan | Feb | Mar | Apr | May | June | July | Aug | Sep | Oct | Nov | Dec |

The American Kestrel is our smallest and most colorful falcon, typically about the size of a robin. Florida is inhabited by a smaller race (*F. s. paulus*), which has been threatened by loss of cavity trees and reduced habitat availability. The threatened status refers to this race. Both sexes and immatures exhibit vertical black streaks behind and in front of the eye. Males have slate-blue crowns and wing coverts, rusty tail with black terminal band, and rufous back. Undersides exhibit black spots on a buff background. Females are browner overall with more heavily marked back, tail, and undersides. Immatures resemble adults with more streaking below. Kestrels are found throughout Florida, usually nesting in abandoned woodpecker holes excavated in pine trees; breeding range is indicated on the range map. A helpful tool for wildlife managers is the artificial nest box that these birds readily use. During spring (March to June) the female incubates three to five eggs while the male hunts and feeds his mate. Insects make up the bulk of the diet, although small mammals and reptiles are frequently taken. Florida experiences a large influx of northern American Kestrels during winter. Some have been known to winter on the Dry Tortugas (one of few land birds to do so). Like the Florida race, these birds often space themselves along telephone wires while hunting, but are distinguished by their larger size.

FAMILY *Falconidae: Caracaras and Falcons*
MERLIN (*Falco columbarius*)   p. 228
LENGTH 12 in (30 cm)   WEIGHT 5.7 oz (0.16 kg)

Other names Pigeon Hawk
Description Dark above, heavily barred tail, no distinct facial markings
Habitat Coastal beaches; salt marshes; dry prairies; wet prairies and marshes; agricultural environments
Range Statewide

Jan	Feb	Mar	Apr	May	June	July	Aug	Sep	Oct	Nov	Dec

Somewhat larger than Kestrels, Merlins are readily distinguished as falcons by their long, pointed wings. Males are blue-gray above while females are brown. White underparts are streaked with brown, and the tail has heavy black bands separated by white. These swift fliers have similar migration and wintering habits to their larger cousin, the Peregrine Falcon. Behaviorally, the Merlin can be considered a miniature Peregrine. They usually take smaller birds (especially shorebirds and passerine birds), but their diet also includes small mammals and insects. They often fly close to the ground with bursts of speed, pursuing prey. Merlins are often seen along the coasts or inland in open landscapes from September through April.

FAMILY *Falconidae: Caracaras and Falcons*

PEREGRINE FALCON (*Falco peregrinus*)

p. 228

LENGTH 16–20 in (41–51 cm)   WEIGHT 1.3 lb (0.64 kg)   STATUS **E**

Other names Duck Hawk

Description Dark crown and nape forming helmet

Habitat Coastal beaches; salt marshes; dry prairies; wet prairies and marshes; agricultural environments

Range Statewide

Jan	Feb	Mar	Apr	May	June	July	Aug	Sep	Oct	Nov	Dec

The Peregrine Falcon had a nearly worldwide distribution, but suffered drastic population declines throughout its range as the result of pesticide contamination. Florida represents an important wintering area, especially for the Arctic subspecies (*F. p. tundrius*). Migrant falcons can be seen in Florida after the first fall cold front and some remain all winter. Peregrine Falcons often are observed along Florida's coasts feeding on migrant shorebirds. Inland lakes and marshes, which are abundant with waterfowl, also attract these spectacular hunters. Peregrines take a wide variety of bird prey, specializing in wetlands species. Peregrines are the largest falcons found in Florida. Adults are slate-gray above with a distinct cheek/eye patch extending over the head. The breast is white with dark barring on the undersides. Immatures are brown above with brown streaking on breast and undersides. Pointed wings and strong, purposeful flight distinguish this spectacular bird overhead. When diving it is considered the fastest bird in the world (200 mph or 322 kmph). Many parts of the eastern United States are experiencing population increases through reintroduction or natural colonization.

ORDER *Galliformes: Gallinaceous Birds*

Chickenlike birds with strong walking legs and short rounded wings.

FAMILY *Phasianidae: Turkeys and Quail*

WILD TURKEY (*Meleagris gallopavo*)

LENGTH 45 in (114 cm)   WEIGHT 16.3 lb (7.39 kg)

p. 231

Description Large, dark, iridescent body; naked head

Habitat Xeric scrub; hardwood swamps; cypress swamps; mesic hammocks; mixed pine and hardwood forests; pine flatwoods; sandhills

Range Statewide

Jan	Feb	Mar	Apr	May	June	July	Aug	Sep	Oct	Nov	Dec

The Wild Turkey is Florida's largest game bird. It has a much more slender appearance than domesticated varieties. The mostly dark plumage occasionally exhibits colorful metallic hues in sunlight. Males are larger, have blue to pink facial skin, spurred heels, and a dark breast tuft (beard). Females and immatures are less ornate and duller in color. The Wild Turkey remains a widely distributed bird in Florida because of abundant forest cover. They have been reintroduced to many parts of their former range in the East and Midwest where adequate woodlands remain or have recovered. Wild Turkeys forage on the ground eating insects and a variety of seeds including tupelo fruits, acorns, and saw palmetto fruits. Turkeys roost in trees at night, usually in small groups. Females incubate about ten eggs in a ground nest located at the base of a tree or in a palmetto thicket. The white eggs are laid between March and May. The characteristic gobble of the male can be heard during courtship from February through May. Breeding range is indicated on the range map. The Wild Turkey is an extremely popular game bird in Florida. It is also preyed on by bobcats, foxes, Great Horned Owls, and Red-tailed Hawks.

FAMILY *Phasianidae: Turkeys and Quail*

NORTHERN BOBWHITE (*Colinus virginianus*)   p. 231

LENGTH 9 in (23 cm)   WEIGHT 6.3 oz (0.18 kg)

Other names Quail, Partridge

Description Mottled reddish-brown with white (male) or buffy (female) throat and eyestripe

Habitat Xeric scrub; dry prairies; mesic hammocks; mixed pine and hardwood forests; urban environments; pine flatwoods; sandhills; agricultural environments

Range Statewide

Jan	Feb	Mar	Apr	May	June	July	Aug	Sep	Oct	Nov	Dec

The call of the Northern Bobwhite is a characteristic summer sound of Florida's flatwoods, fields, and pastures. Associated primarily with agricultural land today, this diminutive game bird was common throughout Florida's once widespread longleaf pine forests. It is still a popular game bird throughout the state, but it has experienced a dramatic decline throughout the southeastern United States since the late 1950s (65% reduction in last 20 years). These declines are likely due to the succession of pastures to forest, more intensive agriculture, and urbanization. Two races occur in Florida, the peninsular bird exhibiting redder plumage than the northern race. White throat patch and eyestripe distinguish males, while female head plumage appears buff. All birds appear rusty with black and white highlights and lighter undersides. Ten to 15 eggs are laid in a ground nest during spring (February through June); second clutches may be attempted through July. Some nests with more eggs may be the result of more than one female's efforts. Eggs and young often fall prey to a variety of predators, including house cats, dogs, skunks, cotton rats, opossums, and even Barred Owls. Fire ants can also be a problem, especially for chicks. Food consists primarily of a variety of grains, field seeds, and insects.

ORDER *Gruiformes: Cranes, Rails, Limpkins*
This order includes the tall long-legged cranes, the smaller coots and
gallinules, and the secretive rails—almost all of which are marsh inhabitants.

FAMILY *Rallidae: Rails, Gallinules, Coots*
YELLOW RAIL (*Coturnicops noveboracensis*)
LENGTH 7 in (18 cm) WEIGHT 2 oz (0.05 kg)

Description Short tail, short bill, buff and black stripes on back
Habitat Freshwater marshes, fields, wet grasslands
Range Statewide

Jan	Feb	Mar	Apr	May	June	July	Aug	Sep	Oct	Nov	Dec

The Yellow Rail is a reclusive wetland bird that is rarely seen in
Florida. It is somewhat smaller than the Sora, exhibiting more yellow
plumage on back and breast, and has a smaller conical bill that is yellow in the adult and dusky
in juveniles. It resides in freshwater marshes and wet grassy areas while in Florida between
October and May. Its call, a series of *ticks,* has been described as resembling the southern cricket
frog—but it is unlikely to be heard in the state. The Yellow Rail consumes insects, snails, seeds,
and tender leaves. Due to its secretive tendencies, it may be more common than the occasional
sightings suggest.

FAMILY *Rallidae: Rails, Gallinules, Coots*
BLACK RAIL (*Laterallus jamaicensis*)
LENGTH 6 in (15 cm)   WEIGHT 1.2 oz (0.03 kg)

p. 232

Other names Jamaican Crake, Little Black Crake
Description Small; black or gray-black with white speckling
Habitat Salt marshes; wet prairies and marshes
Range Statewide, mostly coastal

Jan	Feb	Mar	Apr	May	June	July	Aug	Sep	Oct	Nov	Dec

The Black Rail has been referred to as a "feathered mouse" due to its small
size and extremely secretive habits. This is our smallest rail, about the size of a
sparrow. The plumage is black with a rusty nape, white stripes underneath, a salt-and-pepper
effect on the back, and a bright red eye. The Black Rail is probably much more common than its
infrequent sightings indicate. It is more apt to run from danger rather than fly. Its distinctive call,
kick-key-do, may be heard around dusk. Black Rails apparently breed widely throughout Florida
from May to September, especially near the coasts in extensive marshes. They make their ground
nests in clumps of grass. Six to ten small white eggs, sprinkled with brown, are laid during summer. Food consists of insects and seeds.

FAMILY *Rallidae: Rails, Gallinules, Coots*
CLAPPER RAIL (*Rallus longirostris*)
LENGTH 14 in (36 cm)   WEIGHT 11.4 oz (0.32 cm)

p. 232

Other names Saltwater Marsh Hen,
Mud Hen, Sedge Hen
Description Mottled gray-brown and black back, buff
underparts
Habitat Salt marshes; mangrove
Range Statewide, coastal

| Jan | Feb | Mar | Apr | May | June | July | Aug | Sep | Oct | Nov | Dec |

The Clapper Rail is similar in size and proportion to the King Rail. However, Clappers are duller-colored, exhibiting more gray than their fresh-water relative, and make a longer, less musical call. Loud noises such as hand-clapping can elicit a vocal response. When walking it bobs its head and tail. Strictly a coastal species, the Clapper Rail is a year-round resident in Florida, but northern birds migrate into north Florida marshes during winter. Nesting habits are similar to the King Rail, with breeding activities extending from March to July. Its breeding range is indicated on the range map. Foods consist of small crabs, shrimp, mollusks, insects, and seeds.

FAMILY *Rallidae: Rails, Gallinules, Coots*
KING RAIL (*Rallus elegans*)
LENGTH 15 in (38 cm)   WEIGHT 14.6 oz (0.41 kg)

p. 232

Other names Freshwater Marsh Hen,
Mud Hen
Description Mottled rufous-brown and
black back, cinnamon underparts
Habitat Wet prairies and marshes; agricultural environments
Range Statewide

| Jan | Feb | Mar | Apr | May | June | July | Aug | Sep | Oct | Nov | Dec |

The King Rail is a larger version of the Virginia Rail, but has less gray on the head. Its cinnamon-brown plumage is brighter than the similar Clapper Rail (which some authorities consider the same species). It is more often heard than seen. The loud, resonant notes of this primarily freshwater bird can sometimes be elicited by loud noises such as slamming car doors and hand-clapping. The King Rail is a permanent Florida resident and nests in dense marsh vegetation near the water's surface. It is distributed throughout Florida in freshwater and brackish marshes, where it overlaps with the Clapper Rail. It seems most abundant in central and south Florida, but is rarely seen in salt marshes and in the Florida Keys. Six to a dozen eggs are laid in late January to July. The black, downy chicks leave the nest immediately after hatching, following their parents in search of food such as aquatic insects, seeds, and succulent vegetation. Like most rails, King Rails rarely flush and prefer to escape danger on foot.

FAMILY *Rallidae: Rails, Gallinules, Coots*
VIRGINIA RAIL (*Rallus limicola*)
LENGTH 9 in (23 cm)   WEIGHT 3.1 oz (0.09 kg)

p. 232

Other names Marsh Hen

Description Gray cheeks, chestnut wings

Habitat Wet prairies and marshes, agricultural environments

Range Statewide

Jan	Feb	Mar	Apr	May	June	July	Aug	Sep	Oct	Nov	Dec

The Virginia Rail is a common winter inhabitant of Florida's freshwater and saltwater marshes. It rarely breeds in north Florida. Long legs, stout body, and slightly down-curved bill are used to advantage in muddy, inundated, and densely vegetated habitats. Rosy undersides with vertically striped (black and white) flanks, mottled brown upperparts, and short, pointed tail distinguish both sexes. Like most rails, the Virginia is a secretive bird, more often detected by its staccato notes than by sight. Most birds are found in Florida from October through March. This very active feeder subsists on a variety of invertebrates as well as small fruits.

FAMILY *Rallidae: Rails, Gallinules, Coots*
SORA (*Porzana carolina*)
LENGTH 8 in (20 cm)   WEIGHT 2.6 oz (0.07 kg)

p. 232

Other names Carolina Crake, Meadow Chicken, Ortolan

Description Small; short, thick yellow-green bill

Habitat Wet prairies and marshes; agricultural environments

Range Statewide

Jan	Feb	Mar	Apr	May	June	July	Aug	Sep	Oct	Nov	Dec

This small, short-billed rail is a winter inhabitant of Florida's salt, brackish, and freshwater marshes. Although it is our most abundant rail, it is more often heard than seen, though it can be found in open areas walking with its head down and tail cocked up. Its call, a descending staccato whistle, can often be elicited by hand-clapping near marsh borders. Soras are mostly gray, with black covering the face and throat, and vertically striped undersides. The bill and legs are yellow. Soras can be found in Florida from September through April. They feed primarily on marsh invertebrates and seeds.

FAMILY *Rallidae: Rails, Gallinules, Coots*
PURPLE GALLINULE (*Porphyrio martinica*)
LENGTH 13 in (33 cm)   WEIGHT 9.1 oz (0.26 kg)

p. 233

Other names Blue Peter, Mud Hen, Pond Chicken, Bonnet-walker

Description Purple-blue body, blue forehead shield (adult) or buffy yellow-brown underparts, greenish blue or olive above (immature)

Habitat Wet prairies and marshes; agricultural environments

Range Statewide

Jan	Feb	Mar	Apr	May	June	July	Aug	Sep	Oct	Nov	Dec

The handsome Purple Gallinule is a denizen of Florida's freshwater marshes, overgrown canals, and swamp borders. The adult's metallic green back and purple-blue head, neck, and undersides are unmistakable. The bill is similar to that of the Common Moorhen, but has a white frontal shield. Immatures resemble young moorhens but are more buff and lack white flanks. It uses its extremely long toes to walk across floating vegetation. The Purple Gallinule's voice is also similar to the Common Moorhen. Loosely constructed nests are placed over water in marsh vegetation, usually cattails or sawgrass. Six to eight eggs are usually laid in spring but nesting can last through summer. Purple Gallinules breed throughout most of the state, and in the winter they vacate the northern parts of Florida but remain abundant in the warmer southern counties, as indicated on the range map. One of the best places to see this species is Anhinga Trail in Everglades National Park. It eats frogs, grasshoppers, spiders, other invertebrates, and a variety of aquatic vegetation.

FAMILY *Rallidae: Rails, Gallinules, Coots*
COMMON MOORHEN (*Gallinula chloropus*)

p. 233

LENGTH 14 in (36 cm)   WEIGHT 12 oz (0.34 kg)

Other names Common Gallinule, Florida Gallinule, Pond Chicken, Mud Hen, Pond Guinea

Description Gray-black head and neck, red forehead shield (summer) or dull brown (winter and immature)

Habitat Wet prairies and marshes, urban environments; agricultural environments

Range Statewide

Jan	Feb	Mar	Apr	May	June	July	Aug	Sep	Oct	Nov	Dec

These very common wetland birds are not nearly as secretive as the closely related rails. Common Moorhens are widely distributed in Florida, inhabiting inland freshwater lakes, ponds, canals, and marshes. These chickenlike birds can be seen scrambling through willows and cattails or swimming in open water, often in and around urban areas. Adults are dark gray below and brownish above with a white lateral stripe on the flanks. The bright yellow-tipped red bill and frontal shield are distinctive marks. Immatures are mostly gray with white flanks and lack brightly colored soft parts. Common Moorhens construct nests on floating tussocks, in cattails, or in woody vegetation such as willow and buttonbush trees. It lays six to 14 eggs in an extended breeding season that lasts from spring through summer. The precocial, black, downy young are capable of walking and swimming immediately following hatching. The voice is a variety of chickenlike clucks and noises that may be repeated monotonously. Food consists of aquatic vegetation, seeds, insects, and other invertebrates.

Family *Rallidae: Rails, Gallinules, Coots*
American Coot (*Fulica americana*)
Length 15 in (38 cm)   Weight 1.6 lb (0.73 kg)

p. 233

Other names Mud Hen, Pull-doo, Pond Crow, White-bill, Splatterer, Pelick
Description Black body, white bill with dark band, small reddish-brown forehead shield
Habitat Salt marshes; open saltwater; open freshwater; wet prairies and marshes; agricultural environments
Range Statewide

| Jan | Feb | Mar | Apr | May | June | July | Aug | Sep | Oct | Nov | Dec |

In winter the American Coot is Florida's most abundant wetland bird. Coots breed irregularly but frequently in Florida, especially in the central lake region. Its winter flocks can number in the thousands. The general form of the coot is similar to that of gallinules, but it appears more ducklike on the water. The white bill and white rump contrast with the gray-to-black plumage. No other Florida bird has a white bill. The green legs end in widely lobed toes, which make the Coot a powerful swimmer, both above and below the surface. Nests are placed along wetland edges or on floating vegetation. Eight to 14 finely flecked buff eggs are laid in a loosely constructed nest during spring. Coots feed like grazing cattle on large mats of water hyacinth but also eat algae, aquatic insects, and a variety of other aquatic vegetation. They are often preyed on by Bald Eagles.

Family *Aramidae: Limpkins*
Limpkin (*Aramus guarauna*)
Length 26 in (66 cm) Weight 2.4 lb (1.09 kg)   Status **SSC**

p. 231

Other names Crying bird, Courlan
Description Brown body, streaked with white; slightly decurved bill
Habitat Hardwood swamps; cypress swamps; wet prairies and marshes
Range Statewide, except western Panhandle

| Jan | Feb | Mar | Apr | May | June | July | Aug | Sep | Oct | Nov | Dec |

The North American range of this unusual species is almost totally within Florida and thus it is considered a Sunshine State specialty. Combining characteristics of both cranes and rails, the Limpkin is a typical inhabitant of freshwater streams, swamps, and lake margins. Long, slightly down-curved bill, brown body with white flecking, buff-colored head, and long, dark olive legs distinguish the Limpkin. Its unique call, a raucous *kwr-r-ee-ow, kurr-r-ee-ow, kr-ow, kr-ow*, is given mostly at night. The breeding season in Florida is apparently year-round and seems to depend upon food abundance; breeding range is indicated on the range map. Four to eight large eggs are laid in a nest made of matted aquatic vegetation placed near the water or as high as up to 15 feet (4.5 meters) up a tree. Limpkins, like Snail Kites, seem somewhat dependent upon the apple snail for food; however, a variety of other items are taken, including frogs, worms, insects, crustaceans, and other mollusks. While feeding, Limpkins often twitch their tails and walk with a limping gait (hence its name). Flight is cranelike, with a slight hesitation in the upstroke.

FAMILY *Gruidae: Cranes*
SANDHILL CRANE (*Grus canadensis*)
LENGTH 40 in (102 cm)   WEIGHT 7.4 lb (3.36 kg)   STATUS **T**

p. 231

Other names Whooper
Description Large gray or brown body; red crown and lores (adults only)
Habitat Dry prairies; wet prairies and marshes; agricultural environments
Range Statewide

Jan	Feb	Mar	Apr	May	June	July	Aug	Sep	Oct	Nov	Dec

The nonmigratory Florida Sandhill Crane is an inhabitant of the scattered marshes and wet prairies throughout the state. The Kissimmee Prairie in south central Florida and Paynes Prairie in north central Florida are both noted for their crane populations. Migrant cranes from the Midwest make Florida their home from late fall through winter. Adults are characterized by black legs, gray plumage (sometimes stained reddish-brown), whitish cheeks, and a red crown. Sexes are similar. Immature birds have brown heads and necks. Nesting lasts from January through June. Large nests containing two eggs are located in thick patches of marsh vegetation such as pickerel weed and maidencane. Breeding range is indicated on the range map. Sandhills often are seen in improved pastures and open woodlands feeding on a variety of plants, seeds, and invertebrates. Their rattling, raucous call, usually given in flight, can be heard over long distances.

FAMILY *Gruidae: Cranes*
WHOOPING CRANE (*Grus americana*)
LENGTH 56 in (142 cm)   WEIGHT 12.8 lb (5.80 kg)   STATUS **SSC**

p. 231

Description Very large white body; red face, black primaries
Habitat Dry prairies; wet prairies and marshes
Range Central Florida

Jan	Feb	Mar	Apr	May	June	July	Aug	Sep	Oct	Nov	Dec

This is the largest wading bird in North America, with a wingspan of up to 7.5 feet (2.3 meters). Males can weigh up to 16 pounds (7 kilograms). The Whooping Crane is similar in general appearance to the Sandhill Crane, but is considerably larger and is mostly white with black primaries and a red face. The voice is a trumpetlike *kerloo, kerleeoo.* By 1940 only 22 individuals occurred in North America—the only known

breeding area was in Wood Buffalo National Park, Northwest Territories, Canada. The preferred habitat of the Whooping Crane is freshwater and saltwater marshes, where it feeds on a variety of crustaceans, amphibians, insects, reptiles, seeds, and grains. Population declines were due to over-harvest, the species' intolerance of human activity, and habitat alteration caused by agriculture and wetlands drainage. Recovery of the Whooping Crane has involved the supplementation of wild populations with captive-raised individuals and the creation of a nonmigratory population in Florida. Although good records exist for this endangered species in parts of the southeastern United States, its historical status as a breeding species in Florida is debatable. Regardless, central Florida was chosen as a reintroduction site because of the presence of suitable habitat. The first releases occurred in 1993 on Kissimmee Prairie in the Three Lakes Wildlife Management Area, and the breeding range has expanded from there, as indicated on the range map. Introductions of up to 20 birds per year have continued since then and the Florida population has grown.

Whooping Cranes in Florida first succesfully reproduced in 2002, and recovery planning has set a goal of 25 breeding pairs by 2020. The state now supports about 100 individuals in the central part of the state and is about halfway toward reaching the initial goal of recovery. The North American population totals about 420. Whoopers from the introduced Wisconsin flock were led to Florida by ultra-light aircraft in 2001 to begin the establishment of a new migratory flock, which now numbers about 40. Whooping Cranes are known for their courtship dance that includes pointing bills skyward, flapping wings, and hopping up and down. The nesting season goes from late winter through spring, when one to three eggs are laid and incubated by both parents. Pairs mate for life. Nests are flat mounds of cattails and other coarse vegetation in wet prairies and marshes and are usually surrounded by water.

ORDER *Charadriiformes: Shorebirds, Gulls, Terns*

This large, diverse order is made up of those species called shorebirds: plovers, sandpipers, gulls, and terns—most of which have webbed front toes.

FAMILY *Charadriidae: Plovers*

BLACK-BELLIED PLOVER (*Pluvialis squatarola*)   p. 234

LENGTH 11 in (28 cm)   WEIGHT 7.8 oz (0.22 kg)

Other names Bull-head, Black-breasted Plover, Beetlehead
Description White rump, black under wings, white wing stripe
Habitat Coastal beaches; agricultural environments
Range Statewide, mostly coastal

Jan	Feb	Mar	Apr	May	June	July	Aug	Sep	Oct	Nov	Dec

The Black-bellied Plover makes coastal Florida its winter refuge from Arctic tundra breeding grounds. Fall migration begins in mid-July, and most spring migrants leave Florida in May. This is our largest plover and may be seen singly or with other shorebirds, feeding near the surf. Black-bellied Plovers are regularly seen inland along large lakeshores, fields and sod farms, especially during fall. A heavier bill and large black patches beneath the wings distinguish the Black-bellied from the American Golden-Plover. While at least a few birds may be seen year-round in Florida, most are strictly winter residents. Small crabs, fish, and other marine invertebrates make up its diet.

FAMILY *Charadriidae: Plovers*
AMERICAN GOLDEN-PLOVER (*Pluvialis dominica*)
p. 234
LENGTH 10 in (25 cm)   WEIGHT 5.1 oz (0.14 kg)

Other names Lesser Golden-Plover
Description Golden-yellow mottled upperparts, small bill, dark rump, gray wing linings
Habitat Coastal beaches; agricultural environments
Range North and central Florida

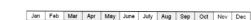

Jan	Feb	Mar	Apr	May	June	July	Aug	Sep	Oct	Nov	Dec

The American Golden-Plover is an unusual fall migrant in Florida, and even more uncommon during spring migration. These long-distance migrants usually fly nonstop from Labrador to the West Indies in fall and appear on Florida's coasts only under unusual weather conditions in spring. American Golden-Plovers are only slightly smaller than the similar-appearing Black-bellied Plover and are best distinguished from their larger relative by the lack of black under the wings and a uniform gray beneath. Golden-Plovers may be seen feeding on insects and invertebrates in plowed fields and mud flats.

FAMILY *Charadriidae: Plovers*
SNOWY PLOVER (*Charadrius alexandrinus*)
LENGTH 6 in (15 cm)   WEIGHT 1.4 oz (0.04 kg)   STATUS **T**

p. 234

Other names Cuban Snowy Plover
Description Pale gray-brown upperparts, incomplete black breast band, gray legs
Habitat Coastal beaches
Range Gulf coast

Jan	Feb	Mar	Apr	May	June	July	Aug	Sep	Oct	Nov	Dec

This diminutive plover is a resident along Florida's Gulf coast. Slightly smaller and considerably paler than the Piping Plover, the Snowy Plover exhibits a dark crescent on the sides of the neck, dark legs, and a slender black bill. Immatures have gray-spotted backs. Snowy Plovers often are difficult to detect, especially when resting on the beach sands with which they blend so well. Snowy Plovers nest from April through July on expansive, sandy beaches—specific locations are indicated on the range map. Three eggs are usually laid in a slight depression on the open beach. Their food consists of worms, insects, and small crustaceans obtained from beaches and tidal flats. Because of extensive human disturbance on these sites, the Snowy Plover has declined and is now considered a state-threatened species. Preservation of extensive Gulf coast beaches and barrier islands, as well as modifying the behavior of people and their dogs, will be necessary to preserve this specialized plover.

FAMILY *Charadriidae: Plovers*
WILSON'S PLOVER (*Charadrius wilsonia*)
LENGTH 8 in (20 cm)   WEIGHT 1.9 oz (0.05 kg

p. 234

Other names Ringneck, Thick-billed Plover
Description Heavy black bill, pinkish legs, brown back
Habitat Coastal beaches
Range Coastal, statewide

| Jan | Feb | Mar | Apr | May | June | July | Aug | Sep | Oct | Nov | Dec |

A wider single neck band, longer, heavier bill, and pinkish or flesh-colored legs distinguish the Wilson's Plover from the other "ringed" plovers. This permanent resident nests fairly commonly on both coasts, as indicated on the range map. Usually three or four darkly marked, cream-colored eggs are laid in a slight depression, occasionally lined with shell fragments. Like the larger Killdeer, a Wilson's Plover will feign a broken wing upon disturbance near the nest. Nesting occurs from April through July. Foods consist of marine and beach invertebrates.

FAMILY *Charadriidae: Plovers*
SEMIPALMATED PLOVER (*Charadrius semipalmatus*)
LENGTH 7 in (18 cm)   WEIGHT 1.7 oz (0.05 kg

p. 234

Other names Ringneck
Description Brown upperparts, orange bill and legs (breeding) or dull yellow (nonbreeding)
Habitat Coastal beaches; agricultural environments
Range Statewide, mostly coastal

| Jan | Feb | Mar | Apr | May | June | July | Aug | Sep | Oct | Nov | Dec |

Slightly larger than the Snowy Plover and smaller than Wilson's Plover, the Semipalmated Plover is a common winter visitor, especially on the coasts. In winter plumage the Semipalmated Plover has clear white undersides, dark brown upperparts, dark collar, dark band through the eye, a black bill, and yellowish legs. This small plover may be seen in great concentrations with other shorebirds on beaches and mudflats. Migrants arrive in Florida as early as July and may remain until May before returning to tundra nesting grounds. Crustaceans and other marine organisms along the coasts, and insects and other terrestrial invertebrates inland, make up the diet.

FAMILY *Charadriidae: Plovers*
PIPING PLOVER (*Charadrius melodus*)   p. 234
LENGTH 7 in (18 cm)   WEIGHT 1.9 oz (0.05 kg)   STATUS **T**

> **Description** Pale gray upperparts, orange legs, white rump
> **Habitat** Coastal beaches
> **Range** Statewide, coastal

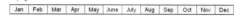

The Piping Plover is a rather nondescript, pale bird of seashore dunes and beaches. Strictly a winter visitor, it is white beneath and pale gray above (the color of wet sand), with a black, incomplete neck band and yellowish legs. The flutelike call is two-noted and musical. Piping Plovers feed in a stop-and-go fashion searching beach sands and flotsam for invertebrate prey. This plover is on the federal list of threatened species.

FAMILY *Charadriidae: Plovers*
KILLDEER (*Charadrius vociferus*)   p. 234
LENGTH 10 in (25 cm)   WEIGHT 3.2 oz (0.09 kg)

> **Other names** Killdee, Meadow Plover
> **Description** Two black breast bands, rufous rump and upper tail
> **Habitat** Coastal beaches; dry prairies; urban environments; agricultural environments
> **Range** Statewide

The Killdeer is the familiar plover of suburbs, fields, and pastures that will readily use areas that have been greatly altered by humans. It also is seen frequently on mud flats and the shores of lakes and rivers. Our largest ringed plover, the Killdeer is a permanent resident and nests throughout Florida. It is distinguishable from similar species by its large size, orange on upper tail, and double neck bands. Its call is a repetition of its name. Nesting occurs from March through July when three to four eggs, buff with dark markings, are laid in a simple depression on the ground. Open sites are preferred for nesting, and gravel rooftops are occasionally used. When nesting birds are confronted with danger they feign a broken wing that may distract potential predators and draw them away from the nest. Killdeer numbers greatly increase during winter when northern migrants arrive. Outside the breeding season the Killdeer is quite social. It may be found close to human dwellings and also is fond of agricultural areas. Food consists mostly of insects and other invertebrates. Killdeer appear to be somewhat susceptible to extremely cold weather.

FAMILY *Haematopodidae: Oystercatchers*
AMERICAN OYSTERCATCHER (*Haematopus palliatus*)
LENGTH 18 in (46 cm)   WEIGHT 1.4 lb (0.64 kg)   STATUS **SSC**

p. 233

Other names Mantled Oystercatcher, Brown-backed Oystercatcher

Description Black hood, heavy red bill, white underparts, pink legs

Habitat Coastal beaches

Range Coastal, statewide

Jan	Feb	Mar	Apr	May	June	July	Aug	Sep	Oct	Nov	Dec

The American Oystercatcher is one of our most unmistakable shorebirds. Strictly a coastal species, this striking bird was once more abundant in Florida. Declining for many years, the American Oystercatcher seems to be maintaining relatively stable numbers on undisturbed Gulf coast beaches and islands, and on dredged material islands and shell bars along the Atlantic Intracoastal Waterway; its breeding range is indicated on the range map. Black head and dark brown upperparts contrast with white undersides. White at the base of the tail and white wing stripes are evident in flight. The long, heavy, red bill, yellow eyes rimmed in red, and pink legs are evident in adults. Two or three mottled eggs are deposited in modest nest scrapes directly on the sand between March and July. Oystercatchers are adept at snatching the soft tissues from slightly open oysters, but also feed on a variety of other mollusks, crustaceans, and invertebrates.

FAMILY *Recurvirostridae: Stilts and Avocets*
BLACK-NECKED STILT (*Himantopus mexicanus*)
p. 233

LENGTH 14 in (36 cm)   WEIGHT 5.9 oz (0.17 kg)

Description Black upperparts, white below, long thin pink or red legs and black bill

Habitat Wet prairies and marshes; agricultural environments

Range Statewide

Jan	Feb	Mar	Apr	May	June	July	Aug	Sep	Oct	Nov	Dec

Long red legs are a distinctive field mark of this common inhabitant of shallow freshwater and saltwater wetlands. Black upperparts, and black, needle-like bill contrast with the pure white undersides. These extremely vocal birds may nest singly or colonially, making shallow nest platforms. Three to seven large, brown-speckled, pointed eggs are laid from April to July. Black-necked Stilts use a number of nesting sites, from freshwater marshes to phosphate mine impoundments. They will scratch out shallow depressions on sand or build elevated stick nests in shallow water. Most stilts leave northern Florida during winter but some may remain all year south of Lake Okeechobee. They feed on aquatic insects and other invertebrates.

FAMILY *Recurvirostridae: Stilts and Avocets*
AMERICAN AVOCET (*Recurvirostra americana*)
LENGTH 18 in (46 cm)   WEIGHT 11.1 oz (0.31 kg)

p. 233

Description Black and white wings, gray (winter) or rusty (spring) head and neck, thin upturned bill
Habitat Wet prairies and marshes; agricultural environments
Range Statewide

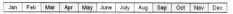

| Jan | Feb | Mar | Apr | May | June | July | Aug | Sep | Oct | Nov | Dec |

The American Avocet regularly wanders through Florida, especially in autumn and spring, but it has been recorded in every month.
Avocets usually appear in Florida in their paler winter plumage with cream-colored head and neck. No other shorebird exhibits such a long, upturned bill and long legs. Black upperparts with a white horizontal wing stripe contrast with light undersides. Avocets may be seen in small flocks feeding in flooded agricultural fields, tidal flats, marshes, and shallow ponds. They quickly sweep their bills back and forth underwater and often submerge their heads and necks while feeding on crustaceans and aquatic insects. It often associates with the Black-necked Stilt.

FAMILY *Scolopacidae: Sandpipers*
GREATER YELLOWLEGS (*Tringa melanoleuca*)
LENGTH 14 in (36 cm)   WEIGHT 6 oz (0.17 kg)

p. 235

Other names Tell-tale Snipe
Description Bill is 2 to 2.5 times width of head; call is a *tew, tew, tew,* repeated three to five times.
Habitat Coastal beaches; salt marshes; wet prairies and marshes; agricultural environments
Range Statewide

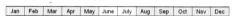

| Jan | Feb | Mar | Apr | May | June | July | Aug | Sep | Oct | Nov | Dec |

This active marsh and shallow lake shorebird is a common winter resident in Florida. As its name implies, this bird has long, yellow legs as well as a needle-like bill (length is 2 to 2.5 times the depth of the head behind the bill), white undersides barred with gray, and darker mottling above. Its voice is a clear, staccato ring, repeated three to five times. It serves as a sentinel for other shorebirds with which it associates. Migrants arrive in late August and may remain through May before returning to tundra breeding grounds. A variety of aquatic and terrestrial organisms are readily eaten. It feeds by skimming the water with its bill instead of probing.

FAMILY *Scolopacidae: Sandpipers*

LESSER YELLOWLEGS (*Tringa flavipes*)   p. 235

LENGTH 10.5 in (27 cm)   WEIGHT 6 oz (0.17 kg)

Other names Tell-tale Snipe

Description Bill is 1 to 1.5 times the width of head

Habitat Coastal beaches; salt marshes; wet prairies and marshes; agricultural environments

Range Statewide

| Jan | Feb | Mar | Apr | May | June | July | Aug | Sep | Oct | Nov | Dec |

Except for its smaller size, the Lesser Yellowlegs is nearly identical to the Greater Yellowlegs. When both species are seen together their size differences make a good field character. When seen singly or in single-species flocks, Lesser Yellowlegs may be identified by a proportionally smaller bill (about 1.5 times the depth of the head behind the bill) and its call, a *tew-tew*, is repeated only one to three times. Both species utilize coastal as well as interior wetlands, where they feed often submerged to their bellies. The Lesser has similar food habits and migration patterns to the Greater Yellowlegs, but is usually more numerous than its larger relative.

FAMILY *Scolopacidae: Sandpipers*

SOLITARY SANDPIPER (*Tringa solitaria*)   p. 236

LENGTH 8.5 in (22 cm)   WEIGHT 1.7 oz (0.05 kg)

Other names Tip-up, Wood Sandpiper

Description White eye ring, dark upperparts speckled with white, greenish legs; bobbing motion

Habitat Hardwood swamps; wet prairies and marshes; agricultural environments

Range Statewide

| Jan | Feb | Mar | Apr | May | June | July | Aug | Sep | Oct | Nov | Dec |

The Solitary Sandpiper is a common migrant and uncommon wintering shorebird in Florida. As its name suggests they are most usually seen singly, or in very small groups. Solitary Sandpipers resemble miniature yellowlegs but with dark legs and darker upperparts. Stream banks, creeks, and edges of ponds and swamps are typical haunts of this bird. Tail-bobbing is a characteristic behavior. Migrants arrive in Florida from sub-Arctic breeding grounds in August and September and usually depart by late April or early May. Food consists of freshwater insects, amphibians, and a variety of invertebrates. They stir up the water with their bills or feet and can be aggressive toward other birds when feeding.

FAMILY *Scolopacidae: Sandpipers*
WILLET (*Catoptrophorus semipalmatus*)   p. 236
LENGTH 15 in (38 cm)   WEIGHT 7.6 oz (0.22 kg)

Other names Stone Curlew, Bill-willie, White-wing Curlew, Pill-willet

Description Long straight bill, gray or brown plumage, black and white wing pattern in flight

Habitat Coastal beaches

Range Statewide, mostly coastal

| Jan | Feb | Mar | Apr | May | June | July | Aug | Sep | Oct | Nov | Dec |

The Willet is a common large shorebird of Florida's coasts. It appears quite plain when at rest or feeding, but displays striking black wing patches and white stripes when in flight. It is somewhat taller and stockier than the Greater Yellowlegs, with a stouter bill, blue-gray legs, and brown-streaked plumage. Willets nest in loose colonies from April to June in sparse to heavy vegetation, but sometimes on open bare ground, laying four large, heavily blotched eggs in a sandy or grass-lined scrape. In winter, plumage is grayer with less streaking. Northern and western birds swell the Florida population, while many Willets migrate through Florida to more southern wintering grounds in Central and South America. Marine invertebrates, crabs, grasshoppers, and other insects make up the diet.

FAMILY *Scolopacidae: Sandpipers*
SPOTTED SANDPIPER (*Actitis macularius*)   p. 236
LENGTH 7.5 in (19 cm)   WEIGHT 1.4 oz (0.04 kg)

Other names Tip-up, Peet-weet, Teeter Snipe, Teeter Tail

Description White wing stripe, stiff-winged flight, teetering motion

Habitat Hardwood swamps; wet prairies and marshes; agricultural environments

Range Statewide

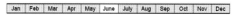

| Jan | Feb | Mar | Apr | May | June | July | Aug | Sep | Oct | Nov | Dec |

Wintering Spotted Sandpipers in Florida have clear white undersides instead of their bold-spotted breeding plumage that appears in late spring. Slightly smaller than the Solitary, Spotted Sandpipers constantly "teeter-totter" when walking. Females are larger and have more spotting. These common shorebirds may be seen singly or in pairs feeding on invertebrates along banks of streams, ponds, and swamp edges. In flight, the wings beat stiffly and rapidly. Migrants arrive in mid-July and return north as late as May.

FAMILY *Scolopacidae: Sandpipers*
UPLAND SANDPIPER (*Bartramia longicauda*)
LENGTH 12 in (30 cm)   WEIGHT 6 oz (0.17 kg)

Description Large ploverlike eye, buff and black mottled back, yellow bill and legs; highly variable calls—alarm is a nasal growl
Habitat Grasslands near water; airport runways; sod fields; golf courses
Range Statewide

Jan	Feb	Mar	Apr	May	June	July	Aug	Sep	Oct	Nov	Dec

The Upland Sandpiper is generally uncommon during spring and fall migration, but it has appeared throughout Florida during its seasonal wanderings to and from South America. Fall birds are generally seen between August and October, spring birds between February and May. It was nearly exterminated in the early 1900s by over-hunting in its Great Plains breeding grounds and is still not common today. Although it is somewhat similar to the Lesser Yellowlegs, it has browner plumage and a yellow bill. The Upland Sandpiper has a habit of perching on exposed fence posts in grassy pastures and on beaches near its breeding grounds. It eats mostly insects and a variety of seeds.

FAMILY *Scolopacidae: Sandpipers*
WHIMBREL (*Numenius phaeopus*) p. 235
LENGTH 17 in (43 cm)   WEIGHT 12.5 oz (0.35 kg)

Other names Hudsonian Curlew
Description Decurved bill, head stripes, grayish underparts
Habitat Coastal beaches; agricultural environments
Range Statewide, mostly coastal

Jan	Feb	Mar	Apr	May	June	July	Aug	Sep	Oct	Nov	Dec

Smaller than the Long-billed Curlew, the Whimbrel has contrasting striping on the head, a shorter, more sharply decurved bill, and mostly brown, mottled plumage. This large, common shorebird is a fall and winter resident along the Atlantic and southern Gulf coasts. The Whimbrel uses its long, curved bill to probe the soft soils of marshes, mudflats, and beaches for shellfish, crabs, worms, and other marine invertebrates. It can be seen inland on mudflats, fields, and lakeshores when it is migrating.

FAMILY *Scolopacidae: Sandpipers*
LONG-BILLED CURLEW (*Numenius americanus*)
p. 235
LENGTH 23 in (58 cm)   WEIGHT 1.2 lb (0.54 kg)

Other names Sickle-bill
Description Very long decurved bill, no head stripes, buff underparts
Habitat Coastal beaches
Range Statewide, coastal

Jan	Feb	Mar	Apr	May	June	July	Aug	Sep	Oct	Nov	Dec

This uncommon but regular winter resident in Florida was extremely rare early in the twentieth century after being very abundant. Numbers have increased since the 1930s. It now can be seen regularly at inlets along the northeast Atlantic coast and on some Gulf beaches probing for burrowing invertebrates with its long, down-curved bill. The unstreaked head and cinnamon wing linings are other good field characters. Long-billed Curlews occur in Florida from September to May, but a few may remain all year. They breed in the Great Plains.

FAMILY *Scolopacidae: Sandpipers*
MARBLED GODWIT (*Limosa fedoa*)
p. 235
LENGTH 18 in (46 cm)   WEIGHT 11.3 oz (0.32 kg)

Description Cinnamon buff underparts, slightly upturned pink bill with dark tip
Habitat Coastal beaches; agricultural environments
Range Statewide, mostly coastal

Jan	Feb	Mar	Apr	May	June	July	Aug	Sep	Oct	Nov	Dec

A once abundant winter resident, the Marbled Godwit is a less common Florida visitor today. It is a large shorebird with a very long, slightly upturned, two-toned bill, and long legs. Its plumage is a light brown barring beneath, and mottled above. The wing linings are a light cinnamon. The very rare **Black-tailed Godwit** (*Limosa limosa*), an Old World visitor, has a whitish belly and white wing linings. The nearly as rare **Bar-tailed Godwit** (*Limosa lapponica*) has been seen occasionally in scattered Florida locations. It is slightly smaller than the Marbled Godwit and is much grayer overall. The rare **Hudsonian Godwit** (*Limosa haemastica*) is distinguished by its smaller size, black and white tail, and cinnamon undersides. The Marbled Godwit prefers saltwater beaches and mud flats where it probes its long bill in search of small invertebrates and tubers. Godwits appear occasionally in late July and August on agricultural muck lands that are being drained for cultivation.

FAMILY *Scolopacidae: Sandpipers*
RUDDY TURNSTONE (*Arenaria interpres*)
p. 237
LENGTH 9 in (23 cm)   WEIGHT 3.9 oz (0.11 kg)

Other names: Calico-back, Rock Plover, Brant Bird

Description Brown head and back, black breast, white belly, orange legs (winter) or rusty upperparts, black and white head (breeding)

Habitat Coastal beaches

Range Statewide, coastal

| Jan | Feb | Mar | Apr | May | June | July | Aug | Sep | Oct | Nov | Dec |

This small, chunky shorebird is a common migrant and winter resident; however, a few nonbreeders remain through summer. They seem most abundant between July and April. While in Florida, Ruddy Turnstones may appear brown above with a black bib and orange legs, but many retain their breeding plumage through winter. Breeding birds develop bright, rusty back feathers and white head feathers. Turnstones exhibit a pied (black and white) appearance in flight. Ruddy Turnstones use coastal habitats and flooded agricultural fields and seem quite tolerant of humans and human activity. They are also seen on bridge railings, docks, and piers, feeding on fish remains. This active bird uses its slightly upturned bill to flip seaweed, shells, and other beach debris in search of invertebrate prey, hence its name.

FAMILY *Scolopacidae: Sandpipers*
RED KNOT (*Calidris canutus*)
p. 237
LENGTH 10 in (25 cm)   WEIGHT 4.4 oz (0.12 kg)

Other names Robin Snipe, Red-breasted Snipe, American Knot, Wah-quoit

Description Dark gray above, white below, short tapered bill, greenish legs (winter) or rufous face and underparts, brown back, mottled with black and white (breeding)

Habitat Coastal beaches

Range Statewide, coastal

| Jan | Feb | Mar | Apr | May | June | July | Aug | Sep | Oct | Nov | Dec |

The Red Knot is smaller than a dowitcher, has a short bill, lacks white tail feathers, and has rather short, greenish legs. During winter, it appears light gray with slight mottling. This gradually turns into its bright summer plumage with robinlike rusty breast feathers. The Red Knot can be an abundant but unpredictable migrant in fall beginning in August and again in spring starting in April. They are seen mostly along sandy coastal beaches, and very rarely in the interior. Some birds remain through summer and flocks of wintering Knots are common. The coquina, a tiny shellfish, is its major food source.

FAMILY *Scolopacidae: Sandpipers*
SANDERLING (*Calidris alba*)   p.238
LENGTH 8 in (20 cm)   WEIGHT 4.2 oz (0.12 kg)

Other names Sand Snipe, Beach Bird, Whiting, Ruddy Plover, Peep
Description Light gray above, white below, black along bend of wing (winter) or
rusty head, back, breast, spotted with black, white below (breeding)
Habitat Coastal beaches
Range Statewide, coastal

Jan	Feb	Mar	Apr	May	June	July	Aug	Sep	Oct	Nov	Dec

This is our most familiar coastal sandpiper. Sanderlings gather in small flocks and follow the advancing and receding surf as potential meals are exposed by wave action. In flight the Sanderling exposes a conspicuous white wing stripe and a light rump. In Florida most birds exhibit light gray plumage above, white below, and black at the bend in the wing. Sanderlings are common on the Gulf and Atlantic coasts from late summer through early spring; some birds can be seen year-round. Food of the Sanderling is mostly marine invertebrates including the common sand flea and the shellfish coquina.

FAMILY *Scolopacidae: Sandpipers*
SEMIPALMATED SANDPIPER (*Calidris pusilla*)   p. 238
LENGTH 6.25 in (16 cm)   WEIGHT 1.1 oz (0.03 kg)

Other names Peep
Description Short stout bill, black legs; brown above, white below (winter) or
rufous, buff mottled above, brown breast streaks, white belly (breeding)
Habitat Coastal beaches; salt marshes; wet prairies and marshes; agricultural environments
Range Statewide, coastal

Jan	Feb	Mar	Apr	May	June	July	Aug	Sep	Oct	Nov	Dec

The Semipalmated Sandpiper is one of the most abundant shorebirds in eastern North America. Black legs, short, stout bill, and gray back differentiate this "peep" from the similar Least and Western Sandpipers with which it is often found. Sometimes it hops along on the beach on one leg. Its most characteristic call is a low-pitched *chirp* or a coarse *cherk*. It occurs in Florida during spring and fall migration, while a few individuals may over-winter in Florida Bay. Most birds winter south of the United States. Foods consist of marine and freshwater invertebrates found on sand and mud flats of beaches, inlets, and lakes.

FAMILY *Scolopacidae: Sandpipers*
WESTERN SANDPIPER (*Calidris mauri*)
p. 238
LENGTH 6.5 in (17 cm)   WEIGHT 0.8 oz (0.02 kg)

Other names Peep

Description Slight droop at tip of black bill, black legs; similar to Semipalmated, with a flight call that is a high *zeep* (winter); rusty wash on crown, ears, back, and V-shaped streakings on breasts to flanks (breeding)

Habitat Coastal beaches; salt marshes; wet prairies and marshes; agricultural environments

Range Statewide, mostly coastal

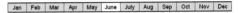

Jan	Feb	Mar	Apr	May	June	July	Aug	Sep	Oct	Nov	Dec

This sandpiper closely resembles the Semipalmated and Least, with which it is often seen. The Western has a longer black bill with a slight droop at the end, and longer black legs; otherwise, in winter plumage it appears identical to the Semipalmated. In fresh breeding plumage, some of which is obtained prior to departing Florida, Westerns have bright tawny patches on the scapulars, back, and sides of the head. When together, Western Sandpipers tend to feed in deeper water than do Semipalmated Sandpipers. Western Sandpipers are abundant during winter and migration. They can be seen foraging for invertebrates on beaches and tidal flats from July through May. A few nonbreeders remain through the summer. Its call is a weak, high-pitched *peet.*

FAMILY *Scolopacidae: Sandpipers*
LEAST SANDPIPER (*Calidris minutilla*)
p. 238
LENGTH 6 in (15 cm)   WEIGHT 0.8 oz (0.02 kg)

Other names Peep

Description Short thin black bill, dull yellow or greenish legs; brown head, back, breast; white belly (winter) or brown, mottled above, dark streaked breast (breeding)

Habitat Coastal beaches; salt marshes; wet prairies and marshes; agricultural environments

Range Statewide

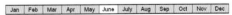

Jan	Feb	Mar	Apr	May	June	July	Aug	Sep	Oct	Nov	Dec

The Least Sandpiper is our smallest "peep" and may be abundant from July through May. It is distinguished from the other peep species chiefly by its yellowish leg color. The back is brown to gray in nonbreeding plumage. The breast is heavily streaked with brown or gray and the belly is white. In flight a narrow white wing stripe is obvious along with a black rump and tail stripe. It is easily confused with Semipalmated and Western Sandpipers, with which it often associates. Its call is a high-pitched *wheet.* Least Sandpipers inhabit coastal as well as inland wetlands. They seem to prefer grassy flats at the edges of salt marshes and freshwater ponds, where they feed on insects, crustaceans, and small mollusks.

FAMILY *Scolopacidae: Sandpipers*
WHITE-RUMPED SANDPIPER (*Calidris fuscicollis*) p. 238
LENGTH 7.5 in (19 cm) WEIGHT 1.2 oz (0.03 kg)

> **Other names** Peep
>
> **Description** White rump, wings extend beyond tail; dusky grey head, breast, back; white eyebrow (winter) or rust on head and ear coverts, dark streaks on white breast and sides (breeding)
>
> **Habitat** Coastal beaches; salt marshes; wet prairies and marshes; agricultural environments
>
> **Range** Statewide

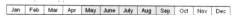

Jan	Feb	Mar	Apr	May	June	July	Aug	Sep	Oct	Nov	Dec

This rather nondescript shorebird is a regular but not abundant fall and late spring migrant in Florida. The White-rumped Sandpiper has dark legs and is gray above and white below, with pale gray mottling on the breast. The best field mark, however, is its clear white rump, seen when the bird flies. White-rumped Sandpipers are found along our coasts and inland and will allow a closer approach than many small shorebirds. Fall birds may be seen between July and September while spring migrants are present in Florida from May through June. Foods are mostly seeds and small aquatic invertebrates.

FAMILY *Scolopacidae: Sandpipers*
PECTORAL SANDPIPER (*Calidris melanotos*) p. 237
LENGTH 9 in (23 cm) WEIGHT 3.5 oz (0.1 kg)

> **Other names** Grass Snipe, Creaker
>
> **Description** Brown upperparts, heavily streaked breast sharply demarcated from white belly
>
> **Habitat** Salt marshes; wet prairies and marshes; agricultural environments
>
> **Range** Statewide

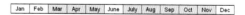

Jan	Feb	Mar	Apr	May	June	July	Aug	Sep	Oct	Nov	Dec

This robin-size sandpiper is common in coastal and inland marshes, flooded fields, and heavily vegetated lake margins. Extensive floating water hyacinth mats occasionally attract large numbers of Pectorals. The streaked, dark breast contrasts with the white belly. It has greenish legs and a slightly down-curved bill. Pectoral Sandpipers are most common during fall (July–November) in freshly drained muck lands around Lakes Apopka and Okeechobee, but may also be seen during spring migration. A variety of invertebrates and seeds are eaten.

FAMILY *Scolopacidae: Sandpipers*
PURPLE SANDPIPER (*Calidris maritima*)
p. 237
LENGTH 9 in (23 cm)   WEIGHT 1.77–3.71 oz (0.05–0.11 kg)

Description Dark gray head, breast, back, white belly, dull orange legs, long drooped bill.

Habitat Coastal beaches; inhabits rock jetties

Range Peninsula coasts

Jan	Feb	Mar	Apr	May	June	July	Aug	Sep	Oct	Nov	Dec

This small dark shorebird is a rare, unpredictable winter visitor in Florida. Most sightings have occurred along the northeast coast. Dark gray head and neck, yellow legs, and yellow base of bill are good field marks. Purple Sandpipers prefer rocky shores and may be seen on rock jetties and breakwaters anywhere along the Atlantic coast, rarely in the Gulf. They eat a variety of invertebrates and algae.

FAMILY *Scolopacidae: Sandpipers*
DUNLIN (*Calidris alpina*)
p. 237
LENGTH 8.5 in (22 cm)   WEIGHT 1.9 oz (0.05 kg)

Other names Red-backed Sandpiper, Sand-snipe

Description Brownish gray above, lighter below, black bill drooped at tip (winter) or white underparts with black belly patch, chestnut back (breeding)

Habitat Coastal beaches; salt marshes; agricultural environments

Range Statewide, coastal

Jan	Feb	Mar	Apr	May	June	July	Aug	Sep	Oct	Nov	Dec

The rather long, slightly down-curved bill is a good field mark of this rather common winter resident. While in Florida, Dunlins usually are gray above and white below, with dark legs. Fall migrants appear in Florida during August and usually depart during May. They migrate in great flocks flying very fast. In late spring some individuals may be seen coming into their distinctive rusty-backed, black-bellied breeding plumage. Dunlins are birds of coastal mudflats, lagoons, and beaches, but may occur inland as well. It is often seen in large flocks, and is probably our most abundant sandpiper. Foods primarily are marine and aquatic invertebrates.

FAMILY *Scolopacidae: Sandpipers*
STILT SANDPIPER (*Calidris himantopus*)
LENGTH 8.5 in (22 cm)   WEIGHT 2 oz (0.06 kg)

Description Gray upperparts, white eyeline, black bill, yellowish legs; smaller and paler than dowitchers (nonbreeding)

Habitat Often associated with other shorebirds at pond edges, beaches, and mud flats

Range Statewide

Jan	Feb	Mar	Apr	May	June	July	Aug	Sep	Oct	Nov	Dec

The Stilt Sandpiper is similar to but smaller than dowitchers, and can be distinguished from Dunlins by its much longer legs. Flying Stilt Sandpipers exhibit an uninterrupted white rump patch. This species can be locally abundant during spring (March–May) and fall (usually July) but its presence is otherwise unpredictable. A few birds over-winter in central and south Florida. They are often seen in the company of other sandpiper species. Stilt Sandpipers inhabit coastal beaches, mud flats, river banks, and lake edges. They feed primarily on invertebrates and occasionally seeds.

FAMILY *Scolopacidae: Sandpipers*
SHORT-BILLED DOWITCHER (*Limnodromus griseus*)   p. 236
LENGTH 11 in (28 cm)   WEIGHT 3.8 oz (0.11 kg)

Other names Red-breasted Snipe

Description Russet underparts, barring on flanks, white belly and vent (breeding) or gray upperparts (winter)

Habitat Coastal beaches; salt marshes; wet prairies and marshes; agricultural environments

Range Statewide

Jan	Feb	Mar	Apr	May	June	July	Aug	Sep	Oct	Nov	Dec

This common migrant and winter resident is found along both coasts but also may be seen regularly along freshwater lakes and marshes. Light-gray underparts, brown above, white rump and tail with dark barring, and very long bill distinguish the Short-billed Dowitcher. Individuals have been seen year-round in Florida with migrations usually peaking in mid-spring and in late summer. The **Long-billed Dowitcher** (*Limnodromus scolopaceus*) is very similar with a slightly longer bill. Both species have greenish-gray legs. While considered uncommon in Florida, this species' actual abundance is difficult to determine because of its close resemblance to the Short-bill. Both species obtain aquatic and marine invertebrates by probing sand and soft mud. In late spring both species have brilliant robin-redbreasts with heavy dark spotting in the neck and breast region of the Long-bill, and little or no spotting on that of the Short-bill. The call of the Short-bill is a loud *tu-tu-tu,* repeated rapidly, while that of the Long-bill is a high pitched *geek,* also repeated rapidly.

FAMILY *Scolopacidae: Sandpipers*
WILSON'S SNIPE (*Gallinago delicata*)
LENGTH 10 in (25 cm)   WEIGHT 4.5 oz (0.13 kg)

p. 236

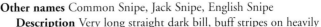

Other names Common Snipe, Jack Snipe, English Snipe

Description Very long straight dark bill, buff stripes on heavily mottled upperparts, striped head, buffy streaked breast, zigzig flight

Habitat Wet prairies and marshes; agricultural environments

Range Statewide

Jan	Feb	Mar	Apr	May	June	July	Aug	Sep	Oct	Nov	Dec

The Wilson's Snipe resembles a dowitcher with its long bill, but has heavier barring on the head, back, and neck, as well as a brown rump and orange tail. An erratic, zigzag flight when flushed is characteristic of this abundant shorebird. Snipes are marsh, wet prairie, and lake edge birds. They probe for worms, insects, and other invertebrates using the flexible tips of their bills. Migrants arrive in September and depart in April or May. This species is less common in south Florida. It permits a close approach when concealed and emits a loud *skape* when flushed. Snipe are a locally popular game bird throughout the southeastern United States.

FAMILY *Scolopacidae: Sandpipers*
AMERICAN WOODCOCK (*Scolopax minor*)
LENGTH 11 in (28 cm)   WEIGHT 6.2 oz (0.18 kg)

p. 236

Other names Timber Doodle

Description Long pale bill, upperparts mottled with black, brown, gray, rust; cinnamon tan below, black crown with buffy cross stripes.

Habitat Mesic hammocks; mixed pine and hardwood forests; wet prairies and marshes; agricultural environments

Range Statewide

Jan	Feb	Mar	Apr	May	June	July	Aug	Sep	Oct	Nov	Dec

This odd-looking, cryptically colored, woodland bird sports a long bill, short legs, and high-set eyes that permit binocular vision in front and behind. Florida is mostly a winter refuge for this species, although Woodcocks breed regularly, if sparsely, throughout north and central Florida. Nests are small depressions on the forest floor, usually containing four camouflaged eggs laid from February to June. The courtship flight of the male is quite spectacular. A nasal *peent* is uttered while the bird spirals upward nearly out of sight; then he plummets downward, uttering a rapid chirping call before returning to his starting point. This pattern is repeated continuously over open fields or wet prairies. Food consists of worms, insects, and other invertebrates. Like the Wilson's Snipe, the Woodcock is a popular game species.

FAMILY *Scolopacidae: Sandpipers*

WILSON'S PHALAROPE (*Phalaropus tricolor*)
LENGTH 9.25 in (23 cm)   WEIGHT 2.1 oz (0.06 kg)

Description Pale gray above, white belly and throat, white above the eye, needle-like, black bill (nonbreeding adult)

Habitat Usually well offshore in open water

Range Central and north Florida

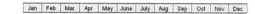

| Jan | Feb | Mar | Apr | May | June | July | Aug | Sep | Oct | Nov | Dec |

Three species of phalarope occur in Florida, but the Wilson's is the most frequently encountered. Phalaropes are unusual in that males incubate the eggs in the absence of the more brightly colored females. These are very active water birds that often spin while feeding in open water. Wilson's Phalaropes appear in Florida mostly between July and September in their nonbreeding plumage: light gray or brown above and white below. The bill is black and needle-like. Sightings of the smaller **Red-necked Phalarope** (*Phalaropus lobatus*) and **Red Phalarope** (*Phalaropus fulicarius*) are mostly pelagic, but they are occasionally seen in coastal areas along the Atlantic Ocean. The Wilson's Phalarope is most likely to be encountered in flooded agricultural fields, bays, lagoons, mud flats. The diet is insects and other invertebrates. Some of these are obtained by stirring up submerged potential prey from muddy lake bottoms.

FAMILY *Laridae: Gulls, Terns, Skimmers* p. 239

SOUTH POLAR SKUA (*Stercorarius maccormicki*)
LENGTH 21 in (53 cm)   WEIGHT 2.5 lb (1.13 kg)

Description Mostly dark, white highlights at base of the primaries; some birds with lighter, buff-colored bodies; skin color is black on feet and bill

Habitat Open saltwater

Range Atlantic ocean

| Jan | Feb | Mar | Apr | May | June | July | Aug | Sep | Oct | Nov | Dec |

This heavy-appearing denizen of the Earth's polar regions is slightly smaller than a Herring Gull. It is mostly dark with white highlights at the base of the primaries. Some birds have lighter, buff-colored bodies. In all forms the skin color is black on feet and bill. The South Polar Skua is not at all common or predictable, but may be seen off the Atlantic Coast and sometimes loafing on beaches between November and February. It scavenges, captures marine prey, follows fishing vessels for discarded scraps, and will sometimes rob other birds of their catch.

FAMILY *Laridae: Gulls, Terns, Skimmers*
POMARINE JAEGER (*Stercorarius pomarinus*)
p. 239
LENGTH 18.5 in (47 cm)   WEIGHT 1.4 lb (0.63 kg)

Description Entirely dark, or with yellowish neck and white chest; bill bicolored—pinkish with a dark tip; tail has twisted central feathers
Habitat Open saltwater
Range Statewide, coastal

Jan	Feb	Mar	Apr	May	June	July	Aug	Sep	Oct	Nov	Dec

This is the most common and largest of the three Jaeger species that visit Florida. It is seen primarily during fall migration but has been reported in every month, especially off the east coast. It is a dark gull about the size of a Ring-billed Gull. Adults can be entirely dark, or can exhibit a yellowish neck and white chest. In any plumage the bill is bicolored—pinkish with a dark tip. The tail shows distinctly twisted central feathers, a feature that is unlike any other jaeger or gull. No inland records are known for Florida. It has been known to eat lemmings near its breeding grounds in Alaska. Elsewhere it scavenges, captures marine prey, and harasses other birds for their catches.

FAMILY *Laridae: Gulls, Terns, Skimmers*
PARASITIC JAEGER (*Stercorarius parasiticus*)
p. 239
LENGTH 16.5 in (42 cm)   WEIGHT 14.9 oz (0.42 kg)

Description Slender wings, slightly peaked crown, narrower bill; body coloration ranges from nearly black to tawny
Habitat Open saltwater
Range Statewide, coastal

Jan	Feb	Mar	Apr	May	June	July	Aug	Sep	Oct	Nov	Dec

The Parasitic Jaeger is about the size of a Laughing Gull. Other than its smaller size, the Parasitic can be distinguished from the Pomarine Jaeger by its more slender wings, slightly peaked crown, and narrower bill. Depending on age and color morph, body coloration can range from nearly black to tawny. It has also been seen throughout the year off of Florida's coasts, but most birds occur in October and November. It is frequently seen chasing other marine birds for their catches.

FAMILY *Laridae: Gulls, Terns, Skimmers*
LONG-TAILED JAEGER (*Stercorarius longicaudus*)   p. 239
LENGTH 15 in (38 cm)   WEIGHT 9.9 oz (0.28 kg)

Description Grayer than the other two jaegers; long central tail feathers; bill short and stout (breeding adult) or white barring and flecking on the upper surfaces of wings and back (immature)

Habitat Open saltwater

Range Peninsula coasts

Jan	Feb	Mar	Apr	May	June	July	Aug	Sep	Oct	Nov	Dec

This is the smallest and least common of Florida's visiting Jaegers. It is grayer than the other two species and breeding adults have very long central tail feathers. The bill is relatively short and stout. Immature birds often show white barring and flecking on the upper surfaces of the wings and back. It looks ternlike in flight and has been known to hover. Its diet is similar to those of the Pomarine Jaeger and Parasitic Jaeger.

FAMILY *Laridae: Gulls, Terns, Skimmers*
LAUGHING GULL (*Larus atricilla*)   p. 240
LENGTH 16 in (41 cm)   WEIGHT 11.5 oz (0.33 kg)

Other names Black-headed Gull

Description Black head, dark gray mantle, dark red bill and legs (adult) or mottled gray head, black bill and legs (winter adult and immature) or brown (juvenile)

Habitat Coastal beaches; salt marshes; open saltwater; open freshwater; urban environments; agricultural environments

Range Statewide

Jan	Feb	Mar	Apr	May	June	July	Aug	Sep	Oct	Nov	Dec

This is the largest of our black-headed gulls as well as our only nesting gull. During summer the adult exhibits a black hood extending from the back of the head to the throat, red bill, reddish legs, and gray wings and back. The immature is dark brown above, with white rump and tail, black tail band, and dark bill and legs. The winter adult has a mottled gray head and dark bill and legs. Laughing Gulls primarily are coastal birds feeding on fish and other marine organisms, but are rather common at landfills and some other inland sites. It may rob other sea birds of their prey. Nests are constructed of grass and other beach plants, usually on a sandy barrier island. The nesting season peaks in late May when three to four dark-colored, splotched eggs are laid.

FAMILY *Laridae: Gulls, Terns, Skimmers*
BONAPARTE'S GULL *(Larus philadelphia)* p. 240
LENGTH 13 in (33 cm)   WEIGHT 7.5 oz (0.21 kg)

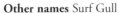

Other names Surf Gull

Description Small black bill, white head with black ear spot, gray mantle with a white wedge on outer wing (winter)

Habitat Coastal beaches; salt marshes; open saltwater; open freshwater; wet prairies and marshes; agricultural environments

Range Statewide

Jan	Feb	Mar	Apr	May	June	July	Aug	Sep	Oct	Nov	Dec

This small gull is a common winter visitor along our coasts and inland. In winter plumage, the Bonaparte's Gull exhibits a white head, gray patch behind the eye, pink legs, dark bill, gray back, white tail, and large white wedges at the ends of otherwise gray wings. Primaries are tipped in black. The immature has a narrow black tail band and incomplete white wedges on the wings. Bonaparte's Gulls are buoyant and ternlike in flight. Foods consist of insects, fish, snails, and other invertebrates. Migrants appear in early fall and may remain through May.

FAMILY *Laridae: Gulls, Terns, Skimmers*
RING-BILLED GULL *(Larus delawarensis)* p. 240
LENGTH 17 in (43 cm)   WEIGHT 1.2 lb (0.54 kg)

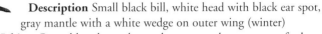

Description Pale gray mantle, black wingtips, yellow bill with black band, yellow legs (adult) or pink bill with black tip, mottled gray-brown, narrow tail band (immature)

Habitat Coastal beaches; salt marshes; open saltwater; open freshwater; wet prairies and marshes; urban environments; agricultural environments

Range Statewide

Jan	Feb	Mar	Apr	May	June	July	Aug	Sep	Oct	Nov	Dec

The Ring-billed is the most common gull in Florida. It may be seen along the coast and inland from October through May. Ring-billed Gulls are smaller than Herring Gulls, have a black band near the end of the bill, yellow legs, and less streaking during winter than Herring Gulls. Immatures are paler overall than Herring Gulls and have a narrower, black tail band. This common gull may be seen in huge flocks near large bodies of water and on sanitary landfills. In addition, they seem particularly fond of shopping center parking lots, roosting on heat-retaining asphalt during cold spells. Foods consist of fish, insects, refuse, and vegetation such as cabbage palm fruits.

FAMILY *Laridae: Gulls, Terns, Skimmers*
HERRING GULL (*Larus argentatus*)
p. 240

LENGTH 25 in (64 cm)   WEIGHT 2.7 lb (1.22 kg)

Description Pale gray mantle, black wingtips, yellow bill, pink legs (adult) or gray-brown, streaked, black tail band, pink legs (immature)

Habitat Coastal beaches; salt marshes; open saltwater; open freshwater; urban environments; agricultural environments

Range Statewide

Jan	Feb	Mar	Apr	May	June	July	Aug	Sep	Oct	Nov	Dec

The Herring Gull is perhaps the most familiar gull in North America. In Florida, this large bird is a common winter visitor especially along the coasts but also may be seen inland. Adults have light gray backs, black wingtips with white spots, pink legs, and gray streaking on the head and neck. First-year birds exhibit dark tails and primaries, and mottled gray-brown upperparts; second-year birds have light gray backs, light head and rump, black-tipped pink bill, and gray-brown wings. Herring Gulls commonly feed on refuse in large garbage dumps as well as on fish, mollusks, carrion, and other debris along our coasts.

FAMILY *Laridae: Gulls, Terns, Skimmers*
LESSER BLACK-BACKED GULL (*Larus fuscus*)
p. 240

LENGTH 21 in (53 cm)   WEIGHT 1.7 lb (0.77 kg)

Other names Scandinavian Lesser Black-backed Gull

Description Dark gray mantle, yellow bill and legs, white head, underparts (adult) or similar to Herring Gull, but more white in head and rump, more black in wings (immature)

Habitat Coastal beaches; open saltwater

Range Peninsula coasts

Jan	Feb	Mar	Apr	May	June	July	Aug	Sep	Oct	Nov	Dec

As the name suggests, the Lesser Black-backed Gull is smaller than the Great Black-backed Gull. Other field marks include a lighter back, yellow legs, thinner bill, and a long-winged appearance. This European visitor has been seen on both coasts of Florida with regularity in recent winters. While uncommon to locally fairly common, it is most likely to be found with other gulls along the Atlantic coast and around garbage dumps.

FAMILY *Laridae: Gulls, Terns, Skimmers*
GREAT BLACK-BACKED GULL *(Larus marinus)*

LENGTH 30 in (76 cm)   WEIGHT 4 lb (1.81 kg)

p. 240

Description Large; black mantle, white head and body; heavy yellow bill, pink legs (adult) or brown or black mottled upperparts, light head (immature)

Habitat Coastal beaches; open saltwater

Range Statewide, coastal

Jan	Feb	Mar	Apr	May	June	July	Aug	Sep	Oct	Nov	Dec

This aggressive, predatory bird, which is our largest "sea gull," appears eagle-like while soaring on thermals. In the United States, the Great Black-backed Gull primarily is a bird of the northeast, but in recent years it has become increasingly common in winter, primarily along Florida's east coast and occasionally the Gulf coast. Adults are distinguished by dark black wings and back, and pink legs. First- and second-year birds have a narrower dark tail band than other large, immature gulls. Like other gulls, the Great Black-backed eats a variety of fish, crustaceans, mollusks, birds, and beach debris.

FAMILY *Laridae: Gulls, Terns, Skimmers*
GULL-BILLED TERN *(Sterna nilotica)*

LENGTH 14 in (36 cm)   WEIGHT 8.2 oz (0.23 kg)

Description Short, stout black bill, black legs and cap   p. 241

Habitat Coastal beaches; salt marshes; wet prairies and marshes; agricultural environments

Range Statewide

Jan	Feb	Mar	Apr	May	June	July	Aug	Sep	Oct	Nov	Dec

As its name suggests this tern has a stouter bill than its relatives. Gull-billed Terns also have a short, notched tail and pale upperparts. The head is black-capped in summer and white-gray in winter. Nest scrapes containing two to three tan eggs colored with black markings often are more elaborate than those of other terns and may contain vegetation and other debris. Nesting occurs along both coasts and near inland freshwater lakes, as indicated on the range map, from May through July. Gull-billed Terns commonly are seen over salt and freshwater marshes feeding on a wide variety of flying insects. Small fish and fiddler crabs also are eaten.

FAMILY *Laridae: Gulls, Terns, Skimmers*
CASPIAN TERN (*Sterna caspia*)
LENGTH 21 in (53 cm)   WEIGHT 1.4 lb (0.64 kg)

p. 241

Description Black cap and forehead, heavy orange-red bill

Habitat Coastal beaches; open saltwater; open freshwater

Range Statewide, mostly coastal

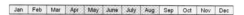

| Jan | Feb | Mar | Apr | May | June | July | Aug | Sep | Oct | Nov | Dec |

This is our largest tern, measuring even larger than the Ring-billed Gull. Nesting Caspian Terns (discovered in Florida in 1962) represent the southeastern breeding limit of the species in North America. Appearing more slender and darker underneath than the Royal Tern, Caspians have a large, blood-red bill and black crown. In winter the tip of the head appears gray or white and slightly crested. Nesting colonies are strictly coastal in Florida—as indicated on the range map—where spoil islands are preferred. Caspian Terns feed on larger fish than their relatives do. Prey species include mullet and menhaden.

FAMILY *Laridae: Gulls, Terns, Skimmers*
ROYAL TERN (*Sterna maxima*)
LENGTH 20 in (51 cm)   WEIGHT 1 lb (0.45 kg)

p. 241

Other names Big Striker, Redbill, Cayenne Tern, Gannet Striker

Description Black cap and crest, often with white forehead, orange-yellow bill

Habitat Coastal beaches; open saltwater

Range Statewide, mostly coastal

| Jan | Feb | Mar | Apr | May | June | July | Aug | Sep | Oct | Nov | Dec |

These large terns are gray above, white below, have a yellow-orange bill, and a black, slightly crested cap. In winter the head is streaked with white and the crest is inconspicuous. Royal Terns nest on islands in the Banana River, Tampa Bay, Charlotte Harbor, on spoil islands near Yankeetown, and irregularly elsewhere along Florida's coasts, as indicated on the range map. These colonial nesters lay one whitish egg covered with spots and blotches in an inconspicuous scrape. Nesting occurs during summer but birds are commonly seen throughout the year. Royal Terns plunge-feed, like most other terns, for a variety of small fish. They often associate with Sandwich Terns.

FAMILY *Laridae: Gulls, Terns, Skimmers*

SANDWICH TERN (*Sterna sandvicensis*)

LENGTH 15 in (38 cm)   WEIGHT 7.3 oz (0.21 kg)

p. 241

Other names Cabot's Tern

Description Black head with crest, slender black bill with yellow tip, black legs

Habitat Coastal beaches; salt marshes; open saltwater

Range Statewide, mostly coastal

Jan	Feb	Mar	Apr	May	June	July	Aug	Sep	Oct	Nov	Dec

This medium-size tern is distinctive, with a yellow-tipped black bill in all plumages. Breeding adults are black-capped with a short, shaggy crest. In winter they develop a white forehead. Sandwich Terns were a more common nester in Florida a century ago. This bird was formerly more abundant in Florida and was apparently extirpated from the state for the bulk of the twentieth century. Recent breeding colonies have been along the coast in extreme northeastern Florida and at a few locations from Tampa Bay to Citrus County, as indicated on the range map. Two eggs are laid in a shallow nest scrape above the high tide line during May or June in mixed colonies with Royal Terns. During winter, birds are frequently seen along both coasts usually from central to south Florida. Like most other terns, Sandwich Terns plunge for small fish.

FAMILY *Laridae: Gulls, Terns, Skimmers*

ROSEATE TERN (*Sterna dougallii*)

LENGTH 15 in (38 cm)   WEIGHT 3.8 oz (0.11 kg)   STATUS **T**

p. 241

Description Black cap and bill, orange-red feet or similar to Common Tern (winter)

Habitat Coastal beaches; open saltwater

Range Central and south Florida, coastal

Jan	Feb	Mar	Apr	May	June	July	Aug	Sep	Oct	Nov	Dec

Roseate Terns have a black bill, are pale gray above, and have a longer, more deeply forked tail and lighter wingtips than Common Terns. This medium-size tern is uncommon as a migrant from its northeastern North American colonies but breeds at scattered locations through the Florida Keys, as indicated on the range map. It once bred regularly in the Dry Tortugas. In Florida, two or three eggs are laid on the ground in shallow scrapes, on bare rock, or in beach debris. Nests are especially sensitive to storms and high tides. Little is known of Florida Keys colonies, but numbers appear to be on the increase. Roseate Terns feed on fish close to shore.

p. 241

FAMILY *Laridae: Gulls, Terns, Skimmers*
COMMON TERN (*Sterna hirundo*)
LENGTH 14 in (36 cm)   WEIGHT 4.2 oz (0.12 kg)

Other names Mackerel Gull
Description Dark nape, dark bar at bend of wing, black feet and bill (winter) or black cap, gray back, black-tipped red bill and legs (breeding)
Habitat Coastal beaches; salt marshes; open saltwater
Range Statewide, mostly coastal

Jan	Feb	Mar	Apr	May	June	July	Aug	Sep	Oct	Nov	Dec

Common Terns primarily are spring and fall migrants in Florida, with a few birds lingering through winter. Occasionally, migrating flocks can number in the thousands. Some nesting has occurred on the coast of the Florida Panhandle. In winter plumage Common Terns have black on nape of neck, black flesh parts, dark wingtips, and forked tail. These birds usually migrate far offshore but occasionally may be seen coastally. Common Terns feed by diving for small fish and crustaceans. The similar **Arctic Tern** (*Sterna paradisaea*) occurs sporadically during migration during spring and fall. It is slightly smaller, has longer wings, and appears more uniformly light gray above than the Common Tern. It is also larger and with a stouter bill than the similar Roseate Tern. Some Arctic Terns migrate between breeding grounds in the Arctic and wintering grounds in Antarctica—a trip of some 11,000 miles. Its pelagic tendencies make it a rare visitor over mainland Florida.

p. 241

FAMILY *Laridae: Gulls, Terns, Skimmers*
FORSTER'S TERN (*Sterna forsteri*)
LENGTH 14 in (36 cm)   WEIGHT 5.6 oz (0.16 kg)

Description White head, black ear-patch, black bill, orange legs (winter) or black-tipped orange bill and legs, primaries lighter than rest of wing and back (breeding)
Habitat Coastal beaches; salt marshes; open saltwater; open freshwater; wet prairies and marshes; agricultural environments
Range Statewide

Jan	Feb	Mar	Apr	May	June	July	Aug	Sep	Oct	Nov	Dec

The Forster's Tern in winter plumage is similar to the Common Tern, but has a black mask extending behind the eye with less or no black on the nape. Some immature birds remain in Florida year-round but are most common during winter months. Forster's Terns can be seen over freshwater and saltwater marshes, inland lakes, and coastal beaches. The call is a grating *zaaap* note. Important foods are primarily insects and small fish.

Family *Laridae: Gulls, Terns, Skimmers*
LEAST TERN (*Sterna antillarum*)

p. 241

Length 9 in (23 cm)   Weight 1.5 oz (0.04 kg)   Status **T**

Other names Sea Swallow, Kill-em Polly, Gaviota Chica, Pigeon de la Mer, Little Tern

Description White forehead, black crown, yellow bill with black tip (adult) or brown back, black nape, black at bend of wing (immature)

Habitat Coastal beaches; salt marshes; open saltwater; open freshwater; wet prairies and marshes; agricultural environments

Range Statewide

Jan	Feb	Mar	Apr	May	June	July	Aug	Sep	Oct	Nov	Dec

This smallest North American tern is a familiar resident in Florida from March through September. Broad, short, swallow-like tail, black cap, white forehead, yellow bill with black tip and rapid wing beat distinguish the Least Tern from its larger relatives. The immature is mottled above with tail more deeply forked than the adult. Historically, Least Terns nested on coastal beaches, dunes, islands, and river shores creating shallow scrapes and laying two to three mottled eggs. Today, most nesting occurs on human-made habitats, including dredged-material islands, construction sites, phosphate mines, and gravel roof tops, from April through August. Their breeding range extends throughout Florida, both inland and on the coast. Least Terns feed by hovering and diving for small fish. Because of competition with humans for recreation and development space, Least Terns are considered a threatened species.

Family *Laridae: Gulls, Terns, Skimmers*
BRIDLED TERN (*Sterna anaethetus*)

p. 242

Length 15 in (38 cm)   Weight 3.4 oz (0.1 kg)

Description Gray upperparts, black cap with white forehead, whitish collar

Habitat Coastal beaches; open saltwater

Range Atlantic coast, Florida Keys

Jan	Feb	Mar	Apr	May	June	July	Aug	Sep	Oct	Nov	Dec

This seagoing tern closely resembles the Sooty Tern but is smaller, with a white forehead patch extending behind the eye, and is lighter above, with a light gray band separating the back and black-capped head. The Bridled Tern is a regular visitor off Florida's Atlantic coast during late summer and early fall. In 1987 two pairs nested in a colony of Roseate Terns in the Florida Keys, the first nesting record for the United States. Since that time it has continued as a Florida breeder. When seen, it is often in the company of Sooty Terns. Bridled Terns catch squid and fish near the surface of offshore waters.

FAMILY *Laridae: Gulls, Terns, Skimmers*
SOOTY TERN (*Sterna fuscata*)
LENGTH 16 in (41 cm)   WEIGHT 6.3 oz (0.18 kg)

p. 242

Description All black above, except for white forehead, white below
Habitat Coastal beaches; open saltwater
Range Dry Tortugas, Atlantic coast

Jan	Feb	Mar	Apr	May	June	July	Aug	Sep	Oct	Nov	Dec

This Florida specialty finds its only regular United States breeding site in the Dry Tortugas, as indicated on the range map. It is the only tern that is black above and white below. Immatures have dark heads, white-flecked upperparts, and shallowly forked tails. About 80,000 adults breed each year in colonies on Bush Key. One egg per nest is laid in a shallow scrape on open sand or under scattered shrubs during late February or early March. After the breeding season, which ends in August, Sooty Terns leave the Tortugas and become strictly pelagic (oceangoing). Sooties do not dive for fish but surface feed, capturing minnows, flying fish, squid, and other top-dwelling species.

FAMILY *Laridae: Gulls, Terns, Skimmers*
BLACK TERN (*Chlidonias niger*)
p. 242
LENGTH 10 in (25 cm)   WEIGHT 2.3 oz (0.07 kg)

Description Black head and body, gray wings and tail, white vent (spring) or dark cap and breast patches, gray mantle (fall)
Habitat Coastal beaches; salt marshes; open saltwater; open freshwater; wet prairies and marshes; agricultural environments
Range Statewide

Jan	Feb	Mar	Apr	May	June	July	Aug	Sep	Oct	Nov	Dec

Migrating Black Terns may arrive in breeding plumage in Florida from northern nesting grounds as early as July. Black head and body, light rump, gray wings, and notched tail are distinctive. In winter, black plumage becomes mostly white with occasional black mottling. Black Terns may be seen over inland and coastal wetlands from April to June and from late July to October. They are rarely seen during winter. Foods include insects and small fish.

FAMILY *Laridae: Gulls, Terns, Skimmers*
BROWN NODDY (*Anous stolidus*)
LENGTH 16 in (41 cm)   WEIGHT 7 oz (0.2 kg)

p. 242

Other names Noddy Tern, Common Noddy, Egg Bird, Booby, Lark

Description All brown, with white cap

Habitat Coastal beaches; open saltwater

Range Dry Tortugas, south Florida

Jan	Feb	Mar	Apr	May	June	July	Aug	Sep	Oct	Nov	Dec

In the United States, the Brown Noddy nests only on Florida's remote Dry Tortugas, as indicated on the range map. This medium-size tern is dark brown overall with a light gray cap that fades toward the nape. Breeding begins in March and may last through summer. During this time they are active around the clock. A single egg is laid in a nest that may be a simple stick platform or an elaborate mound of debris. Brown Noddies remain near their nesting grounds until October or November. Numbers of breeding birds have fluctuated greatly during the past century, but since the 1950s as many as 4,000 pairs have been present. Brown Noddies occasionally are scattered great distances by storms and have been observed in Florida as far away as Jacksonville. Feeding is accomplished by catching small surface fish.

FAMILY *Laridae: Gulls, Terns, Skimmers*
BLACK NODDY (*Anous minutus*)

p. 242

LENGTH 13 in (33 cm)   WEIGHT 4.2 oz (0.12 kg)

Description Smaller than Brown Noddy; dark brown body, sharply defined white cap, slender bill appears slightly decurved

Habitat Coastal beaches; open saltwater

Range Dry Tortugas

Jan	Feb	Mar	Apr	May	June	July	Aug	Sep	Oct	Nov	Dec

The Black Noddy appears most years in the nesting colony on Bush Key in the Dry Tortugas, although none has bred there. It is almost three-fourths the size of the Brown Noddy, with darker plumage and a somewhat longer, more slender bill. They are always associated with the Brown Noddy when seen on Bush Key and can be seen loafing on the Garden Key coaling docks. The Black Noddy is more pelagic than the Brown Noddy outside of the breeding season, but its habits are otherwise similar.

FAMILY *Laridae: Gulls, Terns, Skimmers*
BLACK SKIMMER (*Rynchops niger*)
LENGTH 18 in (46 cm)   WEIGHT 12.3 oz (0.35 kg)   STATUS **SSC**   p. 242

Other names Shearwater, Scissorbill,
Sea-dog, Flood Gull, Razorbill
Description Red and black bill, lower
mandible longer than upper; black upper-
parts, white forehead and underparts
Habitat Coastal beaches; salt marshes
Range Statewide, mostly coastal

Jan	Feb	Mar	Apr	May	June	July	Aug	Sep	Oct	Nov	Dec

Skimmers are unique among birds in that the lower half of the bill is longer than the upper. This long-winged, ternlike bird has black upperparts, white cheeks and neck, red feet, and a red, black-tipped bill. Immatures are browner and more mottled above. Black Skimmers are found along all of the Florida coast. They nest in large colonies, often with tern species—the breeding locations are indicated on the range map. Four to five eggs are laid in a shallow scrape above the high tide line during June or July. Breeding activities may last until September. Skimmers feed by cutting the water's surface with the lower mandible and snatching their fish or shrimp prey with a quick downward snap. Several birds may be seen feeding together in this manner, even after sunset. Development of Florida's coastline has decreased the quantity and quality of nest sites for this unique shorebird. Spoil islands and even gravel rooftops have partly replaced natural breeding substrates for the Black Skimmer in Florida.

ORDER *Columbiformes: Pigeons and Doves*
Pigeonlike land birds with dense, easily shed plumage. Adults produce a milk
in their crops to feed their young.

FAMILY *Columbidae*
ROCK PIGEON (*Columba livia*)   p. 243
LENGTH 12 in (30 cm)   WEIGHT 13 oz (0.37 kg)

Other names Rock Dove, City Pigeon
Description Dark gray body, light gray mantle with black wing
bars, white rump; many variations of blacks, whites, reds, and grays
Habitat Urban environments; agricultural environments
Range Statewide

Jan	Feb	Mar	Apr	May	June	July	Aug	Sep	Oct	Nov	Dec

This is the very familiar pigeon so common in cities, parks, farms, and industrial areas. Rock Pigeons were introduced into North America by early European settlers, and now are common in highly altered human environments. They are now found on every continent except Antarctica. Many color variations occur and may range from slate-gray to brown, white, or a number of combinations. Two black bars across the sides and back characterize the gray form. Rock Pigeons nest year-round on window ledges, under bridges, and in barns or a variety of other structures. Large flocks may be seen circling feeding areas and roosts with upraised wings. The wings often produce a slapping sound when taking off. Rock Pigeons feed mainly on grains and seeds.

FAMILY *Columbidae*
WHITE-CROWNED PIGEON (*Patagioenas leucocephala*)
LENGTH 13 in (33 cm)   WEIGHT 9.2 oz (0.26 kg)   STATUS **T**

p. 243

Other names Baldpate, White-hooded Pigeon
Description Slate-blue overall with white cap; immatures may lack white cap
Habitat Mangrove; mesic hammocks; urban environments
Range South Florida

Although this large pigeon is a sought-after Florida specialty, little is known of its life history. About the size of the Rock Pigeon, the White-crowned Pigeon is mostly dark, with an iridescent nape and a white-crowned head. White-crowned Pigeons nest colonially in coastal mangroves in the Keys and Florida Bay, as indicated on the range map. One or two eggs are laid in a stick nest, usually in late spring. Some birds leave south Florida in late fall or winter, returning the following April or May. Occasionally, large winter roost flocks occur in Everglades National Park or the Keys. White-crowns are mostly inhabitants of dense coastal forests where they feed on a variety of fruits and seeds from tropical plants such as strangler fig, cocoplum, gumbo-limbo, and poisonwood. It is a threatened species in Florida.

FAMILY *Columbidae*
RINGED TURTLE-DOVE (*Streptopelia "risoria"*)
LENGTH 11 in (28 cm)   WEIGHT 4.59–5.86 oz (0.13–0.17 kg)

p. 243

Other names Ringed Dove
Description Light tan or cream to whitish body, white undertail coverts; song is a *cook ca-roo*
Habitat Urban environments; agricultural environments
Range Statewide

The Ringed Turtle-Dove has been bred in captivity for hundreds of years. It and various white varieties are the doves used in research and by magicians, or sold as pets. Today, no natural wild populations are known to exist. However, escaped or released birds were established in St. Petersburg, Florida, and Los Angeles, California. The St. Petersburg population, established in the 1950s, held its own at around 500 birds until the Eurasian Collared-Dove arrived in the 1980s. By that time the population existed in primarily a single flock that was fed mostly at a single household. The combination of interbreeding with the Eurasian Collared-Dove, discontinued feeding at residences, and dispersal of individuals throughout the area has likely led to the virtual disappearance of this species in Florida. Regardless of its status, it had become so variable in appearance because of the variety of plumage types released by dove fanciers that it would be most accurate to refer to it as the Domestic Collared-Dove. The quotation marks around "risoria" suggest that it is not the name of a valid species. Ringed Turtle-Doves are about the size of Mourning Doves but have shorter, square tails, black at the base, and a lighter tan color overall. A narrow black band occurs around the back of the neck in adults. The song is a distinctive, rolling *coo-co-roo* with many repeated syllables. Flimsy nests of sticks are built in trees or shrubs during spring, and two white eggs are laid. Eggs hatch in about 14 days and young fledge 14–15 days later. They primarily are grain feeders.

FAMILY *Columbidae*
EURASIAN COLLARED-DOVE (*Streptopelia decaocto*) p. 243
LENGTH 11.5 in (29 cm) WEIGHT 5.4 oz (0.15 kg)

Other names Collared Turtle-Dove
Description Dark tan upperparts; buffy gray head, neck and underparts; gray primaries and undertail coverts; song is a *ca-coo-cuk*
Habitat Urban environments; agricultural environments
Range Statewide

Jan	Feb	Mar	Apr	May	June	July	Aug	Sep	Oct	Nov	Dec

This Old World species is almost identical to the Ringed Turtle-Dove, except it is a darker tan, slightly larger, its neck band is bordered with white, and undertail coverts are dark. The primaries are distinctively darker than the rest of the wing. Its song is a repeated *ca-coo-cuk,* with brief pauses between phrases. It also gives a Catbirdlike *mew* in flight or upon landing. It first appeared in Florida in the early 1980s shortly after it was introduced into the Bahamas. It now numbers in the millions and breeds throughout the state. It is usually associated with habitats altered by humans, and likely helped eliminate the free-living but domesticated Ringed Turtle-Dove. We predict it will spread throughout North America (it is now breeding west of the Mississippi River) just as it spread throughout Europe from the Middle East in the 1940s. Nests containing two white eggs can be found in trees (especially palms) and shrubs mostly during spring, but nearly year-round. Food consists of grain and weed seeds. It is an important item in the winter diet of the Short-tailed Hawk in the Homestead area.

FAMILY *Columbidae*
WHITE-WINGED DOVE (*Zenaida asiatica*) p. 243
LENGTH 11 in (28 cm) WEIGHT 5.4 oz (0.15 kg)

Other names Eastern White-winged Dove
Description Grayish-brown body; white in bend of wing, which shows at rest
Habitat Urban environments; agricultural environments
Range Statewide

Jan	Feb	Mar	Apr	May	June	July	Aug	Sep	Oct	Nov	Dec

Early records of White-winged Doves in Florida were of birds shot by hunters in the Florida Keys. Band recoveries indicated these birds came from Texas. In the late 1950s numerous captive doves from Mexico that were released in Homestead supposedly spread throughout the Miami area; however, some believe that the species colonized naturally from nearby Caribbean islands. In the early 1970s the Florida Game and Fresh Water Fish Commission captured several hundred of these and released them at various locations as far north as Lake County. This species will probably continue to increase and spread in Florida. Large white wing patches and a long tail highlight an otherwise drab grayish plumage. White-winged Doves behave similarly to the closely related Mourning Dove. One to four eggs are laid in tree nests. Two or more clutches may be raised annually. The song is a distinctive *coo-cuk-ca-roo*. Foods primarily are grains and seeds.

FAMILY *Columbidae*
MOURNING DOVE (*Zenaida macroura*) p. 243
LENGTH 12 in (30 cm)   WEIGHT 4.3 oz (0.12 kg)

Other names Turtle Dove, Carolina Dove, Wood Dove

Description Brown back, buff or tan head and underparts, long white-tipped tail

Habitat Xeric scrub; dry prairies; mesic hammocks; mixed pine and hardwood forests; urban environments; pine flatwoods; sandhills; agricultural environments

Range Statewide

Jan	Feb	Mar	Apr	May	June	July	Aug	Sep	Oct	Nov	Dec

The low, tranquil *coo* of the Mourning Dove is a common sound throughout suburban, rural, and wild Florida. While this bird is an abundant resident, Mourning Dove numbers increase dramatically in winter with the influx of northern migrants. Mourning Doves have an unusually long nesting season which may extend year-round, and, for individual pairs, include as many as three broods. Loosely constructed stick platforms serve as nests that usually contain two eggs. Young are fed a milky solution secreted from their parents' crops. Adults feed mostly on grains and weed seeds. Large flocks often are seen in winter grain fields, feeding on the ground or perched on fences or wires. Smaller than the Rock Pigeon, the Mourning Dove has a long, pointed tail with white-tipped feathers, black-spotted wings, grayish-brown above, a pinkish breast, and an iridescent patch on the sides of the neck. This patch is smaller in females than in males. Juveniles are much darker overall. The rapid whistling of the beating wings is distinctive when this bird takes flight. Mourning Doves are a very popular game bird in Florida as well as the southeastern United States.

FAMILY *Columbidae*
COMMON GROUND-DOVE (*Columbina passerina*)   p. 243
LENGTH 6 in (15 cm)   WEIGHT 1.1 oz (0.03 kg)

Other names Eastern Ground Dove

Description Small; gray-brown with purplish spots on wings; outer half of wings bright rufous

Habitat Coastal beaches; xeric scrub; dry prairies; mixed pine and hardwood forests; pine flatwoods; sandhills; agricultural environments

Range Statewide

| Jan | Feb | Mar | Apr | May | June | July | Aug | Sep | Oct | Nov | Dec |

This is our smallest dove, commonly found in dry, open woodlands, old fields, and pastures. Perhaps even more prolific than the Mourning Dove, Common Ground-Doves may nest practically throughout the year and lay as many as four clutches. Two eggs are usually laid in a loosely constructed nest on the ground, in a shrub, low tree branch, or the abandoned nest of another bird. This chunky bird is mostly gray above with a few black or purplish wing spots, a scalloped appearance on the head and neck, a short tail, and bright chestnut primaries that are visible in flight. Ground-Doves seem to bob their heads continuously and often are seen in pairs. Foods consist of a variety of weed and grain seeds. This species may be locally abundant in some parts of Florida, but is becoming less common in much of the state. Because it nests near the ground it may be vulnerable to feral cat predation.

ORDER *Psittaciformes: Parrots and Parakeets*

Birds with large heads, short necks, down-curved hooked bills with a prominent bulge or cere, and short grasping feet. No native species now exists in Florida, but numerous escaped or released species from elsewhere now live in the state. This mostly tropical group has become increasingly abundant and diverse as the result of the importation of these birds for the pet trade. It is ironic that this tremendous popularity was preceded by the extermination of the United States' sole native breeding parrot, the **Carolina Parakeet** (*Conuropsis carolinensis*), in the early 1900s. The Carolina Parakeet was a denizen of remote virgin cypress swamps, where it nested in cavities. Its tame, trusting nature likely contributed to its demise to "sport" shooters and over-zealous collectors. Until 1992, wild populations of several parrot species were supplemented regularly through the escape and release of wild-captured, imported birds, especially from South America and Central America. Although this trade is now largely illegal, many species are now established—75 species of exotic parrots are known to have occurred outside of captivity in Florida. Of these, 19 species are likely breeding in the state. We anticipate some of these species to continue their colonization of urban and residential areas. Some are even developing hybrid forms. Ten of the most widespread are described here.

FAMILY *Psittacidae: Lories, Parakeets, Macaws, and Parrots*
BUDGERIGAR (*Melopsittacus undulatus*)
LENGTH 7 in (18 cm)   WEIGHT 1 oz (0.03 kg)

p. 244

Other names: Budgie, Parakeet, Shell Parakeet

Description Usually, black and yellow barred head and upperparts, green below, long blue-green tail

Habitat Urban environments

Range Statewide

| Jan | Feb | Mar | Apr | May | June | July | Aug | Sep | Oct | Nov | Dec |

This colorful Australian native breeds locally along Florida's west coast from southwestern Hernando County to northwestern Pasco County, as indicated on the range map. The Budgerigar was once more numerous and widely distributed after its establishment in Florida during the 1960s. The typical plumage is light green underneath, yellow upperparts barred with black. Occasionally, blue-, white-, or yellow-colored individuals may be present in a colony, but the green color predominates. They form flocks in urban settings and are often seen perched on utility wires. Budgerigars are cavity nesters and can compete with native species such as the Purple Martin and Red-bellied Woodpecker, or exotics such as European Starling and House Sparrow, for nest space. Budgies are likely dependent upon supplemental feeding and may be sensitive to extremely low temperatures.

FAMILY *Psittacidae: Lories, Parakeets, Macaws, and Parrots*
ROSE-RINGED PARAKEET (*Psittacula krameri*)
LENGTH 16 in (41 cm)   WEIGHT 5.93–6.6 oz (0.17–0.19 kg)

p. 244

Description Bright green with red bill and long tail; adult male has black chin, pink collar

Habitat Urban environments

Range Central and south Florida, mostly coastal

| Jan | Feb | Mar | Apr | May | June | July | Aug | Sep | Oct | Nov | Dec |

This species is a native of Africa and India, where it is a common inhabitant of lightly wooded areas, farmlands, and gardens around houses. Colonies of breeding Rose-rings occur in St. Augustine, Ft. Myers, and Naples, as indicated on the range map, while individuals have been seen in other Florida cities. The male is mostly green, with yellowish underparts, a black chin, a black stripe across the lower cheeks, and a rose-pink collar around the back of the neck. The nape and long central tail feathers are blue, and the top of the bill is red with a black tip. The female is plain green, lacks the distinctive markings of the male, and has a shorter tail. The call is a loud screeching *kee-ak*. Little is known about its breeding habits in Florida, but in the Old World it nests in tree cavities where it lays two to six eggs. Young fledge six or seven weeks after hatching. It eats a variety of fruits and grains and is considered an agricultural pest in India.

FAMILY *Psittacidae: Lories, Parakeets, Macaws, and Parrots*
MONK PARAKEET (*Myiopsitta monachus*)
LENGTH 11 in (28 cm)   WEIGHT 4.06–5.29 oz (0.12–0.15 kg)

p. 244

Other names Quaker Parakeet
Description Grayish throat and breast, yellow belly, green upperparts, blue primaries
Habitat Urban environments; agricultural environments
Range South and central Florida

Jan	Feb	Mar	Apr	May	June	July	Aug	Sep	Oct	Nov	Dec

The Monk Parakeet is a South American native established in North America by accidental and intentional releases. It is Florida's most abundant parrot. It is larger than the Budgerigar, green above, with blue wings, light gray throat and chest, and yellow belly grading to a green rump. Monk Parakeets may be seen in urban and agricultural settings where their fruit-dominated diet makes them a potential pest. Nesting colonies can contain hundreds of birds; its breeding range is indicated on the range map. Bulky stick nests are built in treetops, telephone poles, athletic field light towers, electrical stations or other tall structures.

FAMILY *Psittacidae: Lories, Parakeets, Macaws, and Parrots*
BLACK-HOODED PARAKEET (*Nandayus nenday*)
LENGTH 12 in (30 cm)   WEIGHT 4.5 oz (0.13 kg)

p. 245

Description Mostly green with black hood, buff eye ring, blue outer tail feathers, and red leg feathers
Habitat Urban and suburban areas
Range Statewide

Jan	Feb	Mar	Apr	May	June	July	Aug	Sep	Oct	Nov	Dec

This distinctive bird is mostly green with a black hood, buff eye ring, blue outer tail feathers, and red leg feathers. This bird is common from Clearwater to Sarasota on the Gulf coast, with smaller numbers in several other cities. Black-hooded Parakeets nest in cavities and consume a variety of seeds, nuts, and fruits. Its breeding range is indicated on the range map.

FAMILY *Psittacidae: Lories, Parakeets, Macaws, and Parrots*
BLUE-CROWNED PARAKEET (*Aratinga acuticaudata*)
p. 245
LENGTH 14.5 in (35.56 cm)   WEIGHT 7 oz (0.2 kg)

Description Similar to Mitred Parakeet in size and color, but has blue crown; lacks red facial feathers
Habitat Urban and suburban areas
Range South Florida

Jan	Feb	Mar	Apr	May	June	July	Aug	Sep	Oct	Nov	Dec

The Blue-crowned Parakeet has been reputed to be a breeding species in the Keys since the 1980s. However, details of its nesting habits and reproduction are sketchy at best. It resembles the Mitred Parakeet in overall size and coloration, but it has a blue crown and lacks red facial feathers. Records also exist for Brevard and Pinellas counties, but it is most common in Ft. Lauderdale. Its diet in Florida is likely similar to that of other parrots and parakeets.

FAMILY *Psittacidae: Lories, Parakeets, Macaws, and Parrots*
RED-MASKED PARAKEET (*Aratinga erythrogenys*)
p. 245
LENGTH 13.5 in (34 cm)   WEIGHT 6 oz (0.17 kg)

Description Red face and red feathers at the bend in each wing
Habitat Urban and suburban areas
Range South Florida

Jan	Feb	Mar	Apr	May	June	July	Aug	Sep	Oct	Nov	Dec

The Red-masked Parakeet is smaller than the Mitred Parakeet and has a red face and red feathers at the bend in each wing. The amount of red on the head is likely related to the age of the bird. The Red-masked Parakeet is known primarily in the Miami and Ft. Lauderdale areas, where it has been seen in flocks of more than 20.

FAMILY *Psittacidae: Lories, Parakeets, Macaws, and Parrots*
MITRED PARAKEET (*Aratinga mitrata*)
p. 245

LENGTH 15 in (38 cm)   WEIGHT 7 oz (0.2 kg)

Description Mostly green above, bluish primaries; lighter green below with buff-colored primaries and secondaries

Habitat Urban and suburban areas

Range South Florida

| Jan | Feb | Mar | Apr | May | June | July | Aug | Sep | Oct | Nov | Dec |

This South American native is mostly green above with bluish primaries. It is lighter green below with buff-colored primaries and secondaries. This large parakeet is found mostly in the Ft. Lauderdale and Miami areas, but has been observed in St. Augustine as well. Like many of its relatives, the Mitred nests in cavities that can be natural or human-made, but details of breeding in Florida are not well known.

FAMILY *Psittacidae: Lories, Parakeets, Macaws, and Parrots*
p. 245
CHESTNUT-FRONTED MACAW (*Ara severus*)

LENGTH 18 in (46 cm)   WEIGHT 15 oz (0.43 kg)

Description Largest Florida parrot; large, heavy, dark bill, long tail, white, featherless cheek patch

Habitat Urban and suburban areas

Range South Florida

| Jan | Feb | Mar | Apr | May | June | July | Aug | Sep | Oct | Nov | Dec |

This largest of the Florida Psittacines nests in the Ft. Lauderdale and Miami areas. Its large, heavy dark bill, long tail, and white, featherless cheek patch, as well as its size, make this introduced species unmistakable. It nests in cavities of large palms and other trees. This gregarious bird feeds on fruits and seeds. Little is known of its breeding and other habits in Florida.

FAMILY *Psittacidae: Lories, Parakeets, Macaws, and Parrots*
RED-CROWNED PARROT (*Amazona viridigenalis*)
LENGTH 12.5 in (32 cm)   WEIGHT 11 oz (0.31 kg)

p. 244

Description Forehead and crown red, body green

Habitat Urban environments

Range Statewide, large urban areas except in Panhandle

Jan	Feb	Mar	Apr	May	June	July	Aug	Sep	Oct	Nov	Dec

Native populations of this parrot are as close as Mexico, but Florida populations around West Palm Beach, Ft. Lauderdale, and Miami derive from releases or escapes. Green plumage is highlighted by a red crown and bright red wing patches that are visible in flight and at rest. Red-crowned Parrots nest in tree cavities or in artificial structures from early spring through summer; its breeding range is indicated on the range map. It eats a variety of fruits including acorns. It appears to have recently declined in the Miami area.

FAMILY *Psittacidae: Lories, Parakeets, Macaws, and Parrots*
WHITE-WINGED PARAKEET (*Brotogeris versicolurus*)
LENGTH 9 in (23 cm)   WEIGHT 2.1 oz (0.05 kg)

p. 244

Description All green with yellow in bend of wing at rest; extensive yellow and white in wings in flight

Habitat Urban environments

Range South and central Florida

Jan	Feb	Mar	Apr	May	June	July	Aug	Sep	Oct	Nov	Dec

This small, mostly green parrot is highlighted with bright yellow and white upper wing patches that appear windowlike when the bird is in flight. From beneath the wing patches are entirely white. This is another South American native introduced from liberated cage birds in the 1960s. The White-winged Parakeet inhabits southeast Florida, especially in the Ft. Lauderdale and Miami areas. It was formerly reported in Ft. Pierce and Sarasota. This colorful parrot is found in small or large groups feeding on fruits and seeds or at evening roosts. They are most common in suburban environments and have been seen nesting in palms. Its breeding range is indicated on the range map. This species appears to have decreased in the 1980s. A very similar species, the **Yellow-chevroned Parakeet** (*Brotogeris chiriri*) lacks the white patch on the upper and lower wing surfaces. Its plumage is somewhat more yellow than the White-winged Parakeet and it has a darker, more reddish bill. Previously these two species were considered the **Canary-winged Parakeet**, a designation that appears in many older field guides. The decline of the White-winged Parakeet may be due in part to the recent success of the Yellow-chevroned Parakeet, but may be more the result of changing importation patterns since the 1980s. Over the last ten years the Yellow-chevroned Parakeet has been on the increase. These two species appear to be hybridizing in the Ft. Lauderdale area.

ORDER *Cuculiformes: Cuckoos*
Long-tailed birds with zygodactylous feet (two toes pointing forward, two toes backward).

FAMILY *Cuculidae: Cuckoos and Anis*
BLACK-BILLED CUCKOO (*Coccyzus erythropthalmus*)   p.246
LENGTH 12 in (30 cm)   WEIGHT 3.6 oz (0.1 kg)
Description Red eye ring, small white spots under tail, all-black bill
Habitat Hardwood swamps; mixed pine and hardwood forests; urban environments
Range Statewide

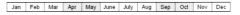

| Jan | Feb | Mar | Apr | May | June | July | Aug | Sep | Oct | Nov | Dec |

The Black-billed Cuckoo is smaller than the Yellow-billed, and is an uncommon migrant in Florida during spring (April–May) and fall (August–December). It has occurred throughout the state, but mostly from central Florida northward. At close range the black bill, red eye ring, less rufous in the primaries, and small white spots under the gray tail separate it from the Yellow-billed Cuckoo. Its song is very different than the Yellow-billed, but it is rarely heard in Florida.

FAMILY *Cuculidae: Cuckoos and Anis*
YELLOW-BILLED CUCKOO (*Coccyzus americanus*)   p. 246
LENGTH 12 in (30 cm)   WEIGHT 3.6 oz (0.1 kg)
Other names Rain Crow
Description Rufous primaries, large white spots under tail
Habitat Xeric scrub; hardwood swamps; cypress swamps; mesic hammocks; mixed pine and hardwood forests; urban environments; pine flatwoods; sandhills
Range Statewide

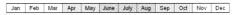

| Jan | Feb | Mar | Apr | May | June | July | Aug | Sep | Oct | Nov | Dec |

The Yellow-billed is the most common of Florida's cuckoos, although it is nowhere abundant. This summer resident is a large secretive woodland bird. Prominent white spots on the black undersides of the tail, yellow lower bill, white undersides, and chestnut-colored wings distinguish both sexes. Yellow-billed Cuckoos breed from Key West through mainland Florida. Loosely constructed stick nests are built during late spring, usually in deciduous hardwoods. Three to six eggs may be laid between May and August. Most individuals depart Florida by early October and return by early April. A variety of insects provide this cuckoo with most of its food. However, when tent caterpillars are particularly abundant, these defoliating insects dominate the diet. The ventriloquial, repeated clucking of the Yellow-billed Cuckoo is a characteristic sound of Florida's hardwood forests.

FAMILY *Cuculidae: Cuckoos and Anis*
MANGROVE CUCKOO (*Coccyzus minor*)   p. 246
LENGTH 12 in (30 cm)   WEIGHT 3.6 oz (0.1 kg)

Other names Black-eared Cuckoo, Rain Crow, Rain Bird

Description Black ear patch, buffy belly, buff may extend onto breast

Habitat Mangrove, mesic hammocks

Range South and west-central Florida, coastal

As its name implies, this cuckoo is an inhabitant of Florida's coastal mangrove forests, but it also utilizes tropical hardwood hammocks. A year-round resident around Florida Bay and the Keys, Mangrove Cuckoos also breed in Pinellas and Hillsborough counties as far north as Tampa Bay along the west coast, as indicated on the range map. This Florida specialty is distinguished from similar species by its buff breast and black mask. The Mangrove Cuckoo is a late spring nester, laying two eggs in a loosely constructed twig platform. Like its relatives, the Mangrove Cuckoo is a caterpillar predator, consuming many bristled species that other birds avoid. These birds are quite secretive and prefer to remain well-hidden among dense growths of vegetation. Its characteristic call is a rapid *ga-ga-gaw*. Other vocalizations include a variety of guttural clucks and notes, as well as calls resembling those of the Yellow-billed Cuckoo.

FAMILY *Cuculidae: Cuckoos and Anis*
SMOOTH-BILLED ANI (*Crotophaga ani*)   p. 246
LENGTH 14 in (36 cm)   WEIGHT 4.2 oz (0.12 kg)

Other names Parrot Blackbird, Black Witch, Tickbird, Cuban Parrot

Description All black with long floppy tail; high ridged, parrotlike bill

Habitat Dry prairies; wet prairies and marshes; urban environments; agricultural environments

Range Central and south Florida

This unusual tropical cuckoo once reached its northern breeding limit at Cape Canaveral and Tampa Bay, where it was of rare to uncommon occurrence. It began breeding in Florida during 1938, but since the early 1970s has experienced dramatic declines. It has now been extirpated from central Florida and the entire west coast. This Florida specialty now seems to be restricted to subtropical Florida. A long floppy tail and ridged, black, parrotlike bill distinguish the Smooth-billed Ani from other "black" birds. Nests are loosely constructed with twigs, leaves, and grass in shrubs, palms, or low tree branches. Anis have a long nesting season that may last from March to September. Apparently, several females may lay eggs in the same nest. Insects form the bulk of the diet. The distinctive call consists of a rising, questionlike note.

FAMILY *Cuculidae: Cuckoos and Anis*
GROOVE-BILLED ANI (*Crotophaga sulcirostris*)
p. 246
LENGTH 13 in (33 cm)   WEIGHT 2.47–3.18 oz (0.07–0.09 kg)

Description All black with long floppy tail; grooves on parrotlike bill, no high ridge
Habitat Urban environments; agricultural environments
Range South Florida, Panhandle

Jan	Feb	Mar	Apr	May	June	July	Aug	Sep	Oct	Nov	Dec

Slightly smaller than the Smooth-billed, the Groove-billed Ani lacks the crest on upper bill, and the bill sometimes exhibits faint grooves. This southern Texas resident wanders widely in winter and is an occasional but rare visitor in Florida. Individuals have been seen throughout the state, especially in the Panhandle.

ORDER *Strigiformes: Owls*
Usually nocturnal birds of prey with large eyes surrounded by a facial disk of feathers; short, hooked bill; strong legs and talons.

FAMILY *Tytonidae: Barn-Owls*
BARN OWL (*Tyto alba*)
p. 247
LENGTH 16 in (41 cm)   WEIGHT 1.1 lb (0.5 kg)

Other names Monkey-faced Owl, White Owl
Description Heartshaped "monkey" face; cinnamon-brown above, white or buff below
Habitat Dry prairies; mesic hammocks; mixed pine and hardwood forests; wet prairies and marshes; urban environments; pine flatwoods; sandhills; agricultural environments
Range Statewide

Jan	Feb	Mar	Apr	May	June	July	Aug	Sep	Oct	Nov	Dec

This large nocturnal predator is not often seen in Florida, yet it is probably common throughout the state. The secretive Barn Owl is more strictly nocturnal than the other "typical" owls. When not hunting for small mammals or insects, Barn Owls retire to secluded tree cavities, abandoned buildings, or other dark recesses. This owl's presence is best confirmed by its eerie nocturnal hissing and screeching. Barn Owls appear to nest throughout the year. As many as 11 rounded eggs are laid in a protected natural or human-made cavity or any flat surface in an attic, barn, shed, or similar structure. The presence of Barn Owls often is revealed by collections of "pellets" beneath a well-used roost. Pellets consist of the indigestible, regurgitated remains of insects, birds, and small mammals, especially the hispid cotton rat.

FAMILY *Strigidae: Typical Owls*
EASTERN SCREECH-OWL (*Megascops asio*)
p. 247
LENGTH 8 in (20 cm)   WEIGHT 5.9 oz (0.17 kg)

Other names Squinch Owl, Death Owl, Cat Owl, Shivering Owl, Mottled Owl

Description Small; ear tufts; gray, red, or brown body streaked with brown and white

Habitat Xeric scrub; hardwood swamps; cypress swamps; mesic hammocks; mixed pine and hardwood forests; urban environments; pine flatwoods; sandhills; agricultural environments

Range Statewide

Jan	Feb	Mar	Apr	May	June	July	Aug	Sep	Oct	Nov	Dec

The Eastern Screech-Owl is Florida's smallest and perhaps best known owl. White undersides are heavily streaked and barred, eyes are yellow, and ear tufts are usually conspicuous. Most Florida Screech-Owls exhibit brown plumage although red morphs and gray morphs are not unusual and all three color morphs may occur in the same nest. Screech-Owls are more often heard than seen, uttering a trembling or quavering call that may sound deceptively distant. Habitat requirements are quite broad. Hollow cavities for nesting may be provided by a variety of forest types or human-made nest boxes. Roosting and hunting grounds may be found in hardwood swamps, pinelands, orange groves, or suburban back yards. Nesting occurs from March to May when about four to five white eggs are laid. It is very defensive of its fledged young. While Screech-Owls consume a variety of small birds and mammals, the majority of their diet consists of insects.

FAMILY *Strigidae: Typical Owls*
GREAT HORNED OWL (*Bubo virginianus*)
p. 247
LENGTH 21 in (53 cm)   WEIGHT 3 lb (1.36 kg)

Other names Cat Owl, Hoot Owl

Description Large with long ear tufts; gray-brown above; black, white, buff below

Habitat Hardwood swamps; dry prairies; mesic hammocks; mixed pine and hardwood forests; wet prairies and marshes; urban environments; pine flatwoods; sandhills; agricultural environments

Range Statewide

Jan	Feb	Mar	Apr	May	June	July	Aug	Sep	Oct	Nov	Dec

The Great Horned is Florida's largest owl, reaching a wingspan of nearly 5 feet (1.5 meters). Prominent ear tufts, yellow eyes, white throat, heavily barred underparts, and dark back distinguish this nocturnal predator. The resonant hoots of this bird may carry a great distance; screamlike calls also are given, especially by juveniles. Great Horned Owls have broad habitat requirements, including a variety of forest and prairie types. Nests, which are fiercely defended, are located in broad forks in trees such as live oaks, in abandoned Bald Eagle or other large raptor nests, and in other secluded sites. With adequate nest sites and food resources these owls may reside in close proximity to humans.

Two rounded eggs usually are laid during winter. Foods consist of rodents, rabbits, skunks, opossums, domestic cats, ducks, and even other owls.

FAMILY *Strigidae: Typical Owls*

BURROWING OWL (*Athene cunicularia*)

LENGTH 9 in (23 cm)   WEIGHT 5.3 oz (0.15 kg)   STATUS **SSC**   p. 247

Other names Ground Owl, Howdy Owl

Description Brown overall with barring and spotting of white and brown, white or gray eyebrows, no ear tufts; usually on ground near burrow

Habitat Dry prairies; urban environments; agricultural environments

Range Statewide

Jan	Feb	Mar	Apr	May	June	July	Aug	Sep	Oct	Nov	Dec

This small, long-legged, ground-dwelling owl is an inhabitant of open, well-drained landscapes ranging from dry prairies and pastures to ballparks and airports. Florida and the Bahamas support the only eastern populations of this typical Great Plains species. It is found in the prairie region to the west and north of Lake Okeechobee, but it is also a very common inhabitant of residential yards in Cape Coral (Lee County). Other breeding locations may be found from Jacksonville to Marathon, as indicated on the range map. Many of these "outlying" individuals use the mowed strips between airport runways. Nests are located 1–3 feet (0.3–0.9 meters) underground where three to seven eggs are laid primarily from March to June. Several nesting pairs often are found in close proximity. Burrowing Owls are mostly nocturnal but also may be seen foraging in daylight. Foods consist primarily of insects, but rodents, amphibians, and small birds are eaten as well. Their name of "Howdy Owl" comes from their repeated bobbing or bowing motion.

FAMILY *Strigidae: Typical Owls*

BARRED OWL (*Strix varia*)   p. 247

LENGTH 20 in (51 cm)   WEIGHT 1.4 lb (0.64 kg)

Other names Swamp Owl, Hoot Owl

Description Rounded gray-brown head (no ear tufts), gray-brown back, lighter below with barring and streaking

Habitat Xeric scrub; hardwood swamps; cypress swamps; mesic hammocks; mixed pine and hardwood forests; wet prairies and marshes; urban environments; pine flatwoods; sandhills; agricultural environments

Range Statewide

Jan	Feb	Mar	Apr	May	June	July	Aug	Sep	Oct	Nov	Dec

Dark eyes and a rounded, earless head distinguish the Barred Owl from the Great Horned Owl. Plumage is brown or grayish with dark scalloped throat feathers, dark streaks underneath, and mottled upperparts. The call, a highly variable but loud *who-cooks-for-you,* is most frequently heard at night but occasionally during the day. Found throughout mainland Florida, it tends to avoid urban areas. The Barred Owl inhabits a variety of forest types but seems to prefer mixed hardwoods and swamps. This bird is a cavity nester, using natural holes in hardwoods or palms, but does build its own nests. Two or three eggs are laid between January and March. Barred Owls are predators of rodents such as cotton rats, flying squirrels, round-tailed muskrats, and deer mice. Barred Owls eat birds and occasionally Screech-Owls, but may fall prey to the larger and more powerful Great Horned Owl.

ORDER *Caprimulgiformes: Goatsuckers*

Nocturnal or crepuscular (active at dusk and dawn) species with long, pointed wings; small, weak feet; and large, gaping mouth.

FAMILY *Caprimulgidae: Goatsuckers*
COMMON NIGHTHAWK (*Chordeiles minor*)   p. 248
LENGTH 9 in (23 cm)   WEIGHT 2.2 oz (0.06 kg)

Other names Bull Bat

Description Mostly black or gray with white throat, long pointed wings with white patch about 1/3 of the distance from tips; call is a drawn-out *peeent*

Habitat Xeric scrub; dry prairies; mesic hammocks; mixed pine and hardwood forests; wet prairies and marshes; urban environments; pine flatwoods; sandhills; agricultural environments

Range Statewide

Jan	Feb	Mar	Apr	May	June	July	Aug	Sep	Oct	Nov	Dec

The Common Nighthawk is the most abundant and familiar of the goatsucker family in North America. A common summer resident throughout Florida, it can be seen in a variety of settings—capturing insects at dusk and early morning over pastures, old fields, wetlands, and cities. It will often rest on a fence, fencepost, or utility wire. Nighthawks also are cosmopolitan in their nesting requirements, using open woodlands, pastures, beaches, disturbed ground, and even gravel rooftops. Between early April and late June, two eggs are laid in the open without protection of a nest. Breeding pairs may raise two clutches each year. Although not secretive while feeding, Common Nighthawks are usually detected by their call, a repeated nasal *peent*. A white stripe is visible beneath each wing in their stiff-winged, buoyant flight. During courtship, males make spectacular dives toward the ground. The wings produce a deep growl or boom as the bird pulls out of its dive. Most birds arrive during late March and April and depart in September, although a few may remain until early November in south Florida.

FAMILY *Caprimulgidae: Goatsuckers*

ANTILLEAN NIGHTHAWK (*Chordeiles gundlachii*)

LENGTH 9 in (23 cm)   WEIGHT 1.8 oz (0.05 kg)

p. 248

Other names Bull Bat, Cuban Nighthawk

Description Similar to common but with a buff or golden wash

Habitat Mesic hammocks; mixed pine and hardwood forests; urban environments; agricultural environments

Range South Florida, Florida Keys

Jan	Feb	Mar	Apr	May	June	July	Aug	Sep	Oct	Nov	Dec

In appearance, the Antillean Nighthawk is virtually indistinguishable from the Common Nighthawk. At close range it appears buffier, but is best identified by its call, a *kitty-kay-dick*. The Antillean Nighthawk breeds in parts of the Florida Keys, as indicated on the range map, and may be seen during spring migration at Ft. Jefferson, Dry Tortugas. Feeding and nesting habits are similar to those of the Common Nighthawk. The dive call of the Antillean Nighthawk male is higher pitched than that of the Common Nighthawk.

FAMILY *Caprimulgidae: Goatsuckers*

CHUCK-WILL'S-WIDOW (*Caprimulgus carolinensis*)

p. 248

LENGTH 12 in (30 cm)   WEIGHT 4.2 oz (0.12 kg)

Other names Dutch Whip-poor-will, Spanish Whip-poor-will

Description Brown or mottled with black, gray, buff; lighter throat bordered by narrow white (male) or buff (female) collar

Habitat Xeric scrub; mesic hammocks; mixed pine and hardwood forests; wet prairies and marshes; pine flatwoods; sandhills

Range Statewide

Jan	Feb	Mar	Apr	May	June	July	Aug	Sep	Oct	Nov	Dec

The Chuck-will's-widow is a typical spring and summer resident throughout most of Florida's woodlands as far south as the upper Keys. Cryptic coloration (mottled brown plumage) and nocturnal habits make this bird inconspicuous. A white throat band is the only obvious contrast to the Chuck-will's-widow's camouflage. Occasionally they are abundant along country roads and can be detected by the reddish glow of their eyes reflected from car headlights. The distinctly four-syllable call is an accurate imitation of its name with an emphasis on the "wid" of widow. These notes may be repeated incessantly (and loudly) throughout the night and into early morning. There is a brief period during spring when the Chuck-will's-widow and the similar Whip-poor-will can be heard together. Although a few birds winter in south Florida, most return to Florida in early spring. Two eggs are laid on the ground in open woodlands from April to early June. Chuck-will's-widows roost along tree limbs that serve as good camouflage. Chucks have very small bills, but relatively enormous bristled mouths that are used for capturing a variety of flying nocturnal insects. Most birds leave Florida for Central and South America by late September.

FAMILY *Caprimulgidae: Goatsuckers*
WHIP-POOR-WILL (*Caprimulgus vociferus*)
LENGTH 10 in (25 cm)   WEIGHT 2 oz (0.06 kg)

p. 248

Other names Eastern Whip-poor-will

Description Mottled gray-brown; black throat bordered by white (buff in female)

Habitat Xeric scrub; mesic hammocks; mixed pine and hardwood forests; wet prairies and marshes; pine flatwoods; sandhills

Range Statewide

| Jan | Feb | Mar | Apr | May | June | July | Aug | Sep | Oct | Nov | Dec |

This rarely encountered winter visitor and transient is a smaller, northern version of our summer resident Chuck-will's-widow. Whip-poor-wills also appear grayer and have a black throat in contrast to the Chuck's buff throat. Whip-poor-wills arrive in Florida in late September during fall migration and some may remain through April, using the same wooded habitats as its Florida relative. Most migrants pass through the state in late February and March. The Whip-poor-will's call is more rapid and the accent is on the last of three syllables. It is behaviorally similar to the Chuck-will's-widow.

ORDER *Apodiformes: Swifts and Hummingbirds*

Two major groups make up this order—the swifts, with long, pointed, stiff wings and tiny, weak feet, spend most of their life in flight; and the hummingbirds, our smallest birds, with the swiftest wing beat and extraordinary ability to hover.

FAMILY *Apodidae: Swifts*
CHIMNEY SWIFT (*Chaetura pelagica*)
LENGTH 5 in (13 cm)   WEIGHT 0.8 oz (0.02 kg)

p. 248

Other names Chimney Swallow, Chimney Bat, Chimney Sweep

Description Brownish-black above; gray throat, breast; narrow, stiff bowed wings

Habitat Xeric scrub; hardwood swamps; cypress swamps; mesic hammocks; mixed pine and hardwood forests; urban environments; pine flatwoods; sandhills

Range Statewide

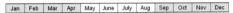

| Jan | Feb | Mar | Apr | May | June | July | Aug | Sep | Oct | Nov | Dec |

A "flying cigar" would be an appropriate description of this nearly tailless, dusky-colored swift. The rapid beat of its relatively long-pointed wings gives the Chimney Swift the appearance of constant motion. Its voice is a continuous staccato chattering that is made during flight. Chimney Swifts are cavity nesters using a variety of natural as well as human-made hollows such as wells and chimneys. Nests, cemented with saliva, are plastered to vertical walls where four to six white eggs are laid between April and July. Roosting birds cling to these same surfaces with extremely small feet and the support of stiff tail bristles. Large numbers of swifts may inhabit a single smoke stack or chimney, where they may appear wheeling around their roost like a cloud in early evening. Chimney Swifts return from South America in March and may remain in Florida until October. They are less frequently observed in south Florida, although they have extended their range southward in recent years to Naples and Miami. Food consists entirely of insects.

FAMILY *Trochilidae: Hummingbirds*   p. 248
RUBY-THROATED HUMMINGBIRD (*Archilochus colubris*)
LENGTH 3.5 in (9 cm)   WEIGHT 0.1 oz (0.002 kg)

Description Iridescent green upperparts, white below; male has a ruby red throat, while female and immature have white throat

Habitat Xeric scrub; mesic hammocks; mixed pine and hardwood forests; urban environments; pine flatwoods; sandhills; agricultural environments

Range Statewide

Jan	Feb	Mar	Apr	May	June	July	Aug	Sep	Oct	Nov	Dec

The Ruby-throated Hummingbird is Florida's smallest bird. Males possess a metallic red throat, green upperparts, whitish undersides, and a dark, slightly forked tail. Females and immatures are green above, white below and have a white-tipped tail. Ruby-throats return to Florida in early March when they feed on nectar produced in early-blooming tubular flowers. While feeding, they hover motionless or move adeptly back and forth. The wings beat so rapidly they are difficult to detect. Some birds remain in central or south Florida throughout the year while others depart in October for Central America. Nectar and small, nectar-eating insects form the diet of the Ruby-throated Hummingbird. The breeding season lasts from May through June when males exhibit an acrobatic, pendulous courtship flight. Its tiny lichen-covered nest, adhered to a small twig, usually contains two pea-size white eggs. Nesting is more likely in north and central Florida than in other parts of the state. Occasionally, other hummingbirds stray into Florida, especially in fall or winter. These include the **Black-chinned Hummingbird** (*Archilochus alexandri*), and **Bahama Woodstar** (*Calliphlox evelynae*). Since about 1988 **Buff-bellied Hummingbirds** (*Amazilia yucatanensis)* are seen in the western Panhandle on an annual basis.

FAMILY *Trochilidae: Hummingbirds*
RUFOUS HUMMINGBIRD (*Selasphorus rufus*)
LENGTH 3.75 in (10 cm)   WEIGHT 0.12 oz (0.003 kg)

Description Similar in size to the Ruby-throated Hummingbird, short wings, orange back, variable throat ranging from white to red to magenta

Habitat Often in suburban gardens and backyards with nectar-producing flowers

Range Statewide

Jan	Feb	Mar	Apr	May	June	July	Aug	Sep	Oct	Nov	Dec

This brightly colored hummingbird of the Pacific Northwest has been increasingly seen in the southeastern United States, especially in coastal areas, since the 1930s. It is most commonly reported in northern Florida during winter. The Rufous Hummingbird is the size of a Ruby-throated Hummingbird, but exhibits much more orange coloration in all plumages. Some adults have orange from the head to back and belly, whereas others are mostly green on the top of the head and back. The very similar **Allen's Hummingbird** (*Selasphorus sasin*) is a potential visitor to Florida. It is slightly smaller with a relatively longer bill. Reports are most likely to originate from the western Panhandle.

ORDER *Coraciiformes: Kingfishers*

Birds of this group all have syndactylous toes, i.e., their front three toes are more or less joined along part of their length.

FAMILY *Alcedinidae: Kingfishers* p. 248

BELTED KINGFISHER (*Ceryle alcyon*)

LENGTH 13 in (33 cm)   WEIGHT 5.2 oz (0.15 kg)

Other names Eastern Belted Kingfisher

Description Blue-gray above, white below; blue breast band, large bill, crested head; female also has a chestnut belly band

Habitat Salt marshes; hardwood swamps; cypress swamps; wet prairies and marshes; agricultural environments

Range Statewide

| Jan | Feb | Mar | Apr | May | June | July | Aug | Sep | Oct | Nov | Dec |

The Belted Kingfisher is a chunky, slate-blue bird with large bill, crested head, and tiny feet. Females, more colorful than the males, are distinguished by a rusty band across their white bellies. They often are seen perched on telephone wires and power lines paralleling flooded roadside ditches. Kingfishers dive headfirst into rivers, lakes, swamps, impoundments, and other open water wetlands. Prey items include small fish such as shiners, killifish, and minnows as well as crayfish, frogs, and insects. Nests are made at the end of a 3- to 15-foot-long (0.9–4.6 meter) tunnel, excavated into a cut-bank, bluff, or spoil pile. Four to five eggs are laid during April or May. Belted Kingfishers can be observed frequently year-round throughout north Florida, and from fall through spring south of Gainesville. Because they require sandy bluffs for burrowing, Kingfishers find the flat terrain of south Florida less suitable for nesting habitat. However, when winter brings numerous northern birds to Florida, Kingfishers become more common throughout the state. They often make a rattling call when in flight.

ORDER *Piciformes: Woodpeckers and Allies*
All members of this order have zygodactylous feet (two toes forward,
two backward), usually inhabit trees, and drill into wood to find insects
and make nest cavities.

FAMILY *Picidae: Woodpeckers*   p. 249

RED-HEADED WOODPECKER (*Melanerpes erythrocephalus*)
LENGTH 9 in (23 cm)   WEIGHT 2.5 oz (0.07 kg)

Other names White-wing, Redhead

Description Entire head is red, as is the neck; black tail and wings with white patches, white belly; immature has brown head

Habitat Xeric scrub; mixed pine and hardwood forests; urban environments; pine flatwoods; sandhills

Range Statewide

Jan	Feb	Mar	Apr	May	June	July	Aug	Sep	Oct	Nov	Dec

The Red-headed Woodpecker is a conspicuous year-round inhabitant of open forests and suburban woodlands throughout most of Florida. Its distribution is patchy, being common in some localities, scarce or absent in others. The bright, entirely red head, white belly, rump and wing patches, and black wings and tail distinguish the adults. Immature birds have brown, mottled heads, darker brown backs, and light, mottled underparts. Hollow cavities in dead trees, limbs, fence posts and utility poles may be used for nest sites. Bluebird nest boxes occasionally are used. The long breeding season extends from May until August; four to seven eggs are laid per clutch and two broods may be raised per season. Vegetation forms the bulk of the Red-headed Woodpecker's diet and may include acorns, berries, and a variety of grains. Insects also are taken. This colorful bird is often seen along suburban and country roads "hawking" for flying and crawling insects.

FAMILY *Picidae: Woodpeckers*   p. 250

RED-BELLIED WOODPECKER (*Melanerpes carolinus*)
LENGTH 9 in (23 cm)   WEIGHT 2.4 oz (0.07 kg)

Other names Zebra Woodpecker, Cham-chack, Guinea Sapsucker, Orange Sapsucker, Ladderback

Description Black and white barring on back; tan or gray underparts; red on head extends from bill to back of neck in male, only on back of head in female

Habitat Xeric scrub; hardwood swamps; cypress swamps; mesic hammocks; mixed pine and hardwood forests; urban environments; pine flatwoods; sandhills

Range Statewide

Jan	Feb	Mar	Apr	May	June	July	Aug	Sep	Oct	Nov	Dec

Although it possesses a red cap from bill to nape, the Red-bellied Woodpecker is named for its often overlooked rosy belly patch. A black and white ladder-striped back characteristic of both sexes. Females lack red on the forehead. The Red-bellied is probably our most widespread woodpecker. This highly adaptable species is found from suburban back yards to a variety of forest types throughout Florida. Cavities in dead and live trees such as cabbage palm, live oak, bald cypress, or slash pine serve as nest sites. They will also occupy bird houses. Breeding occurs from April through June when four to six eggs are laid. Red-bellied Woodpeckers are aggressive birds and may force other cavity nesters (such as Red-cockaded Woodpeckers) from established nest sites. They subsist on a variety of seeds and nuts as well as insects such as ants, grasshoppers, and beetle grubs. It has been known to eat the pulp and juice of ripe oranges, is a common visitor to bird feeders, and is the woodpecker most apt to drum on the drainpipes and windows of houses.

p. 249

FAMILY *Picidae: Woodpeckers*
YELLOW-BELLIED SAPSUCKER (*Sphyrapicus varius*)
LENGTH 8.5 in (22 cm)   WEIGHT 1.8 oz (0.05 kg)

Description White wing stripe on side; striped face; red forehead, crown, throat (male) or red crown, white throat (female)

Habitat Xeric scrub; mangrove; hardwood swamps; cypress swamps; mesic hammocks; mixed pine and hardwood forests; urban environments; pine flatwoods; sandhills

Range Statewide

Jan	Feb	Mar	Apr	May	June	July	Aug	Sep	Oct	Nov	Dec

The Yellow-bellied Sapsucker is a common winter resident in Florida except in the southern reaches of the state. It is the most migratory of our woodpeckers. Year-round reminders of their visits are evident in trees marked with concentric rings of holes. Flowing sap from these holes, and the insects attracted to them, form a part of this colorful woodpecker's diet. They will also eat suet left at feeding stations. An irregular black and white pattern marks the back. Both sexes exhibit a red crown, black and white facial stripes, white wing patches, black bib, and yellowish belly. Males have red throats. Birds in flight exhibit a white rump and white shoulder patches. First-year birds may lack red coloring. Yellow-bellied sapsuckers can be expected in Florida woodlands from October through April.

FAMILY *Picidae: Woodpeckers*
DOWNY WOODPECKER (*Picoides pubescens*)

p. 249

LENGTH 6.5 in (17 cm)   WEIGHT 1 oz (0.03 kg)

Other names Sapsucker

Description Similar to Hairy, but smaller; length of bill is equal to half the width of the head

Habitat Xeric scrub; mangrove; hardwood swamps; cypress swamps; mesic hammocks; mixed pine and hardwood forests; urban environments; pine flatwoods; sandhills

Range Statewide

Jan	Feb	Mar	Apr	May	June	July	Aug	Sep	Oct	Nov	Dec

The Downy is Florida's smallest woodpecker. A daintier, shorter bill (its length is one-half the depth of the head), black spots on outer tail feathers, and a faster, higher-pitched call distinguish the Downy from the Hairy Woodpecker. Downies are more apt to utilize backyard feeders than are Hairy Woodpeckers. Nesting habits are similar to the Hairy's, although smaller trees and snags may be used. Downy Woodpeckers can be seen year-round throughout Florida woodlands, including pinelands and hardwood forests. It is often seen in mixed feeding flocks of chickadees, titmice, and warblers. Its call is a staccato *peek*. The diet consists of beetles, cockroaches, ants, and other insects. Vegetable matter makes up a small portion of the food intake.

FAMILY *Picidae: Woodpeckers*
HAIRY WOODPECKER (*Picoides villosus*)

p.249

LENGTH 9 in (23 cm)   WEIGHT 2.5 oz (0.08 kg)

Other names Sapsucker

Description Black and white with black eye stripe and mustache, red nape on male; length of bill is equal to width of head

Habitat Xeric scrub; hardwood swamps; cypress swamps; mesic hammocks; mixed pine and hardwood forests; urban environments; pine flatwoods; sandhills

Range Statewide

Jan	Feb	Mar	Apr	May	June	July	Aug	Sep	Oct	Nov	Dec

The Hairy Woodpecker can be found throughout Florida woodlands. It is not a common bird, and is much less so in south Florida. Black wings and tail are contrasted against a white belly, neck, and back. The head is striped black and white, and white flecking occurs on the wings. The outer tail feathers usually are pure white (the very similar Downy Woodpecker shows black spots on these feathers). Hairies also have a heavier-appearing bill, the length of which is equal to the depth of the head behind the bill. Males have a red nape patch. Nests are excavated in a variety of dead trees. Eggs, usually three or four, are laid from April through May. The call has been described as a louder version of the Downy's *peek*. Nuts, beetles, and bark-dwelling insects form the bulk of its diet.

Family *Picidae: Woodpeckers*
RED-COCKADED WOODPECKER (*Picoides borealis*)
LENGTH 8 in (20 cm)   WEIGHT 1.6 oz (0.05 kg)   STATUS **SSC**

p. 249

Other names Sapsucker
Description Overall black and white, barred back and wings, large white cheek patch
Habitat Pine flatwoods
Range Statewide

| Jan | Feb | Mar | Apr | May | June | July | Aug | Sep | Oct | Nov | Dec |

Modern timber practices encouraging the harvest of young, plantation-grown pines have created problems for the conservation of this species. The Red-cockaded Woodpecker requires old-growth pine forests—usually longleaf pine—where nest cavities are excavated in living trees infected with the fungal red heart disease. Flowing resin wells are maintained around the nest entrance. These apparently serve as a repellent to egg-eating snakes. The flowing resin often gives these cavity trees a white-washed appearance making them conspicuous members of the forest. The red "cockades" of the males are rarely seen except when birds are in the hand. Red-cockaded Woodpeckers are best identified by their black and white ladder-striped backs, the large, white cheek patches, and their distinctive calls. The Red-cockaded Woodpecker is a highly social bird and exists in small family groups known as clans. Nonbreeding individuals act as helpers during nesting activities. Three to five eggs are laid from April through June in a cavity 20–50 feet (6–15.2 meters) above the ground. Foods consist of fruits, wood-boring beetles, and other insects. The Apalachicola National Forest represents the largest concentration of Red-cockaded Woodpeckers in the world; they also may be seen in scattered locations throughout the peninsula and Panhandle where large expanses of old growth pines persist, as indicated on the range map. It is declining throughout the state and is considered a species of special concern.

Family *Picidae: Woodpeckers*
NORTHERN FLICKER (*Colaptes auratus*)
LENGTH 12 in (30 cm)   WEIGHT 4.8 oz (0.14 kg)

p. 250

Other names Yellowhammer, Highhole, Golden-winged Woodpecker
Description Brown barred with black upperparts, white rump, black-spotted tan below with broad black breast patch, small red spot on nape; male has a black mustache
Habitat Xeric scrub; hardwood swamps; cypress swamps; mesic hammocks; mixed pine and hardwood forests; urban environments; pine flatwoods; sandhills
Range Statewide

| Jan | Feb | Mar | Apr | May | June | July | Aug | Sep | Oct | Nov | Dec |

The Northern Flicker is a large, brightly colored woodpecker of open woods and suburbs. In flight, yellow under the wings is conspicuous. Flickers are brown with black barring above, have a white rump, spotted underparts and black throat patch. Adult males exhibit a black cheek stripe extending from the base of the bill. Northern Flickers are found throughout the state, but are much less common in south Florida and the upper Keys. Nests usually are located in hollow cavities in palms, oaks, or pines at varying heights. About six white eggs are laid from late March to May. In suburban areas Flickers can become something of a nuisance due to their habit of "drumming" on a variety of surfaces from hollow trees to gutters, siding, and windows. Its call is a loud series of *wick* notes. Insects, especially ants, are the most important foods; hence, Flickers may often be seen foraging on the ground.

FAMILY *Picidae: Woodpeckers*

PILEATED WOODPECKER (*Dryocopus pileatus*)   p. 250

LENGTH 16 in (41 cm)   WEIGHT 10.9 oz (0.31 kg)

Other names Lord-god, Good-god, Logcock, Woodcock, Woodchuck, Wood-cady, Cock-o-the-woods

Description Large; black with red crest (less red on female), red or black mustache, white throat, face, neck; no white shows on wing at rest

Habitat Xeric scrub; hardwood swamps; cypress swamps; mesic hammocks; mixed pine and hardwood forests; urban environments; pine flatwoods; sandhills

Range Statewide

The Pileated Woodpecker is one of the most distinctive birds of Florida's deep forests and swamps. But unlike its close relative, the Ivory-billed Woodpecker, the Pileated is very adaptable and often may be seen in close proximity to busy urban areas. It has a red, crested head, white throat, and white stripe from base of bill to the shoulders. The white wing linings, which are frontally located, are conspicuous in flight. The female's red plumage is restricted to a smaller portion of the crest. The raucous call, which resembles a slower, louder Flicker's call, and methodical drumming may carry for long distances. Pileated Woodpeckers excavate rectangular cavities in soft or rotten wood. Eggs, usually three to five, are laid between February and May. Carpenter ants and wood-boring beetles are important food items that are obtained by hammering apart rotten logs and stumps. During fall, a variety of fruits such as swamp tupelo, dogwood, and sugarberry also are eaten.

Family *Picidae: Woodpeckers*

Ivory-billed Woodpecker (*Campephilus principalis*)

p. 250

Length 20 in (51 cm)   Weight 15.89–20.12 oz (0.45–0.57 kg)   Status **E**

Other names Pait

Description Large white wing patch on wing at rest; black face, forehead, throat; ivory bill; white stripe from side of head to side of back

Habitat Cypress swamps

Range Statewide

Jan	Feb	Mar	Apr	May	June	July	Aug	Sep	Oct	Nov	Dec

*

Long thought extinct throughout its range, the Ivory-billed Woodpecker was rediscovered along the White River in Arkansas in 2004. As the largest North American woodpecker, it has been the target of fruitless searches in Southeastern swamps for decades. The virgin cypress swamps throughout the Southeast were the haunts of this impressive bird. Florida was likely one of the last strongholds of this species, but the last convincing records came from the 1930s. Before the recent rediscovery, the last confirmed record in continental North America dates to 1944. Some individuals may have survived in Cuba through the 1950s. The Ivory-billed Woodpecker's original Florida distribution was nearly the entire peninsula with a few records from the panhandle. The combination of widespread logging of large cypress and pine forests and the Ivory-bill's inability to adapt to change caused the drastic range reduction that has nearly exterminated it. Its tendency to utilize very small areas for nesting and foraging may help explain the existence of a few individuals without detection. Now, perhaps with maturing forests that provide better feeding and nesting resources, the species will make a comeback. If so, it will be one of the most dramatic and unlikely recoveries of an endangered species anywhere in the world. Ivory-bills are larger than Pileated Woodpeckers. A heavy, whitish bill and large white wing patches are visible while perched. In flight, the undersides of the wings are bordered in white. Females lack a bright red crest. Its *kent* call was described as if played from a toy trumpet. The diet consists primarily of the wood-boring larvae of long-horned beetles and a variety of fruits such as southern magnolia. Nest cavities are usually built 15–70 feet (4.6–21.3 meters) above the ground in cypress trees, but other tree species are also used. The nest entrance is larger than that of the Pileated Woodpecker's rectangular hole, and it tends to be oval. Both sexes participate in nest construction, incubating, and caring for young, which number from one to five. Although the status of the Ivory-billed Woodpecker is unknown at the time of this writing, its Phoenix-like reappearance provides hope of restoring this charismatic species to its historical range, including Florida.

* Indicates the presumed Ivory-billed Woodpecker breeding season in Florida before its extirpation and what might be expected if it is returned to the state.

ORDER *Passeriformes: Passerine Birds*

This is a large assemblage of birds, called perching birds, including well over half of all the living bird species. All have a foot with three toes forward, one backward, well adapted for gripping a perch.

FAMILY *Tyrannidae: Tyrant Flycatchers*
EASTERN WOOD-PEWEE (*Contopus virens*)
p. 251
LENGTH 6 in (15 cm)   WEIGHT 0.5 oz (0.01 kg)

Description Olive-brown or gray above, whitish wing bars and underparts, no eye ring
Habitat Mesic hammocks; mixed pine and hardwood forests; pine flatwoods; sandhills
Range Statewide

Jan	Feb	Mar	Apr	May	June	July	Aug	Sep	Oct	Nov	Dec

A regular breeder in north Florida, the Eastern Wood-Pewee is often identified by its call, *pee-a-wee,* which closely resembles its name. It is less frequently seen in the open than other flycatchers, preferring the closed canopies of moist woodlands. The plumage is dark olive above, light below with grayish breast, white throat, black tail, and dark wings with pale wing bars. The cup-like nest is constructed of grasses and lichens and located on a tree branch up to 60 feet (18.3 meters) above the ground. Three to four eggs are laid in May or June. Insects make up most of the diet, while small fruits are occasionally eaten. It departs Florida in September, returning in late March.

FAMILY *Tyrannidae: Tyrant Flycatchers*
YELLOW-BELLIED FLYCATCHER (*Empidonax flaviventris*)
LENGTH 5.5 in (14 cm)   WEIGHT 0.4 oz (0.01 kg)

Description Dark wings with two buff to white wingbars, yellowish-green breast, ashy-green above, distinct whitish eyering
Habitat Dense undergrowth of moist to wet woodlands, often near the ground
Range Statewide

Jan	Feb	Mar	Apr	May	June	July	Aug	Sep	Oct	Nov	Dec

With a greenish back, and distinctive wing bars, this migrant species is similar in appearance to the other *Empidonax* flycatchers but it has a yellow eye ring and a yellow wash over the throat and breast. Its song, never uttered in Florida, is an explosive *pse-ek* or a *pur-wee.* During fall some immature Acadian Flycatchers also possess a yellow breast; hence, care must be exercised in identifying these. The Yellow-bellied Flycatcher can be found in woody thickets or understories of hardwood swamps and other woodlands.

FAMILY *Tyrannidae: Tyrant Flycatchers*
ACADIAN FLYCATCHER (*Empidonax virescens*) p. 251
LENGTH 6 in (15 cm)   WEIGHT 0.5 oz (0.01 kg)

Other names Green Crested Flycatcher

Description Olive-green upperparts, lighter below; buffy wings bars and eye ring

Habitat Hardwood swamps; cypress swamps; mesic hammocks; mixed pine and hardwood forests; sandhills

Range Mostly north and central Florida

Jan	Feb	Mar	Apr	May	June	July	Aug	Sep	Oct	Nov	Dec

The Acadian is our smallest breeding flycatcher in Florida. Olive-green head and upperparts, dark wings with buff wing bars, buff eye ring, yellow lower abdomen, and grayish breast characterize the adult. Immatures have a more brown and mottled appearance above with no yellow underneath. The long, broad bill is dark above and yellowish below. The Acadian Flycatcher is an inhabitant of Spanish moss–festooned swamplands and moist woodlands from central Florida through the Panhandle. A canoe trip down any central Florida river in spring will result in seeing or hearing this species. It may be seen from late April through September on its breeding grounds. The frail-looking nests usually are constructed of Spanish moss and hung from a forked branch of an understory tree. Eggs, numbering two to four, are laid during May or June. Its two-syllable call has been described as an explosive *wicky-up* or *peet-sit.* It eats mostly flying insects, but will also snatch spiders and millipedes from the ground.

FAMILY *Tyrannidae: Tyrant Flycatchers*
ALDER FLYCATCHER (*Empidonax alnorum*)
WILLOW FLYCATCHER (*Empidonax traillii*)
LENGTH 5.5 in (14 cm)   WEIGHT 0.5 oz (0.01 kg)

Other names Traill's Flycatcher

Description Larger than Least Flycatcher, smaller than Eastern Wood-Pewee, greenish-backed

Habitat Moist woodlands, shrubby thickets

Range Statewide

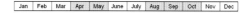

Jan	Feb	Mar	Apr	May	June	July	Aug	Sep	Oct	Nov	Dec

These two flycatchers were once considered a single species, Traill's Flycatcher. Both are brown-olive above, with white throat and olive sides, two white wing bars on each wing, and a white eye ring. The only truly distinguishing feature is their songs, which, unfortunately, are rarely uttered in Florida. The Alder song has been described as *fee-bee-o,* and the Willow, a *fitz-bew.* When singing, they are easy to distinguish from each other. Both occur during spring and fall migration, but are rarely identified beyond an *Empidonax* or Traill's complex flycatcher. They are normally seen in trees and shrubs along rivers, swamps, and other wooded sites.

FAMILY *Tyrannidae: Tyrant Flycatchers*
LEAST FLYCATCHER (*Empidonax minimus*)   p. 251
LENGTH 5 in (13 cm)   WEIGHT 0.4 oz (0.01 kg)

Description Gray-green above, lighter below; buff wing bars and eye ring

Habitat Mesic hammocks; mixed pine and hardwood forests; sandhillls

Range Statewide

Jan	Feb	Mar	Apr	May	June	July	Aug	Sep	Oct	Nov	Dec

This smallest North American flycatcher is seen in Florida during migration to and from its north woods breeding grounds. In recent years several individuals have wintered in southeastern Florida. It is the second most common small flycatcher in Florida (after the Acadian) and is the easiest to identify. The Least Flycatcher is brown to olive-gray above and pale below, with grayish breast and white throat, and has white wing bars and white eye rings. It looks similar to other *Empidonax* flycatchers and is best distinguished from these by its call, a clear, distinctive *whit*. Least Flycatchers are insect eaters and prefer open woodlands.

FAMILY *Tyrannidae: Tyrant Flycatchers*
EASTERN PHOEBE (*Sayornis phoebe*)   p. 251
LENGTH 7 in (18 cm)   WEIGHT 0.7 oz (0.02 kg)

Other names Pee-wee, Tick Bird, Bridge Phoebe

Description Gray-black above, white or yellowish below; dark wash on breast; pumps tail consistently

Habitat Dry prairies; mesic hammocks; mixed pine and hardwood forests; urban environments; sandhills; agricultural environments

Range Statewide

Jan	Feb	Mar	Apr	May	June	July	Aug	Sep	Oct	Nov	Dec

Like most flycatchers, the Eastern Phoebe is seen as a silhouette while sitting on exposed perches. Its habit of rapidly pumping its tail readily identifies this bird even without visible field marks. The Eastern Phoebe is rather nondescript with grayish-brown upperparts, light buff underparts, and black bill. Eastern Phoebes do not usually breed in Florida but are common residents from September through March. The two Florida nesting records occurred in May 1988 and 1990 in northern Okaloosa County. Nests are often placed in human structures and are constructed of mud and plant fibers. Insects are preferred food, often caught in midair, but fruits from sugarberries, hollies, and other trees and shrubs also are eaten. This is a common roadside bird and perches frequently on utility lines and fences, and may often be heard singing its name *phee-bee, phee-bee.*

FAMILY *Tyrannidae: Tyrant Flycatchers*
VERMILION FLYCATCHER (*Pyrocephalus rubinus*)

p. 251

LENGTH 6 in (15 cm)   WEIGHT 0.39–0.49 oz (0.01–0.014 kg)

Description Bright red, black back and eyestripe; female is gray-brown above with streaked belly

Habitat Dry prairies; mesic hammocks; mixed pine and hardwood forests; urban environments; sandhills; agricultural environments

Range Statewide

Jan	Feb	Mar	Apr	May	June	July	Aug	Sep	Oct	Nov	Dec

This native of the southwestern United States and Mexico is seen sporadically in Florida during winter. Most birds have been observed in the Panhandle but individuals have shown up throughout the state. The male is bright red with a black back and black eyestripe. The female is gray brown above with a white belly washed in light pink and streaked with brown. The Vermilion Flycatcher feeds primarily on flying insects and appears partial to perching in hardwood trees near lake shores. Arrivals and departures of the Vermilion are unpredictable but most have been seen between September and April.

FAMILY *Tyrannidae: Tyrant Flycatchers*
GREAT CRESTED FLYCATCHER (*Myiarchus crinitus*)

p. 251

LENGTH 9 in (23 cm)   WEIGHT 1.2 oz (0.03 kg)

Other names Southern Crested Flycatcher, Crested Flycatcher, Freight-bird

Description Olive-brown crest and back, gray throat and breast, yellow belly, rufous on wings and tail, white wing bars

Habitat Xeric scrub; hardwood swamps; cypress swamps; mesic hammocks; mixed pine and hardwood forests; urban environments; pine flatwoods; sandhills; agricultural environments

Range Statewide

Jan	Feb	Mar	Apr	May	June	July	Aug	Sep	Oct	Nov	Dec

About the size of the Eastern Kingbird, the Great Crested Flycatcher is one of our most familiar and vocal woodland birds in Florida. Olive-drab upperparts, ash-gray throat, yellow belly, chestnut tail, and barred wings distinguish this summer resident. Great Crested Flycatchers may be seen in mixed woodlands throughout the state from late March until early fall. Some birds remain in south Florida year-round. This large flycatcher nests in cavities often excavated by woodpeckers and will nest in bird houses. The authors have observed single pairs occupying houses erected for Purple Martins. Nests contain from four to six streaked eggs laid from April through June. A common nest material is shed snake skin. In modern times, clear plastic material that resembles snake skin has been used. A loud *weep* call is frequently made near nest sites and elsewhere throughout the year. Great Crested Flycatchers choose exposed vantage points from which frequent sallies are made for grasshoppers, caterpillars, beetles, and other insects. Small fruits make up a small part of the Great Crested Flycatcher's diet. A similar species, the **Brown-crested Flycatcher** (*Myiarchus tyrannulus*) occasionally winters in extreme southern Florida

(Everglades National Park). It is a duller brown color, with less reddish or chestnut colors in the tail, a paler (almost white) gray throat, and paler yellow underparts. It also has an all-black lower mandible. Another western bird, the **Ash-throated Flycatcher** (*Myiarchus cinerascens*) has started to appear during fall migration along the Panhandle coast, and during winter in the northern peninsula. It is grayer overall and has a paler yellowish belly than the Great Crested Flycatcher.

FAMILY *Tyrannidae: Tyrant Flycatchers*
WESTERN KINGBIRD (*Tyrannus verticalis*)   p. 251
LENGTH 9 in (23 cm)   WEIGHT 1.4 oz (0.04 kg)

Description Gray head and breast, yellow belly, black tail with white outer feathers
Habitat Dry prairies; urban environments; agricultural environments
Range Statewide

Jan	Feb	Mar	Apr	May	June	July	Aug	Sep	Oct	Nov	Dec

This regular winter visitor is seen annually, although unpredictably, throughout Florida. It appears at a time when most other large flycatchers are absent (September–April) and therefore should not be confused with our summer residents, although Western Kingbirds have been reported in every month. They often are seen in open country on exposed perches. The Western Kingbird is gray above with bright yellow underparts, dark wings, and black tail. The red crown patch of the male is seldom observed. A variety of insects forms its diet.

FAMILY *Tyrannidae: Tyrant Flycatchers*
EASTERN KINGBIRD (*Tyrannus tyrannus*)   p. 251
LENGTH 8 in (20 cm)   WEIGHT 1.5 oz (0.04 kg)

Other names Bee Bird, Bee Martin
Description Black upper parts, white below; white-tipped black tail
Habitat Dry prairies; mixed pine and hardwood forests; urban environments; agricultural environments
Range Statewide

Jan	Feb	Mar	Apr	May	June	July	Aug	Sep	Oct	Nov	Dec

Black head, dark upperparts, white underparts, and a black tail with a white terminal band distinguish this common summer resident in Florida. The red patch behind the head is seldom seen. These birds are often conspicuous due to their habit of using exposed perches such as utility lines, telephone poles, treetops, and fences. From these vantage points frequent sallies are made for a variety of insects, many of which are agricultural pests. Fruits are occasionally plucked from branches while hovering. Nests may be placed in shrubs or trees that provide adequate protection from predators. Pine trees are used most often for nest sites. These sites are frequently near water. Three to four eggs are usually laid during May. Eastern Kingbirds typically are seen in Florida from March until October. Their numbers have declined in Florida over the last few decades. They do not breed in the Florida Keys.

FAMILY *Tyrannidae: Tyrant Flycatchers*
GRAY KINGBIRD (*Tyrannus dominicensis*)
LENGTH 9 in (23 cm)   WEIGHT 1.5 oz (0.04 kg)

p. 251

Other names Pipiry Flycatcher

Description Gray above, white below; black ear patch; large dark bill

Habitat Mangroves; mesic hammocks; urban environments

Range Statewide, coastal

| Jan | Feb | Mar | Apr | May | June | July | Aug | Sep | Oct | Nov | Dec |

This Florida specialty breeds in widely scattered localities along the Gulf and Atlantic coasts but seems to be more abundant near mangroves (southern Gulf coast and Keys), as indicated on the range map. The Gray Kingbird is somewhat larger than the Eastern Kingbird, is lighter above with a slightly forked, unbanded tail, and has a larger, heavier bill. Like the Eastern Kingbird, the Gray Kingbird is resident from March through September. Loosely constructed nests are often placed in mangroves overhanging water. Two to three eggs are laid in May or early June. Gray Kingbirds feed on insects from exposed, elevated perches. They are quite tolerant of human activity provided there is ample feeding and nesting habitat. Gray Kingbirds are a common sight perched on power lines through the Keys.

FAMILY *Tyrannidae: Tyrant Flycatchers*
SCISSOR-TAILED FLYCATCHER (*Tyrannus forficatus*)   p. 251
LENGTH 13 in (33 cm)   WEIGHT 1.5 oz (0.04 kg)

Description Very long black and white tail feathers, pale gray overall, dark wings, pinkish-red wash on belly

Habitat Urban environments; agricultural environments

Range Statewide

| Jan | Feb | Mar | Apr | May | June | July | Aug | Sep | Oct | Nov | Dec |

Few Florida birds are as unmistakable as the Scissor-tailed Flycatcher. This medium-size flycatcher has a deeply forked tail that may be 12 inches (84 cm) long, pink wing linings, light gray head and neck, and dark upper wing and tail surfaces. Males have slightly longer tails than do females and the immatures' tails are about half the adult tail length. Scissor-taileds are summer residents in the south-central United States and usually reside in Central America during winter. A few birds, however, winter regularly in the Keys and south Florida as far north as Pasco and Hernando counties, and are occasionally seen in migration along the Gulf coast (rarely on the Atlantic coast). These distinctive birds are most often seen on exposed perches such as utility wires and tall, leafless trees. The diet consists mostly of insects. Birds wintering in Key West often feed on wild bees living in concrete utility poles.

FAMILY *Laniidae: Shrikes*
LOGGERHEAD SHRIKE (*Lanius ludovicianus*)
p. 252
LENGTH 9 in (23 cm)   WEIGHT 1.7 oz (0.05 kg)

Other names Butcher Bird, French Mockingbird, Catbird
Description Hooked bill; gray cap and back, white below; black mask, wings, tail; white in wings and outer tail feathers
Habitat Dry prairies; sandhills; agricultural environments
Range Statewide

Jan	Feb	Mar	Apr	May	June	July	Aug	Sep	Oct	Nov	Dec

This predatory Florida songbird inhabits agricultural lands and other open areas. While it resembles the Northern Mockingbird at a distance, the Loggerhead Shrike is a stockier bird with a bold black mask, black tail, and white wing patches. The heavy bill is short and hooked. The infrequent call consists of short mechanical notes. Its song is more varied and musical. Nests are often in open-growing, thorny shrubs or small trees and are constructed of twigs, feathers, rootlets, and other plant fibers. The Loggerhead Shrike is an early nester, laying an average of five light gray, brown-spotted eggs from February through June. During winter, northern migrants inflate the Florida population. Shrikes often are seen perched on telephone wires and fences while hunting for small animals. Rodents, lizards, small birds, grasshoppers, caterpillars, and other insects make up its completely animal diet. Shrikes are incapable of grasping prey with their small feet but frequently impale food items on long thorns or barbed wire. Because of its heavy dependence upon insects, the Loggerhead Shrike has experienced a decline in numbers due to pesticides.

FAMILY *Vireonidae: Vireos*
WHITE-EYED VIREO (*Vireo griseus*)
LENGTH 5 in (13 cm)   WEIGHT 0.4 oz (0.01 kg)
p. 253

Description Gray-green above, white wing bars, yellow spectacles, white eye (dark in immature), yellowish sides
Habitat Xeric scrub; hardwood swamps; cypress swamps; mesic hammocks; mixed pine and hardwood forests, pine flatwoods; sandhills
Range Statewide

Jan	Feb	Mar	Apr	May	June	July	Aug	Sep	Oct	Nov	Dec

This small vireo is a common resident of Florida's woodlands. Gum swamps, oak hammocks, and pine flatwoods seem equally suitable to the White-eyed Vireo. Greenish upperparts, yellow spectacles, white wing bars, and white irises characterize adults; juveniles have dark eyes. It is a perpetual singer, the song a syncopated series of five to seven notes ending in a staccato *chick*. The nest is composed of grass, bark, Spanish moss, and leaves and is hung from a V-shaped twig that is no more than 8 feet (2.4 meters) off the ground. Three to five brown-spotted, white eggs are laid between April and June. Migrants arrive in Florida in mid-September on their way to South America, although many winter in Florida. Spring migrants pass through in March and April. Foods are mostly insects but also include fruits of greenbriar, dogwood, and other woodland plants.

FAMILY *Vireonidae: Vireos*
YELLOW-THROATED VIREO (*Vireo flavifrons*)
LENGTH 5.5 in (14 cm)   WEIGHT 0.6 oz (0.02 kg)

p. 253

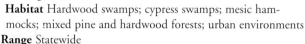

Description Bright yellow throat, breast, spectacles; olive-green back; white wing bars

Habitat Hardwood swamps; cypress swamps; mesic hammocks; mixed pine and hardwood forests; urban environments

Range Statewide

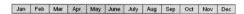

| Jan | Feb | Mar | Apr | May | June | July | Aug | Sep | Oct | Nov | Dec |

The Yellow-throated Vireo is a common summer resident in Florida north of Orlando. It prefers deciduous or mixed deciduous-pine woodlands for nesting. Yellow spectacles, breast, and throat contrast with a white belly, gray rump, and greenish upperparts. The song is a repeated series of two- and three-note phrases resembling the Red-eyed Vireo's, but slower and more deliberate. The nest is a hanging, woven cup placed high in a tall pine or hardwood. Three to five eggs are usually laid in April. Breeding range is indicated on the range map. Yellow-throated Vireos are most common in Florida between March and October. A few birds over-winter in south Florida—their winter range is also indicated on the range map. Insects dominate the diet.

FAMILY *Vireonidae: Vireos*
BLUE-HEADED VIREO (*Vireo solitarius*)
LENGTH 5.5 in (14 cm)   WEIGHT 0.6 oz (0.02 kg)

p. 253

Other names Solitary Vireo

Description Slate-gray head, white spectacles, olive-green back, white wing bars

Habitat Hardwood swamps; cypress swamps; mesic hammocks; mixed pine and hardwood forests; urban environments; pine flatwoods; sandhills

Range Statewide

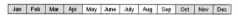

| Jan | Feb | Mar | Apr | May | June | July | Aug | Sep | Oct | Nov | Dec |

The Blue-headed Vireo is a fairly common migrant and winter bird in mainland Florida. Blue-gray head with white spectacles, greenish upperparts, white wing bars, yellowish flanks, and white underparts distinguish this woodland bird. Blue-headed Vireos are found in a variety of wooded situations from pine flatwoods and hardwood hammocks to suburban backyards. It is often seen in mixed flocks with other common wintering birds, though it is most often solitary or in pairs when breeding. Foods are mostly tree-dwelling insects with a few fruits such as dogwood and wax myrtle. Blue-headed Vireos can be found in Florida from mid-October through April.

FAMILY *Vireonidae: Vireos*

RED-EYED VIREO (*Vireo olivaceus*)

LENGTH 6 in (15 cm)   WEIGHT 0.8 oz (0.02 kg)

p. 253

Other names Hanging Bird, Preacher Bird

Description Blue-gray crown bordered with black, white eyebrow, red eye

Habitat Hardwood swamps; mesic hammocks; mixed pine and hardwood forests

Range Statewide

| Jan | Feb | Mar | Apr | May | June | July | Aug | Sep | Oct | Nov | Dec |

In eastern North America the Red-eyed Vireo is one of the most abundant woodland birds. Its distinctive song, *how-are-you? I'm fine,* may be repeated incessantly, and is a characteristic sound of spring and summer. Upperparts are grayish with a black-bordered, white eyestripe. Underparts are white with pale yellow flanks. The red eyes are visible only at close range. In Florida, Red-eyed Vireos are common in mixed hardwood forests throughout central and north Florida. They breed less frequently in south Florida, but are not uncommon in the Fakahatchee Strand of Collier County. Nests are woven cups suspended from a forked branch of a shrub or tree. Three to five eggs are laid during May. Spring migrants arrive in mid- or late March while the last fall migrants pass through during October. The wintering ground of this common species is in South America. Insects form the bulk of the Red-eyed Vireo's diet although fruits such as dogwood and Virginia creeper are also taken.

FAMILY *Vireonidae: Vireos*

BLACK-WHISKERED VIREO (*Vireo altiloquus*)

LENGTH 6 in (15 cm)   WEIGHT 0.6 oz (0.02 kg)

p. 253

Description Gray crown, white eyebrow, black whisker stripe on side of throat

Habitat Mangrove; mesic hammocks

Range South and Central Florida, coastal

| Jan | Feb | Mar | Apr | May | June | July | Aug | Sep | Oct | Nov | Dec |

This Florida specialty is found only along the state's southern coasts and the Keys. It is similar to the Red-eyed Vireo but has a heavier bill and distinctive black "whiskers." The song also resembles the Red-eyed Vireo's but is hoarser and is sung in couplets (two phrases and a pause). The Black-whiskered Vireo is a bird of Florida's mangrove forests and tropical hardwoods. Like other vireos its nest is a shallow woven cup. Eggs usually number three and are white with brown spots. Nesting occurs in May or June. Most birds depart for South America by mid-September and begin their return to Florida in late March. Although breeding occurs only south of Port Charlotte and Miami, as indicated on the range map, migrant Black-whiskered Vireos are frequently seen on the upper Gulf coast. Insects and spiders form the bulk of its diet.

FAMILY *Corvidae: Jays and Crows*
BLUE JAY (*Cyanocitta cristata*)   p. 254
LENGTH 11 in (28 cm)   WEIGHT 3 oz (0.09 kg)

Other names Jaybird, Florida Blue Jay

Description Blue crest, black collar, blue above, white spots on wings and tail, white underparts

Habitat Xeric scrub; hardwood swamps; cypress swamps; mesic hammocks; mixed pine and hardwood forests; urban environments; pine flatwoods; sandhills; agricultural environments

Range Statewide

| Jan | Feb | Mar | Apr | May | June | July | Aug | Sep | Oct | Nov | Dec |

The Blue Jay is one of Florida's most widespread and recognized songbirds. This raucous, animated bird is as often heard as seen. Its calls vary from the typical *jay, jay,* and sometimes convincing Red-shouldered Hawk and Red-tailed Hawk imitations, to a wide range of *clucks, rattles,* and *churrs.* The Blue Jay also has a subdued musical whisper song, rarely heard. Blue Jays are crested, blue above, and whitish below. The face is masked in black while the wings are generously marked with blue, white, and black. The sexes are similar. It is a permanent Florida resident using a wide range of habitats from pine flatwoods and hardwood hammocks to urban environments. Blue Jays seem to have a fondness for acorns but will eat nearly anything smaller than themselves, including insects, rodents, lizards, and other birds. Most nesting takes place between March and late July, and individual pairs may raise more than one brood each year. Nests are placed 10–40 (3–12 meters) feet above ground and are constructed of twigs, Spanish moss, pine needles, paper, and other debris. Eggs, usually numbering three or four, are light green or brown and spotted with dark brown.

FAMILY *Corvidae: Jays and Crows*
FLORIDA SCRUB-JAY (*Aphelocoma coerulescens*)
LENGTH 11 in (28 cm)   WEIGHT 2.8 oz (0.08 kg)   STATUS **T**   p. 254

Other names Florida Jay, Smooth-headed Jay

Description Blue upperparts, gray back, dark eye-ear patch, whitish forehead, white throat, breast with blue-gray streaks, gray underparts

Habitat Xeric scrub

Range Statewide except Panhandle

| Jan | Feb | Mar | Apr | May | June | July | Aug | Sep | Oct | Nov | Dec |

The Florida Scrub-Jay is found only in the dry oak scrublands of peninsular Florida. About the size of the Blue Jay, the Florida Scrub-Jay is crestless and paler in color. Sky blue upperparts and breast band, grayish back, and light gray underparts distinguish both sexes. The Florida species can be separated from its western relatives by the light forehead and eyebrows. The Florida Scrub-Jay's calls are varied but less raucous than the Blue Jay's. In recent decades the range of this permanent Florida resident has been greatly reduced due to spreading urbanization and agriculture. Some of the more extensive patches of suitable habitat remain in the Ocala National Forest, Merritt Island National Wildlife Refuge, and in the uplands west and north of Lake Okeechobee. The Florida Scrub-Jay is considered a threatened species by the U.S. Fish and Wildlife Service and the Florida Fish and Wildlife Conservation Commission. It is dependent on a variety of scrub oaks for nesting as well as food. Its breeding range is indicated on the range map. Eggs are laid between late March and late May. Nests are constructed of twigs and lined with finer material. The average clutch has three greenish, brown-spotted eggs. Florida Scrub-Jays are gregarious and offspring of mated pairs often assist in subsequent nesting activities. Foods, other than acorns, include grasshoppers, beetles, ants, wasps, spiders, and a variety of berries and other fruits.

FAMILY *Corvidae: Jays and Crows*
AMERICAN CROW (*Corvus brachyrhynchos*)   p. 254
LENGTH 17 in (43 cm)   WEIGHT 1 lb (0.45 kg)

Other names Common Crow, Southern Crow, Florida Crow, Cawin' Crow, Corn Crow

Description All black

Habitat Coastal beaches; xeric scrub; hardwood swamps; dry prairies; cypress swamps; mesic hammocks; mixed pine and hardwood forests; urban environments; pine flatwoods; sandhills; agricultural environments

Range Statewide

The American Crow is our largest crow and the one most often found in and around large wooded uplands. This common, permanent resident is unmistakable: entirely black, large heavy bill, and familiar call—a repeated full, broad *caw*. Loosely constructed nests, occasionally abandoned by large birds of prey, are usually located high in a pine or tall hardwood tree. Eggs, averaging four, usually are laid between January and May. During winter the Florida population is augmented by northern migrants. Crows' habit of "mobbing" is often a good clue to finding otherwise secretive birds of prey—the raucous calls give away both the crows' presence and that of the hawk or owl. American Crows have also earned a reputation as crop destroyers and remain a popular game bird in some rural areas. The diet, however, is predominantly nonagricultural and includes a variety of insects, young rabbits, rodents, snakes, lizards, and the eggs and young of reptiles and birds.

FAMILY *Corvidae: Jays and Crows*
FISH CROW (*Corvus ossifragus*) p. 254
LENGTH 15 in (38 cm)   WEIGHT 10.6 oz (0.3 kg)

Description All black

Habitat Coastal beaches; salt marshes; mangrove; mesic hammocks; mixed pine and hardwood forests; urban environments; agricultural environments

Range Statewide

Jan	Feb	Mar	Apr	May	June	July	Aug	Sep	Oct	Nov	Dec

Although the Fish Crow is smaller than the American Crow, identification by size alone is unreliable. The best single field character distinguishing the Fish Crow is its hoarse, nasal voice. The most frequent calls are the two-syllable *uh-oh* and a repetitive *cah*. Fish Crows are abundant in Florida, especially near coastlines, rivers, lakes, and marshes. Nesting habits are similar to the American Crow but egg-laying may occur somewhat later in the spring. The diet is highly variable but includes a large proportion of wetland foods such as crabs, mollusks, crayfish, and the eggs and young of colonial nesting waterbirds such as Wood Storks, Anhingas, and herons.

FAMILY *Hirundinidae: Swallows*
PURPLE MARTIN (*Progne subis*) p. 255
LENGTH 8 in (20 cm)   WEIGHT 1.7 oz (0.05 kg)

Other names Black Martin, Gourd Martin, House Martin

Description Metallic purplish-black, black wings (male) or dull purplish-black upperparts, gray collar, gray underparts (female)

Habitat Mangrove; dry prairies; mixed pine and hardwood forests; wet prairies and marshes; urban environments; agricultural environments

Range Statewide

Jan	Feb	Mar	Apr	May	June	July	Aug	Sep	Oct	Nov	Dec

Perhaps no other North American bird is so strongly sought as a tenant by landowners as the Purple Martin. This attractive gregarious swallow once relied on natural tree cavities for nest sites but because of extensive loss of forests, and its inherent adaptability, it now relies on human-made martin apartments. These range in design from dried gourds (originally used by Indians) to elaborate multi-family manufactured houses on poles. Martins also will occupy a wide range of other human-made structures ranging from commercial signs, street lamps, and traffic lights to operating oil rigs. The most consistently utilized structures, regardless of design or purpose, are located not far from lakes or ponds. The Purple Martin is our largest swallow and the only one with readily distinguished sexes. Males are a dark metallic blue, while females and juveniles are blue-brown above, with a whitish belly. Females also exhibit a blue patch on the back of the head. Martins arrive in Florida during late January and early February. Nesting occurs from late March through early July, when three to six white eggs are laid. Fall migration can begin as early as late June when flocks of several hundred to several thousand Martins may be seen gathering before their trans-Gulf flight to Brazil. Most of the Florida population leaves the state long before northern birds migrate through in late August and September. The diet is composed of a variety of insects, chiefly beetles and dragonflies.

FAMILY *Hirundinidae: Swallows*   p. 255
TREE SWALLOW (*Tachycineta bicolor*)
LENGTH 6 in (15 cm)   WEIGHT 0.7 oz (0.02 kg)

Other names White-bellied Swallow
Description Metallic green or blue upperparts, white below, notched tail
Habitat Coastal beaches; salt marshes; open freshwater; dry prairies; wet prairies and marshes; urban environments; agricultural environments
Range Statewide

Jan	Feb	Mar	Apr	May	June	July	Aug	Sep	Oct	Nov	Dec

The Tree Swallow is most often seen in Florida from fall through spring when this gregarious migrant forms loose flocks of 50 or less, or wheeling clouds numbering in the thousands. Tree Swallows are glossy green (sometimes purple) above and white below. Their tails are slightly forked. Females are less colorful than males, and immatures are grayish above with an indistinct chest band. Insects make up the bulk of the Tree Swallow's diet; however, wax myrtle fruits are consumed in large quantities, especially when cold temperatures reduce insect activity. Migrants may arrive in late August and linger through May.

FAMILY *Hirundinidae: Swallows*   p. 255
NORTHERN ROUGH-WINGED SWALLOW (*Stelgidopteryx serripennis*)
LENGTH 5.5 in (14 cm)   WEIGHT 0.6 oz (0.02 kg)

Other names Sand Martin, Gully Martin, Bank Swallow, Gully Bird
Description Light brown above, whitish below with brownish wash on breast
Habitat Open freshwater; wet prairies and marshes; urban environments; agricultural environments
Range Statewide

Jan	Feb	Mar	Apr	May	June	July	Aug	Sep	Oct	Nov	Dec

This rather nondescript swallow is a moderately frequent migrant and nester throughout Florida. The Northern Rough-winged Swallow is brownish above, with a buff throat grading into a white belly. The tail is slightly notched. Rough-wings are usually cavity nesters, burrowing into the sides of stream banks, canals, and spoil piles, but they will occasionally nest in drain pipes extending from bridges or buildings. Eggs, laid in May or June, number around six and are pure white. Nesting sites of this species are loosely scattered through north and central Florida. Its abundance is likely limited by suitable nest sites, a similar situation to that of the Belted Kingfisher. Regardless, it is not as colonial as Florida's other swallows. Rough-wings are fairly common as migrants from fall through spring in south Florida with a few birds over-wintering. Foods, as with other swallows, are mostly insects.

FAMILY *Hirundinidae: Swallows*

BANK SWALLOW (*Riparia riparia*)

p. 255

LENGTH 5 in (13 cm)   WEIGHT 0.5 oz (0.01 kg)

Other names Sand Martin

Description Dark brown above; white throat with brown band across chest; white belly

Habitat Open freshwater; dry prairies; wet prairies and marshes; urban environments; agricultural environments

Range Statewide

Jan	Feb	Mar	Apr	May	June	July	Aug	Sep	Oct	Nov	Dec

The dull-colored Bank Swallow is a common Florida migrant. Brownish upperparts, dark wings, and white belly with contrasting brown chest band distinguish this small swallow from the similar Northern Rough-winged Swallow. Like many other swallows, the Bank Swallow is gregarious and may be seen in small flocks during migration, especially over agricultural lands, grasslands and herbaceous wetlands. Insects are the mainstay of its diet, fueling these birds to their South American wintering grounds. Spring migrants may be seen between April and May; fall migrants pass through between late August and early October.

FAMILY *Hirundinidae: Swallows*

CLIFF SWALLOW (*Petrochelidon pyrrhonota*)

p. 255

LENGTH 5.5 in (14 cm)   WEIGHT 0.8 oz (0.02 kg)

Description Pale white or buff forehead, blue cap, rufous throat, buff rump

Habitat Open freshwater; urban environments; agricultural environments

Range Statewide

Jan	Feb	Mar	Apr	May	June	July	Aug	Sep	Oct	Nov	Dec

In Florida most Cliff Swallows are strictly migrants, occurring during spring and fall in variable, unpredictable numbers. A square tail, buff or rusty rump patch, dark reddish-brown throat and cream-colored forehead identify this bird. One anomalous colony of Cliff Swallows nested under highway bridges at Port Mayaca on the northeast shore of Lake Okeechobee from the late 1960s to the early 1980s, and another was found near Apalachicola in 1997. Nests are gourd-shaped and constructed of mud. Eggs, usually three to six, are white with brown dots. The nesting season lasts from April through June. Cliff Swallows typically are seen foraging for flying insects over agricultural and other open landscapes. Spring migrants appear between late March and mid-May; fall birds pass through from mid-August through October.

FAMILY *Hirundinidae: Swallows*
CAVE SWALLOW (*Petrochelidon fulva*)
LENGTH 5.5 in (14 cm)   WEIGHT 0.7 oz (0.02 kg)

p. 255

Other names Caribbean Cave Swallow
Description Rufous forehead, dark blue cap, buff throat, rufous rump
Habitat Urban environments; agricultural environments
Range South Florida

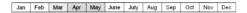

| Jan | Feb | Mar | Apr | May | June | July | Aug | Sep | Oct | Nov | Dec |

Like the similar Cliff Swallow, this species has a square tail and buff rump patch, but it has a buff throat and cinnamon forehead. Up until recently it had been considered an "accidental" in Florida, with numerous sightings chiefly in spring. In 1987, 16 pairs were found nesting under several Florida Turnpike bridges near Homestead (Miami-Dade County), and this population now appears to be increasing and likely resident in southeastern Florida. Nests are gourd-shaped mud structures built in early April. Elsewhere nests also are built under the eaves of buildings, concrete culverts, and rock walls. Eggs number two to five and are white with fine specks of brown. Food primarily consists of flying insects caught over waterways and fields.

FAMILY *Hirundinidae: Swallows*
BARN SWALLOW (*Hirundo rustica*)
LENGTH 7 in (18 cm)   WEIGHT 0.6 oz (0.02 kg)

p. 255

Description Deeply forked tail, blue-black back, buff to cream underparts, chestnut above bill and on throat
Habitat Open freshwater; dry prairies; wet prairies and marshes; urban environments; agricultural environments
Range Statewide

| Jan | Feb | Mar | Apr | May | June | July | Aug | Sep | Oct | Nov | Dec |

This is probably our best known swallow, even though it primarily is a migrant in Florida. The Barn Swallow is distinguished by an extremely deeply forked tail, reddish undersides, pointed wings, and dark blue, metallic upperparts. Juveniles are lighter below and browner above. Most Barn Swallows are seen in Florida as they travel in flocks to wintering grounds in Central America (between July and November) or on their way north (between April and June). However, some birds remain in the state to nest, usually from May to July. In recent years it has extended its range into the Florida Keys where it nests under highway bridges. Two to six eggs are laid in a nest constructed of mud, grass, and feathers and plastered underneath bridges, against houses, or in caves and hollow trees. The diet is mostly insects. Common prey, taken on the wing, includes flies, beetles, ants, and stink bugs. Nesting Barn Swallows appear to be on the increase in Florida.

FAMILY *Paridae: Titmice*

CAROLINA CHICKADEE (*Poecile carolinensis*)   p. 256

LENGTH 4.5 in (11 cm)   WEIGHT 0.4 oz (0.01 kg)

Other names Florida Chickadee

Description Black cap and bib, white cheeks

Habitat Xeric scrub; hardwood swamps; cypress swamps; mesic hammocks; mixed pine and hardwood forests; urban environments; pine flatwoods; sandhills

Range Statewide

Jan	Feb	Mar	Apr	May	June	July	Aug	Sep	Oct	Nov	Dec

This tiny, energetic woodland bird is a common resident except in south Florida. Both sexes are gray above and white below with black cap and throat, and white cheek patch. The Carolina Chickadee is often detected by its voice: a distinctive *chick-a-dee-dee-dee*, or *fee-bee, fee-bay.* Carolina Chickadees use tree cavities and occasionally boxes for nest sites. Breeding occurs in April and May, when five to seven white, brown-flecked eggs are laid. Chickadees tolerate close human contact and are residents in wooded suburbs. They are often seen in mixed feeding flocks with other small woodland bird species. Foods are predominately insects but chickadees are frequent visitors at window and backyard feeding stations. Wild seeds and small fruits also are eaten.

FAMILY *Paridae: Titmice*

TUFTED TITMOUSE (*Baeolophus bicolor*)   p. 256

LENGTH 6 in (15 cm)   WEIGHT 0.8 oz (0.02 kg)

Other names Peter Bird, Peto Bird, Tomtit

Description Gray upperparts and crest, black forehead

Habitat Xeric scrub; hardwood swamps; cypress swamps; mesic hammocks; mixed pine and hardwood forests; urban environments; pine flatwoods; sandhills

Range Statewide

Jan	Feb	Mar	Apr	May	June	July	Aug	Sep	Oct	Nov	Dec

This close relative of the chickadee is slightly larger but similar in habits and distribution, although it occurs as a nesting species into south Florida. The Tufted Titmouse is light gray above, with reddish or chestnut flanks and a prominent crest. Its call is a quickly-repeated *peter-peter-peter.* Other calls are reminiscent of the Carolina Chickadee. Titmice are residents of a variety of forest types such as cypress swamps, hardwood hammocks, longleaf pine sandhills, and wooded suburbs. They are absent from the Keys and the coastal belt south of Cape Canaveral/Tampa Bay. Natural cavities and boxes provide nest sites where five to seven brown-flecked, white eggs are laid during April through June. Nests are composed of leaves, grass, bark, feathers, hair (sometimes from live mammals!), and usually a snake skin or two. The absence of cavities may limit the distribution of this bird. Tufted Titmice are common visitors at feeding stations, especially during winter. Sunflower seeds are a favorite food. Wild foods include a variety of insects, seeds, berries, and acorns.

FAMILY *Sittidae: Nuthatches*
RED-BREASTED NUTHATCH (*Sitta canadensis*)
LENGTH 4.5 in (11 cm)   WEIGHT 0.4 oz (0.01 kg)

p. 256

Description Black (male) or gray (female) crown, white eyebrow, black eyeline, rusty below
Habitat Mixed pine and hardwood forests; pine flatwoods
Range North and central Florida

Jan	Feb	Mar	Apr	May	June	July	Aug	Sep	Oct	Nov	Dec

This typically northern species is smaller than the White-breasted Nuthatch.

Reddish underparts, smaller bill, and black eyestripe set the Red-breasted Nuthatch apart. Females and juveniles are a lighter buff underneath. It feeds along branches and trunks in a variety of positions. The call is more nasal and does not carry as far as that of the White-breasted Nuthatch. Extreme north Florida provides the haunts for this bird, especially during harsh winters. However, it is never common in the state. Red-breasted Nuthatches can be looked for between October and April, but usually during especially cold weather. It prefers pine woods where it can be seen extracting seeds from cones.

FAMILY *Sittidae: Nuthatches*
WHITE-BREASTED NUTHATCH (*Sitta carolinensis*)
LENGTH 5.5 in (14 cm)   WEIGHT 0.7 oz (0.02 kg)

p. 256

Other names Florida Nuthatch, Sapsucker
Description Black crown, white face and underparts
Habitat Mesic hammocks; mixed pine and hardwood forests; pine flatwoods; sandhills
Range North and central Florida

Jan	Feb	Mar	Apr	May	June	July	Aug	Sep	Oct	Nov	Dec

This is our largest nuthatch; it has blue-gray upperparts, black crown and upper neck, stout, needle-like bill, and black eye surrounded by white. Like most nuthatches, the White-breasted spends a considerable amount of time upside down foraging for insects along branches and tree trunks. It is often detected by its call, a nasal *yank-yank*. Formerly widespread in Florida, it has virtually disappeared as a breeding species except in the Red Hills region of the Panhandle, as indicated on the range map, but still occurs in winter. White-breasted Nuthatches once nested in a variety of woodlands north of Lake Okeechobee. Nests are placed in tree cavities made by other birds or sometimes in cavities that they make themselves in rotten wood. Eggs, numbering four to seven, are laid in March or April. At other times they are occasionally seen in south Florida. During fall and winter the most important food is large mast such as acorns and hickory nuts. The meat of these large seeds is obtained by wedging the nut in a crevice and hammering away the outer covering. A variety of smaller seeds and fruits is also eaten. Insect food includes beetles, spiders, moths, ants, and other bark dwellers.

FAMILY *Sittidae: Nuthatches*

BROWN-HEADED NUTHATCH (*Sitta pusilla*)

p. 256

LENGTH 4.5 in (11 cm)   WEIGHT 0.4 oz (0.01 kg)

Other names Cha-cha, Gray-headed Nuthatch, Squeeze-bird

Description Brown head, gray back, whitish throat, buff-gray below

Habitat Pine flatwoods; sandhills

Range Statewide

Jan	Feb	Mar	Apr	May	June	July	Aug	Sep	Oct	Nov	Dec

This inhabitant of Florida's open pine forests is our smallest nuthatch. It nests through-out the state but exhibits a sporadic distribution in south Florida, as indicated on the range map. The species was recently reintroduced to Everglades National Park. A pale gray spot behind the neck separates the brown head from gray back. Underparts are white. The call is a rapid series of mechanical twitterings, which is an aid to locating feeding family groups. Brown-headed Nuthatches are cavity nesters. They excavate their own holes—especially in pine trees—or use abandoned woodpecker holes, fence posts, or boxes. A clutch consists of four to six white, brown-flecked eggs usually laid in March or April, but sometimes as early as February. The Brown-headed Nuthatch feeds on a variety of wood-boring and bark-inhabiting insects and other invertebrates as well as pine seeds. Its preferred flatwoods habitat is often the home of the Red-cockaded Woodpecker.

FAMILY *Certhiidae: Creepers*

BROWN CREEPER (*Certhia americana*)

p. 256

LENGTH 5 in (13 cm)   WEIGHT 0.3 oz (0.01 kg)

Description Brown above, streaked with white; thin decurved bill; white below

Habitat Mesic hammocks; mixed pine and hardwood forests; pine flat-woods; sandhills

Range North Florida

Jan	Feb	Mar	Apr	May	June	July	Aug	Sep	Oct	Nov	Dec

The mottled brown upper surfaces of the Brown Creeper blend with the rough bark surfaces on which it feeds. Stiff tail feathers assist the creeper in its circling ascent searching for bark-dwelling insects, spiders, and other arthropods. The under-sides are white and the bill is narrow and down-curved. The call is a single, high-pitched *seee*. The Brown Creeper is a winter resident of north Florida's woodlands from October through March. Because of its habits and coloration it probably is easily overlooked.

Family *Troglodytidae: Wrens*

CAROLINA WREN (*Thryothorus ludovicianus*)　　　　p. 257
Length 5.5 in (14 cm)　　Weight 0.7 oz (0.02 kg)

Other names Florida Wren

Description Rufous-brown above, white eyebrows, buff below

Habitat Xeric scrub; hardwood swamps; cypress swamps; mesic hammocks; mixed pine and hardwood forests; urban environments; pine flatwoods; sandhills; agricultural environments

Range Statewide

| Jan | Feb | Mar | Apr | May | June | July | Aug | Sep | Oct | Nov | Dec |

This is one of our most abundant and widespread woodland birds. More often heard than seen, the bell-like *tea-kettle, tea-kettle, tea-kettle* song often is the best way of finding the Carolina Wren during any season. Largest of the Florida wrens, it is reddish-brown above, buff below, with a white throat and eyestripe. This year-round resident is a cavity-nester that makes use of small tree holes, upturned roots, open nest boxes, hanging plants, and an unexpected array of human-made objects from hanging laundry to old shoes. The nesting season extends from late February into July or August. Nests are an oven-shaped ball of fine material on a foundation of large leaves and twigs. Three to six white eggs with red-brown spotting are laid, and as many as three broods may be raised by a single pair each year. Carolina Wrens are woodland birds inhabiting dense understory vegetation. They are also very tolerant of human activity, provided nest sites are not disturbed. Food consists almost entirely of insects.

Family *Troglodytidae: Wrens*

BEWICK'S WREN (*Thryomanes bewickii*)　　　　p. 257
Length 5 in (13 cm)　　Weight 0.28–0.42 oz (0.007–0.011 kg)

Description Brownish-gray above, gray below; white eyebrow stripe; white in outer tail feathers

Habitat Mesic hammocks; mixed pine and hardwood forests

Range North Florida

| Jan | Feb | Mar | Apr | May | June | July | Aug | Sep | Oct | Nov | Dec |

This very rare winter visitor is slightly smaller than the Carolina Wren, with white undersides, darker brown upperparts, white eyestripe, and long, fan-shaped tail ending in white spots. Bewick's Wrens have occurred in central and north Florida from October through March, but have decreased in recent years to the point that it may be extirpated in the state. Most records are from the Panhandle. Winter habitats are similar to those of the Carolina Wren, but it seems to prefer relatively hilly country. Insects make up the bulk of the diet.

FAMILY *Troglodytidae: Wrens*
HOUSE WREN (*Troglodytes aedon*)
LENGTH 5 in (13 cm)   WEIGHT 0.4 oz (0.01 kg)

p. 257

Other names Eastern House Wren, Jenny Wren
Description Brown upperparts with fine barring on wings and tail, grayish-white below
Habitat Xeric scrub; mesic hammocks; mixed pine and hardwood forests; urban environments; pine flatwoods; sandhills
Range Statewide

| Jan | Feb | Mar | Apr | May | June | July | Aug | Sep | Oct | Nov | Dec |

House Wrens are common winter visitors throughout Florida from October to April. The drab brown upperparts are marked with subtle black barring. Light gray underparts are barred from lower belly to tail. The mouselike House Wren is common in fence rows, brush piles, suburbs, and in a variety of woodlands. A distinctive chattering call often gives away this small bird's presence. Food consists mainly of insects.

FAMILY *Troglodytidae: Wrens*
WINTER WREN (*Troglodytes troglodytes*)
LENGTH 4 in (10 cm)   WEIGHT 0.3 oz (0.01 kg)

p. 257

Other names Eastern Winter Wren
Description Dark brown above, paler below; heavy barring on flanks; buff eyebrow
Habitat Mesic hammocks; mixed pine and hardwood forests
Range North and central Florida

| Jan | Feb | Mar | Apr | May | June | July | Aug | Sep | Oct | Nov | Dec |

This, our smallest wren, has an extremely stubby tail. Similar in markings to the House Wren, the Winter Wren exhibits more dark barring on the belly. It is seldom seen south of Gainesville, and is uncommon elsewhere in the state. Winter Wrens usually visit between October and March. This secretive bird inhabits a variety of woodlands, searching through shadowy brush piles and dense vegetation for insects.

FAMILY *Troglodytidae: Wrens*
SEDGE WREN (*Cistothorus platensis*)
LENGTH 4.5 in (11 cm)   WEIGHT 0.3 oz (0.01 kg)

p. 257

Other names Short-billed Marsh Wren
Description Brown-tan above, streaked head and back, buff-orange below
Habitat Salt marshes; dry prairies; wet prairies and marshes; agricultural environments
Range Statewide

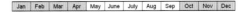

| Jan | Feb | Mar | Apr | May | June | July | Aug | Sep | Oct | Nov | Dec |

Sedge Wrens are common winter residents in Florida and may be seen in a variety of grassy wetlands and dry fields both inland and coastal from

October through April. Rarely, they are seen during summer. Occasionally, drier pastures and fields will contain numerous birds. Sedge Wrens exhibit finer white streaking on the back than Marsh Wrens, and a less distinct eye line. Underparts are mostly buff. When disturbed, Sedge Wrens will flutter a short distance before disappearing into thick grassy cover. Foods are mostly insects.

FAMILY *Troglodytidae: Wrens*

MARSH WREN (*Cistothorus palustris*)　　　　　　　　　　　　p. 257

LENGTH 5 in (13 cm)　　WEIGHT 0.4 oz (0.01 kg)

Other names Long-billed Marsh Wren, Tomtit
Description Dark brown, gray brown, or rusty brown upperparts with white streaks on back, whitish below, white eyebrow
Habitat Salt marshes; freshwater marshes in winter and during migration
Range Statewide, mostly coastal

Jan	Feb	Mar	Apr	May	June	July	Aug	Sep	Oct	Nov	Dec

In Florida, the Marsh Wren inhabits salt marshes on both the Gulf and Atlantic coasts. The dominance of mangrove in south Florida restricts these small wrens to the northern two-thirds of the state. The Marsh Wren is mostly brown above with white eye line, black upper back streaked with white, and mostly white undersides. The breeding wren of our northeastern coast is a dull gray-brown color; that of the Gulf coast subspecies is dark brown. In winter the lighter brown or reddish-brown-plumaged birds are from northern populations and also occur in freshwater marshes. The song consists of a series of bubbly gurgles ending in a trill. Permanent Florida residents build a large, globe-shaped nest made of marsh grasses and attached to stems of *Spartina* or *Juncus*. Pairs of Marsh Wrens often nest in a clumped arrangement, leaving apparently suitable habitat vacant. Several "dummy" or courtship nests are made by the male but lack the lining of finer grasses and feathers. Eggs are brown with dark spots and number three to five. Food consists almost entirely of insects and spiders, with an occasional snail or other small invertebrate.

FAMILY *Pycnonotidae: Bulbuls*

RED-WHISKERED BULBUL (*Pycnonotus jocosus*)

LENGTH 7 in (18 cm)　　WEIGHT 1 oz (0.03 kg)

Description Large black crest, red ear patch, red undertail coverts
Habitat Urban environments
Range Southeast Florida

p. 254

Jan	Feb	Mar	Apr	May	June	July	Aug	Sep	Oct	Nov	Dec

This is one of Florida's more picturesque exotic birds. An inhabitant of greater Miami-Dade suburbs and parks, the Red-whiskered Bulbul is a native of Asia. Its establishment in south Florida followed intentional releases or escapes from captivity in 1960, an origin shared with most of the state's exotic avifauna. Red-whiskered Bulbuls are about the size of Eastern Phoebes. A flycatcher-like bill, long black crest, red ear patch, red undertail coverts, brown upperparts, and white underparts distinguish this species. Immature birds have brown crests and lack red ear patches. Males sing a distinctive musical song of rising and falling notes. Nesting begins in early February after the breakup of large winter roosts. Nests are composed of woven grasses, plant fibers, and bits of refuse. Bulbuls use a variety of small trees and shrubs characteristic of Miami-Dade suburbs. Its breeding range is indicated on the range map. This new Florida resident depends in part on a wide assortment of exotic fruits such as Brazilian pepper, figs, lantana, jasmine, loquat, and blossoms such as bottlebrush, melaleuca, coconut palm, cecropias, and umbrella trees. A variety of insects is also eaten. Fears that this introduced bird may become an agricultural pest have not materialized to date.

FAMILY *Regulidae: Kinglets*
GOLDEN-CROWNED KINGLET (*Regulus satrapa*) p. 252
LENGTH 4 in (10 cm)   WEIGHT 0.2 oz (0.01 kg)

Description Tiny; orange or yellow striped crown bordered by black, whitish underparts, two white wing bars

Habitat Hardwood swamps; cypress swamps; mesic hammocks; mixed pine and hardwood forests; pine flatwoods; sandhills

Range North Florida

Jan	Feb	Mar	Apr	May	June	July	Aug	Sep	Oct	Nov	Dec

Kinglets are tiny birds, about the size of gnatcatchers, with much shorter tails and bills. The Golden-crowned Kinglet is strictly a winter visitor seen most commonly in the Panhandle from October through March. It is absent from south Florida during winter. Greenish upperparts are highlighted with black wings, white wing bars, and striped crown terminating with a brightly colored patch: orange in the male, yellow in the female. Underparts are a dull white. The call is an extremely high-pitched *tsee* that may be difficult to detect. The Golden-crowned Kinglet seems always to be in motion. It feeds primarily upon small forest-dwelling insects.

FAMILY *Regulidae: Kinglets*
RUBY-CROWNED KINGLET (*Regulus calendula*) p. 252
LENGTH 4 in (10 cm)   WEIGHT 0.2 oz (0.01 kg)

Description Olive-green back, two white wing bars, incomplete eye ring, yellowish-gray underparts

Habitat Hardwood swamps; cypress swamps; mesic hammocks; mixed pine and hardwood forests; pine flatwoods; sandhills

Range Statewide

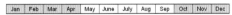

Jan	Feb	Mar	Apr	May	June	July	Aug	Sep	Oct	Nov	Dec

This small active bird is a common winter visitor throughout Florida woodlands. Similar in size to the Golden-crowned Kinglet, the Ruby-crowned Kinglet is greenish above, pale below, with white wing bars, and no distinct facial marks except for a bold white eye-ring. The ruby crown of the male is rarely seen in the field. A two-note, wrenlike call and a habit of flicking its wings are characteristic behaviors. It often associates with chickadees, titmice, and warblers in mixed feeding flocks. Ruby-crowned Kinglets appear in a variety of forest types in early October and may remain through April. Food consists mainly of small insects.

FAMILY *Regulidae: Kinglets*
BLUE-GRAY GNATCATCHER (*Polioptila caerulea*)   p. 252
LENGTH 4.5 in (11 cm)   WEIGHT 0.2 oz (0.01 kg)

Description Tiny; blue-gray above, white below; white eye ring; long black tail with white outer feathers

Habitat Hardwood swamps; cypress swamps; mesic hammocks; mixed pine and hardwood forests; urban environments; pine flatwoods; sandhills

Range Statewide

Jan	Feb	Mar	Apr	May	June	July	Aug	Sep	Oct	Nov	Dec

The Blue-gray Gnatcatcher has often been described as a miniature mockingbird. The male is bluish-gray above with dark wings; long, black tail with white outer tail feathers; black forehead; white eye ring and white undersides. Females and immatures lack black on the head and have a duller bluish cast above. This diminutive forest-dweller is at home in a number of forest types, from live oak hammocks to pine flatwoods and willow swamps. Nests are compact cups of woven grasses, leaves, spider webs, and lichen straddling a horizontal twig. The four to five eggs, bluish with fine brown dots, are laid in April or May. Gnatcatchers are extremely active birds and can be observed cocking and fanning their long tails while calling or pursuing small foliage-dwelling insects. The call is a high-pitched *tsee,* and it often mimics other bird species. South Florida is an important wintering range for many northern gnatcatchers.

FAMILY *Turdidae: Thrushes*
EASTERN BLUEBIRD (*Sialia sialis*)   p. 258
LENGTH 7 in (18 cm)   WEIGHT 1.1 oz (0.03 kg)

Other names Florida Bluebird

Description Blue above, reddish-brown throat and breast, white belly; female duller and grayer; juveniles spotted

Habitat Mixed pine and hardwood forests; pine flatwoods

Range Statewide

Jan	Feb	Mar	Apr	May	June	July	Aug	Sep	Oct	Nov	Dec

In Florida, bluebirds are characteristic of dry pinelands where nest cavities are available. With extensive timber harvesting throughout the state's extensive pinewoods, natural cavities have become less available. However, nest boxes erected in suitable habitats are used readily by these attractive Florida residents. The Eastern Bluebird is less common in extreme south Florida but it was recently reintroduced into Everglades National Park. In the male, bright blue upperparts contrast with the robin-red throat and chest, and white belly. Females are duller overall with a grayish head. During the breeding season from March through June the distinctive *churlee* or *cheerily* song can be heard. Three to five pale blue eggs are laid on a mat of pine needles or grass. Two clutches may be raised each year by the same pair. Bluebirds are fond of sitting on tall exposed perches and are frequently seen gathered above roadsides along telephone wires. During winter, Florida's resident population is augmented by an influx of northern migrants. Food consists of grasshoppers, caterpillars, and other insects during spring and summer, while small fruits dominate the winter diet.

FAMILY *Turdidae: Thrushes*
VEERY (*Catharus fuscescens*)
p. 258
LENGTH 7 in (18 cm)   WEIGHT 1.1 oz (0.03 kg)
Other names Wilson's Thrush
Description Reddish-brown above, gray sides, buff on breast with light spotting
Habitat Mesic hammocks; mixed pine and hardwood forests
Range Statewide

Jan	Feb	Mar	Apr	May	June	July	Aug	Sep	Oct	Nov	Dec

The Veery is a light or tawny-brown thrush with fine, indistinct breast spots and a white belly. These migrants are seen chiefly in spring during April and May and in fall during September and October. It is occasionally heard singing its flutelike, downward-spiraling song in spring. Veeries inhabit mixed deciduous hardwoods and are usually seen on or near the ground. Food habits are similar to other thrushes—a combination of fruits, seeds, and insects.

FAMILY *Turdidae: Thrushes*
GRAY-CHEEKED THRUSH (*Catharus minimus*)
p. 258
LENGTH 7 in (18 cm)   WEIGHT 1.2 oz (0.03 kg)
Description Plain olive-brown above, gray cheeks, indistinct gray eye ring, spotted breast
Habitat Mesic hammocks; mixed pine and hardwood forests
Range Statewide

Jan	Feb	Mar	Apr	May	June	July	Aug	Sep	Oct	Nov	Dec

The Gray-cheeked Thrush is similar to Swainson's Thrush but has grayish cheek patches and lacks any buff coloration. The white undersides are heavily spotted on the breast. Immature Gray-cheeks may possess considerable buff coloring and can be mistaken for Swainson's Thrushes in the fall. Gray-cheeked Thrushes can be seen throughout the state in a variety of wooded areas and are regular visitors during migration at Ft. De Soto Park in Pinellas County and the Dry Tortugas, among other places. Spring birds may be seen in April and May while fall birds pass through the state in September and October. Its song, occasionally heard during spring migration, is series of descending flutelike notes followed by a rising note at the end. Foods include small fruits and insects. In 1995, this species was divided by the American Ornithological Union to recognize a new but very similar species, the **Bicknell's Thrush** (*Catharus bicknelli*). This species nests in the northeastern United States and southeastern Canada, and, like the Gray-cheeked Thrush, probably migrates through Florida in spring and fall. It is somewhat smaller than the Gray-cheeked Thrush and has more yellow at the base of the lower bill. The Bicknell's Thrush winters in the Greater Antilles.

FAMILY *Turdidae: Thrushes*
SWAINSON'S THRUSH (*Catharus ustulatus*)
p. 258

LENGTH 7 in (18 cm)   WEIGHT 1.1 oz (0.03 kg)

Other names Olive-backed Thrush

Description Plain olive-brown above, orange-buff on throat and side of head, buff eye ring, spotted breast

Habitat Hardwood swamps; cypress swamps; mesic hammocks; mixed pine and hardwood forests; pine flatwoods

Range Statewide

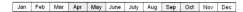

This spring and fall migrant is a rather plain thrush. Olive-brown above and white below, the Swainson's Thrush has a streaked breast and distinct buff eye rings and cheeks. Its habits are somewhat secretive but it can be looked for in moist woodlands and swamp edges from mid-April through early May, then in greater numbers from September into October. Its song is a series of ascending, high-pitched notes that can occasionally be heard in spring. A variety of fruits and insects constitutes this bird's diet.

FAMILY *Turdidae: Thrushes*
HERMIT THRUSH (*Catharus guttatus*)
p. 258

LENGTH 7 in (18 cm)   WEIGHT 1.1 oz (0.03 kg)

Other names Eastern Hermit Thrush, Swamp Sparrow

Description Olive-brown above, reddish tail, spotted breast

Habitat Hardwood swamps; mesic hammocks; mixed pine and hardwood forests

Range Statewide

This common winter visitor is brown above with a moderately spotted breast and a rusty tail that is often bobbed up and down. The Hermit Thrush arrives in late October and may remain in Florida until early May. Single birds can be looked for foraging on the ground within moist woodlands and thickets. Its complex, flutelike song of three or four phrases, each preceded by a long, lower-pitched note, can occasionally be heard in spring. They are usually seen singly or in pairs. They are curious and often can be approached. Foods include insects such as beetles, ants, and grasshoppers as well as fruits of dogwood, holly, and poison ivy. They sometimes hover over their food.

FAMILY *Turdidae: Thrushes*
WOOD THRUSH (*Hylocichla mustelina*)
p. 258
LENGTH 8 in (20 cm)   WEIGHT 1.7 oz (0.05 kg)

Other names Brown Thrush, Swamp Sparrow, Branch Bird

Description Rufous-brown head and nape, olive-brown back and tail, large brown spots on white breast

Habitat Hardwood swamps; mesic hammocks; mixed pine and hardwood forests

Range North and central Florida

Jan	Feb	Mar	Apr	May	June	July	Aug	Sep	Oct	Nov	Dec

The Wood Thrush is similar in appearance to the Brown Thrasher but has a shorter tail and bill. In addition the head is redder than the back and the breast spots are dark and conspicuous. It is somewhat larger than other thrushes that migrate through Florida. The song is a varied, melodious flutelike series of rounded phrases. Breeding birds nest from April to June in deciduous woodlands across north Florida, but they are nowhere abundant in the state. Nests, constructed of twigs, leaves, paper shreds, and plastic are lined with mud, pine needles, and grass, and usually placed in a shrub, but can be as high as 50 feet (15.24 meters) high. Clutches average four greenish-blue eggs. Spring migrants may be seen from March through April, while fall birds usually pass through during October. Foods are similar to those eaten by other thrushes.

FAMILY *Turdidae: Thrushes*
AMERICAN ROBIN (*Turdus migratorius*)
p.258
LENGTH 10 in (25 cm)   WEIGHT 2.7 oz (0.08 kg)

Other names Robin Redbreast

Description Gray-brown above, gray or black head, pale to bright russet breast, incomplete white spectacles, juveniles have speckled breast and back

Habitat Hardwood swamps; cypress swamps; mesic hammocks; mixed pine and hardwood forests; urban environments; pine flatwoods; agricultural environments

Range Statewide

Jan	Feb	Mar	Apr	May	June	July	Aug	Sep	Oct	Nov	Dec

The American Robin is one of Florida's most abundant winter visitors and is becoming an increasingly common nester around some north Florida cities such as Jacksonville, Tallahassee, and Pensacola. Dark gray upperparts, red-orange breast, and yellow bill distinguish this large, familiar songbird. Immatures are spotted below and lighter above. The song is a melodious series of notes: *cheerily-cheery-cheerio*. Nests are placed on horizontal tree limbs or on suitable structures associated with buildings and are constructed of a mixture of mud, grass, and twigs. Three or four greenish-blue eggs may be laid from March through June. Huge flocks are seen frequently throughout Florida during winter as Robins search for abundant food supplies. Winter foods include fruits of swamp tupelo, Brazilian pepper, dahoon holly, gallberry, cabbage palm, sugarberry, mistletoe, and poison ivy. Some birds occasionally become intoxicated after eating fermented fruits. Insects and invertebrates (chiefly earthworms) are eaten more frequently in spring and summer. Winter residents may be seen from November through April. They are often seen in yards pursuing their running and stopping eating style.

FAMILY *Mimidae: Mockingbirds, Thrashers, and Allies*

GRAY CATBIRD (*Dumetella carolinensis*)

p. 257

LENGTH 8 in (20 cm)   WEIGHT 1.3 oz (0.04 kg)

Other names Black Mockingbird

Description All gray, black cap, rufous undertail coverts

Habitat Xeric scrub; hardwood swamps; cypress swamps; mesic hammocks; mixed pine and hardwood forests; urban environments; pine flatwoods

Range Statewide

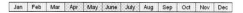

| Jan | Feb | Mar | Apr | May | June | July | Aug | Sep | Oct | Nov | Dec |

This often inconspicuous bird is most abundant during migration but also nests sporadically in north Florida. Because of their secretive habits, Catbirds are more often heard than seen, uttering a distinctive catlike *meow*. Catbirds possess their own musical, jumbled song but are not adept imitators like the closely related Mockingbird. Plumage is mostly dark gray with black tail, black cap, and reddish undertail coverts. The preferred habitats are dense tangles of greenbriar, fetterbush, or other thick growth often associated with large swamps. It breeds locally in scattered locations in extreme north Florida. The nests are loosely constructed cups located near the ground in dense shrubs. Blue eggs number three or four and are usually laid in April or May. Food is mainly vegetable and includes fruits of dogwood, greenbriar, wild grape, and mulberry.

FAMILY *Mimidae: Mockingbirds, Thrashers, and Allies*

NORTHERN MOCKINGBIRD (*Mimus polyglottos*)

p. 257

LENGTH 10 in (25 cm)   WEIGHT 1.7 oz (0.05 kg)

Other names Mockingbird, Eastern Mockingbird

Description Gray above, black wings with white wing bars and white patches, long tail with white outer feathers

Habitat Xeric scrub; dry prairies; mesic hammocks; mixed pine and hardwood forests; urban environments; pine flatwoods; sandhills; agricultural environments

Range Statewide

| Jan | Feb | Mar | Apr | May | June | July | Aug | Sep | Oct | Nov | Dec |

The widely distributed and well-known Mockingbird is Florida's official state bird. A resident of habitat edges, city parks, suburbs, orange groves, and other agricultural areas, Mockingbirds have benefited from humanity's increasing presence in the state. Often described as "ordinary-looking," Mockingbirds are gray above with darker wings and tail, white wing bars and outer tail feathers, and whitish underneath. Perhaps its best known trait is the ability to imitate nearly any sound familiar to it. The calls, usually repeated in threes, most often imitate other birds but may also include domestic animals and a variety of human-made sounds. In spring, the male may sing long into the evening, especially on moonlit nights. Nests, constructed of small twigs, are lined with rootlets or other fine material and usually located within a dense, concealing shrub. Eggs number three to five and are greenish-blue with brown spots and splotches. The breeding season extends from March to August, with some pairs raising two or more clutches. Mockingbirds are vigorous defenders of their nests and the areas around them. Foods include some insects and other invertebrates, and fruits such as greenbriar, dahoon holly, gallberry, Brazilian pepper, elderberry, and cabbage palm. A similar species, the **Bahama Mockingbird** (*Mimus gundlachii*) occasionally appears in southeastern Florida, and a male has built nests on Key West (no reproduction recorded as yet). Its habits are similar to the Northern Mockingbird but it does not mimic other birds and has a more abrupt song with four or five phrases.

FAMILY *Mimidae: Mockingbirds, Thrashers, and Allies*
BROWN THRASHER (*Toxostoma rufum*)   p. 257
LENGTH 11 in (28 cm)   WEIGHT 2.4 oz (0.07 kg)

Other names Brown Thrush, Sandy Mocker, Thrash, Fence Corner Bird
Description Rufous-brown above, white wing bars, gray face, white below streaked with brown; long tail
Habitat Mesic hammocks; mixed pine and hardwood forests; urban environments; sandhills; agricultural environments
Range Statewide

Jan	Feb	Mar	Apr	May	June	July	Aug	Sep	Oct	Nov	Dec

Although it resembles some of our wintering thrushes, the Brown Thrasher is another relative of the Mockingbird. Rusty brown upperparts, tawny wing bars highlighted with black, heavy brown streaking on whitish belly, and long bill and tail distinguish both sexes of this common Florida resident. Brown Thrashers are nearly as skilled at imitating as Mockingbirds, but do not imitate as frequently. Phrases are usually repeated only twice and in a much more musical voice. Nesting occurs in April or May when three to five bluish-white eggs marked with fine brown dots are laid. The nest, constructed with twigs, leaves, and rootlets is usually placed in dense shrubbery or thickets. Brown Thrashers are quite tolerant of humans and may be found in suburban backyards, city parks, citrus groves, and other agricultural lands. In less disturbed settings it is a bird of the edge, inhabiting vegetation on the borders of woodlands and clearings. Foods consist of locally abundant insects and wild fruits.

FAMILY *Sturnidae: Starlings*
EUROPEAN STARLING (*Sturnus vulgaris*)   p. 253
LENGTH 8.5 in (22 cm)   WEIGHT 3.0 oz (0.09 kg)

Other names Blackbird

Description Iridescent black, yellow bill, short tail (summer) or black plumage speckled with white, dark bill (winter)

Habitat Urban environments; agricultural environments

Range Statewide

Jan	Feb	Mar	Apr	May	June	July	Aug	Sep	Oct	Nov	Dec

Starlings are glossy, black birds with needle-like yellow bills, short tails, and reddish legs. Winter birds are generously speckled with white, and the bill is dark. Immature birds are grayish-brown overall. Starlings were introduced into New York City in 1890 and have since spread throughout the North American continent. In Florida they are residents of cities, suburbs, and agricultural lands, where they nest in woodpecker holes or human-made cavities. Twigs, paper, plastic, feathers, and other materials line the nest, where four to seven bluish-green eggs are laid. The nesting season extends from March to July. This aggressive exotic is capable of displacing native cavity nesters from natural and human-made structures. During winter, Starlings may congregate in the thousands, often with other blackbirds. These large, noisy flocks may occur in backyard shade trees, on power lines, or on farm structures. Starlings often imitate other birds but their voice also includes a variety of whistles, squeaks, and clicks. Foods eaten include grasshoppers, earthworms, grains, cherries, and other fruits.

FAMILY *Sturnidae: Starlings*
COMMON MYNA (*Acridotheres tristis*)
LENGTH 9.7 in (25 cm)   WEIGHT 3.7 oz (0.1 kg)

Description Brownish body, white under the tail, dark head with yellow starling-like bill and eye patch, yellow legs

Habitat Urban and suburban yards, parks, and campuses

Range South Florida

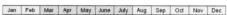

Jan	Feb	Mar	Apr	May	June	July	Aug	Sep	Oct	Nov	Dec

This bird is native to parts of the Middle East, India, and Southeast Asia. It began breeding in Florida in the early 1980s, and now appears to be established as a resident in the southeastern areas of the state. Breeding range is indicated on the range map. It is about the size of a European Starling, but has dark brown plumage, black head and neck, and yellow skin on the face and feet. It is white under the wings and tail. This exotic species is most often associated with agricultural lands and suburbs. It can be a nuisance in areas outside of Florida where it congregates in large numbers. Common Mynas exhibit highly variable songs and vocalizations. They forage on the ground for insects and fruits, and will nest in signs and other artificial cavities. The larger **Hill Myna** (*Gracula religiosa*) has been established in the Miami-Dade area for about 50 years, but has not spread as far as the Common Myna. It is black with white wing patches and yellow wattles. It is a popular cage bird that is skilled at mimicking the human voice. Its diet is primarily fruit obtained in trees and shrubs, and it nests in natural cavities.

FAMILY *Motacillidae: Wagtails and Pipits*
AMERICAN PIPIT (*Anthus rubescens*)
p. 252
LENGTH 6.5 in (17 cm)   WEIGHT 0.8 oz (0.02 kg)

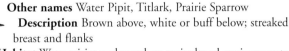

Other names Water Pipit, Titlark, Prairie Sparrow
Description Brown above, white or buff below; streaked breast and flanks
Habitat Wet prairies and marshes; agricultural environments
Range Statewide

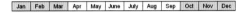

| Jan | Feb | Mar | Apr | May | June | July | Aug | Sep | Oct | Nov | Dec |

Pipits are easily overlooked ground-dwelling birds that superficially resemble sparrows. Buff undersides with brown streaking on breast contrast with greenish-brown upperparts. A thin bill and longish tail bordered in white distinguish the American Pipit from sparrows. Migrants arrive during October and usually depart by March, but are fairly common winter visitors in Florida. Pipits inhabit open landscapes such as plowed fields, lake edges, mud flats, and golf courses in north and central Florida, where they can be seen walking, not hopping, in search of food. The call, a repeated *pip-pit,* is uttered while taking flight or flying. Pipits often feed in flocks of several dozen on agricultural pests such as weevils, beetles, and grasshoppers, as well as weed seeds, grains, and snails and slugs. Occasionally, **Sprague's Pipit** (*Anthus spragueii*) appears in Florida. One has wintered off and on along the causeway to St. George Island, and more recently at the Apalachicola Airport. It is generally lighter in color than the American Pipit, with a scaly-patterned back, a pale buff face with distinct dark eye, and whitish underparts with a buff wash and some streaking.

FAMILY *Bombycillidae: Waxwings*
CEDAR WAXWING (*Bombycilla cedrorum*)
p. 252
LENGTH 7 in (18 cm)   WEIGHT 1.1 oz (0.03 kg)

Other names Cedar Bird, Seal, Hammerlock, Cherry Robin, Canadian Robin
Description Brownish-tan crest and back, black mask, yellowish belly, yellow-tipped tail
Habitat Hardwood swamps; cypress swamps; mesic hammocks; mixed pine and hardwood forests; urban environments; pine flatwoods; sandhills
Range Statewide

| Jan | Feb | Mar | Apr | May | June | July | Aug | Sep | Oct | Nov | Dec |

The Cedar Waxwing is a characteristic winter bird seen in large flocks from suburban backyards to deep, remote swamps throughout the state. A variety of distinctive markings and its call, a high-pitched buzzy squeal, make this elegant bird nearly unmistakable. The light brown body is highlighted with a crest, black mask, yellow belly, and yellow-tipped tail. Wing feathers of some adults bear a red spot that looks like nail polish. Immature birds resemble adults but are streaked above and below. In Florida, Cedar Waxwings are most common in winter and spring when they can be seen in large flocks. They often arrive as early as mid-October and linger until May, but this pattern varies from year to year. Fruits are the mainstay of its diet and include those of the sugarberry, mulberry, holly, cedar, cherry, and greenbriar.

Family *Parulidae: Wood Warblers*
BLUE-WINGED WARBLER (*Vermivora pinus*)   p. 259
Length 4.75 in (12 cm)   Weight 0.3 oz (0.008 kg)

Description Yellow underparts, blue-gray wings with two white wing bars, and a distinct black eye line (migration)

Habitat Mesic hammock; mixed pine and hardwood forests; shrub communities

Range Statewide

Jan	Feb	Mar	Apr	May	June	July	Aug	Sep	Oct	Nov	Dec

This uncommon spring and fall migrant exhibits yellow underparts, blue-gray wings with two white wing bars, and a distinct black eye line. It has been seen throughout the state during migration in a variety of woodlands and shrub communities. Its diet is primarily caterpillars and other small invertebrates. In its Midwest and New England breeding grounds, the Blue-winged Warbler regularly interbreeds with the Golden-winged Warbler. Offspring of these pairings are either the **Brewster's Warbler** (showing white undersides of the Golden-winged and black eye line of the Blue-winged) or **Lawrence's Warbler** (with yellow undersides of the Blue-winged and black mask of the Golden-winged). This hybridizing appears to be negatively affecting the more localized Golden-winged Warbler in its breeding range.

Family *Parulidae: Wood Warblers*
GOLDEN-WINGED WARBLER (*Vermivora chrysoptera*)   p. 259
Length 4.75 in (12 cm)   Weight 0.3 oz (0.08 kg)

Description White underparts, black throat and cheek patch (gray in the female), yellow wing patch (less distinct in the female), and yellow crown (migration)

Habitat Mesic hammock; mixed pine and hardwood forests; shrub communities

Range Statewide

Jan	Feb	Mar	Apr	May	June	July	Aug	Sep	Oct	Nov	Dec

The Golden-winged Warbler is a very uncommon spring and fall migrant throughout Florida. White underparts, black throat and cheek patch (gray in the female), yellow wing patch (less distinct in the female), and yellow crown are good field marks. This warbler feeds in small trees and shrubs and may often hang upside down while probing dead leaves for insects. Because of range-wide population declines, the Golden-winged Warbler is under consideration for federal listing as a threatened species. Hybrids with the Blue-winged Warbler (see previous account) have been observed throughout the state.

FAMILY *Parulidae: Wood Warblers*
TENNESSEE WARBLER (*Vermivora peregrina*)
p. 260
LENGTH 5 in (13 cm)   WEIGHT 0.4 oz (0.01 kg)

Description Olive-green above, blue-gray head, white eyebrow, white or yellowish below, white undertail coverts

Habitat Xeric scrub; mesic hammocks; mixed pine and hardwood forests; pine flatwoods; sandhills

Range Statewide

Jan	Feb	Mar	Apr	May	June	July	Aug	Sep	Oct	Nov	Dec

The Tennessee is a nondescript drab-green warbler with white eye line and yellow-green undersides. It is a common fall migrant during October and again passes through Florida in April. Tennessee Warblers use a variety of woodland and brushy habitats while hunting for insects. It also will consume seeds and small fruits.

FAMILY *Parulidae: Wood Warblers*
ORANGE-CROWNED WARBLER (*Vermivora celata*)
p. 260
LENGTH 5 in (13 cm)   WEIGHT 0.3 oz (0.01 kg)

Description Olive-green overall with yellowish underparts, incomplete eye ring, yellow undertail coverts

Habitat Mesic hammocks; mixed pine and hardwood forests; sandhills

Range Statewide

Jan	Feb	Mar	Apr	May	June	July	Aug	Sep	Oct	Nov	Dec

The Orange-crowned Warbler is greenish-gray above and below with yellow beneath the tail. The breast is faintly streaked and the bill is narrow and slightly down-curved. The orange crown is not visible in the field. The Orange-crowned Warbler is a common winter visitor and can be seen in hardwoods, especially live oaks, as well as in shrubs and tall weeds. It occasionally visits bird feeders, but normally feeds elsewhere on insects and small fruits and seeds. It occurs in Florida from late September to mid-April.

FAMILY *Parulidae: Wood Warblers*

NASHVILLE WARBLER (*Vermivora ruficapilla*)   p. 259

LENGTH 4.75 in (12 cm)   WEIGHT 0.3 oz (0.01 kg)

Description Gray head, white eye ring, yellow undersides, greenish back and wings (migration)

Habitat Mesic hammock; mixed pine and hardwood forests

Range Statewide

Jan	Feb	Mar	Apr	May	June	July	Aug	Sep	Oct	Nov	Dec

This is an uncommon visitor during fall migration and winter primarily in peninsular Florida. The adult male is yellow below, grayish-green above, with a white eye ring and no wing bars. Fall birds (most commonly seen in Florida) are similar to Common Yellowthroats in fall plumage. When seen in Florida it is usually as a single bird in a variety of upland forests with well-developed understories. It feeds mainly on insects.

FAMILY *Parulidae: Wood Warblers*

NORTHERN PARULA (*Parula americana*)   p. 261

LENGTH 4.5 in (11 cm)   WEIGHT 0.3 oz (0.01 kg)

Other names Southern Parula Warbler

Description Blue above, white wing bars, yellow throat and breast; male has rufous-orange and blue band on breast

Habitat Hardwood swamps; mesic hammocks; mixed pine and hardwood forests

Range Statewide

Jan	Feb	Mar	Apr	May	June	July	Aug	Sep	Oct	Nov	Dec

The Northern Parula is widespread in Florida and breeds south to northern Monroe County in hardwood hammocks, mixed pine/hardwood woodlands, and cypress swamps. Although it is our smallest warbler, its bright coloration and loud incessant song, described as an ascending trill increasing in volume towards an explosive *zip,* make this bird conspicuous. Upperparts are bluish with light green back, two white wing bars, and a white eye ring divided by a black eyestripe. The white belly is contrasted by a yellow breast. Reddish and blue bands highlight the adult male's breast. The nest is usually constructed within a hanging clump of Spanish moss. Eggs, numbering two to six, are white with brown spots on the large end, and are laid between early April and June. Fall migrants depart Florida as early as mid-August and begin their return in mid-February. Some Parulas also winter in Florida. Food consists primarily of caterpillars, spiders and small flying insects.

FAMILY *Parulidae: Wood Warblers*
YELLOW WARBLER (*Dendroica petechia*)
LENGTH 5 in (13 cm)   WEIGHT 0.3 oz (0.01 kg)

p. 261

Other names Cuban Golden Warbler, Wild Canary, Summer Yellow-bird

Description Bright yellow below with reddish streakings, yellow-green above (male) or duller with faint or no streaks (female)

Habitat Mangrove; hardwood swamps; agricultural environments

Range Statewide

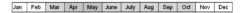

| Jan | Feb | Mar | Apr | May | June | July | Aug | Sep | Oct | Nov | Dec |

Throughout most of Florida the Yellow Warbler is encountered as a fall and spring migrant. However, the West Indies race *(D. p. gundlachi)* is a permanent resident in the Keys where it nests in mangroves—the breeding range for this race is indicated on the range map. The male's golden yellow plumage is highlighted by chestnut streaking on the breast and darker wings. Females are lemon-yellow and unstreaked below. Yellow patches on outer tail feathers help differentiate immatures from immature Hooded Warblers (white patches) and Wilson's Warblers (no patches). The song consists of three to four *sweet* notes followed by several more in rapid succession. Nests constructed of grasslike materials and finished with a soft lining are placed in a forked branch of a dense shrub or tree. The two to four blotched, white eggs are laid in April or May. Migrants are most common during the fall and can be seen from July through October. Spring migrants are seen from early March to early May. It is usually seen in willows but also in old fields and other moderately open vegetation. Yellow Warblers feed mostly on insects.

FAMILY *Parulidae: Wood Warblers*
CHESTNUT-SIDED WARBLER (*Dendroica pensylvanica*)   p. 262
LENGTH 4.5 in (11 cm)   WEIGHT 0.4 oz (0.01 kg)

Description Yellow crown, black and white face, chestnut sides and flanks, yellow wing bars (spring) or yellow-green above, yellow wing bars, chestnut flanks (fall); immatures may lack chestnut

Habitat Mesic hammocks; mixed pine and hardwood forests; sandhills; agricultural environments

Range Statewide

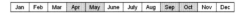

| Jan | Feb | Mar | Apr | May | June | July | Aug | Sep | Oct | Nov | Dec |

The drab fall colors of the Chestnut-sided Warbler are a sharp contrast to its colorful breeding plumage. Greenish head and back, two pale yellow wing bars, and light underparts characterize fall birds. The spring bird has a yellow crown, black eye line and whiskers, white underparts, and chestnut flanks. Females are less boldly marked but have the same pattern. Migrating Chestnut-sided Warblers are not often seen in Florida, but may be seen in mature forests, swamps, and brushy woodlands from April to May. They are generally not seen during fall. It feeds mainly on insects.

FAMILY *Parulidae: Wood Warblers*

MAGNOLIA WARBLER (*Dendroica magnolia*)

p. 261

LENGTH 5 in (13 cm)   WEIGHT 0.3 oz (0.01 kg)

Description Lemon-yellow underparts with
black streaking, gray crown, black face and back, yellow rump (spring)
or gray head and breast, olive-green above, yellow below with faint stripes
(winter)

Habitat Hardwood swamps; mesic hammocks; mixed pine and hardwood
forests

Range Statewide

Jan	Feb	Mar	Apr	May	June	July	Aug	Sep	Oct	Nov	Dec
			Apr	May				Sep	Oct		

In fall, the bright yellow and black breeding plumage of the male
Magnolia Warbler is replaced by much grayer coloring. In Florida males
exhibit yellow undersides with black flecks on the flanks, gray head with faint white eye line,
greenish back, yellow rump, white tail patches, and two white wing bars. Females are grayer overall and lack the white tail patches. Fall migrants arrive in Florida during late September on their
way to Central America. A few birds winter in extreme south Florida. Spring birds are seen occasionally in April and May. Magnolia Warblers seem partial to hardwood habitats where they hunt
insects.

FAMILY *Parulidae: Wood Warblers*

CAPE MAY WARBLER (*Dendroica tigrina*)

p. 261

LENGTH 5 in (13 cm)   WEIGHT 0.4 oz (0.01 kg)

Description Male has chestnut cheek patch, yellow collar and throat, white wing
patch, yellow rump; female lacks chestnut patch and is duller

Habitat Mesic hammocks; mixed pine and hardwood forests;
urban environments

Range Statewide

Jan	Feb	Mar	Apr	May	June	July	Aug	Sep	Oct	Nov	Dec
		Mar	Apr	May				Sep	Oct	Nov	

The burnt-orange or chestnut "ear" of the male Cape May Warbler is its
most distinctive feature. Underparts are bright yellow with heavy black
streaking. Upperparts are olive-green streaked with black. The rump is yellow and the
wings have large white wing bars. The female is duller, but also has a yellow rump, heavily
streaked breast and two white wing bars. In both sexes the bill is slightly down-curved. Cape
Mays are abundant spring migrants passing through Florida during April and May, when they are
often seen in flowering oaks and hickories. Fall migration occurs from late August through
October. A few birds spend the winter in extreme south Florida. It feeds primarily on insects and
is most frequent in deciduous woodlands.

FAMILY *Parulidae: Wood Warblers*
BLACK-THROATED BLUE WARBLER (*Dendroica caerulescens*)   p. 262
LENGTH 5 in (13 cm)   WEIGHT 0.4 oz (0.01 kg)

Description Gray-blue above; black face, throat; white wing patch (male) or olive-green above; white eyebrow, smaller wing patch (female)
Habitat Xeric scrub; hardwood swamps; cypress swamps; mesic hammocks; mixed pine and hardwood forests; urban environments; pine flatwoods
Range Statewide

Jan	Feb	Mar	Apr	May	June	July	Aug	Sep	Oct	Nov	Dec

Audubon considered the female Black-throated Blue Warbler a species distinct from the male. Olive-drab upperparts, white eye line, white wing patch and buff underparts identify the female. Males are dark blue above with black cheeks, throat and flanks, and are white below with white wing patches. The wing patches are the most consistent field mark for both sexes, although some immature females may lack these. During migration it can be seen in a variety of forest types from late August to late October and from mid-March through May. A few over-winter in south Florida. Foods are predominantly insects which are often taken on the wing.

FAMILY *Parulidae: Wood Warblers*
YELLOW-RUMPED WARBLER (*Dendroica coronata*)   p. 261
LENGTH 5.5 in (14 cm)   WEIGHT 0.5 oz (0.01 kg)

Other names Myrtle Warbler, Audubon's Warbler
Description Brownish above, white throat, yellow rump (winter)
Habitat Xeric scrub; hardwood swamps; cypress swamps; mesic hammocks; mixed pine and hardwood forests; urban environments; pine flatwoods; sandhills; agricultural environments
Range Statewide

Jan	Feb	Mar	Apr	May	June	July	Aug	Sep	Oct	Nov	Dec

The Yellow-rumped is the most abundant wintering warbler in Florida. This is in part due to its habit of feeding upon fruit of the widely distributed wax myrtle during colder months. It is a rather drab warbler with brownish upperparts, white eye line, and streaked undersides. The best field mark is the bright yellow rump patch that is characteristic of both sexes. In early spring a few males may exhibit various stages of breeding plumage development, but most birds depart Florida before completing their molt. Yellow-rumps appear in Florida during October and may remain until April. It is not unusual to encounter large flocks of this species particularly during the colder months. Under these circumstances its call, a distinctive chip, is easily identified. It is often seen with other wintering warblers, vireos, titmice and chickadees. Aside from wax myrtle fruit, insects also are eaten.

FAMILY *Parulidae: Wood Warblers*
BLACK-THROATED GREEN WARBLER (*Dendroica virens*)   p. 262
LENGTH 5 in (13 cm)   WEIGHT 0.3 oz (0.01 kg)

Description Olive-green above, yellow face, black on throat and breast (male)

Habitat Xeric scrub; hardwood swamps; mesic hammocks; mixed pine and hardwood forests; urban environments; pine flatwoods

Range Statewide

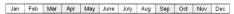

| Jan | Feb | Mar | Apr | May | June | July | Aug | Sep | Oct | Nov | Dec |

This is the only eastern warbler with a black throat and yellow cheek patches. White underparts have black-streaked flanks, upperparts are olive-green, and wings have two white wing bars. Females are similar but less boldly marked. Although the Black-throated Green Warbler nests as close as north Georgia, it is seen only briefly in most of Florida as a migrant. A few birds regularly winter in south Florida and the Keys. Spring birds may be encountered from late March to early May. In fall they migrate through from early September to late October. The Black-throated Green Warbler uses a variety of woodlands and feeds on small insects and a few small fruits.

FAMILY *Parulidae: Wood Warblers*
BLACKBURNIAN WARBLER (*Dendroica fusca*)   p. 262
LENGTH 4.5 in (11 cm)   WEIGHT 0.4 oz (0.01 kg)

Description Bright orange throat, eyebrow, and crown patch; white wing patch; black crown and back (male) or yellow instead of orange, and brownish-olive instead of black (female and fall male)

Habitat Mesic hammocks; mixed pine and hardwood forests

Range Statewide

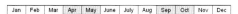

| Jan | Feb | Mar | Apr | May | June | July | Aug | Sep | Oct | Nov | Dec |

A large white wing patch and orange throat (brighter in the male) are the best field marks for the adult Blackburnian Warbler. Upperparts are black, with light undersides and streaked flanks. Immatures and adult females exhibit similar color patterns but are duller overall with two white wing bars. This is not a common bird in Florida, but can be expected in migration in September and October and in April and May. Blackburnians are seen chiefly in deciduous hardwoods while foraging for insects.

Family *Parulidae: Wood Warblers*
YELLOW-THROATED WARBLER (*Dendroica dominica*)
LENGTH 5 in (13 cm)   WEIGHT 0.3 oz (0.01 kg)

p. 262

Other names Sycamore Warbler
Description Black and white head, bright yellow throat
Habitat Mesic hammocks; mixed pine and hardwood forests; urban environments; pine flatwoods
Range Statewide

| Jan | Feb | Mar | Apr | May | June | July | Aug | Sep | Oct | Nov | Dec |

Gray upperparts are highlighted by two white wing bars, white eye line, white ear patch, and black cheeks. Underparts are white with black-streaked flanks and yellow throat and chest. The bill is long in comparison with others of the genus. The song is a series of *sweet* notes with the last three repeated more rapidly than the first three. The Yellow-throated Warbler is a common year-round resident breeding throughout the state except south of Lake Okeechobee, as indicated on the range map. It is most abundant in mixed pine-hardwood forest where it can be seen foraging along trunks and branches probing for insects. Nests are most frequently built in clumps of hanging Spanish moss. The three to five white eggs are marked on the large end with brown and lavender flecking, and are laid in April or early May. The **Sutton's Warbler** (seen only a few times in Florida) is a hybrid between the Yellow-throated Warbler and Northern Parula. This very rare form exhibits a greenish back and little streaking on flanks.

Family *Parulidae: Wood Warblers*
PINE WARBLER (*Dendroica pinus*)
LENGTH 5 in (13 cm)   WEIGHT 0.4 oz (0.01 kg)

p. 263

Other names Pine-creeping Warbler
Description Unstreaked olive-green above, yellow underparts, white wing bars, yellow eyebrow; female paler
Habitat Xeric scrub; mixed pine and hardwood forests; pine flatwoods; sandhills
Range Statewide

| Jan | Feb | Mar | Apr | May | June | July | Aug | Sep | Oct | Nov | Dec |

The male Pine Warbler is greenish above with dark wings, two white wing bars, yellow breast and streaked flanks. Females have grayish undersides while immature birds are browner above than adults. The song is a single-pitched trill—like a musical sewing machine—that carries a considerable distance. Pine Warblers may be seen hawking for flying insects or creeping, nuthatch-fashion, along pine trunks and tree limbs. During the breeding season, from March through April, Pine Warblers are virtually always associated with pine trees. At other times they are less habitat-specific. Nests are concealed cups attached to narrow branches and constructed of pine needles and grass with a lining of finer materials. The three to four eggs are white with brownish spotting on the large end. Pine Warblers are year-round residents throughout Florida. In addition to insects, a variety of small seeds also are eaten.

FAMILY *Parulidae: Wood Warblers*
PRAIRIE WARBLER (*Dendroica discolor*)
LENGTH 4.5 in (11 cm)   WEIGHT 0.3 oz (0.01 kg)

p. 263

Other names Northern Prairie Warbler,
Florida Prairie Warbler

Description Yellow-green above, yellow underparts with black
streaks on sides and face; female is paler; wags tail

Habitat Mangrove; pine flatwoods; agricultural environments

Range Statewide

| Jan | Feb | Mar | Apr | May | June | July | Aug | Sep | Oct | Nov | Dec |

The Prairie Warbler is greenish above with buff wing bars, chestnut streaking on back, a black eye line, yellow undersides, and black streaking on the flanks. Males are somewhat more brightly colored than females and also have a black crescent beneath each eye. Immatures are much duller. The song is an ascending series of flutelike *zee* notes. Its habit of tail-bobbing is a good aid to identification. The two subspecies that occur in Florida are virtually identical in appearance. Despite its name, open grasslands are not used. During the breeding season in Florida the resident Prairie Warbler subspecies (*D. d. paludicola*) is a bird of coastal mangrove swamps. However, a few birds of the eastern subspecies breed at inland locations in north Florida and in the Panhandle among shrubs and young, densely grown pine stands. The breeding ranges of both species are indicated on the range map. Nests are composed of local plant fibers and placed up to 10 feet (3 meters) in a mangrove or other shrub. The three to five white eggs are speckled brown and laid from March through May. Northern birds migrate through Florida from late July through early November and from early March to early May. Prairie Warblers feed mainly on insects.

FAMILY *Parulidae: Wood Warblers*
PALM WARBLER (*Dendroica palmarum*)

p. 263

LENGTH 5 in (13 cm)   WEIGHT 0.4 oz (0.01 kg)

Other names Yellow Palm Warbler, Western Palm Warbler

Description Yellow undertail coverts, wags tail; chestnut crown, yellow
throat and breast, streaked (spring) or brown crown, white eyebrow,
whitish-buff underparts, streaked (fall)

Habitat Xeric scrub; mangrove; hardwood swamps; dry prairies; cypress
swamps; mesic hammocks; mixed pine and hardwood forests; wet prairies and
marshes; urban environments; pine flatwoods; sandhills; agricultural environments

Range Statewide

| Jan | Feb | Mar | Apr | May | June | July | Aug | Sep | Oct | Nov | Dec |

As a winter warbler in Florida, the Palm is second in abundance only to the Yellow-rumped. Spring birds are yellow below with brownish streaking, olive above, with a pale eye line and rufous cap. Fall and winter birds are paler overall with yellow undertail coverts. Palm Warblers continually bob their tails. Fall migrants arrive in late September and may remain through April. They may be seen in a variety of habitats from woodland edges to agricultural lands and marshes.

Foods are mostly insects such as small beetles, caterpillars, and grasshoppers. During colder weather small fruits and seeds are eaten.

FAMILY *Parulidae: Wood Warblers*

BAY-BREASTED WARBLER *(Dendroica castanea)*   p. 263

LENGTH 5 in (13 cm)   WEIGHT 0.5 oz (0.01 kg)

Description Chestnut crown, throat, flanks; buff neck patch (spring) or buff undertail coverts, black legs, olive-green streaked back (fall)

Habitat Mesic hammocks; mixed pine and hardwood forests

Range Statewide

Jan	Feb	Mar	Apr	May	June	July	Aug	Sep	Oct	Nov	Dec

Spring males exhibit chestnut crown, throat and flanks, black face, cream ear patch and undersides, two white wing bars and grayish upper-parts. Females lack the black face and are less boldly colored. While breed-ing individuals are unmistakable, fall birds are olive-gray overall with black wings and two white wing bars. Adult males usually retain some light chestnut coloration on the sides. Bay-breasted Warblers closely resemble the fall Blackpoll Warbler but lack distinct streaking underneath and have black rather than brown or yellowish legs. Fall birds pass through Florida primarily in October. Spring migrants have been recorded from mid-March to early May. The Bay-breasted Warbler is not common in Florida but can be looked for in deciduous hardwoods. Foods are mostly insects.

FAMILY *Parulidae: Wood Warblers*

BLACKPOLL WARBLER *(Dendroica striata)*   p. 263

LENGTH 5 in (13 cm)   WEIGHT 0.5 oz (0.01 kg)

Description Black cap, white cheeks, black and white streaking overall (spring) or olive-green above, yellowish underparts with streaking, pale legs (female and fall male)

Habitat Mesic hammocks; mixed pine and hardwood forests; urban environments; agricultural environments

Range Statewide

Jan	Feb	Mar	Apr	May	June	July	Aug	Sep	Oct	Nov	Dec

White cheeks, two white wing bars, black cap and throat, and streaked undersides distinguish the spring adult male Blackpoll. The female has a greenish-brown head and is less boldly marked. The fall bird has a streaked, greenish-yellow head, back, and throat. During fall it is an uncommon migrant from late September to late October. Spring migrants are abundant and have been recorded from mid-April to late May. As West Indian migrants, they are not often seen in northwestern Florida during either season. The Blackpoll Warbler inhabits a variety of woodland types and may also be seen in gardens, orchards, and wooded suburbs. Like most warblers its food consists mostly of insects.

FAMILY *Parulidae: Wood Warblers*
CERULEAN WARBLER (*Dendroica cerulea*) p. 259
LENGTH 4.75 in (12 cm)   WEIGHT 0.3 oz (0.01 kg)

Description Grayish-blue above, white below with a narrow black throat band (male) or bluish-green crown and is paler (female and migration)

Habitat Mesic hammock; mixed pine and hardwood forests; cypress forests; hardwood swamps; pine flatwoods

Range Statewide

Jan	Feb	Mar	Apr	May	June	July	Aug	Sep	Oct	Nov	Dec

The Cerulean Warbler is a seldom-seen spring and fall migrant throughout the state. The spring male is grayish-blue above, white below with a narrow black throat band. Gray streaking on white flanks and two white wing bars are also characteristic. The female has a bluish-green crown and is otherwise much paler than the male. In its breeding range in the Midwest and northeastern United States. the Cerulean Warbler nests very high in deciduous trees. Range-wide population declines have made this a potential candidate for federal listing as a threatened species. Fall migrants have been observed from July through October. Spring migrants may be encountered between March and May. Cerulean Warblers feed mainly on insects.

FAMILY *Parulidae: Wood Warblers*
BLACK-AND-WHITE WARBLER (*Mniotilta varia*) p. 260
LENGTH 5.25 in (13 cm)   WEIGHT 0.4 oz (0.01 kg)

Description Black and white streaked overall, black (male) or white (female) throat

Habitat Xeric scrub; hardwood swamps; cypress swamps; mesic hammocks; mixed pine and hardwood forests; urban environments; pine flatwoods; sandhills

Range Statewide

Jan	Feb	Mar	Apr	May	June	July	Aug	Sep	Oct	Nov	Dec

Heavy black streaking with white belly and white stripe on the crown distinguish this common winter visitor. The Black-and-white is one of our "creeping" warblers and may be seen hanging upside down, nuthatchlike, on tree limbs. The call is a high, thin, two-noted whistle. Fall migrants arrive in late July, while the last spring migrants depart in May. In Florida, they can be found throughout winter in a variety of habitats but show a preference for hardwoods. Black-and-white Warblers feed exclusively on insects and are often seen in the company of other wintering warblers, chickadees, titmice, and vireos.

FAMILY *Parulidae: Wood Warblers*
AMERICAN REDSTART (*Setophaga ruticilla*)
LENGTH 5 in (13 cm)   WEIGHT 0.3 oz (0.01 kg)   p. 264

Other names Flamebird

Description Black head, back, breast; orange patches on wings and tail (male) or gray-brown with yellow on wings and tail (female)

Habitat Xeric scrub; mangrove; hardwood swamps; cypress swamps; mesic hammocks; mixed pine and hardwood forests; urban environments; pine flatwoods; sandhills; agricultural environments

Range Statewide

| Jan | Feb | Mar | Apr | May | June | July | Aug | Sep | Oct | Nov | Dec |

This colorful warbler is a common spring and fall migrant. It has nested in northwest Florida and is an uncommon winter resident in south Florida—its winter range is indicated on the range map. The adult male is white below and black above with orange patches on the sides, wings, and tail. The female is grayish above with yellow instead of orange patches. The second-year male resembles the female with dark flecking on the throat and light orange side patches. Redstarts make a habit of fanning their tails and exposing these brightly colored feathers. It is frequently seen in hardwood forests and woodland edges. Fall migrants arrive between late July and early November. Spring birds pass through between late March and early June when males can be heard singing *see, see, see, see-ah* in rapid rising and falling phrases. Redstarts actively hawk for flying insects.

FAMILY *Parulidae: Wood Warblers*
PROTHONOTARY WARBLER (*Protonotaria citrea*)   p. 260
LENGTH 5.5 in (14 cm)   WEIGHT 0.5 oz (0.01 kg)

Other names Golden Swamp Warbler, Swamp Yellowbird

Description Bright yellow head, breast, sides; blue-gray wings and tail

Habitat Hardwood swamps; cypress swamps

Range Statewide

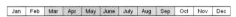

| Jan | Feb | Mar | Apr | May | June | July | Aug | Sep | Oct | Nov | Dec |

The Prothonotary is a stocky, bright yellow warbler with bluish wings and tail. There are no wing bars but the tail has distinctive white patches. The male's song is a series of ringing notes: *sweet, sweet, sweet, sweet, sweet.* This is our only warbler that nests in cavities. Preferred habitats are forested wetlands such as gum swamps, cypress swamps, and hardwood bottomlands in Florida southward to northern Monroe County, but rare in southeastern Florida. Nest boxes are occasionally used. The nest consists of moss, grasses, and small leaves. Eggs, numbering three to five, are cream-colored and boldly speckled. Laying may occur between mid-April and early June. Migrants leave Florida between July and September and return in March. Insects form the bulk of its diet.

FAMILY *Parulidae: Wood Warblers*
WORM-EATING WARBLER (*Helmitheros vermivorum*)
LENGTH 5 in (13 cm)   WEIGHT 0.7 oz (0.02 kg)

p. 260

Description Black and buff head stripes, buff underparts, brown above

Habitat Mesic hammocks; mixed pine and hardwood forests

Range Statewide

Jan	Feb	Mar	Apr	May	June	July	Aug	Sep	Oct	Nov	Dec

Olive-brown back, buff head with two black stripes and buff-orange underparts make this a distinctive warbler. The song is a brief, unmusical *buzz*. In Florida, the Worm-eating Warbler is most often encountered as a migrant from late March to early May and from late August to early October. A few birds over-winter in south Florida—the winter range is indicated on the range map. As a breeder it is found only in the western Panhandle in late April and May. The nest is built of leaves and placed in dense vegetation on the ground, usually in steep, wooded ravines with a well-developed understory. Eggs, numbering four or five, are white with brown flecking on the large end. Worm-eating Warblers are mostly found in deciduous hardwood habitats. Foods are primarily insects and spiders.

FAMILY *Parulidae: Wood Warblers*
SWAINSON'S WARBLER (*Limnothlypis swainsonii*)
LENGTH 5.5 in (14 cm)   WEIGHT 0.7 oz (0.02 kg)

p. 260

Description Brown above, reddish-brown cap, light eyebrow, yellowish-white below

Habitat Hardwood swamps; mesic hammocks; mixed pine and hardwood forests

Range Statewide, mostly Panhandle

Jan	Feb	Mar	Apr	May	June	July	Aug	Sep	Oct	Nov	Dec

This olive-brown warbler is white below with a dark eye line, pale stripe above the eye, and dark crown. The song is a loud, slurred series of five notes ending with two ascending notes. The Swainson's Warbler is an uncommon breeder throughout north Florida, as indicated on the range map. It favors densely vegetated rivers and swamps where it fastens a nest to a shrub, palmetto, cane, or vine. Three to five white eggs are laid in April or May. Fall migration takes place from August through October. Spring birds arrive during late March. Swainson's Warblers frequently forage for a variety of small insects on the ground.

FAMILY *Parulidae: Wood Warblers*

OVENBIRD (*Seiurus aurocapilla*)

p. 265

LENGTH 6 in (15 cm)   WEIGHT 0.7 oz (0.02 kg)

Other names Golden-crowned Thrush

Description Olive-green above, orange crown stripe, white eye ring, streaked breast

Habitat Hardwood swamps; cypress swamps; mesic hammocks; mixed pine and hardwood forests

Range Statewide

| Jan | Feb | Mar | Apr | May | June | July | Aug | Sep | Oct | Nov | Dec |

This ground-dwelling warbler gives the impression of a small thrush. Olive upperparts are highlighted by a black-bordered orange cap. White underparts are marked boldly with black spots. Immatures lack the orange crown. Although less common in north Florida, the Ovenbird is a widespread winter resident. Fall migrants arrive in mid-August; the last birds in spring are seen in late April or early May. Occasionally the male's song, a steadily louder *teacher, teacher, teacher, teacher,* can be heard in spring. Ovenbirds exhibit a preference for deciduous woodlands where they feed on spiders, caterpillars, flies, and other insects. Fruits and seeds are occasionally eaten.

FAMILY *Parulidae: Wood Warblers*

NORTHERN WATERTHRUSH (*Seiurus noveboracensis*)

p. 265

LENGTH 6 in (15 cm)   WEIGHT 0.8 oz (0.02 kg)

Description Brown above, narrow yellow or whitish eyebrow that tapers behind the eye, throat spotted

Habitat Hardwood swamps; cypress swamps; mesic hammocks; mixed pine and hardwood forests

Range Statewide

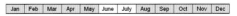

| Jan | Feb | Mar | Apr | May | June | July | Aug | Sep | Oct | Nov | Dec |

This is another ground-dwelling migrant and winter resident warbler. Olive-brown upperparts are contrasted by white or cream underparts that are heavily streaked and lack contrasting flank color. The narrow eyebrow is white or buff. The Northern Waterthrush is a common fall and spring migrant, traveling south from late August through September and north from April through May. A few birds winter in scattered south Florida locations. This is a bird of deciduous or broadleaf woodlands and is usually not far from water. Northern Waterthrushes usually walk instead of hop, and bob the rear part of their body rapidly. The song begins with loud distinctive notes and trails off at the end but is rarely heard in Florida. Insects make up the bulk of its diet.

FAMILY *Parulidae: Wood Warblers*
LOUISIANA WATERTHRUSH (*Seiurus motacilla*)
LENGTH 6 in (15 cm)   WEIGHT 0.7 oz (0.02 kg)

p. 265

Other names Large-billed Waterthrush, Water Wagtail
Description Brown above, white eyebrow that widens behind the eye; white throat unspotted
Habitat Hardwood swamps; cypress swamps; mesic hammocks; mixed pine and hardwood forests
Range Statewide

Jan	Feb	Mar	Apr	May	June	July	Aug	Sep	Oct	Nov	Dec

The Louisiana Waterthrush closely resembles its relative, the Northern Waterthrush. The unspotted white throat, white eyebrow that becomes broader behind the eye, tannish flanks, and a larger bill distinguish the Louisiana from the Northern. The sexes appear similar. While foraging, the Louisiana bobs its head and hind end continuously. The song consists of five to six slurred notes followed by three or four sharper notes. It is an inhabitant of wooded streams and seems to be expanding its breeding range into northwest Florida. Nests are placed in protected spots along stream banks and are constructed of leaves and grass. The four to six white eggs are laid from early May to June. Migration occurs earlier than that of most other warblers. Spring birds pass through Florida in March and early April, while fall migrants are seen from mid-July through September. A few scattered individuals have been reported during winter. Food consists of snails, insects, and other invertebrates that are associated with streams.

FAMILY *Parulidae: Wood Warblers*
KENTUCKY WARBLER (*Oporornis formosus*)
LENGTH 5.25 in (13 cm)   WEIGHT 0.5 oz (0.01 kg)

p. 259

Description Yellow below, olive green above, black mask and yellow eye ring (migration)
Habitat Mesic hammock; mixed pine and hardwood forests; shrub communities
Range Statewide

Jan	Feb	Mar	Apr	May	June	July	Aug	Sep	Oct	Nov	Dec

The Kentucky Warbler is known primarily as a spring and fall migrant, but it also breeds in northwest Florida, as indicated on the range map, and occasionally winters in extreme south Florida. The adult male is yellow below, olive green above, with a black mask and yellow eye ring. The female is similar with a narrower mask. The concealed nest is usually built near the ground at the base of a shrub in moist woodlands and river bottoms. Four to five eggs are laid in May or June. The male's song is reminiscent of the Carolina Wren but is more slurred. Spring migrants arrive as early as March, fall migrants pass through from July through October. The diet consists of spiders, insects, and occasional seeds and small fruits.

FAMILY *Parulidae: Wood Warblers*
CONNECTICUT WARBLER (*Oporornis agilis*)
LENGTH 5.25 in (13 cm)   WEIGHT 0.45 oz (0.01 kg)

Description Buff to gray head with distinct white eye ring, pale yellow undersides, greenish back
Habitat Thick shrubs and understory generally in woodlands
Range Statewide

Jan	Feb	Mar	Apr	May	June	July	Aug	Sep	Oct	Nov	Dec

This spring and fall migrant is not commonly seen in Florida, although it has been recorded from throughout the state. A gray throat and head with white eye ring distinguish this fall warbler from similar *Oporornis* species such as the Mourning and MacGillivray's Warblers, neither of which are seen as often as the Connecticut. None of the species in this group has wing bars. The Connecticut Warbler uses dense undergrowth in a variety of wooded habitats during its migration in Florida. Spring migrants pass through from April to May, fall birds from August to October. The diet consists mostly of insects and other invertebrates.

FAMILY *Parulidae: Wood Warblers*
MOURNING WARBLER (*Oporornis philadelphia*)
LENGTH 5.25 in (13 cm)   WEIGHT 0.45 oz (0.01 kg)

Description Stout, pale to gray head and face, greenish back, yellow belly
Habitat Dense shrubs and understory vegetation in a variety of habitats, usually wooded
Range Statewide

Jan	Feb	Mar	Apr	May	June	July	Aug	Sep	Oct	Nov	Dec

This is a rare migrant that has been seen in scattered locations throughout Florida. It is distinguished from the Connecticut Warbler by being somewhat smaller and with a less distinct eye ring. It is an especially difficult bird to identify during fall. This is exacerbated by having very similar habitat requirements and feeding tendencies as the Connecticut Warbler. The Mourning Warbler is virtually indistinguishable from the even rarer **MacGillivray's Warbler** (*Oporornis tolmiei*). Fall migrants have been seen from August through October, spring birds from March through May.

FAMILY *Parulidae: Wood Warblers*
COMMON YELLOWTHROAT (*Geothlypis trichas*)   p. 265
LENGTH 5 in (13 cm)   WEIGHT 0.4 oz (0.01 kg)

Other names Maryland Yellowthroat
Description Black mask bordered with gray, olive-brown back, yellow below (male) or lacking mask and duller (female)
Habitat Mesic hammocks; mixed pine and hardwood forests; wet prairies and marshes; agricultural environments
Range Statewide

| Jan | Feb | Mar | Apr | May | June | July | Aug | Sep | Oct | Nov | Dec |

This abundant, resident warbler is one of Florida's most widespread birds. Both sexes are olive-green above and yellow below. Males have white-bordered black masks and are brighter yellow beneath. The song is a loud *wichity-wichity,* and the call a *churr-churr.* Nests may be located in marshes, swamps, or dry woodlands, and are usually placed near the ground and constructed of dry grass and stems. The three to four white eggs are speckled around the large end and are laid from early April to early June. The Common Yellowthroat does not breed in the Florida Keys. Many northern birds either winter in Florida or pass through in spring and fall. Common Yellowthroats feed on a variety of aquatic and terrestrial insects and spiders.

FAMILY *Parulidae: Wood Warblers*   p. 264
HOODED WARBLER (*Wilsonia citrina*)
LENGTH 5 in (13 cm)   WEIGHT 0.4 oz (0.01 kg)

Description Black hood, yellow face and underparts, olive-green above, white spots in tail (male) or lacking black hood (female)
Habitat Hardwood swamps; pine flatwoods
Range Statewide

| Jan | Feb | Mar | Apr | May | June | July | Aug | Sep | Oct | Nov | Dec |

The Hooded Warbler is olive-green above, with yellow cheeks, large black eyes, and yellow underparts. Adult males exhibit a distinctive black hood that extends from the top of the head to the throat. The song is a ringing *weet-a, weet-a, wee-tee-o.* In Florida the Hooded Warbler inhabits swamps and moist pine flatwoods in the Panhandle and northern peninsula south to Ocala. Its breeding range is indicated on the range map. Nests are made of woven plant fibers and placed in dense shrubs. Eggs, numbering three or four, are white and splotched in shades of gray and brown. Two clutches are sometimes raised between May and July. During fall migration they are seen in Florida from July through October and in spring from mid-March through April. Foods consist of insects and other invertebrates.

FAMILY *Parulidae: Wood Warblers*
WILSON'S WARBLER (*Wilsonia pusilla*)
p. 264
LENGTH 4.5 in (11 cm)   WEIGHT 0.3 oz (0.01 kg)

Description Black cap, yellow forehead, eyebrow and underparts; olive-green above; no white in tail (male) or lacking lack cap (female)
Habitat Mesic hammocks; mixed pine and hardwood forests; agricultural environments
Range Statewide

| Jan | Feb | Mar | Apr | May | June | July | Aug | Sep | Oct | Nov | Dec |

The Wilson's is an uncommon, unpredictable fall and spring migrant that occasionally also winters in Florida. The male is bright yellow below, greenish above, and has a black cap. The female is similar but lacks black plumage and is duller overall. During migration Wilson's Warblers utilize forest edge and shrub vegetation often near streams while foraging on the wing for insects. They are curious and somewhat tame to humans.

FAMILY *Parulidae: Wood Warblers*
CANADA WARBLER (*Wilsonia canadensis*)
LENGTH 5.25 in (13 cm)   WEIGHT 0.36 oz (0.01 kg)

Description Blue-gray above, yellow below with gray to black necklace and white eye-ring
Habitat Dense shrubs and undergrowth in woodlands and woodland edges
Range Statewide

| Jan | Feb | Mar | Apr | May | June | July | Aug | Sep | Oct | Nov | Dec |

This is another rare migrant from August to October that has been seen throughout the state. It is seen with even less regularity in spring. Fall plumage is yellow below with a gray to black necklace beneath the throat. The white eye line and eye ring should still be visible during the fall. It catches insect prey on the wing in woody habitats with dense understory vegetation.

FAMILY *Parulidae: Wood Warblers*
YELLOW-BREASTED CHAT (*Icteria virens*)
LENGTH 7 in (18 cm)   WEIGHT 0.9 oz (0.03 kg)

p. 265

Description Large; heavy bill; bright yellow
throat, breast; white spectacles; olive above
Habitat Hardwood swamps; mixed pine and hardwood forests
Range Statewide, mostly north Florida

| Jan | Feb | Mar | Apr | May | June | July | Aug | Sep | Oct | Nov | Dec |

This largest of North American warblers is a summer resident in north
Florida. The yellow breast grades to a white underbelly; upperparts are olive
green. The black between the eye and bill is bordered in white. Not only is its
size unusual for a warbler, but its behavior is also unique. Some of the Chat's unusual behavior
includes nighttime singing, song mimicry, and aerial feats of contortion. Hal Harrison described
one variation of the song as "the alarm call of a Wren, a foghorn, and a chuckling, high-pitched
laugh." The nest is usually no more than 6 feet (2 meters) off the ground in dense vegetation and
is a bulky, well concealed structure. The large eggs number three to six, are white with splotches
of brown and lavender, and are laid between May and July. The breeding range is indicated on
the range map. Some migrant birds can be expected to pass through Florida during most of the
year except from January through March. Some Chats over-winter in Florida. Foods include
caterpillars, beetles, wasps, and a variety of fruits and berries.

FAMILY *Coerebidae: Bananaquits*
BANANAQUIT (*Coereba flaveola*)
LENGTH 4 in (10 cm)   WEIGHT 0.35 oz (0.009 kg)

p. 253

Other names Bahama Honeycreeper, Sugarbird
Description Black upperparts; yellow rump and belly; white throat, breast,
eyebrow; decurved bill
Habitat Urban environments
Range South Florida

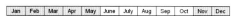

| Jan | Feb | Mar | Apr | May | June | July | Aug | Sep | Oct | Nov | Dec |

Because it is an abundant inhabitant of the Bahama Islands only 50 miles (80.5
km) east of south Florida, it is strange that so few Bananaquits ever reach Florida, and the few
that do remain only a few days before disappearing. The Bananaquit is a warbler-size bird with a
decurved bill. The adult has a black back with a yellow rump, black tail, white eyebrow, and yellow underparts. White highlights appear on the wings and tail. Bananaquits feed primarily on
nectar and nectar-eating insects. They occur in extreme southeastern Florida primarily between
November and March.

FAMILY *Thraupidae: Tanagers*
SUMMER TANAGER (*Piranga rubra*)
LENGTH 7.5 in (19 cm)   WEIGHT 1 oz (0.03 kg)

p. 266

Other names Summer Redbird

Description All red with a large pale bill (male) or yellow-buff overall, darker above with a pale bill (female)

Habitat Mesic hammocks; mixed pine and hardwood forests; pine flatwoods

Range Statewide

Although not so brightly colored as the Scarlet Tanager, this summer resident is one of Florida's most distinctive birds. The Summer Tanager exhibits red plumage, with darker red wings and heavy, whitish bill. Females are orange-yellow below and greenish-brown above. The song is robinlike and the call is a staccato *chick-a-tick-a-tuck.* Nests are usually built in large trees in hardwood hammocks or oak-pine woodlands. The three or four eggs are bluish-green with brown spots and laid in April or May. Nests are constructed with Spanish moss, grass, and other fine materials. Its breeding range is indicated on the range map. Summer Tanagers return to Florida in early March and may remain until early November. A few birds may over-winter. Foods include caterpillars, beetles, wasps, and many small, fleshy fruits. It often catches insects, especially bees and wasps, on the wing.

FAMILY *Thraupidae: Tanagers*
SCARLET TANAGER (*Piranga olivacea*)
LENGTH 7 in (18 cm)   WEIGHT 1 oz (0.03 kg)

p. 266

Description Brilliant red with black wings and tail (male) or olive-green above, yellowish below with dark wings (female)

Habitat Mesic hammocks; mixed pine and hardwood forests

Range Statewide

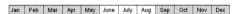

The male Scarlet Tanager is unmistakable with its brightly colored red plumage and contrasting black wings and tail. Females are greenish-yellow below and olive green above. Winter males resemble females with black wings and tail. During fall some males may exhibit red splotches while molting into winter plumage. Scarlet Tanagers are encountered only during migration in Florida. Fall birds can be seen from early September through October. Spring migration lasts from late March through early May. While this bird may be seen throughout the state it seems most common in the Panhandle. Scarlet Tanagers prefer deciduous woodlands and feed upon a variety of insects and spiders.

FAMILY *Thraupidae: Tanagers*
WESTERN TANAGER (*Piranga ludoviciana*)
LENGTH 7.23 in (18 cm)   WEIGHT 1 oz (0.03 kg)

Description Yellow body, black wings with white and yellow wingbars; males may exhibit some orange near base of bill
Habitat Urban environments
Range Statewide

Jan	Feb	Mar	Apr	May	June	July	Aug	Sep	Oct	Nov	Dec

This rare winter visitor and occasional migrant from the western United States turns up throughout the state between October and May, especially along Florida's coast. During winter it occasionally turns up at bird feeders, but is primarily an insect eater. Unlike our breeding tanagers, the male Western is yellow with red head, black wings and white wing bars.

FAMILY *Thraupidae: Tanagers*
WESTERN SPINDALIS (*Spindalis zena*)
LENGTH 6.75 in (17 cm)   WEIGHT 0.75 oz (0.02 kg)

Other names Stripe-headed Tanager
Description Distinct harlequin pattern with white and black patches on wings and face, dull orange rump and breast; small bill for a tanager
Habitat Hardwood hammocks, well-vegetated parks and backyards
Range South Florida

Jan	Feb	Mar	Apr	May	June	July	Aug	Sep	Oct	Nov	Dec

This vagrant from the West Indies is a boldly marked relative of the tanagers that has occurred sporadically throughout the year in extreme southeastern Florida. When in Florida it turns up in hardwood hammocks and wooded residential areas. It feeds on small fruits, including the exotic Brazilian pepper. It is somewhat smaller than our native tanagers but exhibits distinctive white face and wing patches, yellow breast, and dark gray and chestnut upperparts.

FAMILY *Emberizidae: Towhees and Sparrows*
EASTERN TOWHEE (*Pipilo erythrophthalmus*)

p. 267

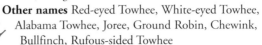

LENGTH 8 in (20 cm)   WEIGHT 1.5 oz (0.04 kg)

Other names Red-eyed Towhee, White-eyed Towhee, Alabama Towhee, Joree, Ground Robin, Chewink, Bullfinch, Rufous-sided Towhee

Description Black head, breast, upperparts, rufous sides and flanks, white belly (male) or brown instead of black (female)

Habitat Xeric scrub; mesic hammocks; mixed pine and hardwood forests; pine flatwoods; sandhills

Range Statewide

The Eastern Towhee is a widespread resident in a variety of Florida woodlands and wooded suburbs with dense undergrowth. The male is black above, white below, with orange-red flanks, and white wing and tail spots. Females have brown plumage in place of the males' black. Juveniles are brownish-gray with streaking above and below. Towhees in Florida exhibit red eyes in the extreme western Panhandle, yellowish eyes from there eastward to the peninsula, and pale or white eyes in most of peninsular Florida—this distribution is indicated in the range map. Wintering Towhees from northern areas have red eyes. Intergradations between shades of red and white also occur. The song is a ventriloquial *drink-your-teeee,* and the call an ascending *tuwee.* Towhees nest in dense shrubbery or palmettos in pine flatwoods, deciduous hardwoods, xeric scrub, and other forested uplands. The cupped nest is made of leaves, twigs, bark, and other plant fibers. Each of as many as three annual clutches usually contain three eggs that are pink-white with brown markings. The breeding season extends from April to early September. This extremely active and inquisitive bird often gives the impression of a larger animal as it noisily scratches through dry leaves and palmetto fronds in search of a meal. It moves both feet together when it scratches. Foods include ground-dwelling beetles, grubs, ants, earthworms, and a variety of seeds and berries.

FAMILY *Emberizidae: Towhees and Sparrows*
BACHMAN'S SPARROW (*Aimophila aestivalis*)

p. 268

LENGTH 6 in (15 cm)   WEIGHT 0.7 oz (0.02 kg)

Other names Pine-woods Sparrow

Description Reddish-brown above, buff or grayish below, buff eyebrow, brown line behind eye

Habitat Pine flatwoods

Range Statewide

As its other name indicates, the Bachman's Sparrow is a resident of dry pine-dominated woodlands and treeless dry prairies. Brown upperparts are highlighted with gray; underparts are unstreaked with white belly and gray breast.

The crown is dark brown with gray streaks, and gray cheeks are bordered with brown. The musical song is a long, high whistle followed by an extended trill. Its ending is reminiscent of the trill of the Eastern Towhee. Nests are grassy domes placed on or near the ground in a palmetto clump or dense shrub. Eggs, numbering three to five, are white and laid from early April through July, during which time up to three broods are raised. The Bachman's Sparrow is a permanent resident throughout Florida north of Lake Okeechobee in scattered locations usually dominated by longleaf pine, wire grass, and saw palmetto. Its breeding range is indicated on the range map. A few birds winter in extreme south Florida. Foods include seeds, especially in winter, and a variety of insects and other invertebrates.

FAMILY *Emberizidae: Towhees and Sparrows*
CHIPPING SPARROW (*Spizella passerina*)   p. 268
LENGTH 5.5 in (14 cm)   WEIGHT 0.4 oz (0.01 kg)

Description Rufous cap (brown in winter), white eyebrow, black eye line and lores
Habitat Dry prairies; urban environments; agricultural environments
Range Statewide

Jan	Feb	Mar	Apr	May	June	July	Aug	Sep	Oct	Nov	Dec

This abundant winter resident is also an infrequent nester in the Panhandle of Florida. Upperparts are brown and underparts are gray. The head is gray with black eye line, white eyebrow, and rufous cap. Winter birds have less distinct head plumage. Juveniles are streaked below. The song is a single-pitched trill, like a sewing machine. Nests are placed low in small trees or shrubs. Eggs are greenish-blue with brown-red markings, and are laid from early April through June. Chipping Sparrows are much more likely to be seen as wintering residents from mid-October through mid-May. They are usually seen in small flocks in weedy fields, woodland edges, and suburban lawns and gardens. It is often a visitor of backyard feeders. Foods include caterpillars, beetles, ants, grains, and weed seeds.

FAMILY *Emberizidae: Towhees and Sparrows*
CLAY-COLORED SPARROW (*Spizella pallida*)
LENGTH 5.5 in (14 cm)   WEIGHT 0.4 oz (0.01 kg)

Description Buffy breast, gray nape of neck, brown rump, distinctly patterned face with dark mustache
Habitat Weed fields, shrubby woodland edges
Range Statewide

Jan	Feb	Mar	Apr	May	June	July	Aug	Sep	Oct	Nov	Dec

The Clay-colored Sparrow is seen occasionally throughout Florida as a migrant and winter resident. They are seen primarily between September and May. It can be distinguished from the similar Chipping Sparrow by its more buff undersides, whiter stripes on the head, and buffy rather than gray rump. Small numbers and individuals may be seen in groups of Chipping Sparrows. They use similar habitats and have comparable diets.

FAMILY *Emberizidae: Towhees and Sparrows*
FIELD SPARROW (*Spizella pusilla*)
LENGTH 5.5 in (14 cm)   WEIGHT 0.4 oz (0.01 kg)

p. 269

Other names Grass Sparrow
Description Pink bill, rusty crown, white eye ring
Habitat Dry prairies; agricultural environments
Range Statewide

The Field Sparrow is primarily a winter visitor but also nests in the Panhandle and north Florida, as indicated on the range map. Upperparts are brown and gray with white wing bars. Underparts are buff-gray, and the head is gray with light brown face high-lights and reddish-brown crown. The immature bird is browner overall with a streaked breast. The song is a series of slow whistles increasing to a trill. Nests are made of grasses or other fibers and placed in a tall shrub, bush, or on the ground. Three or four eggs are laid from early April through June, and are bluish-green with brown spots. Most birds in Florida are northern visitors from early November through early April. They are less apt to visit feeders than other sparrows. Field Sparrows use pastures, old fields, woodland edges, and other open areas where they feed upon weed seeds and insects. In winter they often may be seen in the company of Chipping Sparrows.

FAMILY *Emberizidae: Towhees and Sparrows*
VESPER SPARROW (*Pooecetes gramineus*)
LENGTH 6 in (15 cm)   WEIGHT 1 oz (0.03 kg)

p. 268

Description Gray-brown streaked above, streaked breast, white outer tail feathers
Habitat Dry prairies; pine flatwoods; agricultural environments
Range Statewide

This large sparrow is streaked brown and buff above, and white below with streaking on breast and sides. White outer tail feathers are conspicuous when in flight and distinguish it from the similar Savannah Sparrow. Vesper Sparrows remain close to the ground in dry grasslands, woodland edges, road-sides, and other open areas. Winter visitors are found primarily in north Florida from early October through early April. The Vesper Sparrow is so named as it usually sings at twilight. It walks on the ground and runs from danger instead of flying away. It can often be seen taking a dust bath. Foods in winter are primarily seeds and waste grains.

FAMILY *Emberizidae: Towhees and Sparrows*
LARK SPARROW (*Chondestes grammacus*)
LENGTH 6.5 in (17 cm)   WEIGHT 1 oz (0.02 kg)

Description Chestnut cheek patch bordered in black and white, a slender-appearing sparrow; white breast with dark central spot
Habitat Grassy areas with sparse shrubs such as road edges and vacant lots
Range Statewide

| Jan | Feb | Mar | Apr | May | June | July | Aug | Sep | Oct | Nov | Dec |

This distinctive sparrow is not a common visitor in Florida, but it has been seen throughout the state. Its head is boldly marked with chestnut patches and black and white stripes. The unstreaked pale to white breast contains a central dark spot. Most occurrences have been between August and April. The Lark Sparrow uses weedy lots, pastures, and shrubby habitats where it consumes a variety of seeds.

FAMILY *Emberizidae: Towhees and Sparrows*
SAVANNAH SPARROW (*Passerculus sandwichensis*)   p. 267
LENGTH 5.5 in (14 cm)   WEIGHT 0.8 oz (0.02 kg)

Description Brown upperparts and white breast heavily streaked, pinkish legs, yellowish eyebrow
Habitat Dry prairies; agricultural environments
Range Statewide

| Jan | Feb | Mar | Apr | May | June | July | Aug | Sep | Oct | Nov | Dec |

This winter resident is a common inhabitant of grasslands, sand dunes, old fields, and other dry, open areas. The breast is heavily streaked and the back varies from light to medium brown with dark streaking. A light yellowish eyebrow is visible at close range. When disturbed, Savannah Sparrows often fly a short distance then run. The call note is a staccato *chip*. Migrants arrive in Florida in late September and may remain through early May. The Savannah Sparrow is primarily a weed seed eater.

FAMILY *Emberizidae: Towhees and Sparrows*
GRASSHOPPER SPARROW (*Ammodramus savannarum*)
LENGTH 5 in (13 cm)   WEIGHT 0.8 oz (0.02 kg)   STATUS **E**

p. 267

Other Names Florida Grasshopper Sparrow
Description Striped head, plain buff face and underparts, streaked buff-brown back
Habitat Dry prairies
Range Statewide

| Jan | Feb | Mar | Apr | May | June | July | Aug | Sep | Oct | Nov | Dec |

This highly variable, widespread sparrow is represented in Florida by an isolated endangered subspecies (the Florida Grasshopper Sparrow (*A. s. floridanus*)), as a migrant, and as a regular but uncommon winter resident. The Florida resident is darker than other forms with a white crown stripe, orange lores, buff breast, white belly and thinly streaked flanks. The juvenile is less colorful with streaking on the breast. The song consists of two *chips* followed by a grasshopper-like *buzz*. Grasshopper Sparrows are not easily viewed and if flushed, fly a short distance, then run. The breeding season extends from March through August when three or four white, brown-speckled eggs are laid; the breeding range is indicated on the range map. Nests are constructed of fine grass and placed on the ground. Preferred habitat is treeless and poorly drained with saw palmetto, cordgrass, and scattered shrubs. Grasshopper Sparrows apparently were abundant in south-central Florida, but now have a patchy distribution. The conversion of their nesting habitat to cattle range-land has caused this species to decline. Northern birds may be seen throughout the state from mid-October through early May. Foods shift from insects during summer to seeds during winter.

FAMILY *Emberizidae: Towhees and Sparrows*   p. 267
HENSLOW'S SPARROW (*Ammodramus henslowii*)
LENGTH 5 in (13 cm)   WEIGHT 0.5 oz (0.01 kg)

Description Olive, almost green, head; heavily streaked back; rust on wings; streaked breast and sides

Habitat Dry prairies; pine flatwoods

Range Statewide, mostly north Florida

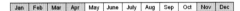

| Jan | Feb | Mar | Apr | May | June | July | Aug | Sep | Oct | Nov | Dec |

The Henslow's Sparrow is an extremely secretive bird, rarely assuming an exposed perch. The greenish, flat-topped head has a yellowish central stripe with black borders. The brown upperparts are streaked with white and black. Underparts are white with buff breast streaked with brown. Henslow's Sparrows prefer open grasslands with scattered shrubs or small trees. The wet savannahs of Apalachicola National Forest are a typical wintering ground. They can be expected in north and central Florida from early November through mid-April. Foods include, seeds, insects, and other small invertebrates.

FAMILY *Emberizidae: Towhees and Sparrows*
LE CONTE'S SPARROW (*Ammodramus leconteii*)
LENGTH 5 in (13 cm)   WEIGHT 0.45 oz (0.01 kg)

Description Small sparrow with small bill, buff chest and sides with dark streaks, face a burnished brown-orange with distinct patterning on head, neck and back

Habitat Grassy fields with few shrubs

Range Statewide

| Jan | Feb | Mar | Apr | May | June | July | Aug | Sep | Oct | Nov | Dec |

This small sparrow has a white crown stripe bordered by black, with a pale orange eyebrow, gray ear patch, buff breast and sides with dark streaks. A scaly-appearing back with faintly streaked nape separate it from the similar Sharp-tailed Sparrow. This rarely seen wintering species prefers to run rather than fly in its preferred habitat of moist, grassy fields that usually contain broomsedge, a tall grass. Le Conte's Sparrows may be found in north and central Florida between November and early May. Weed seeds and insects are eaten.

Family *Emberizidae: Towhees and Sparrows*
Saltmarsh Sharp-tailed Sparrow (*Ammodramus caudacutus*)   p. 267
Length 5 in (13 cm)   Weight 0.67–0.74 oz (0.02–0.021 kg)

Description Gray crown stripe and nape; buff-orange and gray face; buffy breast and sides

Habitat Salt marshes

Range Statewide, coastal

Jan	Feb	Mar	Apr	May	June	July	Aug	Sep	Oct	Nov	Dec

This is a relatively common but secretive sparrow that winters in salt marshes along both coasts of Florida. Upperparts are reddish-brown with white streaking, the belly is white, and sides and breast are buff with faint brown streaking. The tail is short and pointed. An orange triangle surrounds a gray cheek patch in birds from the northeast. In all forms, a gray crown is bordered by broad, dark brown stripes. Saltmarsh Sharp-tailed Sparrows can be seen from mid-October through May in Florida. Foods consist of marsh grass seeds, spiders, grasshoppers, and other insects. The very similar **Nelson's Sharp-tailed Sparrow** (*Ammodramus nelsoni*) is also a winter resident. It has less contrast between streaked and light breast feathers, it has a smaller, rounder head, and is grayer. It is found in similar habitats as the Saltmarsh Sharp-tailed Sparrow.

Family *Emberizidae: Towhees and Sparrows*
Seaside Sparrow (*Ammodramus maritimus*)   p. 268
Length 5.5 in (14 cm)   Weight 0.8 oz (0.02 kg)   Status **E, SSC**

Other names (subspecies) Dusky Seaside Sparrow, Cape Sable Seaside Sparrow, Scott's Seaside Sparrow, Northern Seaside Sparrow, Wakulla Seaside Sparrow, Louisiana Seaside Sparrow, MacGillavray's Seaside Sparrow

Description Varies from grayish-olive to dark brown above with a light grayish breast marked with buff or plain streaking. Dark whisker stripe on white throat

Habitat Salt marshes

Range Coastal, almost statewide (absent from South Florida, except for Cape Sable Seaside Sparrow in and around the Everglades)

Jan	Feb	Mar	Apr	May	June	July	Aug	Sep	Oct	Nov	Dec

The Seaside Sparrow is an inhabitant of coastal saltwater marshes from Massachusetts to Texas. Variability in plumages has led to the description of nine subspecies, seven of which occur in Florida (see other names, above). Seaside Sparrows on the Atlantic coast are grayish-olive above, with a light grayish breast marked with faint streaking. On Gulf coast marshes adults are darker with brown backs and more buff-colored breasts. The **Cape Sable Seaside Sparrow** appears more greenish-gray than the other subspecies—the Endangered status in the statistics above refers to this subspecies. Both the **Scott's Seaside Sparrow** and the **Wakulla Seaside Sparrow** are species of special concern. The most distinctive race of Seasides in Florida—the black and white streaked **Dusky Seaside Sparrow** from Merritt Island and the St. Johns valley in Brevard County—became extinct in 1987. All races have a dark whisker stripe on a white throat and yellow lores. The tail is short and pointed and the bill is relatively long and conical. Because Seasides molt only once annually in late summer or early fall, feathers are heavily worn by May and June, at which time the adult appears dull brown with a dark gray breast. The song is a *buzzy spitsch-sheer* that resembles the song of a distant Red-winged Blackbird. Nests are constructed of marsh grass and often have a roof or canopy woven over the top. Three or four white, brown-spotted eggs are laid from March through August. Florida nesters are year-round residents while northern migrants over-winter from November through March. The breeding range is indicated on the range map. Foods primarily are snails, spiders, grasshoppers, small crabs, beetles, and seeds.

FAMILY *Emberizidae: Towhees and Sparrows*
FOX SPARROW (*Passerella iliaca*)
LENGTH 7 in (18 cm)   WEIGHT 1.1 oz (0.03 kg)

Description Brown-reddish wings, back and chest with gray and white streaks; gray face patch, pale white wing bars

Habitat Variable—weedy fields, dense cover in woodlands

Range North Florida

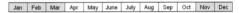

This is a species of the far north that occasionally winters in north Florida. It derives its name from its reddish plumage. The Fox Sparrow has a gray head streaked with brown, reddish rump and tail, heavily streaked underparts, and a large breast spot. It inhabits dense undergrowth of mixed hardwood-pine forests, usually between November and February. Seeds and insects are eaten while scratching through leaf litter.

FAMILY *Emberizidae: Towhees and Sparrows*
SONG SPARROW (*Melospiza melodia*) p. 269
LENGTH 6 in (15 cm)   WEIGHT 0.7 oz (0.02 kg)

Description Brown and gray streaked head, heavily streaked breast with large central spot, heavy dark stripe borders white throat

Habitat Dry prairies; mixed pine and hardwood forests; sandhills; agricultural environments

Range Statewide

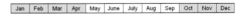

This familiar northern songbird is a common winter resident in Florida. Brown upperparts are contrasted by white undersides. The heavily streaked flanks and breast usually surround a large, central spot. The white throat is bordered by dark stripes and the head is streaked brown with a lighter central stripe. The tail is long and rounded and pumped in flight. In Florida only its call note, a staccato *chip,* can be heard. Song Sparrows are regular winter visitors except in the southern third of the state. They may be seen in grasslands, woodland edges, and old fields from early October through April. Foods include insects and a variety of weed seeds.

FAMILY *Emberizidae: Towhees and Sparrows*

LINCOLN'S SPARROW (*Melospiza lincolnii*)

LENGTH 5.75 in (15 cm)   WEIGHT 0.6 oz (0.01 kg)

Description Smaller than Song Sparrow; buffy chest and flanks with dark streaking, white throat streaked with black, mottled brown-black-gray back

Habitat Dense grassy areas, brush piles, woodland edges

Range Statewide

Jan	Feb	Mar	Apr	May	June	July	Aug	Sep	Oct	Nov	Dec

A few individuals of this northern sparrow are seen each year in Florida during winter or while migrating. The adult has a buff breast band with fine brown streaks, white belly, gray-brown upperparts, gray central crown stripe bordered in reddish-brown, and a wide gray eyebrow. It usually is seen along brushy ditches, canal banks, and thickets. The diet consists of seeds and insects.

FAMILY *Emberizidae: Towhees and Sparrows*

SWAMP SPARROW (*Melospiza georgiana*)   p. 269

LENGTH 5.5 in (14 cm)   WEIGHT 0.8 oz (0.02 kg)

Description Chestnut crown, gray face, white throat, reddish-brown wings

Habitat Hardwood swamps; dry prairies; wet prairies and marshes; agricultural environments

Range Statewide

Jan	Feb	Mar	Apr	May	June	July	Aug	Sep	Oct	Nov	Dec

The Swamp Sparrow is a common winter resident in Florida using brushy fields, lake borders, swamp edges, freshwater and saltwater marshes, and other wet areas. Brown upperparts are highlighted with reddish wing patches, white throat, gray cheeks, and gray crown. Underparts are grayish with brown streaking on breast and flanks. The call is a metallic *chip*. Swamp Sparrows can be seen in Florida from early October to April. They may form flocks in winter, but more are secreted in dense vegetation. Weed seeds and insects make up most of its diet.

FAMILY *Emberizidae: Towhees and Sparrows*
WHITE-THROATED SPARROW *(Zonotrichia albicollis)* p. 269
LENGTH 6.5 in (17 cm)   WEIGHT 0.9 oz (0.03 kg)

Description Black and white or black and tan striped head, white throat, yellow lores

Habitat Hardwood swamps; dry prairies; mesic hammocks; mixed pine and hardwood forests; urban environments; pine flatwoods; sandhills; agricultural environments

Range Statewide, mostly north Florida

Jan	Feb	Mar	Apr	May	June	July	Aug	Sep	Oct	Nov	Dec

Unstreaked, grayish underparts, bright white throat patch and head stripes distinguish this winter visitor. The immature has a buff throat patch and head stripe. The call is a thin *zeep*. Occasionally its song, *old-sam-peabody, peabody, peabody,* is heard on warm winter days. White-throated Sparrows are common in north Florida and rare in central Florida from late October through April. They can be found in a variety of habitats from hardwood forest and swamp edges to old fields and suburban backyards. Foods include seeds, small fruits, and insects.

FAMILY *Emberizidae: Towhees and Sparrows*
WHITE-CROWNED SPARROW *(Zonotrichia leucophrys)* p. 269
LENGTH 6.5 in (17 cm)   WEIGHT 1 oz (0.03 kg)

Description Black and white head; gray face, neck, breast; head is brown and buff striped in immatures

Habitat Dry prairies; mixed pine and hardwood forests; agricultural environments

Range Statewide

Jan	Feb	Mar	Apr	May	June	July	Aug	Sep	Oct	Nov	Dec

Black and white striped crown, gray unstreaked underparts, and grayish-brown upperparts distinguish this unpredictable winter visitor. Immatures are browner and duller overall, without the white striped crown. White-crowned Sparrows use woodland edges, brushy fields, and other open areas. Although uncommon, this large sparrow may be looked for from early October through early May. Foods are mostly seeds but include a variety of insects when available.

Family *Emberizidae: Towhees and Sparrows*
DARK-EYED JUNCO (*Junco hyemalis*)　　　　　　　　　　p. 268
LENGTH 6 in (15 cm)　　WEIGHT 0.7 oz (0.02 kg)

Other names Slate-colored Junco, Blue Snowbird, White-tailed Sparrow

Description Gray head, back, breast; white belly; pink bill; white outer tail feathers; female is duller

Habitat Dry prairies; urban environments; pine flatwoods; agricultural environments

Range North and central Florida

Jan	Feb	Mar	Apr	May	June	July	Aug	Sep	Oct	Nov	Dec

The Dark-eyed Junco winters in unpredictable numbers in Florida. Its nonsparrowlike plumage is slate-gray with white belly and white outer tail feathers. The bill is flesh-colored. Wintering flocks may be seen, primarily in north Florida, from late October through April. Juncos occasionally may use backyard feeding stations but are more often seen in open woodlands, grain fields, dry grasslands, and brushy vegetation. Dark-eyed Juncos forage on the ground in search of exposed seeds and insects.

Family *Emberizidae: Towhees and Sparrows*
LAPLAND LONGSPUR (*Calcarius lapponicus*)
LENGTH 6.25 in (16 cm)　　WEIGHT 1 oz (0.02 kg)

Description Boldly patterned with rust, buff, gray and white; dark breastband, white belly

Habitat Open grassy areas near beaches, airports, and roadsides

Range North Florida

Jan	Feb	Mar	Apr	May	June	July	Aug	Sep	Oct	Nov	Dec

A rare winter visitor to Florida, this longspur has a broad buff eye brow, a buff ear patch with black border, reddish-brown nape and neck, white belly, and streaked flanks. The male has black barring on the chest while the female exhibits a buff chest. Lapland Longspurs have been seen in Florida on sand dunes, at airports, in pastures, and along grassy road shoulders.

Family *Emberizidae: Towhees and Sparrows*
SNOW BUNTING (*Plectrophenax nivalis*)
LENGTH 6.75 in (17 cm)　　WEIGHT 1.5 oz (0.04 kg)

Description Stout, pale sparrow with clear white belly, reddish buff cheek patches and top of head; bright white wing patches in flight; buff and black mottled back

Habitat Coastal dunes, beaches

Range North Florida

Jan	Feb	Mar	Apr	May	June	July	Aug	Sep	Oct	Nov	Dec

During some winters, this Arctic species spends a few days or weeks in northeast Florida in the grassy dune area of Ward's Bank (now called Huguenot Memorial

Park) between the St. Johns River and Ft. George River Inlets. Its winter plumage is mostly white with a buff or rusty cap, black and white wings, and a black and white streaked tail. Its occurrence in Florida is unpredictable.

FAMILY *Cardinalidae: Cardinals and Grosbeaks*
NORTHERN CARDINAL (*Cardinalis cardinalis*)
p. 270
LENGTH 8 in (20 cm)   WEIGHT 1.6 oz (0.05 kg)

Other names Redbird

Description All red, with crest, black face, orange bill (male) or all brown or buff; reddish crest, wings, tail; black face; orange bill (female); immature is like female, but with dark bill

Habitat Xeric scrub; mesic hammocks; mixed pine and hardwood forests; urban environments; pine flatwoods; sandhills; agricultural environments

Range Statewide

Jan	Feb	Mar	Apr	May	June	July	Aug	Sep	Oct	Nov	Dec

One of our most common suburban inhabitants and backyard feeder visitors, the Northern Cardinal is also one of our most easily recognized birds. The bright red plumage of the male is highlighted by a black mask. Females are brown overall with red highlights. Both sexes are heavy-billed and crested. The song—a rich, whistled *cheer, cheer, cheer*—is performed by both the male and female. Cardinals are nonmigratory inhabitants of woodland edges, gardens, and suburbs. Nests are loosely constructed of small twigs, leaves, and grasses, and are usually placed in a wild or landscaped shrub. Eggs, numbering two to five, are greenish-blue with brown and reddish markings and can be found from March through August. Up to three broods can be raised each year by a single pair. Cardinals are primarily seed and fruit eaters, but also will eat insects when abundant and when feeding their young. In particular, fruits of dogwood, beautyberry, sugarberry, cherry, poison ivy, and holly are eaten. Sunflowers are favorite items at feeding stations.

FAMILY *Cardinalidae: Cardinals and Grosbeaks*
ROSE-BREASTED GROSBEAK (*Pheucticus ludovicianus*)
p. 270
LENGTH 8 in (20 cm)   WEIGHT 1.6 oz (0.05 kg)

Description Black head and underparts, red breast, white belly and rump, white patches on wing, pale bill (male) or brown above, striped head, white eyebrow and underparts, streaked with brown (female)

Habitat Xeric scrub; mesic hammocks; mixed pine and hardwood forests; urban environments; pine flatwoods

Range Statewide

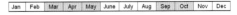

Jan	Feb	Mar	Apr	May	June	July	Aug	Sep	Oct	Nov	Dec

This large finch is seen uncommonly in Florida during migration on its way to and from South America. The male is black above with white rump and wing patches. Underparts are white with a red breast. The female is brown with white wing bars, white eye line, and streaked, buff-colored underparts. Rose-breasted Grosbeaks are seen in open woodlands, swamps, and second-growth timber, especially in the Panhandle. Spring migrants occasionally can be heard singing their robinlike song. They can be seen from late March through early May, and in fall from early September through October. Some birds over-winter. Foods include a variety of fruits, seeds, and insects.

FAMILY *Cardinalidae: Cardinals and Grosbeaks*
BLUE GROSBEAK (*Passerina caerulea*)
LENGTH 6 in (15 cm)   WEIGHT 1 oz (0.03 kg)

p. 270

Description All blue with rusty wing bars, large stout bill (male) or all brown with rusty wing bars (female)

Habitat Mesic hammocks; mixed pine and hardwood forests; agricultural environments

Range Statewide, mostly North Florida

Jan	Feb	Mar	Apr	May	June	July	Aug	Sep	Oct	Nov	Dec

The Blue Grosbeak is a summer resident in north Florida inhabiting brushy vegetation bordering streams, marshes, fields, woodlands, and roadsides. Males are purplish-blue with a black face mask and chestnut wing bars. Females are light brown with dark wings, buff wing bars, and dark tail. Blue Grosbeaks are somewhat larger and heavier-billed than the similar Indigo Bunting. The song is a series of long melodious warbles. Nests are found in shrubs or small trees and are constructed with grass, leaves, hair, and other pliable material. Three to five light blue eggs are laid from late April through July. Breeding records occur southward into Pinellas and Orange counties, as indicated on the range map. Migrants return to Florida in early or mid-April and the last fall migrants depart in September. A few birds will over-winter. Insects, spiders, snails, weed seeds, and grains are eaten.

FAMILY *Cardinalidae: Cardinals and Grosbeaks*
INDIGO BUNTING (*Passerina cyanea*)
LENGTH 5.5 in (14 cm)   WEIGHT 0.5 oz (0.01 kg)

p. 270

Other names Indigo Bird, Swamp Bluebird

Description Indigo blue with blackish wings (male) or all brown with faint breast streakings (female)

Habitat Mixed pine and hardwood forests; agricultural environments

Range Statewide

Jan	Feb	Mar	Apr	May	June	July	Aug	Sep	Oct	Nov	Dec

No other Florida bird is entirely blue or as iridescent as the male Indigo Bunting. The female is mostly brown with faint streaks on breast and back and has faint blue plumage on tail and wings. Winter adult males resemble females but have more blue. The song is a musical series of paired phrases. Indigo Buntings are summer residents in north Florida, nesting in open woodlands, field edges, and old fields. The breeding range is indicated on the range map. They are often seen singing from exposed treetops or from utility wires. The song has been variably described, including *fire, fire–where, where–here, here–see-it, see-it*. The cupped nest is woven with fine grasses and leaves. The two to four pale blue eggs are laid from May to August. Spring migrants return to Florida in mid-April while fall birds are seen from August through October. A few over-winter in central and south Florida. Indigo Buntings primarily are seed eaters but also will consume a variety of berries and insects.

FAMILY *Cardinalidae: Cardinals and Grosbeaks*
PAINTED BUNTING (*Passerina ciris*)
p. 271
LENGTH 5 in (13 cm)   WEIGHT 0.8 oz (0.02 kg)

Other names Nonpareil

Description Blue head, greenish-yellow back, green wings and tail, red rump, underparts and red eye ring (male) or greenish above, yellowish below with yellow eye ring (female)

Habitat Mesic hammocks; mixed pine and hardwood forests; urban environments; pine flatwoods

Range Statewide

Jan	Feb	Mar	Apr	May	June	July	Aug	Sep	Oct	Nov	Dec

The Painted Bunting is one of Florida's most colorful birds. The male has a blue head, red under-sides and rump, greenish-yellow back, and dark wings and tail. Females are dull yellow below and green above. First-year males look similar to females. The song is a loud, high-pitched and varied warble. Painted Buntings prefer dense, brushy vegetation along roads, woodland edges, and back-yard gardens. It breeds from northern Brevard County northward along the St. Johns River and the Atlantic coastal counties. Nests are similar to those of Indigo Buntings, usually placed at the end of a branch in Spanish moss. Eggs, numbering two to five, are white with brown speckling, and are laid from May through June. Foods are primarily seeds but may include small fruits and insects. In some locations Painted Buntings are frequent visitors at feeding stations. Although numerous birds over-winter in central and south Florida, most Painted Buntings leave the state by late October. Spring migrants begin their return in mid-April.

FAMILY *Cardinalidae: Cardinals and Grosbeaks*
DICKCISSEL (*Spiza americana*)
p. 271
LENGTH 6 in (15 cm)   WEIGHT 1 oz (0.03 kg)

Description Gray head, black V on yellow breast, rufous shoulders (male) or browner, less yellow, no V on breast (female)

Habitat Dry prairies; urban environments; agricultural environments

Range Statewide

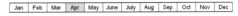

Jan	Feb	Mar	Apr	May	June	July	Aug	Sep	Oct	Nov	Dec

This sparrow-size finch is a regular migrant in Florida, and a few individuals over-winter. They are often found with House Sparrows. Upperparts are brown above and light below with yellow eye line and yellow breast. The male shows a gray to black throat patch. Immatures are duller overall and are streaked below. The song is *dick, dick, dickcissel.* Dickcissels are inhabitants of grasslands, prairies, old fields, and suburbs during their visits to Florida. Migrants are seen primarily during April along the west coast. A few pairs bred near Lake Apopka in 1999. Foods are mostly seeds and grains.

FAMILY *Icteridae: Blackbirds and Orioles*
BOBOLINK (*Dolichonyx oryzivorus*)   p. 264
LENGTH 7 in (18 cm)   WEIGHT 1.7 oz (0.05 kg)

Other names Ricebird

Description Black head and underparts, yellow-buff nape, white scapulars and rump (spring) or buffy with dark streaks on back, rump, sides; striped head (female and fall male)

Habitat Dry prairies; wet prairies and marshes; agricultural environments

Range Statewide

| Jan | Feb | Mar | Apr | May | June | July | Aug | Sep | Oct | Nov | Dec |

During spring the male Bobolink is the only North American songbird that is black below and light above. Fall males and juveniles resemble females and are buff-colored with a dark eye line and head streaks, darker wings and tail, and streaking on the flanks. During migration Bobolinks travel high overhead in large flocks (sometimes in the thousands) emitting a characteristic *clink* call. They are found in Florida from mid-April through late May and in lower numbers from late August through October. Preferred habitats include agricultural lands, pastures, and green grasslands. They are sometimes seen on highway edges and medians. During fall principal foods include grains and seeds. Insects also are taken when available.

FAMILY *Icteridae: Blackbirds and Orioles*   p. 272
RED-WINGED BLACKBIRD (*Agelaius phoeniceus*)
LENGTH 8 in (20 cm)   WEIGHT 2.3 oz (0.07 kg)

Other names Florida Red-wing, Redwing

Description All black with red and yellow shoulder patch (male) or smaller, dark brown, heavily streaked (female)

Habitat Salt marshes; dry prairies; wet prairies and marshes; agricultural environments

Range Statewide

| Jan | Feb | Mar | Apr | May | June | July | Aug | Sep | Oct | Nov | Dec |

This is one of North America's most widespread and abundant birds. In Florida it is found throughout the state from salt and freshwater marshes to agricultural lands. Males are a glossy black with bright red wing patches or epaulets bordered in golden yellow. Females and immatures are sparrowlike, brown above, and streaked below. Females are somewhat smaller than males. The male's song is a melodious *konk-ler-eee,* which may vary in different parts of the state. Nests are woven-grass structures attached to shrubs or tall annuals. Eggs, numbering three or four, are bluish with black and purple markings and laid from April to June. During fall and winter, migrant and resident Red-wings congregate in huge numbers with other blackbirds (starlings, cowbirds, grackles). Flocks with thousands of individuals can be seen feeding in agricultural fields (where they are know to damage crops) and grasslands or descending upon productive marshes. Food consists of seeds such as rice, corn, oats, and wild grasses as well as grasshoppers, dragonflies, and other insects.

FAMILY *Icteridae: Blackbirds and Orioles*
EASTERN MEADOWLARK (*Sturnella magna*)
p. 272
LENGTH 9 in (23 cm)   WEIGHT 3.6 oz (0.10 kg)

Other names Field Lark, Southern Meadowlark
Description Throat, breast, belly yellow with a black V on breast; striped head
Habitat Dry prairies; agricultural environments
Range Statewide

Jan	Feb	Mar	Apr	May	June	July	Aug	Sep	Oct	Nov	Dec

Bright yellow underparts accented by a broad, black bib are the most obvious field marks of the resident Eastern Meadowlark. The head is marked in alternating brown and buff streaks, the back appears mottled brown, and the flanks are streaked. When flying, the Meadowlark displays conspicuous white borders on the tail. The male's song, consisting of two descending, ventriloquial phrases, is often sung from an exposed perch such as a fence post or tree top. Meadowlarks are grassland birds that construct a woven grass nest on the ground. Eggs are white with brownish spots and number from three to five. Egg laying occurs as early as February and as late as June. Insects such as crickets, grasshoppers, beetles, and caterpillars form the bulk of its diet. Small seeds and grains also are eaten.

FAMILY *Icteridae: Blackbirds and Orioles*
YELLOW-HEADED BLACKBIRD (*Xanthocephalus xanthocephalus*)
p. 273
LENGTH 9.5 in (24 cm)   WEIGHT 2.3 oz (0.06 kg)

Description Black, bright yellow head, neck, and upper breast, white wing patches (male) or smaller with yellow throat and no white in the wings (female) or brownish with a pale yellow head (immature males)
Habitat Pastures, cropland, golf courses, freshwater marshes
Range Statewide

Jan	Feb	Mar	Apr	May	June	July	Aug	Sep	Oct	Nov	Dec

This western species usually appears somewhere in Florida each winter, often as a single bird, in a flock of Red-winged Blackbirds or Common Grackles at a cattle feed lot, a horse barn, or pasture. Adult males are black with a bright yellow head, neck, and upper breast, and have white wing patches that show in flight. Females are smaller with yellow throat and no white in the wings. Immature males are brownish with a pale yellow head. Foods consist of grains, seeds, and insects.

FAMILY *Icteridae: Blackbirds and Orioles*
RUSTY BLACKBIRD (*Euphagus carolinus*)
p. 273
LENGTH 9 in (23 cm)   WEIGHT 2.3 oz (0.06 kg)

Description Glossy green with yellow eye (male) or grayish with yellow eye (female)

Habitat Mesic hammock; mixed pine and hardwood forests; pastures

Range Statewide

Jan	Feb	Mar	Apr	May	June	July	Aug	Sep	Oct	Nov	Dec

The Rusty Blackbird occasionally is seen in flocks of mixed blackbird species during winter in central and north Florida. The feathers of wintering birds are rust-edged. Females exhibit buff undersides. By spring the rusty tips wear away leaving a glossy green plumage in the male and a grayish plumage in the female. A bright yellow eye is present in all plumages.

These fruit and insect eaters can be seen in a variety of open habitats and woodlands and swamps from October through April.

FAMILY *Icteridae: Blackbirds and Orioles*
BREWER'S BLACKBIRD (*Euphagus cyanocephalus*)
p. 273
LENGTH 9 in (23 cm)   WEIGHT 2.2 oz (0.06 kg)

Description Glossy, purple-green plumage, yellow eyes (male) or gray-brown with dark eyes (female)

Habitat Pastures, cropland, golf courses

Range Statewide

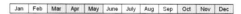

Jan	Feb	Mar	Apr	May	June	July	Aug	Sep	Oct	Nov	Dec

Brewer's Blackbirds can occasionally be seen singly or in small flocks or with Red-winged Blackbirds in pastures, cropland, golf courses, or parks from November through April. Most sightings are in north Florida. Males have glossy, purple-green plumage and yellow eyes, while females are gray-brown with dark eyes. A variety of seeds and insects is eaten.

Family *Icteridae: Blackbirds and Orioles*
BOAT-TAILED GRACKLE (*Quiscalus major*)
LENGTH 15 in (38 cm)   WEIGHT 7.5 oz (0.21 kg)

p. 272

Other names Jackdaw
Description Large; glossy black with long keeled tail,
eyes may be yellow or brown (male) or smaller, buff
breast, dark brown above (female)
Habitat Salt marshes; wet prairies and marshes; urban environments; agricultural environments
Range Statewide

Jan	Feb	Mar	Apr	May	June	July	Aug	Sep	Oct	Nov	Dec

This large grackle appears still larger with its long, deep-keeled tail. Males are black with a purplish iridescence. Females are smaller and brown with dark wings and a shorter, dark tail. The population in peninsular Florida south of Gainesville has brown eyes, unlike the yellow-eyed birds of the northeast coast and western Panhandle. The male's song consists of a complicated array of noisy twitters, clucks, and rattles. Boat-tailed Grackles are common year-round residents except in the extreme northern Panhandle and the Keys. They nest in loose colonies in freshwater and saltwater marshes as well as along lake and stream borders and in towns. Grasses are used to construct a bulky nest placed in trees and other vegetation. Eggs are white with purplish mottling and number two to three. The nesting season extends from February through July; however, Boat-tails occasionally will nest again in October through December. Foods include beetles, crayfish, crabs, corn, and other grains and insects. Boat-tailed Grackles will frequent service stations and rest areas along interstates where they extract dead insects from the grills of automobiles.

Family *Icteridae: Blackbirds and Orioles*
COMMON GRACKLE (*Quiscalus quiscula*)
LENGTH 12 in (30 cm)   WEIGHT 4.5 oz (0.13 kg)

p. 272

Other names Jackdaw, Florida Grackle, Crow Blackbird
Description Black with iridescent purple; yellow eyes;
keeled tail; female is similar, but duller in color
Habitat Dry prairies; mesic hammocks; mixed pine and hardwood forests; urban environments; agricultural environments
Range Statewide

Jan	Feb	Mar	Apr	May	June	July	Aug	Sep	Oct	Nov	Dec

This blackbird is smaller and shorter-tailed than the similar Boat-tailed Grackle. The male is black with a purplish head and bronze iridescence elsewhere. Females appear duller, and immatures are brownish. The eyes have light-colored irises. This permanent resident is distributed throughout Florida. Nesting occurs in a variety of habitats from open woodlands to citrus groves, prairies, and buildings. The bulky, mud-lined nests are placed in tree cavities, forked branches, shrubs, or human-made structures. Eggs number three to six, are greenish-white with splotches of black, gray, and brown, and are laid from mid-March through early July. During winter Common Grackles may form large flocks with other blackbirds. The diet is highly variable and includes many insects, mollusks, crustaceans, berries, wild seeds and cultivated grains.

FAMILY *Icteridae: Blackbirds and Orioles*
SHINY COWBIRD (*Molothrus bonariensis*)   p. 273
LENGTH 7 in (18 cm)   WEIGHT 1.4 oz (0.03 kg)

Other names Glossy Cowbird

Description Head, breast, and upper back glossy purple (black from a distance); the lower back, wings, and tail duller black (male); the female and immature are nearly indistinguishable from the female and immature Brown-headed Cowbird

Habitat Suburban backyards, feeders, grassy roadsides, agricultural areas

Range South Florida and the Florida Keys

Jan	Feb	Mar	Apr	May	June	July	Aug	Sep	Oct	Nov	Dec

This species first arrived in North America from the Caribbean in 1985 when a lone male was seen near Marathon in the Florida Keys. Since then numerous pairs and several immatures have been reported in peninsular Florida and the Panhandle. The adult male is similar in size to the Brown-headed Cowbird, but appears thinner because of its longer tail and longer, less conical bill. The head, breast, and upper back are glossy purple (black from a distance); the lower back, wings, and tail a duller black. The female and immatures are almost indistinguishable from female and immature Brown-headed Cowbirds, except for the longer, less conical bill. Some female Shiny Cowbirds exhibit a faint but distinct eyestripe. It is now fairly common on the Keys where it is a brood parasite like the Brown-headed Cowbird, but breeding there has not yet been confirmed. Host species are usually larger than the Shiny Cowbird. It eats seeds, grains, and a variety of insects.

FAMILY *Icteridae: Blackbirds and Orioles*
BRONZED COWBIRD (*Molothrus aeneus*)   p. 273
LENGTH 8.5 in (22 cm)   WEIGHT 2.2 oz (0.06 kg)

Other names Red-eyed Cowbird

Description Black, bronze gloss on head and back, blue-black wings and tail, bright red eyes (male) or dull black (female) or brown with less distinctive red eyes (immatue)

Habitat Pastures and suburban yards

Range Statewide

Jan	Feb	Mar	Apr	May	June	July	Aug	Sep	Oct	Nov	Dec

The frequency of recurrence of this species in Florida has been increasing and in winter the Bronzed Cowbird may show up anywhere in the state. The male is black with a bronze gloss on the head and back, blue-black wings and tail, and bright red eyes. The female is dull black, and immatures are brown with less distinctive red eyes. Bronzed Cowbirds are inhabitants of open country in their native southwestern United States. They now breed as far east as Louisiana. In Florida they can be seen with other blackbirds in pastures and suburban yards. Foods consist of seeds and insects.

FAMILY *Icteridae: Blackbirds and Orioles*
BROWN-HEADED COWBIRD (*Molothrus ater*)

p. 272

LENGTH 7 in (18 cm)   WEIGHT 1.7 oz (0.05 kg)

Description Brown head, black glossy body (male) or smaller, buff breast, dark brown above (female)

Habitat Xeric scrub; dry prairies; mesic hammocks; mixed pine and hardwood forests; wet prairies and marshes; urban environments; pine flatwoods; sandhills; agricultural environments

Range Statewide

| Jan | Feb | Mar | Apr | May | June | July | Aug | Sep | Oct | Nov | Dec |

The Brown-headed Cowbird is a small blackbird with brown head and greenish-black body. Females are gray overall with faint streaks below. The male's song is a series of thin, wavering squeaks. Brown-headed Cowbirds are most often seen in Florida as fall and winter visitors; however, breeding birds have been found in nearly every county. The Cowbird has earned a notorious reputation because of its parasitic nesting habits. Rather than building its own nest, the female lays four to five white, brown-spotted eggs each in a different bird's nest. The victimized species include a variety of warblers, vireos, tanagers, buntings, orioles, and sparrows. As such, during the nesting season it is found in a wide range of habitats where potential host species are available. Because the egg and young cowbird is larger than its nest mates, it is often the only nest survivor. The diet is mostly grains and seeds, but also includes grasshoppers and other insects. Brown-headed Cowbirds often congregate with other flocking blackbirds during autumn and winter.

FAMILY *Icteridae: Blackbirds and Orioles*
ORCHARD ORIOLE (*Icterus spurius*)

p. 266

LENGTH 7 in (18 cm)   WEIGHT 0.7 oz (0.02 kg)

Description Black head, throat, and upperparts; chestnut rump and underparts (male) or olive-green above, yellow below (female); first year males are same as female, but with black throat and breast

Habitat Mesic hammocks; mixed pine and hardwood forests; urban environments; agricultural environments

Range Central and north Florida

| Jan | Feb | Mar | Apr | May | June | July | Aug | Sep | Oct | Nov | Dec |

The Orchard Oriole is a characteristic summer resident in open deciduous woodlands and suburbs in north Florida. The adult male's black head, breast, tail, back, and wings contrast with rusty red undersides, flanks, and rump. Females are greenish-yellow with grayish wings and buff wing bars. First-year males resemble females but sport a black bib. The song is a musical warble ending with a down-slurred note. The Orchard Oriole has been extending its breeding range southward in Florida and now breeds in and around Orlando, as indicated on the range map. Nests are usually high off the ground and may be concealed in a clump of Spanish moss. They are constructed of fine grasses that contain three to five light blue eggs streaked with brown and purple. Laying may occur from early April through June. Migrants pass through Florida from mid-March through early May and in fall from late August through October. The diet is composed mostly of insects.

FAMILY *Icteridae: Blackbirds and Orioles*
SPOT-BREASTED ORIOLE (*Icterus pectoralis*)
LENGTH 9 in (23 cm)   WEIGHT 1.6 oz (0.05 kg)

p. 266

Description Orange overall with black throat, back, wings, tail;
spots on breast; orange and white patches on wings
Habitat Urban environments
Range Southeastern Florida

| Jan | Feb | Mar | Apr | May | June | July | Aug | Sep | Oct | Nov | Dec |

South Florida's only regularly breeding oriole is the exotic Spot-breasted. Introduced in the 1950s, this Central American native makes its home in heavily landscaped yards in Miami-Dade, Broward, and Palm Beach counties. The song is a series of loud, bubbling, and musical whistles. The male is orange with black tail and back, and black wings with white patches. The black bib separates into scattered spots above the breast. Females are similar but somewhat duller. Juveniles are yellowish below, with no spotting on the breast. Spot-breasted Orioles build pendulous nests in their native tropical haunts, but in Florida, nests are cup-shaped structures placed in a tree or shrub. Eggs, numbering three to five, are pale blue with brown spots and can be found from May through September. This colorful exotic is an inhabitant of Florida's urbanized southeast coast and does not seem to have displaced any native species. Its breeding range is indicated on the range map. Foods include a variety of tropical fruits and insects.

FAMILY *Icteridae: Blackbirds and Orioles*
BALTIMORE ORIOLE (*Icterus galbula*)   p. 266
LENGTH 8.5 in (22 cm)   WEIGHT 1.2 oz (0.03 kg)

Other names Northern Oriole, Bullock's Oriole
Description Black head, throat, back, wings; orange rump and
underparts, white bars on wings (male) or olive-brown above,
orange-yellow below, white wing bars (female)
Habitat Mesic hammocks; mixed pine and hardwood forests; urban
environments; agricultural environments
Range Statewide

| Jan | Feb | Mar | Apr | May | June | July | Aug | Sep | Oct | Nov | Dec |

The distinctively marked male Baltimore Oriole has a black hood, tail, and wings with contrasting orange undersides, rump, and outer tail feathers. The female is dull orange to yellow with dark tail, back, head, and wings. Both sexes show white barring on the wings. Spring migrants can be seen in Florida from early April through mid-May. Fall birds are not commonly seen here and wintering birds occur at scattered locations throughout the state. One nesting record exists for a pair in Key West in the 1970s. Foods consist of insects, seeds, and small fruits. It occasionally will appear at feeding stations if orange sections are offered. Each year a few individuals of the similar **Bullock's Oriole** (*Icterus bullockii*) winter in Florida. This western vagrant is distinguished from the Baltimore by a large white wing patch, orange cheeks, and a black eye line. Females are very similar to female Baltimore Orioles.

FAMILY *Fringillidae: Finches*

PURPLE FINCH (*Carpodacus purpureus*)

p. 271

LENGTH 6 in (15 cm)   WEIGHT 1.2 oz (0.03 kg)

Description Rosy red head, throat, breast, back; notched tail (male) or overall brown with heavily streaked white breast; brown and white striped head (female)

Habitat Hardwood swamps; cypress swamps; urban environments; agricultural environments

Range North and central Florida

Jan	Feb	Mar	Apr	May	June	July	Aug	Sep	Oct	Nov	Dec

The Purple Finch can be seen in large numbers during some winters in north Florida, and in south Florida during particularly cold winters. Males are rose red, especially on the head, rump, and breast. The back is streaked with brown and the tail is distinctly notched. The female is brown above with heavy streaking on a white breast, and has a distinctive white eyebrow and brown ear patch. The diet primarily consists of tree seeds found in a variety of woodland habitats. Purple Finches can be frequent visitors at feeding stations.

FAMILY *Fringillidae: Finches*

HOUSE FINCH (*Carpodacus mexicanus*)

p. 271

LENGTH 5.5 in (14 cm)   WEIGHT 0.7 oz (0.02 kg)

Description Brown cap with red forehead, throat, and breast; brown face and back with heavily streaked underparts; square tail (male) or brown streaked with unpatterned head (female)

Habitat Urban environments; agricultural environments

Range North Florida and urban southeastern Florida

Jan	Feb	Mar	Apr	May	June	July	Aug	Sep	Oct	Nov	Dec

This western species was introduced on Long Island, New York, in the early 1940s when 100 birds were apparently released by a department store. It now breeds throughout most of the continental United States. Wintering flocks were found in Florida in the early 1980s and it is now an established breeder in the upper two-thirds of the state, as indicated on the range map, and its range is expanding southward. House Finches are similar to Purple Finches; however, the male has a brown cap with a red forehead, throat, and breast along with brown-streaked underparts. The female is brown streaked and lacks the ear patch and white eyebrow characteristic of the female Purple Finch. In both sexes the tip of the tail is square, not notched as in the Purple Finch. The song is a very musical series of three-note phrases that occasionally can be heard in winter. In some parts of the east, the House Finch has become the most frequent visitor at feeders. As its name implies, it adapts well to urban and suburban settings, wherever trees and shrubs abound. Nests, constructed of grass and small twigs, are built in conifers and artificial cavities. Clutches consist of two to six eggs. In the absence of evergreens House Finches will nest on ledges of porches, sheds, barns, and other structures. Food consists primarily of seeds.

p. 271

FAMILY *Fringillidae: Finches*
PINE SISKIN (*Carduelis pinus*)
LENGTH 5 in (13 cm)   WEIGHT 0.5 oz (0.01 kg)

Description Brown upperparts and white underparts heavily
streaked; yellow at base of primaries
Habitat Urban environments; pine flatwoods
Range Statewide

Jan	Feb	Mar	Apr	May	June	July	Aug	Sep	Oct	Nov	Dec

The Pine Siskin's sharp, pointed bill is uncharacteristic for a finch. The boldly streaked plumage is grayish-brown above and white or buff below. The dark wings and tail are highlighted with bright yellow bands. Pine Siskins are unpredictable winter visitors in Florida, but are usually seen between October and May. Severe northern weather seems to account for occasionally high numbers in the state. Most birds remain in north Florida during their stay, although a few have been recorded in south Florida. Its undulating flight pattern is reminiscent of the closely related American Goldfinch. Pine Siskins feed chiefly on pine and sweetgum seeds, and in south Florida, Australian pine seeds.

p. 271

FAMILY *Fringillidae: Finches*
AMERICAN GOLDFINCH (*Carduelis tristis*)
LENGTH 5 in (13 cm)   WEIGHT 0.5 oz (0.01 kg)

Other names Wild Canary, Thistle Bird, Eastern Goldfinch

Description Black cap, wings, tail; yellow body; white wing bars (spring male) or
olive-brown above, no cap, yellowish head (winter male) or dull olive-yellow; black wings, tail; no cap (female)
Habitat Mixed pine and hardwood forests; urban environments; pine
flatwoods; sandhills; agricultural environments
Range Statewide

Jan	Feb	Mar	Apr	May	June	July	Aug	Sep	Oct	Nov	Dec

This colorful bird appears in its drab winter plumage during its stay in Florida. The male has yellow cheeks and throat, brown back, black wings and tail, and white wing bars. Females are duller overall. Its call, *chick-chick-a-ree,* is often given in flight. When the bird is perched, its call is a question: *chick-a-ree?* Flocks of goldfinches can be seen from early November through April in most parts of Florida. It is a bird of open woodlands, brushy areas, and old fields, and may be an abundant visitor at feeding stations. Foods include seeds of sunflowers, pines, buttonbush, thistle, and other weeds. A few insects also are taken.

FAMILY *Fringillidae: Finches*

EVENING GROSBEAK (*Coccothraustes vespertinus*)   p. 270

LENGTH 8 in (20 cm)   WEIGHT 1.87–2.61 oz (0.05–0.07 kg)

Description Dark brown and yellow; large pale bill; white in black wings, tail (male) or grayish-tan; white in wings and tail (female)
Habitat Mixed pine and hardwood forests; urban environments; pine flatwoods
Range North Florida

Jan	Feb	Mar	Apr	May	June	July	Aug	Sep	Oct	Nov	Dec

This large, chunky finch is an unpredictable visitor from Canada and New England but can be expected during some cold winters and has occurred southward to Gainesville. The male is yellow with black wings and tail, brown head with yellow eyebrow, and a white inner wing patch. The female is buff-colored with an additional white wing patch. Evening Grosbeaks will visit backyard feeding stations stocked with sunflower seeds as well as pine and hardwood forests. Seeds and fruits form the bulk of its diet.

FAMILY *Passeridae: Old World Sparrows*

HOUSE SPARROW (*Passer domesticus*)   p. 264

LENGTH 6 in (15 cm)   WEIGHT 1 oz (0.03 kg)

Other names English Sparrow, Weaver Finch
Description Black throat and breast, gray crown, white cheek, chestnut nape (male)
Habitat Urban environments; agricultural environments
Range Statewide

Jan	Feb	Mar	Apr	May	June	July	Aug	Sep	Oct	Nov	Dec

The House Sparrow was released at hundreds of locations in eastern North America during the late 1800s. This European native now is widespread in the Western Hemisphere, especially in urban settings. A study of residential birds in St. Petersburg, Florida, in the 1960s revealed that House Sparrows comprised 45% of the avian population. This percentage has declined considerably in recent decades. The male has a black bib, gray cap, white cheeks, dirty white belly, brown and black streaked back and wings with a single white wing bar. Females and immatures are dingy brown with a faint eyestripe. In Florida nests may be found at any time, although most breeding occurs from March to September. Nests are bulky masses of dry grass, pine straw, feathers, plastic, paper, and string, and are built in bird houses, crevices in buildings, signs, light fixtures, rain gutters, and in leafy tree branches. The three to five whitish eggs are heavily speckled with brown and black. Several broods may be raised each year. Young remain in the nest until almost fully grown, enhancing their survivorship. Adults usually mate for life. Its vocalizations are generally unmusical chatterings. It feeds primarily on seeds and grains but also is fond of bread crumbs and other food discarded by people. During nesting young birds are fed insects.

Common Loon
14 in (36 cm)
p. 29

summer

winter

Horned Grebe
12–15 in (30–38 cm)
p. 30

Pied-billed Grebe p. 30
13.5 in (34 cm)

winter

breeding

American White Pelican
62 in (158 cm)
p. 36

nonbreeding

immature

breeding

nonbreeding

Brown Pelican
48 in (122 cm)
p. 36

Wilson's Storm-Petrel
7.25 in (18 cm)
p. 33

Audubon's Shearwater
12 in (30 cm)
p. 32

above

Greater Shearwater
18 in (46 cm)
p. 32

below

Cory's Shearwater
18 in (46 cm)
p. 31

215

White-tailed Tropicbird
30 in (76 cm)
p. 33

Magnificent Frigatebird
40 in (102 cm)
p. 38

male

female

Northern Gannet p. 35
37 in (94 cm)

immature

adult

Brown Booby p. 3
30 in (76 cm)

immature

adult

Masked Booby
32 in (81 cm)
p. 34

female

Anhinga
35 in (89 cm)
p. 38

first-year

Double-crested Cormorant
32 in (81 cm)
p. 37

Black-crowned Night-Heron
25 in (64 cm)
p. 45

adult

immature

Yellow-crowned Night-Heron
24 in (61 cm)
p. 46

adult

immature

American Bittern
28 in (71 cm)
p. 39

Least Bittern
13 in (33 cm)
p. 39

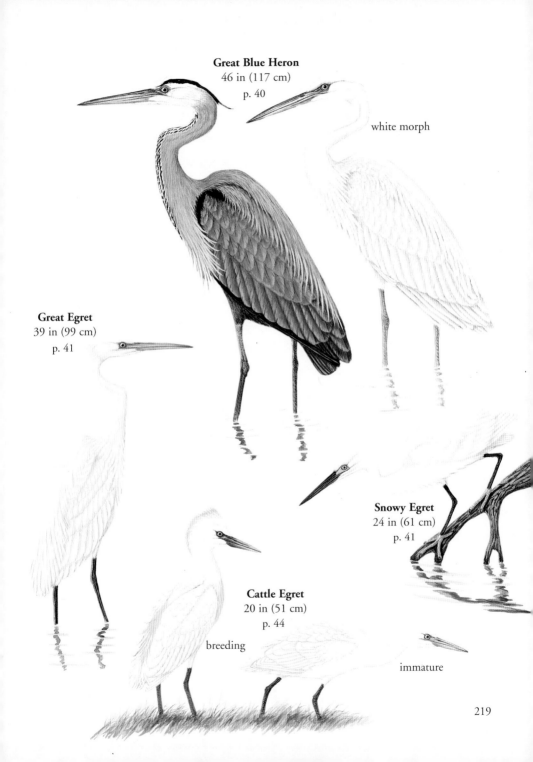

Great Blue Heron
46 in (117 cm)
p. 40

white morph

Great Egret
39 in (99 cm)
p. 41

Snowy Egret
24 in (61 cm)
p. 41

Cattle Egret
20 in (51 cm)
p. 44

breeding

immature

Reddish Egret
30 in (76 cm)
p. 43

white phase

dark phase

Tricolored Heron
26 in (66 cm)
p. 42

Little Blue Heron
24 in (61 cm)
p. 42

immature

molting

adult

Green Heron
18 in (46 cm)
p. 44

Wood Stork
40 in (102 cm)
p. 48

Greater Flamingo
46 in (117 cm)
p. 50

Roseate Spoonbill
32 in (81 cm)
p. 47

White Ibis
25 in (64 cm)
p. 46

immature

adult

Glossy Ibis
23 in (58 cm)
p. 47

221

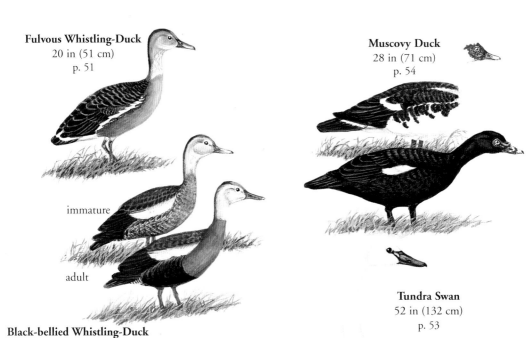

Fulvous Whistling-Duck
20 in (51 cm)
p. 51

Muscovy Duck
28 in (71 cm)
p. 54

immature

adult

Black-bellied Whistling-Duck
21 in (53 cm)
p. 51

Tundra Swan
52 in (132 cm)
p. 53

Snow Goose
28 in (71 cm)
p. 52

blue

white

Canada Goose
40 in (102 cm)
p. 52

female

Green-winged Teal
14 in (36 cm)
p. 60

male

Wood Duck
18 in (46 cm)
p. 54

male

female

Mottled Duck
22 in (56 cm)
p. 57

American Black Duck
23 in (58 cm)
p. 56

male

female

Mallard
23 in (58 cm)
p. 57

female

male

Northern Pintail
20–26 in (51–66 cm)
p. 59

223

Blue-winged Teal
16 in (41 cm)
p. 58

male

female

Northern Shoveler
19 in (48 cm)
p. 59

female

male

Gadwall
20 in (51 cm)
p. 55

male

female

male

American Wigeon
19 in
(48 cm)

male

male

p. 55

Canvasback
21 in (53 cm)
p. 60

female

male

female

Redhead
19 in (48 cm)
p. 61

female

male

Ring-necked Duck
17 in (43 cm)
p. 61

female

male

Lesser Scaup
17 in (43 cm)
p. 62

female

male

Hooded Merganser
18 in (46 cm)
p. 65

female

male

Red-breasted Merganser
23 in (58 cm)
p. 66

female

male

Ruddy Duck   15 in (38 cm)
p. 66

male

female

225

Black Scoter
19 in (48 cm)
p. 63

female

White-winged Scoter
21 in (53 cm)
p. 63

female

male

male

Surf Scoter
20 in (51 cm)
p. 62

male

female

Bufflehead
13 in (33 cm)
p. 64

female

male

Long-tailed Duck
22 in (56 cm)
p. 64

male

female

Common Goldeneye
18 in (46 cm)
p. 65

male

female

Black Vulture
25 in (64 cm)
p. 49

Turkey Vulture
27 in (69 cm)
p. 49

Bald Eagle   p. 70
31–37 in (79–94 cm)

immature

Northern Harrier
20 in (51 cm)
p. 71

male

female

adult

immature

Golden Eagle
30–40 in (76–102 cm)
p. 74

adult

227

American Kestrel p. 75
10 in (25 cm)

male

Crested Caracara
23 in (58 cm)
p. 75

male

female

male

Osprey
24 in (61 cm)
p. 67

female

Merlin
12 in (30 cr
p. 76

male

immature

adult

Peregrine Falcon p. 77
16–20 in (41–51 cm)

Mississippi Kite
14 in (36 cm)
p. 69

adult

immature

Snail Kite
17 in (43 cm)
p. 69

male

female

Swallow-tailed Kite
23 in (58 cm)
p. 68

Cooper's Hawk
14–20 in (36–51 cm)
p. 72

male

immature

Sharp-shinned Hawk
10–14 in (25–36 cm)
p. 71

immature

male

229

Red-tailed Hawk
22 in (56 cm)
p. 74

adult

immature

Broad-winged Hawk
16 in (41 cm)
p. 73

adult

immature

Short-tailed Hawk
16 in (41 cm)
p. 73

dark phase

light phase

Red-shouldered Hawk
19 in (48 cm)
p. 72

adult

immature

Wild Turkey
45 in (114 cm)
p. 77

male

female

Limpkin
26 in (66 cm)
p. 83

male

female

Northern Bobwhite
9 in (23 cm)
p. 78

Whooping Crane
56 in (142 cm)
p. 84

Sandhill Crane
40 in (102 cm)
p. 84

King Rail
15 in (38 cm)
p. 80

Clapper Rail
14 in (36 cm)
p. 80

Virginia Rail
9 in (23 cm)
p. 81

Sora
8 in (20 cm)
p. 81

Black Rail
6 in (15 cm)
p. 79

Common Moorhen
14 in (36 cm)
p. 82

immature

adult

American Coot
15 in (38 cm)
p. 83

Purple Gallinule
13 in (33 cm)
p. 82

adult

immature

American Avocet
18 in (46 cm)
p. 90

winter

American Oystercatcher
18 in (46 cm)
p. 89

Black-necked Stilt
14 in (36 cm)
p. 89

233

American Golden-Plover
10 in (25 cm)
p. 86

winter

Semipalmated Plover
7 in (18 cm)
p. 87

winter

breeding

winter

Killdeer
10 in (25 cm)
p. 88

Black-bellied Plover
11 in (28 cm)
p. 85

breeding

winter

Piping Plover
7 in (18 cm)
p. 88

Wilson's Plover
8 in (20 cm)
p. 87

female

male

breeding

Snowy Plover
6 in (15 cm)
p. 86

234

Greater Yellowlegs
14 in (36 cm)
p. 90

Lesser Yellowlegs
10.5 in (27 cm)
p. 91

Whimbrel
17 in (43 cm)
p. 93

Long-billed Curlew
23 in (58 cm)
p. 94

Marbled Godwit
18 in (46 cm)
p. 94

Solitary Sandpiper
8.5 in (22 cm)
p. 91

Willet
15 in (38 cm)
p. 92

breeding

American Woodcock
p. 101   11 in (28 cm)

summer

Spotted Sandpiper
7.5 in (19 cm)
p. 92

Wilson's Snipe
10 in (25 cm)
p. 101

winter

Short-billed Dowitcher
11 in (28 cm)
p. 100

winter

Ruddy Turnstone
9 in (23 cm)
p. 95

winter

breeding

Purple Sandpiper
9 in (23 cm)
p. 99

Pectoral Sandpiper
9 in (23 cm)
p. 98

Red Knot
10 in (25 cm)
p. 95

winter

Dunlin
8.5 in (22 cm)
p. 99

breeding

Least Sandpiper
6 in (15 cm)
p. 97

White-rumped Sandpiper
7.5 in (19 cm)
p. 98

winter

Sanderling
8 in (20 cm)
p. 96

winter

Western Sandpiper
6.5 in (17 cm)
p. 97

Semipalmated Sandpiper
6.25 in (16 cm)
p. 96

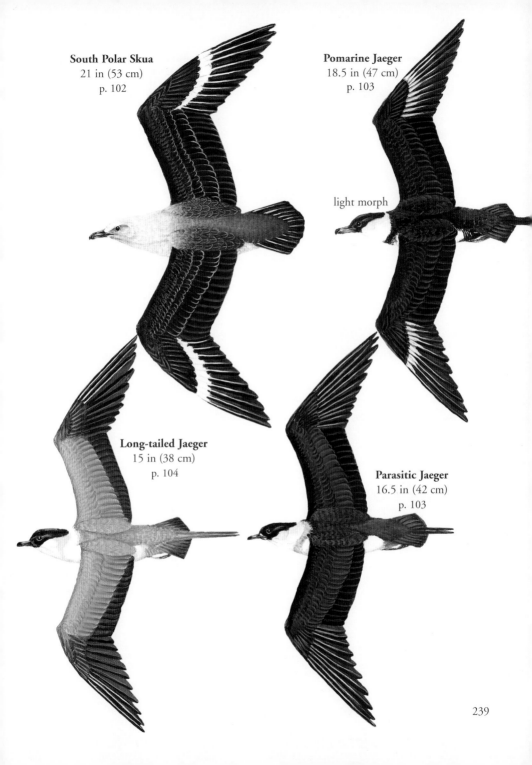

South Polar Skua
21 in (53 cm)
p. 102

Pomarine Jaeger
18.5 in (47 cm)
p. 103

light morph

Long-tailed Jaeger
15 in (38 cm)
p. 104

Parasitic Jaeger
16.5 in (42 cm)
p. 103

Great Black-backed Gull
30 in (76 cm)   p. 107

adult

immature   second winter

Laughing Gull
16 in (41 cm)
p. 104

Lesser Black-backed Gull
21 in (53 cm)
p. 106

Bonaparte's Gull
13 in (33 cm)
p. 105

Herring Gull   p. 106
25 in (64 cm)
first winter

Ring-billed Gull   p. 105
17 in (43 cm)

first winter

adult   adult

240

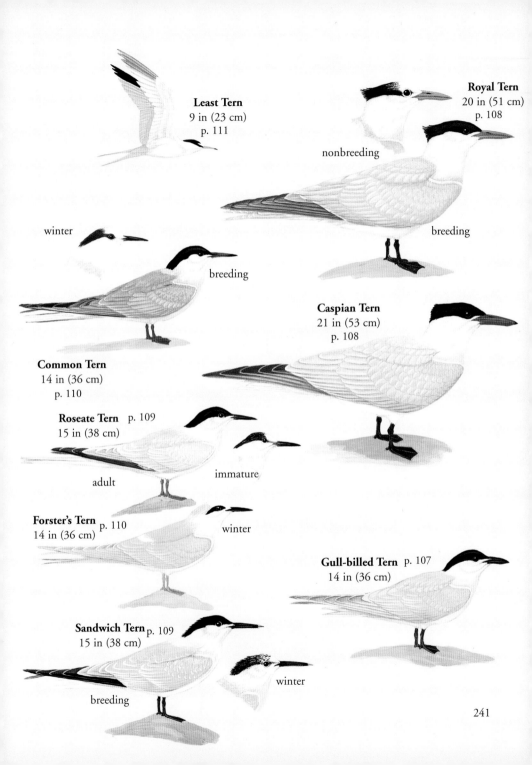

Least Tern
9 in (23 cm)
p. 111

Royal Tern
20 in (51 cm)
p. 108

nonbreeding

winter

breeding

Caspian Tern
21 in (53 cm)
p. 108

breeding

Common Tern
14 in (36 cm)
p. 110

Roseate Tern p. 109
15 in (38 cm)

adult

immature

Forster's Tern p. 110
14 in (36 cm)

winter

Gull-billed Tern p. 107
14 in (36 cm)

Sandwich Tern p. 109
15 in (38 cm)

winter

breeding

241

Black Tern
10 in (25 cm)
p. 112

spring

fall

Bridled Tern
15 in (38 cm)
p. 111

Sooty Tern
16 in (41 cm)
p. 112

Black Noddy
13 in (33 cm)
p. 113

Brown Noddy
16 in (41 cm)
p. 113

Black Skimmer
18 in (46 cm)
p. 114

Common Ground-Dove
6 in (15 cm)
p. 118

Ringed Turtle-Dove
11 in (28 cm)
p. 115

White-Crowned Pigeon
13 in (33 cm)
p. 115

Eurasian Collared-Dove
11.5 in (29 cm)
p. 116

Rock Pigeon
12 in (30 cm)
p. 114

White-winged Dove
11 in (28 cm)
p. 116

Mourning Dove
12 in (30 cm)
p. 117

243

Monk Parakeet
11 in (28 cm)
p. 120

Rose-ringed Parakeet
16 in (41 cm)
p. 119

Budgerigar
7 in (18 cm)
p. 119

White-winged Parakeet
9 in (23 cm)
p. 123

Red-crowned Parrot
12.5 in (32 cm)
p. 123

Blue-crowned Parakeet
14.5 in (35.56 cm)
p. 121

Red-masked Parakeet
13.5 in (34 cm)
p. 121

Mitred Parakeet
15 in (38 cm)
p. 122

Chestnut-fronted Macaw
18 in (46 cm)
p. 122

Black-hooded Parakeet
12 in (30 cm)
p. 120

Mangrove Cuckoo
12 in (30 cm)
p. 125

Yellow-billed Cuckoo
12 in (30 cm)
p. 124

Black-billed Cuckoo
12 in (30 cm)
p. 124

Smooth-billed Ani
14 in (36 cm)
p. 125

Groove-billed Ani
13 in (33 cm)
p. 126

Eastern Screech-Owl p. 127
8 in (20 cm)

gray phase

red phase

brown phase

Great Horned Owl
21 in (53 cm)
p. 127

Barn Owl
16 in (41 cm)
p. 126

Barred Owl
20 in (51 cm)
p. 128

Burrowing Owl
9 in (23 cm)
p. 128

Chuck-will's-widow
12 in (30 cm)
p. 130

Whip-poor-will
10 in (25 cm)
p. 131

Common Nighthawk
9 in (23 cm)
p. 129

Antillean Nighthawk
9 in (23 cm)
p. 130

Belted Kingfisher
13 in (33 cm)
p. 133

male

female

Chimney Swift
5 in (13 cm)
p. 131

Ruby-throated Hummingbird
3.5 in (9 cm)
p. 132

male

female

Yellow-bellied Sapsucker
8.5 in (22 cm)   p. 135

male

female

Red-cockaded Woodpecker
8 in (20 cm)
p. 137

male

male

Red-headed Woodpecker
9 in (23 cm)
p. 134

adult

Hairy Woodpecker
9 in (23 cm)
p. 136

female

juvenile

male

Downy Woodpecker
6.5 in (17 cm)
p. 136

249

Pileated Woodpecker
16 in (41 cm)
p. 138

male

female

Ivory-billed Woodpecker
20 in (51 cm)
p. 139

male

Northern Flicker
12 in (30 cm)
p. 137

male

female

Red-bellied Woodpecker
9 in (23 cm)
p. 134

250

Eastern Kingbird
8 in (20 cm)
p. 144

Gray Kingbird
9 in (23 cm)
p. 145

Scissor-tailed Flycatcher
13 in (33 cm)
p. 145

Eastern Phoebe
7 in (18 cm)
p. 142

Western Kingbird
9 in (23 cm)
p. 144

Acadian Flycatcher
6 in (15 cm)
p. 141

Least Flycatcher
5 in (13 cm)
p. 142

Vermilion Flycatcher
6 in (15 cm)
p. 143

Eastern Wood-Pewee
6 in (15 cm)
p. 140

Great Crested Flycatcher
9 in (23 cm)
p. 143

251

Ruby-crowned Kinglet
4 in (10 cm)
p. 161

female

male

Golden-crowned Kinglet p. 161
4 in (10 cm)

male

female

Blue-gray Gnatcatcher
4.5 in (11 cm)
p. 162

Loggerhead Shrike
9 in (23 cm)
p. 146

American Pipit
6.5 in (17 cm)
p. 169

Cedar Waxwing
7 in (18 cm)
p. 169

Yellow-throated Vireo
5.5 in (14 cm)
p. 147

Blue-headed Vireo
5.5 in (14 cm)
p. 147

Bananaquit p. 188
4 in (10 cm)

European Starling
8.5 in (22 cm)
p. 168

winter

summer

Red-eyed Vireo
6 in (15 cm)
p. 148

Black-whiskered Vireo p. 148
6 in (15 cm)

White-eyed Vireo
5 in (13 cm)
p. 146

Florida Scrub-Jay
11 in (28 cm)
p. 149

Blue Jay
11 in (28 cm)
p. 149

American Crow
17 in (43 cm)
p. 150

Fish Crow
15 in (38 cm)
p. 151

Red-whiskered Bulbul
7 in (18 cm)
p. 160

Bank Swallow
5 in (13 cm)
p. 153

Northern Rough-winged Swallow
5.5 in (14 cm)
p. 152

Cliff Swallow
5.5 in (14 cm)
p. 153

Barn Swallow
7 in (18 cm)
p. 154

Cave Swallow
5.5 in (14 cm)
p. 154

Tree Swallow
6 in (15 cm)
p. 152

Purple Martin
8 in (20 cm)
p. 151

male

Tufted Titmouse
6 in (15 cm)
p. 155

Carolina Chickadee
4.5 in (11 cm)
p. 155

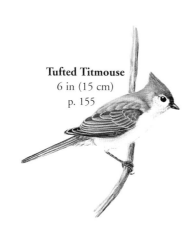

Red-breasted Nuthatch
4.5 in (11 cm)
p. 156

Brown-headed Nuthatch   p. 157
4.5 in (11 cm)

White-breasted Nuthatch
5.5 in (14 cm)
p. 156

Brown Creeper
5 in (13 cm)
p. 157

Northern Mockingbird
10 in (25 cm)
p. 166

Brown Thrasher
11 in (28 cm)
p. 167

Gray Catbird
8 in (20 cm)
p. 166

Carolina Wren
5.5 in (14 cm)
p. 158

Bewick's Wren
5 in (13 cm)
p. 158

House Wren
5 in (13 cm)
p. 159

Marsh Wren
5 in (13 cm)
p. 160

Sedge Wren
4.5 in (11 cm)
p. 159

Winter Wren
4 in (10 cm)
p. 159

Hermit Thrush
7 in (18 cm)
p. 164

Wood Thrush
8 in (20 cm)
p. 165

American Robin p. 165
10 in (25 cm)

adult

juvenile

Swainson's Thrus
7 in (18 cm)
p. 164

Gray-cheeked Thrush
7 in (18 cm)
p. 163

male

Veery
7 in (18 cm)
p. 163

female

Eastern Bluebird
7 in (18 cm)
p. 162

Cerulean Warbler
4.75 in (12 cm)
p. 180

male

female

Nashville Warbler
4.75 in (12 cm)
p. 172

male

female

male

Golden-winged Warbler
4.75 in (12 cm)
p. 170

female

female

Kentucky Warbler
5.25 in (13 cm)
p. 184

male

male

Brewster's Warbler
4.75 in (12 cm)
p. 170

Blue-winged Warbler
4.75 in (12 cm)
p. 170

female

Lawrence's Warbler
4.75 in (12 cm)
p. 170

259

Black-and-white Warbler
5.25 in (13 cm)
p. 180

male

female

Prothonotary Warbler
5.5 in (14 cm)
p. 181

male

Tennessee Warbler
5 in (13 cm)
p. 171

immature

Swainson's Warbler
5.5 in (14 cm)
p. 182

Orange-crowned Warbler
5 in (13 cm)
p. 171

Worm-eating Warbler
5 in (13 cm)
p. 182

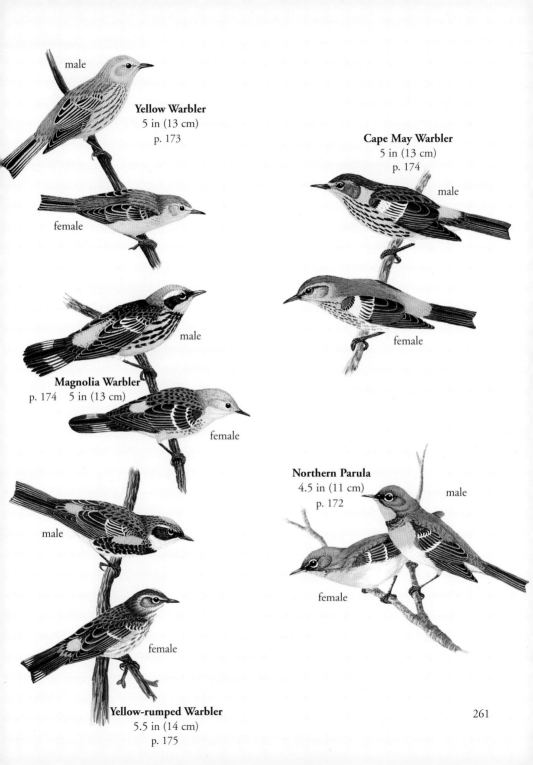

Yellow Warbler
5 in (13 cm)
p. 173

male

female

Cape May Warbler
5 in (13 cm)
p. 174

male

female

male

Magnolia Warbler
p. 174   5 in (13 cm)

female

Northern Parula
4.5 in (11 cm)
p. 172

male

female

male

female

Yellow-rumped Warbler
5.5 in (14 cm)
p. 175

261

Black-throated Green Warbler p. 176
5 in (13 cm)

female

male

Yellow-throated Warbler
5 in (13 cm)
p. 177

Blackburnian Warbler p. 176
4.5 in (11 cm)

male

female

Black-throated Blue Warbler
5 in (13 cm)
p. 175

male

female

spring

Chestnut-sided Warbler
4.5 in (11 cm)
p. 173

fall

Blackpoll Warbler
5 in (13 cm)
p. 179

male

female

Bay-breasted Warbler p. 179
5 in (13 cm)

winter

female

Prairie Warbler
4.5 in (11 cm)
p. 178

male

Pine Warbler
5 in (13 cm)
p. 177

male

female

breeding

Palm Warbler
5 in (13 cm)
p. 178

winter

263

Hooded Warbler
5 in (13 cm)
p. 186

male

female

Wilson's Warbler
4.5 in (11 cm)
p. 187

male

female

male

American Redstart
5 in (13 cm)
p. 181

female

House Sparrow
6 in (15 cm)
p. 213

male

female

immature male

female

Bobolink
7 in (18 cm)
p. 204

male (spring)

Common Yellowthroat
5 in (13 cm)
p. 186

male

female

immature male

Yellow-breasted Chat
7 in (18 cm)
p. 188

Northern Waterthrush
6 in (15 cm)
p. 183

Ovenbird
6 in (15 cm)
p. 183

Louisiana Waterthrush
6 in (15 cm)
p. 184

265

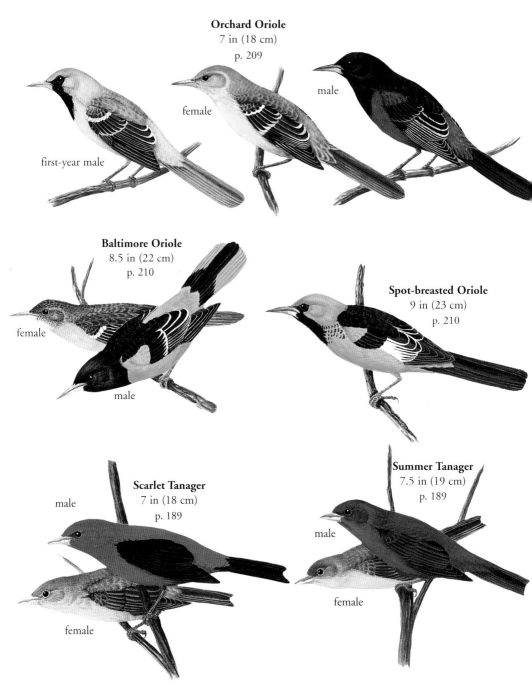

Orchard Oriole
7 in (18 cm)
p. 209

first-year male

female

male

Baltimore Oriole
8.5 in (22 cm)
p. 210

female

male

Spot-breasted Oriole
9 in (23 cm)
p. 210

Scarlet Tanager
7 in (18 cm)
p. 189

male

female

Summer Tanager
7.5 in (19 cm)
p. 189

male

female

Saltmarsh Sharp-tailed Sparrow
5 in (13 cm)
p. 196

Grasshopper Sparrow
5 in (13 cm)
p. 194

Savannah Sparrow
5.5 in (14 cm)
p. 194

Henslow's Sparrow
5 in (13 cm)
p. 195

Eastern Towhee
8 in (20 cm)
p. 191

male

female

Vesper Sparrow
6 in (15 cm)
p. 193

Dark-eyed Junco
6 in (15 cm)
p. 200

Bachman's Sparrow
6 in (15 cm)
p. 191

Seaside Sparrows
5.5 in (14 cm)
p. 196

Dusky

Cape Sable

Northern

Scott's

Chipping Sparrow
5.5 in (14 cm)
p. 192

breeding

winter

Field Sparrow
5.5 in (14 cm)
p. 193

White-throated Sparrow
6.5 in (17 cm)
p. 199

immature

adult
(tan-striped phase)

adult

immature

adult

White-crowned Sparrow
6.5 in (17 cm)
p. 199

Swamp Sparrow
5.5 in (14 cm)
p. 198

Song Sparrow
6 in (15 cm)
p. 197

Rose-breasted Grosbeak
8 in (20 cm)
p. 201

male

female

Evening Grosbeak
8 in (20 cm)
p. 213

male

Northern Cardinal
8 in (20 cm)
p. 201

female

Indigo Bunting
5.5 in (14 cm)
p. 202

male

female

Blue Grosbeak
6 in (15 cm)
p. 202

male

female

Purple Finch
6 in (15 cm)
p. 211

male

male

female

House Finch
5.5 in (14 cm)
p. 211

Pine Siskin
5 in (13 cm)
p. 212

Painted Bunting
5 in (13 cm)
p. 203

male

female

male

spring male

American Goldfinch
5 in (13 cm)
p. 212

winter male

Dickcissel
6 in (15 cm)
p. 203

female

271

Red-winged Blackbird
8 in (20 cm)
p. 204

male

immature male

female

Boat-tailed Grackle
15 in (38 cm)
p. 207

female

male

male

Brown-headed Cowbird
7 in (18 cm)
p. 209

female

Common Grackle
12 in (30 cm)
p. 207

Eastern Meadowlark
9 in (23 cm)
p. 205

Brewer's Blackbird
9 in (23 cm)
p. 206

female

fall variant
male

male

Rusty Blackbird
9 in (23 cm)
p. 206

fall male

fall female

female

male

Yellow-headed Blackbird
9.5 in (24 cm)
p. 205

female

male

Shiny Cowbird
7 in (18 cm)
p. 208

immature

adult
male

Bronzed Cowbird
8.5 in (22 cm)
p. 208

273

BIRDING

In historic times the term *birding* meant bird hunting or shooting, but today, it refers to the act of watching birds. Some people prefer the term bird watching to birding and bird watcher to birder, and occasionally, if you introduce yourself to a nonbirding person as a birder, you have to explain the term. Were you to say "I am a bird watcher," no further explanation would be necessary. Take your choice, both terms are acceptable.

Birding has become a major outdoor activity, and its growth has stimulated much economic activity in sales of binoculars, spotting scopes, bird guides, bird seed, feeders, and associated items, as well as in the nature-tour business. This "nonconsumptive" economy has been valued at nearly $30 billion dollars annually in the United States. One can engage in this "sport" at any desired level, ranging from simply observing birds frequenting a backyard feeder, to spending most of your waking hours visiting birding spots and chasing rarities throughout your state or region, to taking expert-guided tours to various parts of the world.

BASIC EQUIPMENT

Basic equipment for birding includes a good pair of binoculars and a field guide covering the birds of the region. As your interest and involvement develop, you will want to acquire a good spotting scope for observing some birds—ducks, shorebirds, and raptors, for example—from a distance.

Many brands and models of binoculars are available, ranging from useless dime-store glasses costing under $75, to good binoculars at moderate prices costing $75–$400, to top-of-the-line glasses especially designed for birding costing from $500–$1000 or more. Before purchasing binoculars you should know a few basic facts about them. Power of magnification, the first number listed in a description, indicated by 7x, 8x, or 10x, for example, means that the object being viewed is enlarged by a factor of 7, 8, or 10, respectively. Magnification above 10 requires such large glasses and such steady hands that a tripod may be required, thus making them impractical for most bird watching.

The second number, 35 up to 50 (7x35, 7x50, for example), refers to the diameter (in millimeters) of the opening, and thus to the light-gathering ability of the lenses. The higher the number, the more light is admitted, and, thus, the better one can see in dim conditions. Thus a 7x35 (say "7 by 35") binocular magnifies seven times and the diameter of the opening is 35mm. However, wider openings mean a larger and heavier binocular. Thus, in addition to the price, you need to consider the size and weight with which you are most comfortable. Because of the greater light-gathering ability, 7x50 binoculars are probably the best type; however, the size and weight are undesirable for most folks. Good binoculars in the range of 7x35 to 10x42 will suffice for most people, for either casual or more intensive birding. Price should range from $100 to $400 or thereabouts. Occasionally, dealers may offer used higher-priced binoculars available at considerably reduced prices.

The best source of information for suggestions and advice about binoculars is from experienced birders. Your local Audubon Society chapter probably has several active birders among its membership who would be willing to assist. Several periodicals catering to birders occasionally publish articles comparing the advantages and disadvantages of the most popular brands and models. A list of these publications appears in the Resources section.

BIRD FINDING IN FLORIDA

Birds occur in almost every habitat on earth, in cities as well as in fields and forests, so a good beginning point to observe birds is in your own backyard and neighborhood. Every Florida town is home to an array of species—the NORTHERN MOCKINGBIRD, NORTHERN CARDINAL, BLUE JAY, MOURNING DOVE, RED-BELLIED WOODPECKER, COMMON GRACKLE, and the ever-present ROCK PIGEON, EUROPEAN STARLING, and HOUSE SPARROW, just to mention a few of the more common species. A bird feeder and a bird bath will attract many species and allow close-up viewing.

Ponds and lakes, especially if the shoreline vegetation has not been totally obliterated by aggressive landowners or park departments, provide habitat for GALLINULES, DUCKS, WADERS, and other species. In most communities, city or county parks and old cemeteries provide good bird watching habitat. Regionally, state and national parks and national wildlife refuges are easily accessible. Inlets and bays attract large numbers and varieties of birds.

One of the best ways to learn bird identification is to accompany experienced birders in the field. Audubon of Florida has chapters located throughout the state. Each chapter schedules monthly, sometimes more frequent, field trips to nearby birding areas, holds monthly meetings, and usually publishes a monthly newsletter. Newcomers are always welcomed. The address of the chapter nearest to your town may be obtained from your local Chamber of Commerce, or by contacting Audubon of Florida.

Many county and state parks conduct periodic guided tours to observe their birds and other wildlife. Contact your county park department, or visit the Florida State Parks website at http://www.dep.state.fl.us/parks/ or http://www.floridastateparks.org for an alphabetical listing of all Florida parks, calendar of events, and access to state park information by geographical location and recreational activities. Chapters of the Sierra Club and the Nature Conservancy also sponsor field trips to various parts of the state.

The use of a SCREECH-OWL call is often most helpful in calling birds to the observer. For some reason, many species respond to the call of the SCREECH-OWL when given during daylight hours. It is one way to learn what species are in the neighborhood. Another technique, especially effective during the breeding season when males are defending territories, is to play a tape of the song of the species you desire to see. Territorial males

25 BIRDING HOTSPOTS IN FLORIDA

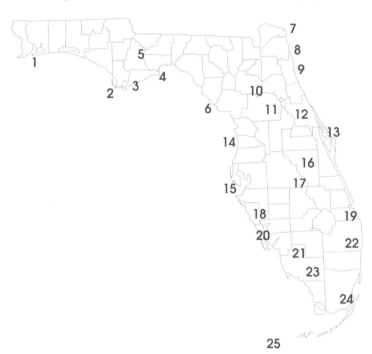

1. Gulf Island National Seashore: gulls, terns, Snowy Plover and other shorebirds

2. St. Joseph Peninsula State Park: a variety of shorebirds, Common Loon, migrating Peregrine Falcons, and many neotropical migrant warblers

3. St. George Island State Park: Migrating songbirds (especially during spring), nesting Bald Eagles, many shorebird species

4. St. Marks National Wildlife Refuge: wintering and migrant waterfowl (many duck species), shorebirds, migrating and wintering songbirds

5. Apalachicola National Forest: Red-cockaded Woodpecker, Brown-headed Nuthatch, wintering songbirds

6. Lower Suwanee National Wildlife Refuge: waterfowl, Wild Turkey, Swallow-tailed Kite, wintering White Pelicans, a variety of shorebirds

7. Fort Clinch State Park: gulls, terns, shorebirds, Brown Pelican, resident and migrant songbirds

8. Huguenot Memorial Park: terns, gulls, shorebirds, Northern Gannet, Common Loon

9. Guana River Wildlife Management Area and State Park: Purple Gallinule, White Pelican, a variety of waterfowl, migrant shorebirds, Peregrine Falcon, and Merlin

10. Paynes Prairie Preserve State Park: Sandhill Crane, Bald Eagle, Northern Harrier, woodland songbirds, egrets and ibises

11. Ocala National Forest: Florida Scrub Jay, Limpkin, Swallow-tailed Kite, Summer Tanager, woodland songbirds

12. Lake Woodruff National Wildlife Refuge: many wintering waterfowl, Bald eagle, Osprey, Limpkin, woodland songbirds

13. Merritt Island National Wildlife Refuge: Roseate Spoonbill, Black-necked Stilt, wintering waterfowl, shorebirds, migrant falcons, herons, ibises, shorebirds

14. Weekiwachee Preserve: Swallow-tailed Kite, woodland songbirds, Red-shouldered Hawk

15. Fort DeSoto County Park: excellent for spring migrant warbler viewing, Black Skimmer, migrant falcons, herons, plovers and other shorebirds

16. Joe Overstreet Landing: Burrowing Owl, Crested Caracara, Eastern Bluebird, Snail Kite, Glossy Ibis, Swallow-tailed Kite, and possibly the newly resident Whooping Crane

17. Lake Kissimmee State Park: Sandhill Crane, Wild Turkey, Florida Grasshopper Sparrow, Snail Kite

18. Myakka River State Park: Limpkin, Wood Duck, Sandhill Crane, Swallow-tailed Kite, White Ibis, wintering waterfowl, Mottled Duck, herons

19. Jonathan Dickinson State Park: Wood Stork, Sandhill Crane, Bald Eagle,

woodpeckers, Florida Scrub-Jay, pineland songbirds

20. J. N. Ding Darling National Wildlife Refuge: Mangrove Cuckoo, Gray Kingbird, Yellow-crowned Night-Heron, Roseate Spoonbill, herons, egrets, and woodland songbirds

21. Corkscrew Swamp Sanctuary: Wood Stork, Red-shouldered Hawk, Barred Owl, Pileated Woodpecker, Swallow-tailed Kite, Carolina Wren, White-eyed Vireo, herons and egrets

22. Arthur R. Marshall Loxahatchee National Wildlife Refuge: Purple Gallinule, Fulvous Whistling-Duck, waterfowl, Anhinga, Limpkin, herons, ibises

23. Fakahatchee Strand State Preserve: Northern Parula, Barred Owl, Red-eyed Vireo, Red-shouldered Hawk, Limpkin, Chuck-will's Widow, woodland songbirds

24. Everglades National Park: White-crowned Pigeon, Short-tailed Hawk, Anhinga, Bald Eagle, Osprey, Reddish Egret, American Bittern, Red-shouldered Hawk, Swallow-tailed Kite, Roseate Spoonbill, white morph of the Great Blue Heron, other herons, ibises

25. Dry Tortugas National Park: Sooty Tern, Brown Noddy, Masked Booby, Magnificent Frigatebird, White-tailed Tropicbird, Antillean Nighthawk, migrant songbirds especially in late April and early May.

will usually respond immediately to the "intruder." Great care must be taken not to play the song so frequently that it disturbs breeding activities. In some areas, such as Everglades National Park, the use of a tape recorder to attract birds is prohibited.

During spring migration in April and May (the peak period in Florida is mid-April to mid-May) several places in Florida are worth visiting to see the transients passing through the state on their way to their northern breeding grounds. One of the best is Fort De Soto Park on Pinellas County's southern peninsula. Also called Mullet Key, this site is famous for the variety and number of birds that occur there in migration.

Other spring "traps" for migrating birds are St. George Island State Park in the Panhandle; Ft. Pickens State Park on Santa Rosa Island on the upper Gulf coast; Cedar Key on the Gulf coast, about halfway up the peninsula; and the Dry Tortugas National Park (including Fort Jefferson), 67 miles west of Key West.

One of the better fall migration sites worth visiting early in October for transient VIREOS, WARBLERS, TANAGERS, and GROSBEAKS, is Saddle Creek Park, a former phosphate mine, now a Polk County park near Lakeland. Another site is Bill Baggs Cape Florida State Recreation Area on Key Biscayne, near Miami, where numerous raptors, including ACCIPITERS, BUTEOS, and FALCONS may be seen migrating south toward the Keys in late September and early October.

In winter, excellent birding is found at Merritt Island National Wildlife Refuge in Brevard County; Loxahatchee National Wildlife Refuge in Palm Beach county; Everglades National Park in Miami-Dade and Monroe counties; National Audubon's Corkscrew Swamp Sanctuary, near Immokalee, Collier county; Ding Darling National Wildlife Refuge on Sanibel Island in Lee county; St. Marks National Wildlife Refuge and Edward Ball Wakulla Springs State Park, both in Wakulla county.

FLORIDA SPECIALTIES

Visiting birders from other states usually want to see those species that are either restricted to Florida or are easier to find here. For example, in North America, the SNAIL KITE, SHORT-TAILED HAWK, SMOOTH-BILLED ANI, MANGROVE CUCKOO, BLACK-WHISKERED VIREO, FLORIDA SCRUB-JAY and WHITE-CROWNED PIGEON occur regularly only in the Sunshine State. Florida is the only state in eastern North America where the CRESTED CARACARA and BURROWING OWL may be seen.

A list of the Florida specialties in our opinion should include the following:

White-tailed Tropicbird	Mottled Duck
Magnificent Frigatebird	Masked Duck
White morph of the Great Blue Heron	Swallow-tailed Kite
Reddish Egret	Snail Kite
Roseate Spoonbill	Short-tailed Hawk
Wood Stork	Crested Caracara
Greater Flamingo	Limpkin

Sooty Tern
Brown Noddy
Black Noddy
White-crowned Pigeon
Mangrove Cuckoo
Smooth-billed Ani
Burrowing Owl
Antillean Nighthawk
Red-cockaded Woodpecker

Gray Kingbird
Cave Swallow
Black-whiskered Vireo
Florida Scrub-Jay
*Red-whiskered Bulbul
Cape Sable Seaside Sparrow
*Spot-breasted Oriole

To this list some birders would probably add a number of other exotic species (we list only two of these, with asterisk *) now breeding in Florida.

The following are a few of the most sought-after species and suggested places to look for them.

Snail Kite

When water levels are up in south Florida and apple snails are plentiful, Snail Kites tend to concentrate and breed in the water conservation areas and near Lake Okeechobee. At this time a good place to see Snail Kites is near the Shark Valley entrance to Everglades National Park and the Miccosukee Indian Restaurant on the Tamiami Trail (U.S. 41) on the southern edge of Conservation Area 3A (between Miami and Big Cypress National Preserve near Forty Mile Bend).

In recent years, Snail Kites have been reoccupying more of their former range in central Florida and may now be seen on Lake Kissimmee where State Road 60 crosses the southern outlet of the lake. Kites are now being seen in Lake Tohopekaliga and East Lake Tohopekaliga in Osceola County, and in the Fellsmere marshes on the northwest quadrant of the intersection of State Road 60 and County Road 512 in Indian River County. During times of severe drought, Snail Kites may concentrate in certain surviving wetland sites. One such place in the mid-1980s was the Palm Beach County Water Catchment Area along the Florida Turnpike, where over 300 kites—nearly half of the Florida population—fed and roosted for several weeks.

Limpkin

This species is widespread throughout central Florida and may be seen along many lakes and streams, but one of the surest places is the Wekiva River Marina, north of Orlando. Limpkins are often seen along the grassy shores of Lake Alice on the University of Florida campus in Gainesville. In south Florida they may be seen at the edge of wooded canals along State Road 29 and U.S. 41.

FLORIDA KEYS SPECIALTIES

Birding in Florida is not complete without one or more trips to Florida Bay, the Florida Keys, and the Dry Tortugas to see the various species that for the most part are seen only there. An excellent Keys birding guide called "Birding in the Florida Keys" has been produced by National Audubon's Tavernier Science Center and the Florida Keys Audubon Society. It can be obtained from the National Audubon Society, 115 Indian Mound Trail, Tavernier, FL 33070, phone 305-852-5092. The Science Center is located just off U.S. 1, at Mile Marker 89.

The WHITE MORPH OF THE GREAT BLUE HERON is found only in the Caribbean area, and may be seen feeding along the shoreline and in Florida Bay throughout the Keys. Part of its population has become adept at panhandling fish from fishermen in the Keys.

REDDISH EGRETS, both dark morph and white morph, are fairly common along the edges of Florida Bay and in shallow ponds on the Keys.

ROSEATE SPOONBILLS are more commonly seen in upper Florida Bay near Flamingo in Everglades National Park, but from November to March they nest on the Cowpens, a small group of islands just west of Tavernier.

Four Caribbean species are found wherever mangroves and tropical hammocks occur. The WHITE-CROWNED PIGEON and a few MANGROVE CUCKOOS are year-round residents, while the ANTILLEAN NIGHTHAWK and BLACK-WHISKERED VIREO occur only during the breeding season from April through August. WHITE-CROWNED PIGEONS inhabit all of the Keys from Key Largo to Key West, and are locally abundant in places. The Antillean Nighthawk is best seen in early evening at Marathon Airport and the Key West Airport. COMMON NIGHTHAWKS also occur throughout the Keys, and the only way to separate the two species as they fly overhead is by their different calls. The Common Nighthawk's call is a long, drawn-out *peeent* while that of the Antillean is a three- or four-note *kity-kay-dick,* distinctively different from that of the Common.

Throughout the Keys, BLACK-WHISKERED VIREOS sing their two-phrase song *cheer-lip, cheer-lip* followed by a pause before another repetition. They are dooryard birds in residential areas, as well as being common in undeveloped tropical hammocks.

The MANGROVE CUCKOO is considerably less common and takes more time and effort to locate. It too can occur in residential areas but is best searched for in the still-undeveloped tropical hardwoods and mangrove habitats of the lower Keys, especially Big Pine Key, No-Name Key, Sugarloaf Key, and Saddlebunch Key. In late April and May it often responds to a recorded playback of its call. A fifth subtropical species, abundant in the Keys during the spring and summer, is the GRAY KINGBIRD. It also occurs along the Atlantic coast north to St. Augustine (occasionally to Fernandina Beach), and on the Gulf coast north to the Panhandle. Watch for these on utility lines.

A trip to the Dry Tortugas to see its specialties—the SOOTY TERN, BROWN NODDY, MASKED BOOBY, BROWN BOOBY, and WHITE-TAILED TROPICBIRD—is best undertaken in late April or early May because that is the time of peak migration for numerous transients.

The Tortugas are accessible by boat, ferry, or sea-plane. Several organizations, including Audubon of Florida, the Florida Ornithological Society, the Sierra Club, and a number of commercial nature tour groups, organize trips of several days' duration to the Tortugas in late April or early May each year to observe these species and the numerous landbird migrants that stop to rest and feed en route from the tropics. Boat tour prices depend on length of stay and whether or not board and lodging are included in the price. You may contact the Key West Chamber of Commerce for additional information on traveling to the Dry Tortugas at 402 Wall Street, Key West, Florida 33040, phone 305-294-2587, http://www.keywestchamber.org. In all the years we have been visiting the Dry Tortugas, we have never met anyone who was not ecstatic about visiting these unique islands.

FLORIDA SCRUB-JAY

This threatened species is restricted to xeric oak scrub habitat in central Florida. The largest populations occur on Merritt Island and Cape Canaveral, Ocala National Forest, and the remnant patches of scrub habitat on the Lake Wales Ridge in Polk and Highlands counties. On Merritt Island one may see Florida Scrub-Jays along the road to Canaveral National Seashore. In Highlands County a healthy population lives on the grounds of Archbold Biological Station, south of Lake Placid where decades of field work have detailed the natural history of this species. Scattered populations occur from Flagler County south to Palm Beach County on the east coast, and from Levy County south to Collier County on the west coast. Check with your local Audubon chapter to learn of specific locations in your immediate area.

RED-COCKADED WOODPECKER

This endangered species occurs in mature pine flatwoods, especially longleaf and slash pine, throughout the state, but is becoming increasingly scarce. Most of the remaining active colony sites are not readily accessible to birders. The largest populations occur in our three national forests: the Apalachicola (which has the healthiest population), the Ocala, and the Osceola (both of whose populations are dwindling). You should check with your local Audubon chapter to learn of any observable colonies in your vicinity.

SHORT-TAILED HAWK

This tropical species breeds throughout peninsular Florida but is so uncommon that it is rarely seen on a regular basis during the nesting season unless someone has pinpointed a breeding pair. In winter up to six or more birds inhabit the Flamingo area of Everglades National Park. From November to late February one or more birds might be seen soaring high overhead along the road to Flamingo. Both color morphs, dark and light, occur together. Breeding has been documented as far north as Avon Park in Highlands County. Occasionally they can be seen soaring over pastures and forest patches in the ranch country northwest of Lake Okeechobee.

SMOOTH-BILLED ANI

This Caribbean species first appeared on the Florida mainland near Lake Okeechobee in the early 1950s, then spread throughout the southern half of the peninsula as far north as Merritt Island on the east coast and the Tampa Bay area on the west coast. It remains relatively uncommon and patchy in distribution and may be on the verge of disappearing from the state (for reasons unknown). It inhabits brushy thickets in residential areas and agricultural fields. Anis are frequently seen at Loxahatchee National Wildlife Refuge, and the western edges of Miami and Homestead. It is the three-letter answer to the common crossword puzzle clue, "black bird."

EXOTIC SPECIES

Like many humans who come to Florida to visit, then end up staying permanently, numerous species of birds from South America, Africa, Asia, and Australia are taking up residence in south Florida. Many of these are the colorful psittacines (parrots). For a partial list, see the chapter devoted to exotics in Florida. The urban/suburban belt from Homestead north to Palm Beach has become home to dozens of species of escaped and released birds. A mild climate, numerous plantings of exotic flowering and fruiting trees and shrubs, and feeding stations supplied by humans all combine to make living in Florida a successful experience for these birds.

Several members of the Tropical Audubon Society in Miami have become experts in locating and identifying most of these species. Information on free field trips and birdwalks guided by leaders from the Tropical Audubon Society may be obtained from Tropical Audubon Society, 5530 Sunset Drive, Miami, FL 33143, phone 305-667-7337, http://www.tropicalaudubon.org. Reservations are usually required for beginners and botany walks, as well as overnight and pelagic trips.

BIRD STUDY

Because birds are so widespread and so visible—unlike most other vertebrates—people have observed and studied them for centuries. The earliest students of birds probably were hunters whose main interest in learning their habits was to obtain them or their eggs for food, and their feathers for ornamentation and clothing. Much of the early information on the natural history of birds was recorded by egg collectors, or oologists—people who collected eggs as a hobby (now illegal) in the 1800s and early 1900s.

Biologists study birds as subjects of research in anatomy, physiology, endocrinology, evolution, behavior, and ecology. The American Ornithologists' Union, organized in 1883, is the professional organization for ornithologists in North America, and publishes *The Auk,* a quarterly journal. For information about AOU membership and publications, write to AOU, 1313 Dolley Madison Blvd., Suite 402, McLean, VA 22101, or visit http://www.aou.org.

Several institutions of higher education in Florida offer educational programs in ornithology leading toward undergraduate and advanced degrees in biology, wildlife ecology, and zoology. These include the University of Florida in Gainesville, Florida State University in Tallahassee, Florida Atlantic University in Boca Raton, University of Central Florida in Orlando, University of South Florida in Tampa, the University of Miami in Coral Gables, and the Florida Institute of Technology in Melbourne. Most of these universities also maintain research collections of bird skins, skeletons, and eggs.

Three institutions, one public and two private, that maintain study collections and foster research are the Florida Museum of Natural History (FMNH) in Gainesville, Archbold Biological Station near Lake Placid, and Tall Timbers Research Station near Tallahassee. The FMNH also houses one of the top collections in North America of bird sounds, both songs and calls. Sound clips are available for download at FMNH's website, http://www.flmnh.ufl.edu.

The abundance and visibility of birds has enabled a large number of amateurs to make important contributions to the science of ornithology. National organizations that foster amateur participation in the field are the Wilson Ornithological Society, which publishes the quarterly *Wilson Bulletin;* the Cooper Ornithological Society, which publishes the quarterly *Condor;* and the Association of Field Ornithologists, which publishes the *Journal of Field Ornithology.* The majority of the membership of the three major bird banding organizations in the United States (Eastern, Inland, and Western Bird Banding Associations) is comprised of amateurs. These associations jointly publish the *North American Bird Bander.*

High interest in bird watching and bird study has led to the organization of state ornithological societies. In 1972, Florida Audubon Society sponsored the founding of the Florida Ornithological Society (F.O.S.) to promote the study and enjoyment of birds by professional and amateur ornithologists and in Florida. The F.O.S. publishes a quarterly journal, the *Florida Field Naturalist,* as well as a quarterly newsletter and a special publication series. It holds semiannual meetings in the spring and fall at various localities in the state, and annually considers applications for grants-in-aid of ornithological research and/or environmental education with an ornithological emphasis. The F.O.S. used to sponsor a Rare Bird Alert, a telephone circuit to inform participants about the appearance of rare species in Florida. Today there are listservers (e-mail discussion groups) which serve the same purpose and are much more timely. F.O.S.'s website, http://www.fosbirds.org, offers a list of Internet links to several statewide and regional bird listservers. The organization's permanent address is Florida Ornithological Society, Florida Museum of Natural History, University of Florida, Gainesville, FL 32611, but the best way to reach its members is through the website.

BIRD BANDING

Sometimes, in the study of birds, it is desirable or necessary to be able to identify individuals in a population. This can be done by placing a numbered band on one leg, so that it can be observed and recorded the next time it is captured, or with the use of additional colored bands one may be able to identify marked individuals without needing to physically recapture them. This study technique is called bird banding (bird ringing in Europe), and in North America the banding program is administered jointly by the U.S. Department of the Interior and the Canadian Wildlife Service. In the U.S., the United States Geological Service Bird Banding Laboratory issues permits and bands to qualified persons and research facilities and maintains the records of *wild* birds banded annually. We have emphasized the word "wild" because the USGS does not maintain records of banded pet-store birds or pigeons. Neither does the USGS maintain records of state game department bandings of nonmigratory game birds, however, even though they are indeed wild birds. In Florida such nonmigratory game birds are the NORTHERN BOBWHITE and the WILD TURKEY.

Bands provided by the Bird Banding Laboratory are made of aluminum and inscribed "Call 1–800–327-BAND" and "Write Bird Band Laurel MD 20708 USA," followed by a unique eight or nine digit number. Older bird bands had the legend "Avise Bird Band Wash DC." In the event a banded bird is recovered by recapture, death, or injury, the finding can be reported by calling the 800 number on the band from anywhere in the United States, Canada, and most parts of the Caribbean. Finders may also send the band and report directly to the USGS Patuxent Wildlife Research Center, Bird Banding Laboratory, 12100 Beech Forest Road, Laurel, MD 20708-4037, or submit the report by e-mail to bandreports@patuxent.usgs.gov. Do not remove a band from a live bird if it can be rehabilitated and released back to the wild. The following information should accompany the band or report: the date found, location (including state, county, and nearest city), circumstances, if known, and your name and address if you desire a report on where and when the bird was banded. Finders may also give the band and information to any ornithologist, bird bander, or local office of the USGS or Florida Fish and Wildlife Conservation Commission (FWC) and ask them to send it on to Washington.

Over the years the banding program has contributed much knowledge about the migratory habits of birds, including distances traveled, directions and routes, wintering and breeding sites (and fidelity to these), and age and longevity. The first inkling about where the CHIMNEY SWIFT wintered in South America came from the observation of Indians in the high Andes wearing necklaces made of bird bands. For further information and resources such as the North American Bird Banding Manual, visit the Banding Laboratory's website at http://www.pwrc.usgs.gov/bbl/.

It may be a bit more difficult to track down banded pigeons. Several organizations of pigeon fanciers administer this program—among them the American Racing Pigeon Union (AU) and the International Federation of Homing Pigeon Fanciers (IF). Annually, the secretary of each local club in these organizations is issued a series of numbered bands to be placed on a leg of each nestling being raised for racing by individual club members. Often, a pigeon is seen with additional markers—usually a colored rubber band placed on the bird just prior to being released for a race. Ideally, when the bird is released it flies straight home, enters its coop, and is a "winner." Sometimes obstacles may be encountered: a storm or adverse winds may exhaust the flyer, or a predator may cripple it. If a tired bird appears in your yard, feed it some bird seed and water for a day or two and it will probably recover and fly home. If injured it should be taken to a rehabilitation center and treated or put out of its misery. A report of your finding can be made to the national secretary of the organization that issued the band. For bands with the letters AU followed by a combination of letters and numbers, contact The American Racing Pigeon Union, Inc., P.O. Box 18465, Oklahoma City, OK 73154-0465, phone (405) 848-5801, www.pigeon.org. For bands with the letters IF followed by a combination of letters and numbers, contact International Federation of American Homing Pigeon Fanciers, Inc., Lost & Found Coordinator, 62 Oak Hill Dr., Toms River, NJ 08753, phone (732) 255-3041, http://www.ifpigeon.com. Other organizations that band pigeons are the National Pigeon Association (NPA), National Birmingham Roller Club (NBRC), American Racing Pigeon Union (IPB), and Canadian Pigeon Union (CU or CRPU).

ATTRACTING AND FEEDING WILD BIRDS

L ike all creatures, birds have three basic needs—food, water, and shelter. Shelter includes nest sites and cover for protection from predators and the elements. If your yard provides one or more of these needs, you should have some birds frequenting it. The more variety of foods and plants in your yard, the greater variety of birds you should be able to attract.

Before we suggest ways to attract birds to your property, we should discuss two basic questions that often arise concerning the feeding of wild birds. These are: (1) Is it necessary to provide food for wild birds? and (2) If I should start feeding, will it be fatal to birds if I stop feeding them? In Florida, the answer to both questions is no. In the absence of snow and ice, birds find sufficient natural foods to sustain them through the winter. Occasionally, when an Arctic air mass penetrates Florida and we have several days of frigid temperatures, some of the insect-eating species, such as VIREOS, WARBLERS, KINGLETS, and WRENS, may suffer losses, and for some of these a bird feeder provisioned with the proper foods could be life-saving.

In some urban areas, such as St. Petersburg, for example, where several tons of bird seed are sold each week, supplemental feeding has undoubtedly enabled larger populations of birds to exist. The three species that appear to have benefited the most from bird feeders are the HOUSE SPARROW, EUROPEAN STARLING, and MOURNING DOVE. Three other species living in St. Petersburg that are dependent on human food subsidies are the ROCK PIGEON, MONK PARAKEET, and EURASIAN COLLARED-DOVE.

We are not aware of any evidence that shows avian mortality has resulted when a person who has been feeding birds suddenly stops feeding them. It is conceivable that this could occur in the north where occasional mild winters and a large number of feeding stations may have encouraged some individuals of species that usually migrate south to remain through the winter. Those individuals, however, probably have several feeding stations to choose from in the neighborhood.

In summary, no one need fear that if they don't provide unlimited food supplies, or if they stop feeding, that our wild birds will suffer. For our native species, sufficient natural foods occur in Florida so that cessation of artificial feeding will have no adverse effect on local populations.

In Florida, the primary reason for providing food for birds is to attract them to our yards where we can more readily see and enjoy them. The best way to do this is to help them meet their food, water, and shelter needs. By providing a variety of foods you should attract a variety of birds. By planting a variety of trees and shrubs you provide both food and shelter for birds.

Numerous species of birds have adapted well to living with humans in cities, residential suburbs, and agricultural areas, and a bird feeder will attract most of them. They include NORTHERN MOCKINGBIRD, BLUE JAY, MOURNING DOVE, NORTHERN CARDINAL, COMMON and BOAT-TAILED GRACKLE, TUFTED TITMOUSE, HOUSE SPARROW, RED-WINGED BLACKBIRD, and EUROPEAN STARLING. Depending on the variety of foods provided, geographic location, and surrounding habitat, several additional species may also frequent feeders: NORTHERN BOBWHITE, RED-BELLIED and DOWNY WOODPECKERS, NORTHERN FLICKER, CAROLINA CHICKADEE, CAROLINA WREN, BROWN THRASHER, GRAY CATBIRD, COMMON GROUND-DOVE, BROWN-HEADED COWBIRD, EASTERN TOWHEE, INDIGO and PAINTED BUNTINGS, PURPLE and HOUSE FINCHES, AMERICAN GOLDFINCH, PINE SISKIN, and, chiefly in north Florida, several species of SPARROWS.

FEEDERS

Some species, such as NORTHERN BOBWHITES, EASTERN TOWHEES, and SPARROWS, prefer to feed on the ground, although some of them will fly up to platform feeders or a tree stump close to the ground. Other species prefer hanging feeders, or feeders fastened to trees. So, a variety of feeder types will attract more species. In addition, it will allow more birds to feed at the same time. Often, when you maintain only one feeder, one or two individuals may exclude other visitors to the feeder.

The simplest feeder is a tray or platform either hanging from a branch or clothesline or installed atop a 2 inch by 4 inch (5 cm by 10 cm) or 4 inch square (10 cm square) post. It should be roofed to protect the seed from rain and should have a raised edge to keep the wind from blowing the seed away. The tray could be a piece of marine plywood or any piece of scrap wood. Another idea is to make a rectangular frame and to nail window screening to this for the bottom. This allows rain to drain through and obviates the need for a roof. A piece of quarter-inch hardware cloth can be fastened beneath the screening to give it support. If the city cuts down an old oak in your neighborhood, you might request a 1- or 2-foot (30 or 61 cm) section of the trunk (if it is solid wood and not rotten) and use this as a feeding platform.

A large variety of commercial feeders can be purchased. Some of these are expensive, but like many expensive things, they last far longer than do the cheap feeders. If you have squirrels in the neighborhood, do not buy cheap plastic feeders, because the squirrels will make short work of them.

Feeders can be made of household items, such as half-gallon or gallon-size milk cartons and jugs, bleach jugs, large plastic soda bottles, etc. Natural materials in the yard can be used such as a small log with holes drilled in it or a pinecone stuffed with suet and peanut butter. These can be hung with clothes hanger wire. Again, if you have squirrels, do not use string or plastic cord.

Food

Wild Bird Seed

Mixes of wild bird seed can be purchased at most supermarkets, pet stores, feed stores, and discount department stores, and nowadays most of these are satisfactory for use in Florida. It is usually a mixture of white proso millet, milo, wheat, and sunflower seeds. Higher-priced mixes are available from garden supply and feed stores. These usually contain more sunflower seeds and less milo and wheat. Many birds like finely cracked corn and this is not found in most mixes. We recommend purchasing a bag of baby chick starter scratch from a feed store and mixing this with the wild bird seed. You may also want to add more sunflower seed to the mix. Two kinds of sunflower seeds are available, the small black oil seed, preferred by most birds, or the larger black and white striped seed. Often, both kinds come in the same package. These can be added to the wild bird seed mix or fed separately in special feeders.

Nyjer, sometimes called thistle, is a preferred food of American Goldfinches and Pine Siskins. It is also a very expensive seed and one cannot expect these birds except during cold winters and in the northern parts of the state.

If you feed birds on the ground, be sure to periodically rake and clean up old seed and fecal material. It would not hurt to change feeding locations periodically to prevent the development or spread of fungal diseases.

If you store your bird seed out of doors or in an open shed, be sure it is in a secure container so that squirrels and rats cannot chew their way into it. Moisture can cause the seed to go moldy or germinate, and flour beetles can quickly turn it into powder, so do not store large amounts over a long period of time.

Suet

Many species of birds will eat suet (the dry hard fat from beef cattle), especially from around the heart and kidneys. This is usually available from your butcher, either free or very inexpensively. You have to ask for it specifically as it is not out on the shelves.

Fat turns rancid, especially in Florida's warm climate, so only small amounts at a time should be provided in mesh bags (onion or citrus bags) or in hardware cloth baskets placed on a tray feeder or fastened to the trunk of a tree. If the suet is cut into small pieces many birds that do not usually come to your feeder will come especially during cold spells. Brown Thrashers,

CAROLINA WRENS, HOUSE WRENS, YELLOW-RUMPED WARBLERS, RUBY-CROWNED KINGLETS—all usually insect-eating birds—have been seen eating suet.

A number of ingredients can be added to melted fat to produce a "cake" readily eaten by many birds. Wild bird seed mix, corn meal, white or whole wheat flour, oatmeal, crushed dried dog food, chopped nuts, raisins, peanut butter—almost anything edible—can be added. The resulting cake can be poured into molds, shaped into balls, stuffed into pinecones or into holes drilled in logs. It can be refrigerated or frozen. Following are two basic recipes:

> 1 cup chopped suet
> 1 cup peanut butter
> 2 cups corn flour
> 1/2 cup wheat flour
> Melt the suet in a pan and stir in peanut butter. Set aside to cool. Mix dry ingredients well and add to the cooling suet mixture. Shape into balls.
>
> or
>
> 1 cup oatmeal
> 1/2 lb. suet (any fat will do)
> 1/2 cup peanut butter
> Corn meal, raisins, chopped nuts, dry cereal, etc.
> Cook oatmeal. While hot, add fat and peanut butter. Then add other ingredients. Form into balls. Place in mesh bags.

You should try various combinations of ingredients until you find one that your birds prefer. Empty pint-size ice cream cartons are ideal for storing suet mix.

Peanut Butter

This can be fed straight or mixed with suet, corn meal, bird seed, etc., and stuffed into holes in a log or in a pinecone. Several years ago some birds were found dead at a feeder with peanut butter in the esophagus, and since then some folks have felt that straight peanut butter is dangerous for small birds.

No additional evidence has been found to confirm this. Nonetheless it should cause no problem when mixed with other foods.

Nuts

Peanuts and pecan pieces or crumbs are readily eaten by a number of species, especially JAYS, WOODPECKERS, and TITMICE.

Fruit

Dried fruits, such as raisins and currants, are loved by MOCKINGBIRDS and WAXWINGS. Most birds like fresh fruits (i.e., apples, pears, grapes, bananas, and citrus) quartered or sliced. Wintering BALTIMORE ORIOLES will frequent feeders to feed on orange halves. A good way to offer these is to hammer one or two long nails through a board, turn the board over and impale orange halves on the points.

Doughnuts and Bread

Day-old doughnuts can be purchased from doughnut shops and placed on a dowel nailed to a board on the feeder, or suspended from an overhead wire. Small pieces and crumbs of most kinds of breads are readily eaten by several species of birds. White bread is not as nutritious as the dark breads, but may be used sparingly.

Sugar Water for Hummingbirds

HUMMINGBIRDS are attracted to specially designed feeders built to hold sugar solution—a mixture of one part granulated sugar to three parts water. The water should be boiled first and the mixture stored in the refrigerator. Feeders should be thoroughly cleaned at least weekly, but do not use a detergent. Do not allow the sugar solution to remain in the feeder so long that mold starts growing in it. Honey should not be used because it sometimes fosters a fungus growth that can be fatal to hummingbirds.

Although most of our RUBY-THROATED HUMMINGBIRDS migrate to Central and South America for the winter, some over-winter in Florida, and several western RUFOUS HUMMINGBIRDS and other species winter in Florida as well. Hence, it is worthwhile to maintain a feeder all winter long in some areas. Wintering hummingbirds have occurred in Pensacola, Destin, Tallahassee, Gainesville, Orlando, and southward.

Occasionally, other species, such as BALTIMORE ORIOLE, some WARBLERS, and TANAGERS, will attend a hummingbird feeder. Ants can become a problem at times, but a little grease or petroleum jelly on the wire suspending the feeder should solve that problem.

For more information on feeding birds, see the recommended reading list at the end of this chapter.

BIRD FEEDER PROBLEMS

Bully-birds or Hog-birds

When one or two birds seem to be hogging all the food, install several feeders to spread out the feast. Use a variety of feeder types—tray, hanging tubular, domed, etc. A cage of 1-inch by 2-inch (3-cm by 5-cm) weldwire fencing built around a feeder will allow the smaller birds to enter but excludes the larger species. By squeezing every other pair of wires you can adjust the size of the openings.

Your yard is probably within the territory of a NORTHERN MOCKINGBIRD, and he (or she—in the winter females also defend a territory) may try to exclude other species from the yard. By providing several feeders in different parts of the yard, your mocker's attention is so divided that it cannot exclude every visitor.

Occasionally, BLUE JAYS or RED-WINGED BLACKBIRDS will thresh seed out of the reservoir of a feeder while searching for sunflower seeds. If you have too few ground-feeding birds to pick the spilled seeds and the seed is going to waste, you need to stop this behavior. This is easily accomplished by boring holes spaced 1 inch (3 cm) apart in a 3/8 inch x 4 inch by 3/4 inch (0.95 cm x 1 cm x 2 cm) piece of wood to insert 3-inch (8-cm) lengths of wire cut from a clothes hanger. This strip is then attached to the front of the food tray. The wires prevent the birds from swinging their heads sideways and sweeping seed out of the reservoir, yet they can still feed. (This is the suggestion of Roy M. Hoover, Apalachee Audubon Society.)

If you feel that one particular species is overwhelming your feeders, observe what those birds are eating, then stop providing those items for a week or so. Some people feed only sunflower seed and this attracts only those species that can shell and eat those seeds.

Hawks

If you have a feeder that caters to small birds, sooner or later one of the bird-eating hawks, usually a SHARP-SHINNED HAWK or COOPER'S HAWK (small, trim, long-legged, long-tailed bluish or brownish raptors) will find your yard. You have created a concentration of their favorite prey items and they are taking advantage of it. This is, of course, natural behavior for their species and they have a right to live also. But, of course, you may not want to be the cause of birds being killed in your back yard. What do you do? The best thing is to cease providing food for a few days. As soon as the small birds stop coming to the feeder, the hawk will move on to a better feeding area. Next, check to insure that you have sufficient cover in your yard to allow small birds to escape from a predator. The feeder should be no farther than 10–15 feet (3–4.5 meters) from shrubbery or a brushpile.

Cats

Cats will be cats, regardless of how well fed, and they will kill birds. You can train a dog not to do something that is in its nature to do, but rarely is this possible with a cat. Domestic cats can kill a tremendous number of birds and other small prey. An individual cat has been known to kill over 1,000 birds in a year. In England, house cats have been implicated in the loss of more than 300 million small birds and mammals annually. In Wisconsin over 200 million birds are lost per year—imagine what the losses must be for the entire United States! So you need to assist the birds in escaping a cat's attempt to capture them. You can do this by making sure the cat is not able to sneak up undetected on birds feeding or bathing on the ground. Do not place a feeder or birdbath immediately next to dense shrubbery or ground cover. You can also bell your cat (although there is little evidence that this really works). If you try it you may wish to use two bells; some cats can learn to adjust their movements to silence a single bell. Of course, if you own a cat, the best way to reduce depredations on birdfeeders is to simply keep your cat inside at all times (this, by the way, is the best method to reduce flea infestations in the home—that is, eliminating access to the outside source of the fleas).

If you are having problems with a neighbor's cat, speak to the neighbor about the problem and see what can be worked out. Cats hate water. A garden hose might discourage the cat from entering your yard. If it is an unclaimed stray, simply stop feeding and attracting birds to your yard. Or, try trapping it to turn over to the local animal control department or the Humane Society. See this website for more information on bird-killing cats and the need to reduce this global source of bird mortality: http://www.abcbirds.org/cats/.

Squirrels

The gray squirrel is one of our common native mammals that has learned to adapt well to humans. They have as much right to live in our yards as do the birds we want to attract. However, they can monopolize a feeder and eat a lot of food. They have all day to learn how to outsmart your every attempt to foil them. Sometimes all you can do is keep trying. There are some excellent commercial feeders on the market designed to exclude squirrels and larger birds by closing shut whenever an animal above a certain weight settles on them. They are expensive, but effective.

An inverted cone of metal placed under a feeder supported by a post will prevent a squirrel from climbing the post, and a cone over a hanging feeder will prevent access from above. But squirrels can easily jump to a feeder if it is placed only a few feet from a tree or shrub. When hanging a feeder use strong wire because a squirrel can easily chew through string or plastic.

Sometimes people trap and cart squirrels several miles away. This might solve your problem temporarily, but may be adding to the squirrel population in someone else's yard. And it is only a temporary solution because there are sufficient squirrels in the area to fill in any empty territories that occur. The senior author once decided that he had to remove the five or six squirrels in his Orlando yard, so he set a trap and over the next 15 days proceeded to capture a squirrel a day, and still had several squirrels coming to the feeder!

You can either spend your time trying to outwit them or resign yourself to feeding them, too. They are interesting animals in their own right, and what would our cities be like without squirrels?

WATER

All birds require water for drinking and bathing. Thus, a source of water will attract several species that aren't particularly interested in the expensive food you might lay out for them. Bird baths can range from a simple inverted trashcan lid set on the ground to a commercially constructed concrete pedestal bath or a custom-built rock-walled pool or grotto with waterfalls and recycling water.

Some birds, especially WARBLERS, are attracted to water dripping into a shallow basin, and many birds love to bathe in a fine misty spray directed at a leafy branch. The water drip is easily made by poking a small pinhole in a gallon plastic jug and suspending it over the bird bath.

It is important to clean the bird bath weekly, and every once in a while clean it with a weak solution of bleach. As with feeders, the location of the bird bath should not be too close to dense vegetation, yet not be farther than 10–15 feet (3–4.5 meters) from safe cover.

COVER AND FOOD PLANTINGS

If you want to attract a variety of birds to your yard, you may first need to change some of your present agricultural practices. Do you use a lot of pesticides? If so, either cease doing this or do all you can to chase birds out of your yard. Some judicious use of pesticides, especially the safer varieties, is sometimes acceptable, but for the most part, if you want to attract wildlife you need to become unhooked on pesticides.

Do you maintain an extremely manicured yard and remove all leaves, clippings, twigs, etc, from around every tree and shrub? If so, you need to stop doing this. It is fine to be neat and trim up to a point, but leaf litter should be left under shrubs. It is good for the shrubs as well as for ground-dwelling birds. Dead trees and snags should be left in place unless they pose a danger to structures, vehicles, or people.

If you have an extensive yard consider allowing some of it to revert to the wild. You can do this and still have a beautiful yard, including a lawn near the house. Expert advice about the use of native plants in home landscaping is available. Some nurseries now specialize in this and members of local chapters of the Florida Native Plant Society are willing to assist homeowners in the use of native species.

Fruit-producing trees, shrubs, and vines attract many birds, and numerous species of these are available for landscape plantings in each of the various climatic regions of Florida. However, by all means, avoid planting exotic species that may be noxious invasives. The FWC makes available a free guide entitled "Planting a Refuge for Wildlife: How to create a backyard habitat for Florida's birds and beasts," which can be ordered from the FWC's website, http://www.floridaconservation.org. It can also be requested from Planting a Refuge, P.O. Box 6181, Tallahassee, FL , 32314-6181, with a donation to support the fund administered by the Florida Wildlife Federation for the FWC, which supports schoolyard projects throughout Florida. You can download the order form from the FWC website.

Do you live on the edge of a pond or lake? If so, do not remove all of the shoreline vegetation. The emergent vegetation along the lake edge provides important habitat for LEAST BITTERNS, GREEN HERONS, COMMON MOORHENS, RED-WINGED BLACKBIRDS, and BOAT-TAILED GRACKLES. Insects produced from the lake and surrounding lands are important foods for numerous birds, including PURPLE MARTINS in summer and TREE SWALLOWS in winter.

A lake shore is an ideal place to install a Purple Martin apartment house on a pole in the water, on a dock, or on the nearby land. Wood Duck boxes can be installed on a post in the lake or in trees on the uplands.

In 2001, during one of the worst droughts in Florida's history, the Department of Environmental Protection began an initiative to identify ways to increase water-use efficiency. The Florida Water Conservation Initiative offers a wealth of water conservation information for those trying to attract birds to their back yards, including downloadable color brochures about efficient lawn irrigation, fertilizer facts, and xeriscaping, on their website http://www.swfwmd.state.fl.us/conservation.

HOUSING FOR BIRDS

Each species of bird has a particular preference for a nest site. Some species prefer the branches of trees (for example, BLUE JAYS, EASTERN KINGBIRDS, BLUE-GRAY GNATCATCHERS). Others prefer cavities in trees (WOODPECKERS, TUFTED TITMICE, CAROLINA CHICKADEES, EASTERN SCREECH-OWLS) or shrubs (NORTHERN MOCKINGBIRDS, BROWN THRASHERS, NORTHERN CARDINALS). Some prefer crevices and crannies (CAROLINA WRENS, HOUSE SPARROWS) or ground cover (EASTERN MEADOWLARKS, NORTHERN BOBWHITES). Several of the species that nest in tree cavities will also nest in artificial bird houses. Installation of bird houses on your property won't guarantee their occupancy, but chances are good that sooner or later one species or another will nest in one. Houses may be made out of scrap lumber, but it should be a good wood that will last several years in the outdoors. If you paint the houses, paint only the external surfaces and use a brown or green color. Tops should be hinged and fastened with a hook and eye so that the boxes can be checked and cleaned periodically. Detailed designs for house construction may be found in some of the references in the Resources section.

CAROLINA WRENS will nest in all sorts of containers—hanging plants and baskets, shelving, ledges, kegs, large coffee and juice cans, etc.—but rarely in a bird house. We have used No. 10 juice cans successfully in a maple swamp where natural crevices were scarce. A rectangular box, 8–10 inches (20–25 cm) long and 5 inches x 5 inches (13 x 13 cm) wide with one end left open may attract this species.

Numerous references dealing with attracting and feeding birds have been written, and several of these are listed in the Resources section. The first two listed are, in our opinion, the best of the lot, and should be read by everyone with a serious interest in this subject.

Following are some suggested dimensions of houses for several Florida species:

Species	Width of Floor	Depth of Cavity	Entrance Diameter	Entrance above floor	Height above ground or water
Barred owl*	12 x 12 in 30 x 30 cm	19–24 in 48–61 cm	6 in 15 cm	10–16 in 25–41cm	12–30 ft 4–9 m
Barn Owl*	12 x 18 in 30 x 46 cm	17–19 in 43–48 cm	6 x 9 in 15–23 cm	0–7 in 0–18 cm	12–30 ft 4–9 m
Carolina Chickadee & Tufted Titmouse	4 x 4 in 10 x 10 cm	8–10 in 20–25 cm	1.25 in 3 cm	6–8 in 15–20 cm	5–15 ft 1–5 m
Eastern Bluebird	5 x 5 in 13 x 13 cm	8–12 in 20–30 cm	1.5 in 4 cm	6–10 in 15–25 cm	5–6 ft 1–2m
Great Crested Flycatcher	6 x 6 in 15 x 15 cm	8–10 in 20–25 cm	2 in 5 cm	6–8 in 15–20cm	8–20 ft 2–6 m
Red-bellied & Red-headed Woodpeckers*	6 x 6 in 15 x 15 cm	12–15 in 30–38 cm	2 in 5 cm	9–12 in 23–30 cm	8–10 ft 2–3 m
Northern Flicker*	7 x 7 in 18 x 18 cm	16 in 41 cm	2.5 in 6 cm	14 in 36 cm	6–12 ft 2–4 m
American Kestrel & Eastern Screech-Owl*	7 x 7 in 18 x 18 cm	16 in 41 cm	3 in 8 cm	14 in 36 cm	10+ ft 3+ m
Prothonotary Warbler	4 x 4 in 10 x 10 cm	6 in 15 cm	1.5 in 4 cm	4 in 10 cm	4–12 ft (land) 1–4 m 3 ft (water) 1 m
Purple Martin**	6 x 6 in 15 x 15 cm	6 in 15 cm	2.5 in 6 cm	1–2 in 3–5 cm	15–20 ft 5–6 m
Wood Duck*	10 x 10 in 25 x 25 cm	24 in 61 cm	3 x 4 in 8 x 10 cm	18 in 46 cm	10–25 (land) 3–8 m 5–25 (water) 1–8 m

*Place sawdust in box.
**Build as multiple apartment house, or gourds may be substituted.

Sick, Injured, and Orphaned Birds

As more and more people populate Florida, interactions between humans and birds increase. For example, more automobiles result in more bird hits, and more buildings with mirrored windows result in higher frequency of bird strikes. At the same time, a greater awareness by people of the plight of wildlife causes them to see and rescue more injured or helpless birds. As a result, greater expenditures in both time and money are being spent on the care, treatment, and rehabilitation of birds in Florida.

Most of these injured and orphaned birds, of course, belong to the most widespread and abundant species in the state—NORTHERN MOCKINGBIRD, BLUE JAY, MOURNING DOVE, NORTHERN CARDINAL, and various CROWS, just to mention a few—and we would be hard-pressed to prove that efforts in rehabilitation had the slightest beneficial impact on those populations. On the other hand, we can say that the expertise, experience, and interest now exists to assist the injured or orphaned individuals of rare, threatened, and endangered species that occasionally come to wildlife rehabilitators because of their experience with the more common species.

We can also point out that most of these rehabilitators are involved with environmental education efforts in their communities, spreading greater awareness of human impact on wildlife. Wildlife rehabilitators perform a worthwhile and valuable service to the community as well as to their wildlife patients. Few of them receive any tax dollars, and most of them end up spending their own funds to support their efforts. They need your financial support and welcome your volunteer services.

Your local Animal Control Department, Humane Society, or Audubon chapter can direct you to your nearest wildlife rehabilitator. Because both state and federal regulations govern the possession of migratory birds, game birds, and many other forms of wildlife, rehabilitators must have permits authorizing them to possess and care for the creatures in their charge. In Florida the Florida Fish and Wildlife Conservation Commission issues these permits and can provide a list of names of rehabilitators in your area. Gradually, most of the rehabilitators are becoming members of the Florida Wildlife Rehabilitation Association, which may be contacted at P.O. Box 1449, Anna Maria, FL 34216, http://www.fwra.org.

Most of Florida's wildlife rehabilitators did not learn their profession in school, but through on-the-job training, which probably began with the first injured or orphaned bird brought to them by a neighborhood kid. Many of them are still learning, but after many failures and successes most know the basics of bird care. A reference that we highly recommend is *Wild Orphan Babies: Mammals and Birds: Caring for Them, Setting Them Free* by William J. Weber, a Leesburg, Florida, veterinarian. (See the recommended reading list in the Resources section.)

SICK AND INJURED BIRDS

It usually takes a person with professional training and experience, such as a veterinarian, to diagnose and treat sick and injured birds. A broken wing or leg must be properly set or the limb will not heal correctly. Most rehabilitators rely on a local veterinarian interested in wildlife medicine for assistance. Many of these vets provide thousands of dollars' worth of free service annually for wildlife. Severely injured or diseased birds may require euthanasia to put them out of their misery. Hence, any birds that appear ill or injured should be delivered to your local wildlife rehabilitator for care.

Fish-hooked Birds

Several species of fish-eating waterbirds, especially the BROWN PELICAN, DOUBLE-CRESTED CORMORANT, and ROYAL TERN, frequently take bait fish on a fisherman's line and get hooked in the process. When this occurs, do not cut the line and allow the bird to fly off trailing a streamer of monofilament line. That is a death sentence for the bird because the line usually becomes entangled in trees where pelicans and cormorants roost and nest, or, for the tern, it becomes wrapped around its body. Instead, reel in the bird, and with another person to assist you with the larger birds, grab it by the bill, fold the wings against the body, and carefully remove the hook without further injuring the bird. You may have to cut off the barbed end first. If the hook has been swallowed, leave it in the bird, but cut the monofilament line as short as possible. Then release the bird.

Monofilament line, even without a hook, snags and kills many creatures along our waterways. Florida fishermen lose and discard miles of monofilament annually. Everyone should get into the habit of picking up this dangerous litter and disposing of it properly.

Oiled Birds

Florida's long coastline, ports of commerce, and tanker shipping lanes on both the Gulf and Atlantic coasts make it extremely vulnerable to oil spills. The 1989 *Exxon Valdez* spill dumped 11 million gallons of crude oil in Prince William Sound in Alaska, killing a massive number of seabirds and marine mammals. Over a decade later, only two species—the BALD EAGLE and the river otter—had recovered from the spill, according to government scientists who worked on the *Exxon Valdez* Oil Spill Trustee Council. Since 2000 there have been two much more massive spills with tens of thousands of birds affected, one off France, the other off Cape Town, South Africa. These all point to the need for contingency planning for a similar tragedy someday in Florida's coastal waters. The question is not if; it is *when.*

Regular Dawn® Dishwashing Detergent can be used to clean oiled birds but the procedure is complicated and should be done by experts. The International Bird Rescue Research Center, an organization dedicated to mitigating the human impact on aquatic birds and other wildlife, has developed procedures, protocols, and techniques for the treatment of oiled birds. Its website, http://www.ibrrc.org, offers a history of oil spills, procedures for treating oiled birds, and other useful information. IBRRC's central office is located at 4369 Cordelia Road, Fairfield, CA 94534, phone 707-207-0380.

When an oil spill occurs, speed in responding is of the essence. If you should spot an extensive sheen of oil or tar on a body of water**,** do not assume that someone else has reported it. The following numbers should be called:

National Response Center (NRC): 1-800-424-8802

U.S. Coast Guard Atlantic Area Command Center: 757-398-6390

Florida Department of Environmental Protection, Bureau of Emergency Response: 850-245-2010

Finding and Reporting Sick or Dead Birds

Occasionally some calamity occurs that results in the illness or death of birds. This could be caused by a naturally occurring disease—avian botulism, pox, or aspergillosus, for example—or by a lethal pesticide with which the birds have come in contact, such as diazinon sprayed on lawns to control mole crickets. If birds should land on a lawn shortly after it has been sprayed with this chemical—and in the dry season birds are sometimes attracted to a wet lawn—it is fatal to them. Because of this the Environmental Protection Agency has banned the use of diazinon on golf courses and sod farms. The EPA is also phasing out its use on home lawns. Occasionally GRACKLES, NORTHERN MOCKINGBIRDS, and AMERICAN ROBINs have been killed in Florida because of this chemical, which is one reason of many that its use is being discontinued.

During spring and fall migration birds occasionally strike TV towers and tall buildings, especially during severe weather fronts. Events such as the one that occurred at the Crystal River power plant on the Gulf coast in the early 1980s can kill thousands of birds in a single night. Other birds strike picture windows and windows coated with highly reflective materials, and others are hit by cars.

Finding an occasional sick or dead bird is generally no cause for alarm, but since the West Nile Virus (WNV) was first documented in the United States in 1999, the FWC (Florida Fish and Wildlife Conservation Commission) and the Florida Department of Health maintain a bird mortality database to monitor the virus, which can cause disease in humans, birds, and other vertebrates. If you find a number of sick or dead birds, especially crows, contact the FWC. You can do this by filling out the Surveillance for Wild Bird Die-offs form online at http://www.wildflorida.org/bird/default.asp or by calling your local FWC office.To learn more about the West Nile Virus, see the website of the Center for Disease Control and Prevention, www.cdc.gov, or of the Florida Department of Health, http://www.doh.state.fl.us/.

Fresh dead birds are valuable, not only because they can be studied for possible cause of death, but as material for other biological studies and for museum and educational specimens. Ornithologists located at most of the state's major universities always welcome fresh dead birds in good condition, as long as information showing date and locality and possible cause of death, if known, accompanies the specimen.

ORPHANED BIRDS

Each year during the baby bird season—chiefly the spring and summer—newly fledged birds, some too young to fly well, appear in our neighborhoods, and many people think they are abandoned and in need of human assistance. The best policy is to leave them alone. Their parents are nearby and are still caring for them. If the baby is in some immediate danger of predation or being run over by traffic, then it should be picked up and placed in a nearby shrub or small tree. Touching it will not cause the parents to abandon it. If the baby appears too young and wobbly, then place it in a small container, such as a berry box, and fasten it to a branch of the tree or shrub. Most of the time this should be sufficient and the parents will continue caring for the fledgling. If you have doubts about the well-being of the bird, observe it from a distance over the next hour or two to see if a parent has returned to it before you decide to rescue it permanently. Only after you have determined that the baby bird is truly abandoned should you remove it from the wild. Baby birds require frequent feeding of specialized diets and several weeks of care until they are independent. Only as a last resort should anyone take on the task of rearing one. Do everything you can to get the baby to a rehabilitator. (Once you have gone through the experience of rearing a baby bird you will better appreciate this bit of advice!) If you must rear the bird, the first thing you need to do is determine which species it is so you will know what to feed it. Most likely it will be one of the more common species nesting in your neighborhood—NORTHERN MOCKINGBIRD, BLUE JAY, NORTHERN CARDINAL, COMMON GRACKLE, or MOURNING DOVE.

The above species, and most of the other bird species you may care for, are called altricial birds. They hatch helpless, usually naked and blind, and are dependent upon the parents for warmth and food for two or three weeks until they become fully-grown and independent. Species whose babies are fully developed when they hatch—with downy feathers, open eyes, and strong legs—are called precocial birds.

Within a few hours after hatching they can run about or swim and feed themselves, although they still require adult protection and guidance and warmth for a few days until their contour (body) feathers form. Chickenlike birds such as the NORTHERN BOBWHITE and all DUCKS and SHOREBIRDS are precocial.

CARE OF ALTRICIAL ORPHANS

Shelter

The baby bird should be placed in a small container lined with a soft cloth or paper towel and several sheets of tissue. A quart-size berry box or any similar container will do. As the tissue becomes soiled, replace it. Warmth can be provided by a 40- or 60-watt light bulb with the distance of the bulb being adjusted until temperature is just above 95°F if the baby is naked, and 70–75° if feathered. Once the nestling is fully feathered and the ambient nighttime temperature remains in the 70's, then no additional heat is required. Instead of a light bulb, a heating pad could be used. In both cases, be sure not to overheat the bird.

The nest container should be placed inside a larger carton to protect the bird from accidental tipovers or a household pet or, in the case of an older fledgling, from premature escape. When the fledgling begins moving around, the nest container can be placed in a wire mesh cage, or if you have a secure screened porch, it can be given a corner of the porch with a perch (a tree branch) over newspaper.

Food

A number of baby bird diets have been developed by various rehabilitators, but the following, devised by Dr. Weber, is a good basic diet for most altricial birds that is relatively easy to prepare and feed. Soak pieces of dry Purina Cat Chow in one egg yolk mixed into 6 ounces of homogenized milk. The pieces of cat food should soak in a small amount of formula only until they have absorbed sufficient moisture to soften them, but not be mushy. The softened pieces may be picked up with a pair of blunt forceps or a toothpick and placed into the back of the throat of the begging bird. Feed the bird as much as it will take at a feeding. Younger birds need to be fed every 20–30 minutes; older birds, once filled, can go an hour between feedings. Generally, the babies will let you know when they are hungry.

Other Foods and Supplements

Offer pieces of grape, apple, banana, mulberries, blackberries, blueberries (whatever is in season), insects captured in the yard (but only in pesticide-free yards), mealworms (golden grubs, available from fish bait or pet stores), crickets, and shelled sunflower seeds, peanuts, and pecans. Once or twice a week add a drop of liquid vitamins—the kind sold in pet shops for cagebirds—on a food pellet. Also about once a week crush a tablet of Vitamin B-1 and sprinkle this on a few pellets before feeding.

Water

Most baby bird diets contain sufficient water that they do not need to be given water directly. However, occasionally after you have fed the nestling, you may dip your finger in water and touch it to the tip of the beak so that it dribbles water into the mouth. This is the only way to provide water; do not use a dropper as you could accidentally place water into the air passage.

Mourning Doves

Doves feed their young a "milk" formed in the crop. An excellent substitute for this is Hi Protein baby cereal mixed with water to a soupy consistency, just thin enough to be taken up by a medicine dropper. Insert the dropper down the back of the mouth and fill the crop. Do this several times. Feed every two hours or so, depending on the hunger of the dove. As the dove becomes feathered, begin feeding it by hand a mixture of bird seed and baby chick starter scratch, but first remove the unshelled sunflower seeds and shell these before feeding them to the dove. Also provide a few grains of canary or parakeet grit with the bird seed mixture. Gradually reduce the cereal diet and increase the seed diet, but continue providing some cereal until the dove is feeding itself and drinking from a water dish. Be sure to wipe off with a damp cloth any cereal spilled on the head and neck after each feeding.

Hawks and Owls (Raptors)

Orphaned raptors should be taken to a rehabilitator who is trained in the care of this highly specialized group of birds. Far too many orphaned raptors have been brought to Audubon of Florida's Center for Birds of Prey suffering from vitamin/mineral deficiencies as a result of inadequate nutrition. A temporary diet that can be fed to raptors prior to transfer to a raptor center is the same one designed for altricial birds. Thin strips of beef heart sprinkled with a calcium-vitamin-mineral powder (Vionate, available from drug stores and some pet stores) can supplement this diet.

CARE OF PRECOCIAL ORPHANS

Because they tend to be flighty and high-strung, it is sometimes difficult to successfully rear wild quail and ducks, but with care and patience, it can be done.

Northern Bobwhite

The cage should be a wooden or heavy cardboard box about 12–15 inches (30–28 cm) wide and 24–30 inches (61–76 cm) long. Insert a wire or string across the top of the box about 8 or 10 inches (20–25 cm) from one end. Over this drape a piece of cloth to form an inner chamber. The cloth should leave about a 2-inch (5-cm) gap above the floor to allow chicks to run in and out of the chamber. Fasten a small mirror on the wall of this chamber. The mirror functions as a sibling—another chick is always there when needed.

This is especially important if you have only one chick. The heat source can be a heating pad under the box or a 40-watt light bulb. Temperature should be about 90–95°F in the chamber.

Line the floor with several layers of newspaper and several layers of paper towels above this. The towels will be replaced daily, the newspapers once a week, depending on need. Do not allow papers to become too wet or messy. Ideally, have two identical containers so that you can alternate their use. This way you need handle the chicks only once a week when you transfer them from one box to the other.

Feed turkey starter food. In an emergency, baby chick starter will suffice, but it is lower in protein content. After a few days begin adding a few grains of baby chick starter scratch. Also begin adding small bits of grass and clover blades, lettuce, and any insects that you can capture, including small mealworms and crickets. Always keep some canary or parrot grit on the floor of the cage or in the food dish. The water dish should be the kind used for baby chicks, although a very shallow jar lid will suffice if only a few chicks are present. As the quail become larger and fully feathered, you will need to build an outdoor predator-proof pen that allows them contact with the ground.

Wood Duck

Food and care of ducklings is similar to that for quail, except you need to provide a larger source of water and you will have to clean the cage almost daily. After the ducklings are several days old, add a shallow pan of water no more than 1 inch (3 cm) deep and allow the ducklings to play in it for 10–15 minutes, perhaps once or twice daily, but do not let them become soaked and chilled. After two or three weeks you will need to provide a large outdoor pen with a permanent pool of water (a pan buried in the dirt, or one above ground with a ramp). Be sure the ducklings can easily get out of the pool. To predator-proof a cage, the outer covering should be made of two or three thicknesses of chicken wire or hardware cloth. Once the ducklings are about three-fourths grown and are fully feathered, including wing primaries, they may be released in suitable habitat—usually a pond where you have seen other Wood Ducks.

BIRD CONSERVATION

If we enjoy seeing birds, if we appreciate their role and value as living creatures, then it follows that we should become involved with their welfare and conservation. Ever-expanding human development is destroying the habitats of numerous wildlife species in Florida, especially those that depend on natural forests, scrublands, prairies, and wetlands. Each new homesite, subdivision, or shopping plaza destroys the habitat and displaces the animals that lived there. In the past we could rationalize this by thinking, "Oh, there are plenty of undeveloped areas nearby that they can move to." This is no longer true in our highly urbanized and suburbanized landscapes. Most of the vacant undeveloped properties scattered here and there are being developed, and few "vacant" habitats remain nearby; if there are any, they are probably already occupied by wildlife.

When a community buys parklands for the recreational needs of its citizens—ball parks, tennis courts, picnic facilities—it too often ignores the needs of wildlife and of those citizens who enjoy passive recreation such as bird watching, nature photography, or just hiking through the woods. Wildlife, which has just as much right to live on the land as do the humans who "own" it, do not have any say about their fate. They neither vote nor pay taxes, but they do pay a high price for human development with their lives, and, sometimes, with the extinction of their species. The need for pristine natural space and wildlife habitat within our communities and on our own lands is as important to humans as it is to wildlife.

What can you as an individual do about all this? At the very least, you can join one or more of the environmental organizations in your area that are actively promoting the preservation and conservation of wildlife habitat. It takes no more effort than simply writing a check and mailing in your annual membership.

If you are willing and able to do more, you can become an active participant in the work of the organization. You can also take a few moments to write or phone to let your elected officials know of your interest and concern about what they are doing or not doing on behalf of wildlife. Show your support for programs and initiatives that encourage wise management of growth and development on the regional, state, and national level. You cannot assume that the agencies responsible for the management of a public resource will always do what is "right" in the discharge of their stewardship. Continual vigilance by the public is necessary to ensure the protection of our wildlife resources. It is an undertaking that is well worth the effort. The beauty and wonder of nature are rewards in themselves, and they are a precious legacy for future generations. You, individually, may feel helpless to change the course of things, but through membership in environmental organizations your name and your annual dues multiply your influence.

BIRDS AND THE LAW

Both state and federal laws regulate the disturbance and taking of birds in Florida. All native and nongame migratory birds—except blackbirds, grackles, cowbirds, and crows, which cause damage to trees, crops, livestock, or wildlife—are protected. Established exotic birds such as the HOUSE SPARROW, EUROPEAN STARLING, ROCK PIGEON, and MUSCOVY DUCK are not protected. The Florida Fish and Wildlife Conservation Commission (FWC) publishes the list of species designated endangered, threatened, or of special concern by the federal and state governments. Please check with the commission for current information and details. You can learn more about Florida hunting regulations, permits, special opportunity hunts, game seasons, bag limits, and much more at FWC's hunting website, www.wildflorida.org/hunting/default.asp.

Many cities have ordinances prohibiting the firing of weapons within city limits. The state also has a law dealing specifically with children and guns (including air rifles or BB guns) which reads partly as follows:

(1) The use for any purpose whatsoever of BB guns, air or gas-operated guns, or electric weapons or devices, by any minor under the age of 16 years is prohibited unless such use is under the supervision and in the presence of an adult who is acting with the consent of the minor's parent.

(2) Any adult responsible for the welfare of any child under the age of 16 years who knowingly permits such child to use or have in his or her possession any BB gun, air or gas-operated gun, electric weapon or device, or firearm in violation of the provisions of subsection (1) of this section commits a misdemeanor of the second degree, punishable as provided (by law). Section 790.22, Florida Statutes.

If you know of a child shooting at birds, make an effort to talk with the child and/or the parents about the situation and the law. If the child persists and the parents won't cooperate, then speak to your local wildlife enforcement officer or the police or sheriff. Don't expect them to become excited and rush out to arrest the violator. Most of them feel that they have more important criminals to deal with than a kid with a BB gun. But if the child is killing or injuring numerous birds, then be persistent. Ask the officials at least to speak with the child's parents. Fortunately, with greater environmental awareness and conservation issues being taught in elementary schools, fewer children are inclined to kill birds.

The Florida Fish and Wildlife Conservation Commission maintains the Wildlife Alert program, which has been highly successful since its inception in 1979, resulting in over 20,000 arrests and $300,000 in rewards ranging from $25 to $1,000 each. Anyone seeing a violation of fish and wildlife laws can call the Wildlife Alert Hotline at 1-888-404-FWCC (3922) to report the illegal activity. This number will connect any caller to the appropriate office in the state of Florida, and can be found inside the front cover of most phone directories.

Town Bird Sanctuaries

With the state and federal laws that already protect birds, and with the prohibitions against discharging weapons within most city limits, each municipality is automatically a bird sanctuary. Officially designating a particular area a bird sanctuary is done primarily for publicity purposes and to enhance environmental awareness among schoolchildren and the general public.

The city council of a legally incorporated municipality can declare the town a bird sanctuary by a resolution drawn up by the city attorney. For an unincorporated community, the resolution must be passed by the board of county commissioners. For a housing subdivision, a majority vote of the property owners' association can declare the area a bird or wildlife sanctuary. Such a declaration is meaningless, however, without accompanying publicity, educational efforts, and appropriate signs.

To submit a request to establish a bird sanctuary in a particular developed area, the local governmental body with jurisdiction over the area should write to the Bureau of Nongame Wildlife, Florida Fish and Wildlife Conservation Commission, 620 S. Meridian Street, Tallahassee, FL 32399-1600.

Florida's Nongame Wildlife Efforts

Prior to the 1980s, the primary efforts of the Florida Game and Fresh Water Fish Commission dealt with the management of game species—white-tailed deer, wild hog, Wild Turkey, and Northern Bobwhite. In the early 1980s, the legislature established a nongame wildlife program and the Nongame Wildlife Trust Fund to finance it. The trust fund has supported and funded many bird programs, including, for example, the Breeding Bird Atlas and the reintroduction of the Whooping Crane. Trust fund monies are derived chiefly from a $4.00 first-time auto registration fee paid by new residents who transfer their vehicle registrations from another state. Current citizens of Florida may also contribute to the fund by adding $1.00 to their annual auto registration renewals. The fund also accepts donations from the public.

In 1999 the Florida Game and Freshwater Fish Commission was merged with the Marine Fisheries Commission to become the Florida Fish and Wildlife Conservation Commission (FWC). The commission is a huge state organization with many divisions, and part of their work deals with birds. They are in charge of research and management for wildlife listed as endangered, threatened, or of special concern. One project of the FWC is the Great Florida Birding Trail, a 2000-mile highway trail combining highway signs identifying birding trail sites with a map showing good birding areas (see www.floridabirdingtrail.com). They also run the Wings Over Florida program of award levels for birders keeping life lists of birds seen. Each month in *Florida Monthly* magazine they publish "Wildlife Watching with the Florida Fish and Wildlife Conservation Commission."

ENDANGERED AND THREATENED SPECIES

In 1972 the Florida Audubon Society and Florida Defenders of the Environment founded the Florida Committee on Rare and Endangered Plants and Animals (FCREPA). The committee prepared a list of the species in Florida that were endangered, threatened with endangerment, or otherwise of special concern. Six special subcommittees of biologists covering each major group—plants, invertebrates, fishes, amphibians and reptiles, birds, and mammals—were organized to perform the work. The end products of this effort were the volumes of the *Rare and Endangered Biota of Florida* series, originally published between 1978 and 1982 by the University Presses of Florida. Most of the volumes were rewritten in the 1990s to reflect changes in Florida's wildlife populations.

Rare and Endangered Biota of Florida Series, Ray E. Ashton, Jr., Series Editor (Gainesville: University Press of Florida)

Vol. 1. *Mammals,* edited by Stephen R. Humphrey (1992)

Vol. 2. *Fishes,* edited by Carter R. Gilbert (1992)

Vol. 3. *Amphibians and Reptiles,* edited by Paul E. Moler (1992)

Vol. 4. *Invertebrates,* edited by Mark Deyrup and Richard Franz (1995)

Vol. 5. *Birds,* edited by James A. Rodgers, Jr., Herbert W. Kale II, and Henry T. Smith (1996)

Vol. 6. *Plants,* edited by Daniel B. Ward (1979) (out of print as of the date of this publication)

The list of endangered and threatened species is reviewed annually and revised as needed under Florida Administrative Code, Chapter 39, Rules 39–27.003 (endangered species), 39–27.004 (threatened species), and 39–27.005 (species of special concern). The Florida Fish and Wildlife Conservation Commission maintains the list and consolidates state and federal official lists of endangered species, threatened species, and other species categorized in some way by the respective jurisdictional agencies as meriting special protection or consideration. A copy of this list may be obtained from the FWC's website at http://www.wildflorida.org. (Click on Imperiled Species.)

Because recovery of the state's endangered species depends upon the knowledge and actions of the people who visit or live in Florida, we briefly discuss here some of these species and their special problems.

WOOD STORK

This species thrives in wetland habitats that undergo periodic flooding and drying. During wet periods, fish populations spread out, reproduce, and grow. In dry seasons, the fish concentrate in pools and are available to many wading species of birds. Because of overdrainage of wetlands and the manipulation of water levels by humans, the stork population has declined from a high of about 75,000 in 1930 to today's population: statewide annual populations fluctuate between 3,500 and 5,500 birds. Continued loss of wetlands and improper management of water levels can only result in continued declines of this species.

SNAIL KITE

This species, formerly called the Everglade Kite, depends for its very existence on a single food source, the Apple Snail (*Pomacea paludosa*). The snail is widespread throughout the Florida peninsula but is available to the kite only in open freshwater marshes that retain water throughout the year. When a marsh dries out, as occasionally happens in drought periods, the snails disappear and the kites must move elsewhere; but if they cannot find suitable habitat with snails, the kites are doomed. With the drainage of much of south Florida's wetlands and the unnatural manipulation of water levels in the remaining marshes, the kite population fluctuates widely from year to year. Once a marsh dries out, even if only temporarily, it may take several years of adequate water levels to replenish the snail population so that kites can return to the marsh. The kite population fluctuates from 200 to 700 birds, depending on water conditions the previous nesting season. Recently, over 1000 kites were recorded in central and south Florida.

BALD EAGLE

The Bald Eagle was originally listed on February 14, 1978, as an endangered species throughout the lower 48 states, except in Minnesota, Michigan, Wisconsin, Washington, and Oregon, where it was listed as a threatened species. Effective August 11, 1995, the U.S. Fish and Wildlife Service reclassified the Bald Eagle from endangered to threatened in the lower 48 states. In those states where the species was already listed as threatened, it remains classified that way.

Outside of Alaska, more Bald Eagles occur in Florida than in any other state. In addition, Florida supports the largest number of breeding Bald Eagles of any southeastern state. Approximately 70% of the occupied nesting territories in the Southeast are in Florida. Unfortunately, Florida's growing human population and development efforts across the state are continually encroaching on eagle nest sites. The U.S. Fish and Wildlife Service and the Florida Fish and Wildlife Conservation Commission have issued guidelines for the protection of eagle nests. These guidelines provide for an inviolate primary zone with a 750–1,500 foot radius, as well as a secondary zone with certain use and activity restrictions covering a 1-mile maximum radius. Because a nest tree can be felled in minutes, and a primary zone bulldozed in several hours, citizen vigilance is important for the protection of eagle nests. Learn where eagles are nesting in your area and be alert to any proposed development plans near these sites. As part of a project to determine the success rates of eagle nests found in developed areas, the FWC website offers a searchable database of all eagle nests it has verified in the state of Florida since 1998. Contact the FWC if you spot a new nest, or if any threat to an existing one appears imminent.

CRESTED CARACARA

Formerly called Audubon's Caracara, this species once occurred from Volusia south to Collier County, but is now restricted for the most part to the Kissimmee Prairie region from Osceola County south to Lake Okeechobee and northern Collier County. It has been declining as native prairie habitat has been converted to citrus groves and improved pastures. The Florida population now numbers about 400 birds. If landowners were encouraged to leave patches of native prairie and scattered stands of cabbage palms (its preferred nest site) when converting to improved pasture, it may be possible to retain this magnificent species in the Florida landscape.

AMERICAN KESTREL

Florida is an important wintering area for American Kestrels from the north; they may be seen on utility poles and wires along most state highways from October through April. But the resident breeding population, the Southeastern Kestrel, which is smaller in size than its northern cousin, is relatively scarce and is declining in most parts of the state. The chief reason for the decline in central Florida is believed to be a reduction in the number of dead trees and snags that provide the cavities needed by the kestrel as nest sites. An intervention that may help increase the kestrel population is the installation of nesting boxes in suitable habitat throughout the state. This would be a good project for local Audubon chapters and Eagle Scouts.

FLORIDA SANDHILL CRANE

The resident race of the Sandhill Crane occurs throughout most of the Florida peninsula in wet prairies, marshy lake edges, and low-lying pastures wherever it can find food, suitable nesting habitat, and low human disturbance. This crane will tolerate some human proximity, but not near nest sites. They can survive on improved pasturelands as long as isolated shallow-water ponds and marshes are not destroyed.

SNOWY PLOVER

This inhabitant of Florida's Gulf coast requires expansive, dry sandy beaches for breeding and both dry and tidal sand flats for foraging. Increased human activity, vehicles, and pet dogs and cats on beaches, especially near passes and inlets during spring and early summer when the plovers nest, have caused a great reduction in the number of Snowy Plovers in Florida. Most of the breeding pairs of Snowy Plovers are found on Panhandle beaches.

LEAST TERN

This tern appears in Florida in middle to late March to breed, then returns to South America by mid-September. It prefers to nest on sandy or shelly islands, isolated beaches, and sand spits where vegetation is sparse or absent. Such sites are also preferred by humans for many recreational activities. In recent years, the Least Tern has been hard-pressed to find sufficient ground for nesting. Fortunately, it has found substitute nesting sites on flat, gravel-covered roofs of shopping plazas, warehouses, schools, and apartment buildings. These sites are relatively free of disturbance by humans and their pets, raccoons, and tidal flooding, although they present other hazards (temporary flooding after heavy downpours, unfenced dropoffs, and roofing tar). The terns nest only on lightly-colored substrates (white crushed limestone pearock, and cream, yellow, or tan river pebbles) and avoid roof areas covered with gray crushed traprock.

Tern colonies on beaches, dunes, and causeways can often be protected from humans by posting the site with stakes, engineering tape, and signs identifying the colony and requesting that people remain away during the nesting season. Your regional FWC wildlife biologist can assist in posting the site and providing the proper signs. Rooftop colonies do not require posting, but it is a good idea to contact building owners or managers and encourage them to allow the birds to remain undisturbed. Where rooftop colonies cause a nuisance, refer to the next chapter for possible solutions.

RED-COCKADED WOODPECKER

This highly specialized woodpecker, found only in open, mature pine forests, requires old, living trees (60–120 years or older) in which to excavate a nest cavity. Most commercial forests in Florida are harvested on rotations of only 20–40 years; hence the Red-cockaded has been on a steady decline for the past several decades while most of the older timber stands are being harvested. It is only in our national and state forests and refuges that this species has the best chance to escape extinction, and then only if the forests are managed in such a way to enhance woodpecker survival. Unfortunately, public forest policy has been mostly directed toward maximum harvest rather than protection of wildlife. This attitude has been gradually shifting, especially after lawsuits brought by environmental organizations. Whether or not new management practices will be sufficient and timely remains to be seen. Meanwhile the Red-cockaded Woodpecker continues to decline.

Because there is little hope of preserving any woodpeckers on privately owned commercial forest lands, management efforts must be conducted in our publicly owned forests, and this will not happen without strong public support and vigilance.

FLORIDA SCRUB-JAY

This jay is a threatened species because its oak scrub habitat is prime land for housing subdivisions, shopping malls, and citrus groves. In fact, the Florida scrub is becoming the most endangered habitat in the state. The largest colonies of jays occur on public and other conservation lands on Merritt Island National Wildlife Refuge, at Cape Canaveral Air Station, Ocala National Forest, and Archbold Biological Station near Lake Placid. The jay will survive at these sites only if the habitat is periodically burned to maintain certain stages of the oak scrub community. The Florida Scrub-Jay was listed as threatened in 1987. By 1993, populations had declined an estimated 90% to about 10,000 individuals. Since then, further severe declines have been documented throughout the state.

Anyone observing Florida Scrub-Jays on public lands outside of the previously mentioned sites, or on privately owned lands, is urged to report the sighting to Audubon of Florida, a local Audubon chapter, or to a regional wildlife biologist from the FWC. To learn about the Florida Scrub-Jay Population Monitoring and Habitat Restoration Project, visit the Audubon of Florida website, http://www.audubonofflorida.org.

CAPE SABLE SEASIDE SPARROW

Though it is widely distributed over a large area of south Florida and it continues to occupy much of its historically known range in Collier, Miami-Dade, and Monroe Counties, the population of this small, olive-gray subspecies of the Seaside Sparrow appears quite ephemeral except for two core populations in and near Taylor Slough and in Big Cypress Swamp/Everglades National Park (Kushlan and Bass 1983). The population estimate in 1992 was 6,450 birds. In 1993, it numbered 3,347 and in 1994 it totalled 2,800 birds. The decrease may be linked to the effects of Hurricane Andrew in August 1992. A 2004 survey suggested some recovery from the lows of the early 1990s, with an estimate of about 3,600 birds. The bird should theoretically be secure and well protected in Everglades National Park. Unfortunately, the park is threatened by all the forces impacting natural waterflows from the northern Everglades region. The Dusky Seaside Sparrow became extinct in the 1980s, and though it has persisted, the Cape Sable Seaside may not be far behind.

DUSKY SEASIDE SPARROW

We will conclude this chapter with the Dusky Seaside Sparrow, a population no longer considered to be endangered, but only because it is now extinct. It was the most distinctive race of Seasides because of its black and white streaked undersides. First discovered in 1873 near Salt Lake in the St. Johns River valley in Brevard County, it was considered a separate species until 1973 when, based on biological evidence, it was designated a subspecies, or race, closely related to all the other Seaside Sparrows on the Atlantic and Gulf coasts. By this time it occurred only in the marshes of northern Merritt Island and the St. Johns River valley west of Titusville.

Adverse impacts of human activities on the Dusky probably began with early efforts to drain marshes in the 1920s. In the late 1940s DDT was sprayed on Merritt Island marshes, and in the late 1950s these marshes were diked and impounded for mosquito control, which effectively destroyed the Dusky's habitat. State and county road construction and canal excavation by General Development Corporation destroyed more habitat in the St. Johns marsh. Governmental inertia in restoration of habitat and the invasion of shrubby vegetation due to overdrainage intensified wildfires set by ranchers each winter to improve cattle pasture.

These cumulative adverse impacts over five decades finally brought the Dusky to the edge of extinction and by 1979 only seven males remained in the marsh. Six of these were captured in 1979–80 and brought into captivity. Over the next several years, in a cooperative effort involving the Wildlife Research Laboratory of the Florida Game and Fresh Water Fish Commission (now FWC), the Santa Fe Community College Teaching Zoo, the Florida Museum of Natural History, Florida Audubon Society, and Walt Disney World's Discovery Island Zoological Park, the Duskies were mated with female Scott's Seaside Sparrows, a closely related subspecies from the Gulf coast. Although a few young were produced, it was a matter of too little, too late, and the last Dusky Seaside Sparrow died on June 16, 1987.

BIRD/HUMAN PROBLEMS AND SOLUTIONS

A s Florida becomes more developed with each passing year, interactions between birds and humans increase. Some of these are simply temporary annoyances, such as a noisy bird singing outside a bedroom window at night, but others can be more serious, such as a woodpecker persistently drilling holes into the wooden siding of a house. In many cases the problem is short-term or can easily be solved. That night-singing bird may be a NORTHERN MOCKINGBIRD—the state bird of Florida—singing a song of passion for his beloved during a few moonlit nights in spring. Or it may be a CHUCK-WILL'S-WIDOW that doesn't need any moonlight to stimulate his loud song in April, May, and June. As passions cool, so does the singing. And the flocks of noisy GRACKLES or RED-WINGED BLACKBIRDS that suddenly descend on a lawn in late winter will be there only a day or so before moving on. Patience and a concern for the welfare of wildlife, both in short supply in the modern world, help to minimize many of these "problems."

Many times, it is the bird that experiences the problem. For example, the windows of many new office buildings are coated with a highly reflective material to reflect heat and light. Surroundings—sky, clouds, trees—are also reflected, and flying birds can strike these windows.

The following paragraphs discuss several of these problems. One solution that we do not recommend is the killing of problem birds. In addition to being illegal unless a permit has been issued for this by both state and federal agencies, it is often only a temporary solution because sooner or later another bird will appear to replace the removed bird. For problems that you are not able to solve peacefully, we urge you to contact the nongame wildlife biologist at your regional office of the Florida Fish and Wildlife Conservation Commission (see your phonebook or http://www.floridaconservation.org).

BIRDS AND NOISE

In Florida, GRACKLES, frogs, and MOCKINGBIRDS—like cockroaches and mosquitoes—are ever-present facts of life. For humans who can't stand the presence and noise of nature, whether it is the noise of a flock of grackles, a chorus of frogs, or a lone, midnight-singing MOCKINGBIRD, we seriously recommend that they consider moving to an upper floor of an apartment or condominium building.

315

For those who really don't mind living in the midst of nature, but still would like to get that persistent singer just outside their bedroom window to move off a bit, we recommend the following. In the evening, at dusk, when birds are going to roost, stand by the tree or shrub where the singer roosts and create enough disturbance to discourage the bird from using that site. You may need to do this several evenings in a row. A helium-filled balloon with an eye painted on it tied to the roost tree might be sufficient to discourage the bird from roosting there.

Second (or you might try this first), tie a line to one or two of the leafy branches and extend this into your house through the nearest window or porch. You might tie a helium-filled balloon containing a few grains of round gravel or unpopped corn to this line. When the bird begins singing, yank the line a few times. The disturbance should succeed in making the bird move to another tree.

A third solution is to close up the house and turn on your air conditioning.

CHIMNEY SWIFTS

Chimney Swifts, as their name suggests, are fond of nesting in chimneys. Formerly, they nested in hollow trees, and perhaps still do in some localities where chimneys are absent. They build delicate nests of tiny twigs fastened together and to the inside wall of the chimney with a sticky saliva that hardens into a secure glue. (Bird nest soup is made from the nest of a swift in China.)

After the young hatch, they become quite noisy when being fed by the parents. To an unsuspecting person down in the living room, the sound can suggest a rattlesnake in the chimney! The birds do no damage; indeed, they eat thousands of flying insects daily and are valuable to have about. We suggest that you close the damper just above the fireplace to reduce the noise and to prevent any young accidentally falling into the room. (If you have ever chased a soot-covered fledgling around the house you can appreciate this advice.) After about two weeks or so the birds should fledge and leave the chimney.

If you would prefer not to have the swifts in your chimney in the future, we suggest that you have a cover of weldwire cloth placed over the top of your chimney in early winter after the swifts have departed for South America.

WOODPECKERS

Generally, woodpeckers pose no problems to humans, but once in a while an individual woodpecker begins excavating holes in the wood sidings of buildings, most often a relatively new building. The first thing to do is check the wood for the presence of insects. If the wood is infested with wood borers, for example, the woodpecker is simply responding to the presence of a food source in a part of your house that needs upkeep. Replacing the infested wood should solve the problem.

Sometimes a bird is damaging the wood framing of a window. This could be a response to the woodpecker seeing his reflection in the glass. The destruction of wood is displacement behavior in response to an intruder that refuses to leave. Try covering the window with some material such as plastic or cardboard so he does not see his reflection. Perhaps the woodpecker is excavating a hole in the siding for a nest or roost cavity. In this case, cover the damaged area with a sheet of opaque plastic and allow it to flap loosely in the breeze. This is the kind of plastic used at construction sites to cover wood and other supplies and used by painters as a cover cloth. It is too smooth for the woodpecker to grasp, and the free flapping end should help discourage further pecking. Another possible solution is to attach helium-filled balloons, with a large eye painted on each, near the site. Another item that may work is a plastic toy pinwheel fastened so that it faces into a prevailing breeze and spins.

Be sure that there are sufficient natural nesting sites in your neighborhood. Woodpeckers excavate cavities in snags or dead branches of living trees and in trunks of dead trees. This is a good reason to leave a few dead trees, or at least a 10- to 20-foot section of the trunk of the tree, standing—as long as it will not damage buildings or vehicles when it finally does fall. RED-BELLIED WOODPECKERS, RED-HEADED WOODPECKERS, and NORTHERN FLICKERS will nest in bird houses, and the placement of one or more of these in your yard and neighborhood may encourage them to nest there instead of in your house.

Most woodpeckers "drum" to demarcate territory and to attract a mate, usually during the spring months. Like any drummer, they seek a good surface that will resonate well. Utility pole condensers and the metal flashing on chimneys and roof peaks make excellent surfaces and sounds, except, of course, to the human in the bedroom below at 6 A.M. Covering the site with opaque plastic with a free end to flap in the breeze or attaching one or two one-eyed balloons may solve the problem. Or perhaps you could reschedule your wake and sleep cycle in the spring months to coincide with that of your romantic neighbor.

DOMESTIC DUCKS

When residences are built around lakes in Florida, sooner or later someone decides that the lake needs some ducks. There may already be some native WOOD DUCKS living on the lake, but these may not be sufficiently visible or tolerant of human activity. The only ducks available for stocking are usually domesticated MALLARDS or MUSCOVY DUCKS, or combinations thereof. After several years, as both the duck and human populations increase, the neighborhood fights begin between those who love and feed the ducks and those who complain about aggressive drakes and messy guano in driveways and swimming pools.

The best means of population control is to find nests and remove eggs. Do not remove all the eggs; allow one or two to remain and hatch. Otherwise the female will quickly renest and lay another full complement of eggs, and this time you may not find the nest. Not every young duckling grows up to become a pet or pest. Our lakes are also home to fish, turtles, and alligators, all of which consider a baby duck fair game, and, occasionally, a hawk or an otter will take a duckling. As distressing as this may seem, it is all part of the game of life. (You might think about this the next time you enjoy a piece of fried chicken.)

Do not capture the ducks and transport them to another lake. It is illegal to release any exotic species into the wild in Florida, even if you captured the birds in the wild initially. The ducks and their fresh eggs are edible and could be donated to shelters to provide food for people or other animals.

BIRD ROOSTS

Some species of birds gather into large flocks at the end of the day and roost together in large concentrations. In Florida we have all seen crows, gulls, or herons flying to roost in the evening. Most of these roosts are not too near human centers and do not cause any problems. Roosting blackbirds usually do not present the problems in Florida that they do farther north in Tennessee and Kentucky, where roosts containing a million or more birds—chiefly EUROPEAN STARLINGS, RED-WINGED BLACKBIRDS, COMMON GRACKLES, and BROWN-HEADED COWBIRDS—often appear in winter near human habitations. Generally, an active roost does not pose any problems to humans, but there can be some health problems associated with disturbance of the ground under an abandoned roost weeks or months afterwards.

If a blackbird roost, or any roost for that matter, is causing some concern, the first thing to do is call on the expertise of the U.S. Fish & Wildlife Service. Each roost is unique and requires individual study to determine its potential threat, if any, to human welfare.

BIRDS AND WINDOWS

Large picture windows and windows coated with reflective materials can cause injury or death for birds, especially during spring and fall migration. The vast expanses of reflective glass on modern office buildings look just like open sky to a flying bird, or, closer to the ground, like the surrounding landscape. What can be done to reduce the incidence of strikes? Anything that masks the reflection will help. In some instances, wide mesh netting can be hung over the glass. This can appear decorative and is not as aesthetically objectionable as opaque plastic sheeting. Silhouettes of an avian predator such as a falcon, or cutouts of large "eyes," can be strategically placed on windows.

Dark or bronze-colored window coatings tend to be more visible and less reflective than the silver-colored coatings, and fewer birds strike these darker windows. This fact should be brought to the attention of those involved in planning and construction of buildings.

Most injuries received from window strikes are concussions and are usually fatal. Occasionally a bird will be found in lethargic condition under a window. If placed in a small box for an hour or so and kept in a quiet place, it may recover and be released. If it has not recovered within several hours then it should be taken to a wildlife rehabilitator for care. You can find one near you at the website of the National Wildlife Rehabilitators Association, http://www.nwrawildlife.org. Dead birds should be given to the nearest museum or university biology department.

Roof-nesting Tern Colonies

We have already discussed efforts needed to protect and encourage tern colonies in Florida on both beaches and rooftops (see Bird Conservation chapter). Occasionally, rooftop colonies can cause some problems for people living or working below or next door to the colony. For example, a colony of 100 or 200 terns can deposit a large number of droppings on automobiles parked in an adjoining lot or into a swimming pool of a condominium or motel.

Once a colony has become established nothing can be done legally to remove the terns from the roof and the best course of action is to grin and bear it for a few more weeks. Their droppings are not a health menace and the only damage done is the temporary inconvenience of putting up with them and cleaning them up. A colony that forms in early May should end breeding for the most part by the end of June or early July, if the colony cycle has not been disrupted by disturbance and egg loss. If attempts are made to illegally destroy or remove eggs, the terns will persistently renest and the period of colony activity will be extended several weeks.

This was dramatically illustrated several years ago by two adjacent rooftop colonies near Daytona Beach. One colony atop a three-story condominium was inaccessible from the roof and, although the condo owners complained about droppings in their pool area (fortunately, their automobiles were protected by a covered roof), they were not sufficiently agitated to overcome the roof access problem and they left the terns undisturbed. Within two or three weeks after they had called for help, most of the young had fledged and the problem disappeared.

Next door was a rental apartment complex with a rooftop colony of terns next to an uncovered parking lot. The apartment manager responded to his tenants' complaints by going onto the roof and removing the eggs. He continued to do this periodically and each time the terns would renest, so that three weeks after the undisturbed terns on the next-door condominium had vacated, the terns atop the apartment complex were still going strong.

As precarious as the Least Tern's status is, we would hope that most owners or managers of buildings suitable for rooftop nesting would welcome the chance to host a colony. However, if it is important to prevent a colony from forming on a particular roof, then several actions can be taken prior to the arrival of the terns in early spring.

Because the terns will not nest on a dark substrate—for example, black, gray, or green—we recommend the stones or gravel on the roof be sprayed a dark color. If this is not a feasible option, then place several helium-filled balloons, each with a large eye painted on it, at several locations on the roof. Or stretch several lengths of clothesline across the roof and drape these with flapping plastic flags, the kind seen in automobile dealer lots.

At the same time you are taking steps to discourage nesting on a rooftop, take some positive actions to encourage the birds to nest elsewhere. Is there another roof nearby that could be enhanced to provide the terns with an alternate site? Is there some open vacant land nearby that could be scraped of vegetation and fenced to exclude dogs, raccoons, and people?

All colonies of LEAST TERNS, both natural and rooftop, should be reported to your regional nongame wildlife biologist and he or she should be contacted if the terns present any problems or are faced with any threats.

PIGEONS

Most pigeons in North America are the feral population of the domesticated form of the OLD WORLD ROCK PIGEON. Pigeons were brought to the New World by early colonists for food, for pets, as a means of communication, and for recreational racing (homing pigeons). Pigeon racing is still pursued by many people and two national organizations, the American Racing Pigeon Union and the International Federation of Homing Pigeon Fanciers, foster the sport. Even though the pigeon is an exotic species, hence does not enjoy the full protection of the Migratory Bird Treaty Acts, at least the fact that some free-flying pigeons may belong to someone should make one pause before harming one. In most instances an owned pigeon will bear one or more obvious leg bands.

Pigeons cause nuisance problems when they become too numerous in a particular site—entrances to public buildings, schools, warehouses, feedlots, etc. They perch and nest on horizontal surfaces such as eaves, gables, and ledges, and their droppings fall on the ground below. They can sometimes be forced to move elsewhere by blocking or covering these perch/nest sites with chicken wire or any material that will prevent perching.

The population can be reduced by trapping and removing the birds. However, because they are homing pigeons they cannot be released elsewhere as they will promptly return to the capture site. Occasionally, birds held in captivity for several weeks at a site far from the capture point will "home" in on the new site. Sometimes a pigeon fancier may be willing to take the birds. Or there may be no alternative except to humanely dispose of the birds. We do not recommend the use of drugged baits to capture pigeons because of the danger of injuring or killing native species that might be attracted to the bait.

EXOTIC SPECIES

South Florida's climate is subtropical and with the massive development of cities, numerous tropical species of flowering and fruiting trees and shrubs have been planted in landscaping around homes, subdivisions, and parks, providing a niche for animals from other lands. With a large pet trade to provide a source of birds, it is not surprising that numerous species have been released, or have escaped, and now survive in south Florida. Some of these species are reproducing; others may simply be populations of long-lived individuals living out their lifespan without breeding. A number of species are successfully breeding and expanding their populations. At least 17 species of Psittacines (parrots and parakeets), two species of mynas, a bulbul, an oriole, and a swamphen (see list below) now breed in the Ft. Lauderdale and Miami areas. Quite a few of these have spread elsewhere in the state and we have included these in our species accounts, but for the most part we omit the relatively recent exotic species that have been introduced by people, either deliberately or accidentally. As time passes we learn of more additions to the list of exotic avifauna now breeding in the state. Many tourist attractions feature live birds, which inevitably escape from time to time; these birds, too, may survive for a time in the wild. Hence, the sighting of a SCARLET IBIS *(Eudocimus ruber)*, or a KING VULTURE *(Sarcoramphus papa)*, or an EGYPTIAN GOOSE *(Alopochen aegyptiacus)* in central Florida should not be too startling or unexpected nowadays.

Bill Robertson and Glen Woolfenden observed in their 1992 annotated list of *Florida Bird Species*, "Unfortunately, few places on earth rival southern Florida in number and variety of free-flying, non-native birds." Generally, their impacts have been minor to undetectable, but in many urban areas they are likely more numerous than their native counterparts. At least 150 exotic bird species have been reported in Florida, including about 60 that have nested in the state. The number of established exotic species in Florida will certainly continue to rise as urban environments become more hospitable, especially for birds of tropical origin.

INTRODUCED EXOTIC BIRDS BREEDING IN FLORIDA

Mute Swan (*Cygnus olor*)
Black Swan (*Cygnus atratus*)
Muscovy Duck (*Cairina moschata*)
Common Peafowl (*Pavo cristatus*)
Purple Swamphen (*Porphyrio porphyrio*)
Rock Pigeon or Domestic Pigeon
    (*Columba livia*)
Eurasian Collared-Dove
    (*Streptopelia decaocto*)
Budgerigar (*Melopsittacus undulatus*)
Rose-ringed Parakeet (*Psittacula krameri*)
Blue-and-yellow Macaw (*Ara ararauna*)
Chestnut-fronted Macaw (*Ara severus*)
Blue-crowned Parakeet
    (*Aratinga acuticaudata*)
Green Parakeet (*Aratinga holochlora*)
Mitred Parakeet (*Aratinga mitrata*)
Red-masked Parakeet (*Aratinga erythrogenys*)
White-eyed Parakeet
    (*Aratinga leucophthalmus*)

Dusky-headed Parakeet (*Aratinga weddellii*)
Black-hooded Parakeet *(Nandayus nenday)*
Monk Parakeet (*Myiopsitta monachus*)
White-winged Parakeet
    (*Brotogeris versicolurus*)
Yellow-chevroned Parakeet
    (*Brotogeris chiriri*)
White-fronted Parrot (*Amazona albifrons*)
Red-crowned Parrot (*Amazona viridigenalis*)
Blue-fronted Parrot (*Amazona aestiva*)
Yellow-naped Parrot (*Amazona auropalliata*)
Orange-winged Parrot (*Amazona amazonica*)
Red-whiskered Bulbul (*Pycnonotus jocosus*)
Hill Myna *(Gracula religiosa)*
Common Myna *(Acridotheres tristis)*
European Starling (*Sturnus vulgaris*)
House Sparrow (*Passer domesticus*)
House Finch (*Carpodacus mexicanus*)
Spot-breasted Oriole *(Icterus pectoralis)*

RESOURCES

BOOKS

Attracting and Feeding Birds

Attracting Birds and Other Wildlife to Your Yard by William J. Weber, DVM. Dover Publications, New York, NY. 1982.

The Audubon Society Guide to Attracting Birds by Stephen Kress. Charles Scribner's Sons, New York, NY. 1985.

Banquets for Birds by Patrice Benneward and Constance Stallings. National Audubon Society, New York, NY. 1983.

A Complete Guide to Bird Feeding, Revised Ed. by John V. Dennis. Alfred A. Knopf, New York, NY. 1994.

Feeding the Birds by Jan Mahnken. Wings Books, New York, NY. 1983.

Homes for Birds, Revised Ed. U.S. Dept. of Interior. (Available from U.S. Govt. Printing Office, Washington, DC. 1992.)

How to Attract Birds, Revised Ed. by Michael McKinly. Ortho Books, San Francisco, CA. 1995.

The New Handbook of Attracting Birds by Thomas P. McElroy, Jr. W.W. Norton Co., New York, NY. 1984.

Planting a Refuge for Wildlife: How to create a backyard habitat by Susan Cerulean, Celeste Botha, and Donna Legare. Florida Fish and Wildlife Conservation Commission. 1987. (Available from www.floridaconservation.org.)

The Wildlife Gardener by John V Dennis. Alfred A. Knopf, New York, NY. 1985.

Biology of Birds

The Audubon Society Encyclopedia of North American Birds by John K. Terres. Wings Books: Distributed by Outlet Book Co., New York, NY. 1991.

Bird Migration by Chris Mead. Facts on File Publs., New York, NY. 1987.

Birds: Their Life, Their Ways, Their World by Christopher Perrins and C.J.O. Harrison. Reader's Digest Assoc., Inc. Pleasantville, NY. 1979.

The Dictionary of American Bird Names (Rev. Ed.) by Ernest A. Choate, revised by R. A. Paynter, Jr. The Harvard Common Press, Boston, MA. 1985.

A Dictionary of Birds edited by Bruce Campbell and Elizabeth Lack. Buteo Books, Vermillion, SD. 1985.

Fundamentals of Ornithology, 2nd Ed., by Josselyn Van Tyne and Andrew J. Berger. John Wiley & Sons, New York, NY. 1976.

A Guide to Bird Behavior, Vol. I, by Donald W Stokes. Little, Brown & Co., Boston, MA. 1979.

A Guide to Bird Behavior, Vol. II, by Donald W Stokes and Lillian Q. Stokes. Little, Brown & Co., Boston, MA. 1983.

A Guide to Bird Behavior, Vol III, by Donald W Stokes and Lillian Q. Stokes. Little, Brown & Co., Boston, MA. 1989.

A Guide to Bird Biology: Secrets of Bird Life, Rev. Ed., by Ron Freethy. Blandford Press, Sterling Publ. Co., New York, NY. 1990.

An Introduction to Ornithology, 3rd Ed., by George J. Wallace and H. D. Mahan. MacMillan Co., New York, NY. 1975.

The Life of Birds, 4th Ed., by Joel Carl Welty and Luis F Baptista. W B. Saunders, New York, NY. 1988.

Ornithology. 2nd Ed. by Frank B. Gill. W. H. Freeman and Co., New York, NY. 1995.

Ornithology: An Ecological Approach, by John Faaborg. Prentice Hall, Englewood Cliffs, NJ. 1988.

Ornithology in Laboratory and Field, 5th Ed., by Olin Sewall Pettingill, Jr. Academic Press, Orlando, FL. 1985.

Treasury of North American Birdlore edited by Paul S. Eriksson and Alan Pistorius. Paul S. Eriksson Publ., Middlebury, VT. 1987.

The Wonder of Birds edited by Robert M. Poole. National Geographic Society, Washington, DC. 1983.

Words for Birds: A Lexicon of North American Birds with Biographical Notes by Edward S. Gruson. Quadrangle Books, New York, NY. 1972.

Bird Identification

We highly recommend readers to obtain a copy of one or more of the following excellent and complete field guides to the birds of eastern North America, usually available through most bookstores or Internet vendors (listed in alphabetical order):

Birds of North America: A Guide to Field Identification, Revised Edition by Chandler S. Robbins, Bertel Bruun, and Herbert S. Zim. Golden Press, New York, NY. 2001.

A Field Guide to the Birds of Eastern and Central North America 5th Ed. by Roger Tory Peterson. Houghton Mifflin Co., Boston, MA. 2002.

National Geographic Field Guide to the Birds of North America, 4th Ed. edited by Mel Baughman. National Geographic Society, Washington, DC. 2002.

The Sibley Guide to Birds by David A. Sibley. Knopf, New York, NY. 2000 (now also available as separate guides for eastern and western North America).

There are a number of guides dealing with specific groups of birds. These are most helpful in identification of similar-appearing species that are difficult to separate in the field in some plumages. Among these references are:

Common Coastal Birds of Florida and the Caribbean by David W. Nellis, Pineapple Press, Sarasota, FL. 2001.

A Field Guide to Hawks of North America, 2nd Ed. by William S. Clark and Brian K. Wheeler. Houghton Mifflin Co., Boston, MA. 2001.

A Field Guide to Warblers of North America, by Jon L. Dunn and Kimball L. Garrett. Houghton Mifflin Co., Boston, MA. 1997.

Gulls: A Guide to Identification, 2nd Ed., by Peter J. Grant. Academic Press, Harcourt Brace, Boston, MA. 1994.

Hawks in Flight: The Flight Identification of North American Migrant Raptors by Pete Dunne, David Sibley, and Clay Sutton. Houghton Mifflin Co., Boston, MA. 1989.

Shorebirds: An Identification Guide to the Waders of the World by Peter Hayman, John Marchant, and Tony Prater. Houghton Mifflin Co., Boston, MA. 1991.

Seabirds: An Identification Guide by Peter Harrison. Houghton Mifflin Co., Boston, MA. 1991

Sick, Injured, and Orphaned Birds

"The Care of Orphaned Birds" by Herbert W. Kale, II. *Florida Naturalist* 52(2): 6–12 (1979).

Care of Uncommon Pets by William J. Weber, DVM. Holt, Rinehart and Winston, New York, NY. 1979.

The Complete Care of Orphaned or Abandoned Baby Animals by C.E. Spaulding, DVM, and Jackie Spaulding. Rodale Press, Emmaus, PA. 1979.

"Saving Oiled Seabirds." International Bird Rescue Research Center. American Petroleum Institute, Washington, DC. 1978.

"What do I do with this baby bird?" A free brochure available from Suncoast Seabird Sanctuary, Inc., 18328 Gulf Blvd., Indian Shores, FL 33785. www.seabirdsanctuary.org

Wild Orphan Babies: Mammals and Birds: Caring for Them, Setting Them Free by William J. Weber, DVM. 2nd Ed. Holt, Rinehart and Winston, New York, NY. 1978.

Wild Orphan Friends by William J. Weber, DVM. Holt, Rinehart and Winston, New York, NY. 1976.

Birding

A.B.A. Checklist: Birds of Continental United States and Canada American Birding Association, P.O. Box 6599, Colorado Springs, CO 80934 (www.americanbirding.org).

A Birder's Guide to Florida, by Bill Pranty. American Birding Association, Colorado Springs, CO. 1996.

The Birder's Handbook: A Field Guide to the Natural History of North American Birds by Paul R. Ehrlich, David S. Dobkin, and Darryl Wheye. Simon & Schuster, Inc., New York, NY. 1988.

Birds of South Florida: An Interpretive Guide by Connie Toops and Willard E. Dilley. River Road Press, Conway, AR. 1986.

Checklist of Florida's Birds by Henry M. Stevenson, Updated 2002. Florida Fish and Wildlife Conservation Commission. (Available free from the FWC's Wings Over Florida Program. See www.wld.fwc.state.fl.us/wof for further information)

Checklist of North American Birds, 7th Ed. American Ornithologists' Union. Washington, DC. 1998.

Common Coastal Birds of Florida and the Caribbean by David W. Nellis. Pineapple Press, Inc., Sarasota, FL. 2001.

The Complete Birder: A Guide to Better Birding by Jack Conner. Houghton Mifflin Co., Boston, MA. 1988.

Everything you need to know about Birding and Bird Attraction by Alan Pistorius. Houghton, Boston, MA. 1998.

First Guide to Birds by Roger Tory Peterson. Houghton Mifflin Co., Boston, MA. 1986.

Florida Bird Life by Alexander Sprunt, Jr. Coward-McCann, Inc. New York, NY. 1954 (Out of print, but occasionally available from some dealers.)

A Guide to the Nests, Eggs, and Nestlings of North American Birds, 2nd Ed. by Paul J. Baicich and Colin Harrison. AP Natural World, San Diego, CA. 1997.

The Habitat Guide to Birding by Thomas P. McElroy, Jr. N. Lyons Books, New York, NY. 1987.

How to Know the Birds, 2nd Ed. by Roger Tory Peterson. Gramercy Pub. Co., New York, NY. 1986.

The Illustrated Bird Watcher's Dictionary by Donald S. Heintzelman. Winchester Press, Tulsa, OK. 1980.

An Introduction to Bird Life, for Bird Watchers by Aretas A. Saunders. Dover Publs., Inc., New York, NY. 1964.

SCANS Key to Birdwatching by Virginia C. Holmgren. Timber Press, Portland, OR. 1983.

Vertebrates of Florida: Identification and Distribution by Henry M. Stevenson. University Presses of Florida, Gainesville, FL. 1976.

Watching Birds: An Introduction to Ornithology by Roger F Pasquier. Houghton Mifflin Co., Boston, MA. 1977.

PERIODICALS ON BIRDING

Bird Watcher's Digest. Box 110, Marietta, OH 45750.
http://www.birdwatchersdigest.com. Subscriptions: bwd@birdwatchersdigest.com
or (800) 879–2473.

Birder's World. Kalmbach Publishing, P.O. Box 1612, Waukesha, WI 53187–1612.
http://www.birdersworld.com Subscriptions: (800) 533–6644.

Birding. American Birding Association, P.O. Box 6599, Colorado Springs, CO 80934.
http://www.americanbirding.org Subscriptions: member@aba.org.

Living Bird. Cornell Laboratory of Ornithology, Membership Department, P.O. Box 311,
Ithaca, NY 14851.

Nature Society News. P.O. Box 390, Griggsville, IL 62340. http://www.naturesociety.org
This is devoted to the Purple Martin.

North American Birds. American Birding Association. PO Box 6599, Colorado Springs,
CO 80934. http://www.americanbirding.org or (800) 850–2473.

WildBird. 3 Burroughs, Irvine, CA 92618.
http://www.animalnetwork.com/wildbird/print/wbdefault.asp

OTHER RESOURCES ON BIRD FINDING

An excellent guide to birding sites in Florida that we recommend to every serious birder
is *A Birder's Guide to Florida,* 4th Ed. by Bill Pranty (original text by James A. Lane and
Harold R. Holt). Copies are available from bookstores and Internet vendors as well as
from the American Birding Association website, http://www.americanbirding.org.

The Florida Fish and Wildlife Conservation Foundation offers a wealth of informa-
tion on Florida birds and birding links through its website, www.floridaconservation.org.
The FWC sponsors several birdwatching programs. One of them is Wings Over Florida
(WOF), a free awards program open to amateur or experienced, resident or non-resident
Florida birdwatchers. Participants identify birds and send in their findings to the FWC.
Full-color certificates are awarded at five levels of achievement, starting at 50 species
(Beginner) through 350 species (Elite Florida Birder). Anyone can order a free application
packet, which includes an application sheet, the guide "Bird Watching Basics" on field
equipment and bird identification tips, and an up-to-date Florida bird checklist.

There is also a Wings Over Florida Junior Birder Program. The program was developed to help teachers introduce third- and fourth-grade students to birdwatching. It
offers teachers a guide with resources, directions, and a "Bird Detective" activity guide
which introduces nearly 50 species of common birds found in Florida. The activities cover
important science and language arts benchmarks for Sunshine State Standards and FCAT
writing prompts. When students have identified and listed 15 birds, they receive the
Hummingbird certificate.

To request a WOF application packet, download Junior Birder teacher and student resources, and obtain additional information on Wings Over Florida and the Junior Birder Program, visit http://www.wld.fwc.state.fl.us/wof/. Questions can be e-mailed to wof@fwc.state.fl.us

Traditionally, only local birders knew about the great birding sites in their area. Most publicity went to the federal and state sites, such as the J.N. "Ding" Darling National Wildlife Refuge and Everglades National Park. The FWC, through an ambitious program called Great Florida Birding Trail, aims to combine more prominent birding sites with smaller local sites in groups that will spread out casual birdwatchers and their ecotourism dollars into the surrounding communities.

Supported in part by the Florida Department of Transportation and the Wildlife Foundation of Florida, the Great Florida Birding Trail is a 2000-mile highway trail that unifies existing and new birding sites throughout Florida. Modeled after the successful Great Texas Coastal Birding Trail, it combines special highway signs identifying Birding Trail sites with a detailed map showcasing birding opportunities in Florida. The Trail is a work in progress, and will consist of a series of clusters, each containing five to ten sites, highlighting communities and special ecosystems such as the Lake Wales Ridge.

To download a map of the trail or request one by mail, visit www.floridabirdingtrail.com. To receive updates on the progress of the Great Florida Birding Trail and participate in the site nomination process, send your name, address, phone number and e-mail address to Birding Trail Coordinator, FWC, 620 S. Meridian St., Tallahassee, FL 32399-1600.

Organizations and Agencies

Conservation Organizations in Florida

In addition to the following statewide organizations (many with both local and national affiliates), several regional and local organizations also exist. To learn of one in your community, check your phone directory, local chamber of commerce, or the Internet.

1000 Friends of Florida. A watchdog organization, founded to see that the growth planning process fulfills the long-term needs of Florida. 926 East Park Avenue, P.O. Box 5948, Tallahassee, FL 32314-5948, http://www.1000friendsofflorida.org

Florida Conservation Foundation. This organization operates the Environmental Information Center, publishes ENFO News on various environmental issues, and organizes conferences and workshops. 1251B Miller Avenue, Winter Park, FL 32789. No website available at time of publication.

Florida Defenders of the Environment. This organization specializes in scientific and economic studies of environmental issues dealing with river and lake protection, water quality, and public lands. 4424 NW 13th Street, Suite C-8, Gainesville, FL 32609-1885, http://www.fladefenders.org

Florida Native Plant Society. Members of this group are interested in the preservation and enjoyment of native plants and in their utilization in landscape plantings. P.O. Box 278, Vero Beach, FL 32902-0278, http://www.fnps.org

Florida Wildlife Federation. An affiliate of the National Wildlife Federation, this organization includes hunters, anglers, and other outdoor recreationalists, all with an interest in conservation and wise use of wildlife and the environment. P.O. Box 6870, Tallahassee, FL 32314, http://www.fwfonline.org

National Audubon Society/Audubon of Florida. Formerly an independent corporation founded in 1900, the Florida Audubon Society united its efforts with the National Audubon Society in 1999 to become Audubon of Florida. Audubon of Florida boasts 40,000 members in 45 community-based chapters throughout the state. The mission of National Audubon and Audubon of Florida is to conserve and restore natural ecosystems by focusing on birds and other wildlife for the benefit of humanity and the Earth's biological diversity. 444 Brickell Avenue, Suite 850, Miami, FL 33131, http://www.audubonofflorida.org

The Nature Conservancy. The primary cause of this organization is the preservation of high-quality natural plant and animal habitat throughout the state through purchase or gift. Most of the acquired lands are turned over to a state or federal land agency for protection and management, while some are retained as Conservancy sanctuaries. Florida Chapter: 222 S. Westmonte Drive Suite 300, Altamonte Springs, FL 32714. http://www.nature.org

The Sierra Club. This organization focuses on a wide range of environmental concerns including air and water quality, wildlife, and scenic habitat protection. It maintains two offices in Florida. Florida Regional Field Office: 475 Central Ave Suite M1, St. Petersburg, FL 33701; South Florida Regional Office, 2700 SW 3rd Ave, Suite 2F, Miami, FL 33129; http://www.sierraclub.org

Many of Florida's birds spend a large part of their lives in the neotropical regions of Central and South America. Thus, we cannot ignore the impacts of the habitat degradation now taking place in these countries. Again, the individual can enlarge his or her ability to solve environmental problems through membership in organizations working in the region, or in a particular country. **BirdLife International**, formerly the International Council for Bird Preservation, fosters numerous programs in bird conservation throughout the world out of its Cambridge, U.K., headquarters and its regional offices in the Americas, Asia, the European Union, and the Middle East. Individuals can assist in this effort through membership in the **World Bird Club**. Write to: World Bird Club Subscriptions, BirdLife International, Wellbrook Court, Girton Road, Cambridge CB3 0NA, UK, or contact the BirdLife Partner Designate for the US, the National Audubon Society, at 700 Broadway, New York, NY 10003-9562. For more information about BirdLife International, visit http://www.birdlife.net.

STATE GOVERNMENT AGENCIES

Several state and federal agencies deal with land and water resources that have a direct or indirect impact on birds. The most important of these are listed here:

Florida Department of Environmental Protection. Water quality of lakes and rivers, ground water, sewage, municipal and hazardous wastes, dredge and fill, mining, etc. 3900 Commonwealth Boulevard, Tallahassee, FL 32399. http://www.dep.state.fl.us

Florida Fish and Wildlife Conservation Commission. This organization came into existence in 1999. It integrates the former Game and Fresh Water Fish Commission, the former Marine Fisheries Commission, and elements of the Divisions of Marine Resources and Law Enforcement of the Florida Department of Environmental Protection. The commissioners exercise the regulatory and executive powers of the state with respect to wild animal life, freshwater aquatic life and marine life. The FWC's website is www.floridaconservation.org. It maintains five regional offices as follow:

Northwest Region, 3911 Hwy. 232, Panama City, FL 32409-1658, 850-265-3676, 24-Hour Law Enforcement: 850-233-5150

North Central Region (formerly Northeast Region), Route 7, Box 440, Lake City, FL, 32055-8713, 386-758-0525, 24-Hour Law Enforcement: 386-758-0529

Northeast Region (formerly Central Region), 1239 S.W. 10th Street, Ocala, FL 34474-2797, 352-732-1225, 24-Hour Law Enforcement: 352-732-1228

Southwest Region (formerly South Region), 3900 Drane Field Road, Lakeland, FL 33811-1299, 863-648-3203, 24-Hour Law Enforcement: 863-648-3200

South Region (formerly Everglades Region), 8535 Northlake Boulevard, West Palm Beach, FL 33412, 561-625-5122, 24-Hour Law Enforcement: 561-625-5122

Water Management Districts

These are large and influential organizations that directly impact birdlife because of the vast acreages that they manage. Increasingly, the water management districts are involved in the management of wetland and upland habitats for the benefit of wildlife.

Northwest Florida Water Management District, 81 Water Management Drive, Havana, FL 32333, phone 850-539-5999. http://www.nwfwmd.state.fl.us

Suwannee River Water Management District, 9225 CR 49, Live Oak, FL 32060, phone 904-362-1001. http://www.srwmd.state.fl.us

St. Johns River Water Management District, P.O. Box 1429, Palatka, FL 32178-1429, phone 904-329-4500. http://sjr.state.fl.us

Southwest Florida Water Management District, 2379 Broad Street, Brooksville, FL 34609-6899, phone 352-796-7211. http://www.swfwmd.state.fl.us

South Florida Water Management District, 301 Gun Club Road, West Palm Beach, FL 33416-4680, phone 561-686-8800. http://www.sfwmd.gov/site/index.php?

FEDERAL AGENCIES

U.S. Fish & Wildlife Service. **For general information, visit** www.fws.gov.

Pertinent offices in the Southeast:

Division of Migratory Birds and Endangered Species, Southeast Region, 1875 Century Blvd., Suite 240, Atlanta, GA 30345-3319, 404-679-7189

Jacksonville Ecological Services Field Office, Wildlife and Habitat Management Office, 6620 Southpoint Drive South, Suite 310, Jacksonville, FL 32216-0958, 904-232-2580

Panama City Ecological Services Field Office, 1601 Balboa Avenue, Panama City, FL 32405-3792 , 850-769-0552

South Florida Ecological Services Field Office, 1339 20th Street, Vero Beach, FL 32960-3559, 772-562-3909

Environmental Protection Agency, Region 4, Sam Nunn Atlanta Federal Center, 61 Forsyth Street, SW, Atlanta, GA 30303-3104, phone 800-241-1754, Fax 404-562-8174. http://www.epa.gov

US Army Corps of Engineers. For general information, visit www.usace.mil/
Jacksonville District, P.O. Box 4970, 400 West Bay Street, Jacksonville, FL 32232-0019. phone 904-232-2568. http://www.saj.usace.army.mil
Mobile District, P.O. Box 2288, Mobile, AL 36628-0001, phone 251-471-5966. http://sam.usace.army.mil

CHECKLIST

Florida's avifauna is constantly in a state of flux, its collection of species increasing and decreasing as a result of changing climate, expanding and shrinking habitats, and human activities. The Florida bird checklist includes 467 species, including those that nest in, winter in, and migrate through the state. This total should be viewed as a minimum. The list identifies those species that have been introduced (25), are rare (42), are pelagic (10), or that occur here in such low numbers and with such irregularity that they are considered accidental (81). It also includes two that are extinct in the state because one (Ivory-billed Woodpecker) may someday be reintroduced into Florida and because the other (Dusky Seaside Sparrow) may have been seen by living birders before its disappearance. Additionally, the list includes a handful of distinct subspecies and color morphs, which are not included in the species total and appear as indented entries. Bird species that breed in the state are indicated by bold text. Florida has approximately 183 nesting species. Of the 25 that have been introduced, at least 11 are parakeets or parrots. Clearly, Florida's bird diversity is high, but most species do not breed here and occur in the state only for the winter or briefly during migration. It is during these times that the variety of Florida birds is the highest.

a = accidental

e = extinct

i = introduced

p = pelagic

r = rare

bold = species breeding in Florida

- ❑ Red-throated Loon (r)
- ❑ Pacific Loon (a)
- ❑ Common Loon
- ❑ Least Grebe (a)
- ❑ **Pied-billed Grebe**
- ❑ Horned Grebe
- ❑ Red-necked Grebe (a)
- ❑ Eared Grebe (a)
- ❑ Yellow-nosed Albatross (p)
- ❑ Black-capped Petrel (p)
- ❑ Cory's Shearwater (p)
- ❑ Greater Shearwater (p)
- ❑ Sooty Shearwater (p)
- ❑ Manx Shearwater (p)
- ❑ Audubon's Shearwater (p)
- ❑ Wilson's Storm-Petrel (p)
- ❑ Leach's Storm-Petrel (p)
- ❑ Band-rumped Storm-Petrel (p)

- ❑ White-tailed Tropicbird
- ❑ Red-billed Tropicbird (r)
- ❑ **Masked Booby**
- ❑ Brown Booby
- ❑ Red-footed Booby (r)
- ❑ Northern Gannet
- ❑ American White Pelican
- ❑ **Brown Pelican**
- ❑ **Double-crested Cormorant**
- ❑ Great Cormorant (r)
- ❑ **Anhinga**
- ❑ **Magnificent Frigatebird**
- ❑ **American Bittern**
- ❑ **Least Bittern**
- ❑ **Great Blue Heron**
  - ❑ **Great White Heron**
  - ❑ **Würdemann's Heron**
- ❑ **Great Egret**

- ❑ **Snowy Egret**
- ❑ **Little Blue Heron**
- ❑ **Tricolored Heron**
- ❑ **Reddish Egret**
- ❑ **Cattle Egret**
- ❑ **Green Heron**
- ❑ **Black-crowned Night-Heron**
- ❑ **Yellow-crowned Night-Heron**
- ❑ **White Ibis**
- ❑ Scarlet Ibis (a)
- ❑ **Glossy Ibis**
- ❑ White-faced Ibis (a)
- ❑ **Roseate Spoonbill**
- ❑ **Wood Stork**
- ❑ **Black Vulture**
- ❑ **Turkey Vulture**
- ❑ Greater Flamingo

❒ **Fulvous Whistling-Duck**
❒ **Black-bellied Whistling-Duck**
❒ Greater White-fronted Goose (a)
❒ Snow Goose
❒ Canada Goose
❒ Brant
❒ Tundra Swan
❒ Mute Swan (i)
❒ **Muscovy Duck** (i)
❒ **Wood Duck**
❒ Gadwall
❒ Eurasian Wigeon (r)
❒ American Wigeon
❒ American Black Duck
❒ Mallard
❒ **Mottled Duck**
❒ **Blue-winged Teal**
❒ Cinnamon Teal (a)
❒ Northern Shoveler
❒ White-cheeked Pintail (a)
❒ Northern Pintail
❒ Green-winged Teal
❒ Canvasback
❒ Redhead
❒ Ring-necked Duck
❒ Greater Scaup
❒ Lesser Scaup
❒ King Eider (a)
❒ Common Eider (a)
❒ Harlequin Duck (a)
❒ Surf Scoter
❒ White-winged Scoter
❒ Black Scoter
❒ Long-tailed Duck
❒ Bufflehead
❒ Common Goldeneye
❒ **Hooded Merganser**
❒ Common Merganser
❒ Red-breasted Merganser
❒ Masked Duck (r)

❒ **Ruddy Duck**
❒ **Osprey**
❒ **Swallow-tailed Kite**
❒ **White-tailed Kite**
❒ **Snail Kite**
❒ **Mississippi Kite**
❒ **Bald Eagle**
❒ Northern Harrier
❒ Sharp-shinned Hawk
❒ **Cooper's Hawk**
❒ Northern Goshawk (a)
❒ **Red-shouldered Hawk**
❒ **Broad-winged Hawk**
❒ **Short-tailed Hawk**
❒ Swainson's Hawk (a)
❒ **Red-tailed Hawk**
❒ Ferruginous Hawk (a)
❒ Rough-legged Hawk (a)
❒ Golden Eagle (r)
❒ **Crested Caracara**
❒ **American Kestrel**
❒ Merlin
❒ Peregrine Falcon
❒ **Wild Turkey**
❒ **Northern Bobwhite**
❒ Yellow Rail (r)
❒ **Black Rail**
❒ **Clapper Rail**
❒ **King Rail**
❒ Virginia Rail
❒ Sora
❒ **Purple Gallinule**
❒ **Common Moorhen**
❒ **American Coot**
❒ **Limpkin**
❒ **Sandhill Crane**
❒ **Whooping Crane** (i)
❒ Black-bellied Plover
❒ American Golden-Plover
❒ **Snowy Plover**
❒ **Wilson's Plover**
❒ Semipalmated Plover

❒ Piping Plover
❒ **Killdeer**
❒ Mountain Plover (a)
❒ **American Oystercatcher**
❒ **Black-necked Stilt**
❒ American Avocet
❒ Greater Yellowlegs
❒ Lesser Yellowlegs
❒ Solitary Sandpiper
❒ **Willet**
❒ Spotted Sandpiper
❒ Upland Sandpiper (r)
❒ Whimbrel
❒ Long-billed Curlew
❒ Black-tailed Godwit
❒ Hudsonian Godwit
❒ Bar-tailed Godwit (a)
❒ Marbled Godwit
❒ Ruddy Turnstone
❒ Red Knot
❒ Sanderling
❒ Semipalmated Sandpiper
❒ Western Sandpiper
❒ Least Sandpiper
❒ White-rumped Sandpiper
❒ Baird's Sandpiper (r)
❒ Pectoral Sandpiper
❒ Sharp-tailed Sandpiper (a)
❒ Purple Sandpiper
❒ Dunlin
❒ Curlew Sandpiper (a)
❒ Stilt Sandpiper (r)
❒ Buff-breasted Sandpiper (r)
❒ Ruff (r)
❒ Short-billed Dowitcher
❒ Long-billed Dowitcher
❒ Wilson's Snipe
❒ **American Woodcock**
❒ Wilson's Phalarope
❒ Red-necked Phalarope (r)
❒ Red Phalarope (r)

❏ Great Skua (r)
❏ South Polar Skua
❏ Pomarine Jaeger (r)
❏ Parasitic Jaeger (r)
❏ Long-tailed Jaeger (r)
❏ **Laughing Gull**
❏ Franklin's Gull (a)
❏ Little Gull (a)
❏ Bonaparte's Gull
❏ Ring-billed Gull
❏ California Gull (a)
❏ Herring Gull
❏ Thayer's Gull (a)
❏ Iceland Gull (a)
❏ Lesser Black-backed Gull
❏ Glaucous Gull (a)
❏ Great Black-backed Gull
❏ Sabine's Gull (a)
❏ Black-legged Kittiwake (r)
❏ **Gull-billed Tern**
❏ **Caspian Tern**
❏ **Royal Tern**
❏ **Sandwich Tern**
❏ **Roseate Tern**
❏ Common Tern
❏ Arctic Tern (r)
❏ Forster's Tern
❏ **Least Tern**
❏ **Bridled Tern**
❏ **Sooty Tern**
❏ Black Tern
❏ **Brown Noddy**
❏ Black Noddy
❏ **Black Skimmer**
❏ Dovekie (a)
❏ Common Murre (a)
❏ Thick-billed Murre (a)
❏ Razorbill (a)
❏ Atlantic Puffin (a)
❏ **Rock Pigeon** (i)
❏ **White-Crowned Pigeon**
❏ **Ringed Turtle-Dove** (i)

❏ **Eurasian Collared-Dove** (i)
❏ **White-winged Dove** (i)
❏ **Mourning Dove**
❏ **Common Ground-Dove**
❏ Key West Quail-Dove (a)
❏ **Budgerigar** (i)
❏ **Rose-ringed Parakeet** (i)
❏ **Monk Parakeet** (i)
❏ **Black-hooded Parakeet** (i)
❏ **Blue-crowned Parakeet** (i)
❏ **Red-masked Parakeet** (i)
❏ **Mitred Parakeet** (i)
❏ **Chestnut-fronted Macaw** (i)
❏ **Red-crowned Parrot** (i)
❏ **White-winged Parakeet** (i)
❏ **Yellow-chevroned Parakeet** (i)
❏ **Yellow-billed Cuckoo**
❏ Black-billed Cuckoo
❏ **Mangrove Cuckoo**
❏ **Smooth-billed Ani**
❏ Groove-billed Ani
❏ **Barn Owl**
❏ Flammulated Owl (a)
❏ **Eastern Screech-Owl**
❏ **Great Horned Owl**
❏ **Burrowing Owl**
❏ **Barred Owl**
❏ Short-eared Owl (r)
❏ Northern Saw-whet Owl (a)
❏ Lesser Nighthawk (a)
❏ **Common Nighthawk**
❏ **Antillean Nighthawk**
❏ **Chuck-will's-widow**
❏ Whip-poor-will
❏ White-collared Swift (a)
❏ **Chimney Swift**
❏ Vaux's Swift (a)
❏ Antillean Palm Swift (a)

❏ Cuban Emerald (a)
❏ Bahama Woodstar (a)
❏ **Ruby-throated Hummingbird**
❏ Black-chinned Hummingbird (a)
❏ Buff-bellied Hummingbird (a)
❏ Rufous Hummingbird (a)
❏ Allen's Hummingbird (a)
❏ **Belted Kingfisher**
❏ **Red-headed Woodpecker**
❏ **Red-bellied Woodpecker**
❏ Yellow-bellied Sapsucker
❏ **Downy Woodpecker**
❏ **Hairy Woodpecker**
❏ **Red-cockaded Woodpecker**
❏ **Northern Flicker**
❏ **Pileated Woodpecker**
❏ Ivory-billed Woodpecker (e)
❏ Caribbean Elaenia (a)
❏ Olive-sided Flycatcher (r)
❏ **Eastern Wood-Pewee**
❏ Yellow-bellied Flycatcher
❏ **Acadian Flycatcher**
❏ Alder Flycatcher
❏ Willow Flycatcher
❏ Least Flycatcher
❏ Eastern Phoebe
❏ Black Phoebe (a)
❏ Say's Phoebe (a)
❏ Vermilion Flycatcher
❏ Ash-throated Flycatcher (a)
❏ **Great Crested Flycatcher**
❏ Brown-crested Flycatcher (a)
❏ La Sagra's Flycatcher (a)
❏ Couch's Kingbird (a)
❏ Cassin's Kingbird (a)

❒ Western Kingbird
❒ **Eastern Kingbird**
❒ **Gray Kingbird**
❒ Loggerhead Kingbird (a)
❒ Scissor-tailed Flycatcher
❒ Fork-tailed Flycatcher (a)
❒ **Loggerhead Shrike**
❒ **White-eyed Vireo**
❒ Thick-billed Vireo (a)
❒ Bell's Vireo (a)
❒ **Yellow-throated Vireo**
❒ Blue-headed Vireo
❒ Warbling Vireo (r)
❒ Philadelphia Vireo (r)
❒ **Red-eyed Vireo**
❒ Yellow-green Vireo (r)
❒ **Black-whiskered Vireo**
❒ **Blue Jay**
❒ **Florida Scrub-Jay**
❒ **American Crow**
❒ **Fish Crow**
❒ Horned Lark (r)
❒ **Purple Martin**
❒ Cuban Martin (a)
❒ Tree Swallow
❒ Violet-green Swallow (a)
❒ Bahama Swallow (a)
❒ **Northern Rough-winged Swallow**
❒ Bank Swallow
❒ **Cliff Swallow**
❒ **Cave Swallow**
❒ **Barn Swallow**
❒ **Carolina Chickadee**
❒ **Tufted Titmouse**
❒ Red-breasted Nuthatch
❒ **White-breasted Nuthatch**
❒ **Brown-headed Nuthatch**
❒ Brown Creeper
❒ Rock Wren (a)
❒ **Carolina Wren**

❒ Bewick's Wren
❒ House Wren
❒ Winter Wren
❒ Sedge Wren
❒ **Marsh Wren**
❒ **Red-whiskered Bulbul** (i)
❒ Golden-crowned Kinglet
❒ Ruby-crowned Kinglet
❒ **Blue-gray Gnatcatcher**
❒ Northern Wheatear (a)
❒ **Eastern Bluebird**
❒ Veery
❒ Gray-cheeked Thrush
❒ Bicknell's Thrush
❒ Swainson's Thrush
❒ Hermit Thrush
❒ **Wood Thrush**
❒ **American Robin**
❒ Varied Thrush (a)
❒ **Gray Catbird**
❒ **Northern Mockingbird**
❒ Bahama Mockingbird (a)
❒ Sage Thrasher (a)
❒ **Brown Thrasher**
❒ **European Starling** (i)
❒ **Common Myna** (i)
❒ **Hill Myna** (i)
❒ American Pipit
❒ Sprague's Pipit (r)
❒ Cedar Waxwing
❒ Bachman's Warbler (r)
❒ Blue-winged Warbler (r)
❒ Brewster's Warbler (r)
❒ Lawrence's Warbler (r)
❒ Golden-winged Warbler (r)
❒ Tennessee Warbler
❒ Orange-crowned Warbler
❒ Nashville Warbler (r)
❒ **Northern Parula**
❒ **Yellow Warbler**
❒ Chestnut-sided Warbler

❒ Magnolia Warbler
❒ Cape May Warbler
❒ Black-throated Blue Warbler
❒ Yellow-rumped Warbler
❒ Black-throated Gray Warbler (a)
❒ Golden-cheeked Warbler (a)
❒ Black-throated Green Warbler
❒ Townsend's Warbler (a)
❒ Blackburnian Warbler
❒ **Yellow-throated Warbler**
❒ Sutton's Warbler
❒ **Pine Warbler**
❒ Kirtland's Warbler (a)
❒ **Prairie Warbler**
❒ Palm Warbler
❒ Bay-breasted Warbler
❒ Blackpoll Warbler
❒ Cerulean Warbler (r)
❒ Black-and-white Warbler
❒ **American Redstart**
❒ **Prothonotary Warbler**
❒ **Worm-eating Warbler**
❒ **Swainson's Warbler**
❒ Ovenbird
❒ Northern Waterthrush
❒ Louisiana Waterthrush
❒ **Kentucky Warbler** (r)
❒ Connecticut Warbler (r)
❒ Mourning Warbler (r)
❒ MacGillivray's Warbler (a)
❒ **Common Yellowthroat**
❒ Bahama Yellowthroat (a)
❒ **Hooded Warbler**
❒ Wilson's Warbler
❒ Canada Warbler
❒ **Yellow-breasted Chat**
❒ Bananaquit
❒ **Summer Tanager**

- ❐ Scarlet Tanager
- ❐ Western Tanager (a)
- ❐ Western Spindalis (a)
- ❐ Black-faced Grassquit (a)
- ❐ **Eastern Towhee**
- ❐ **Bachman's Sparrow**
- ❐ **Chipping Sparrow**
- ❐ Clay-colored Sparrow (r)
- ❐ **Field Sparrow**
- ❐ Vesper Sparrow
- ❐ Lark Sparrow (r)
- ❐ Black-throated Sparrow (a)
- ❐ Lark Bunting (a)
- ❐ Savannah Sparrow
- ❐ **Grasshopper Sparrow**
  - ❐ **FloridaGrasshopper Sparrow**
- ❐ Henslow's Sparrow
- ❐ Le Conte's Sparrow
- ❐ Saltmarsh Sharp-tailed
- ❐ Sparrow
- ❐ Nelson's Sharp-tailed Sparrow
- ❐ **Seaside Sparrow**
  - ❐ **Cape Sable Seaside Sparrow** (r)
  - ❐ Dusky Seaside Sparrow (e)
- ❐ Fox Sparrow
- ❐ Song Sparrow
- ❐ Lincoln's Sparrow
- ❐ Swamp Sparrow
- ❐ White-throated Sparrow
- ❐ Harris' Sparrow (r)
- ❐ White-crowned Sparrow
- ❐ Dark-eyed Junco
- ❐ Lapland Longspur
- ❐ Chestnut-collared Longspur (a)
- ❐ Snow Bunting
- ❐ **Northern Cardinal**

- ❐ Rose-breasted Grosbeak
- ❐ Black-headed Grosbeak (a)
- ❐ **Blue Grosbeak**
- ❐ Lazuli Bunting (a)
- ❐ **Indigo Bunting**
- ❐ **Painted Bunting**
- ❐ Dickcissel
- ❐ Bobolink
- ❐ **Red-winged Blackbird**
- ❐ Tawny-shouldered Blackbird (a)
- ❐ **Eastern Meadowlark**
- ❐ Western Meadowlark (a)
- ❐ Yellow-headed Blackbird
- ❐ Rusty Blackbird
- ❐ Brewer's Blackbird
- ❐ **Boat-tailed Grackle**
- ❐ **Common Grackle**
- ❐ **Shiny Cowbird**
- ❐ Bronzed Cowbird
- ❐ **Brown-headed Cowbird**
- ❐ **Orchard Oriole**
- ❐ **Spot-breasted Oriole** (i)
- ❐ Baltimore Oriole
- ❐ Purple Finch
- ❐ **House Finch** (i)
- ❐ Pine Siskin
- ❐ American Goldfinch
- ❐ Evening Grosbeak
- ❐ **House Sparrow** (i)

INDEX OF SCIENTIFIC NAMES

INDEX OF SUBJECTS

(Includes birds when they appear on any page other than the species accounts or plates.)

ILLUSTRATED INDEX OF COMMON NAMES

The green page number to the left refers to the Species Account. The brown page number to the right refers to the Plate on which the bird appears.

Anhinga		Ani		Ani		Avocet		Bananaquit	
		Groove-billed		Smooth-billed		American			
38	217	126	246	125	246	90	233	188	253

Bittern		Bittern		Blackbird		Blackbird		Blackbird	
American		Least		Brewer's		Red-winged		Rusty	
39	218	39	218	206	273	204	272	206	273

Blackbird		Bluebird		Bobolink		Bobwhite		Booby	
Yellow-headed		Eastern				Northern		Brown	
205	273	162	258	204	264	78	231	35	216

Booby		Brant		Budgerigar		Bufflehead		Bulbul	
Masked								Red-whiskered	
34	216	53		119	244	64	226	160	254

345

Bunting	Bunting	Bunting	Canvasback	Caracara
Indigo	Painted	Snow		Crested
202 270	203 271	200	60 224	75 228

Cardinal	Catbird	Chat	Chickadee	Chuck-will's-widow
Northern	Gray	Yellow-breasted	Carolina	
201 270	166 257	188 265	155 256	130 248

Coot	Cormorant	Cowbird	Cowbird	Cowbird
American	Double-crested	Bronzed	Brown-headed	Shiny
83 233	37 217	208 273	209 272	208 273

Crane	Crane	Creeper	Crow	Crow
Sandhill	Whooping	Brown	American	Fish
84 231	84 231	157 256	150 254	151 254

Cuckoo	Cuckoo	Cuckoo	Curlew	Dickcissel
Black-billed	Mangrove	Yellow-billed	Long-billed	
124 246	125 246	124 246	94 235	203 271

Dove Common Ground-	**Dove** Eurasian Collared-	**Dove** Ringed Turtle-	**Dove** Mourning	**Dove** White-winged
118 / 243	116 / 243	115 / 243	117 / 243	116 / 243

Dowitcher Short-billed	**Duck** American Black	**Duck** Black-bellied Whistling-	**Duck** Fulvous Whistling-	**Duck** Long-tailed
100 / 236	56 / 223	51 / 222	51 / 222	64 / 226

Duck Mottled	**Duck** Muscovy	**Duck** Ring-necked	**Duck** Ruddy	**Duck** Wood
57 / 223	54 / 222	61 / 225	66 / 225	54 / 223

Dunlin	**Eagle** Bald	**Eagle** Golden	**Egret** Cattle	**Egret** Great
99 / 237	70 / 227	74 / 227	44 / 219	41 / 219

Egret Reddish	**Egret** Snowy	**Falcon** Peregrine	**Finch** House	**Finch** Purple
43 / 220	41 / 219	77 / 228	211 / 271	211 / 271

Flamingo	**Flicker**	**Flycatcher**	**Flycatcher**	**Flycatcher**
Greater	Northern	Acadian	Alder	Great Crested
50 · 221	137 · 250	141 · 251	141	143 · 251

Flycatcher	**Flycatcher**	**Flycatcher**	**Flycatcher**	**Flycatcher**
Least	Scissor-tailed	Vermilion	Willow	Yellow-bellied
142 · 251	145 · 251	143 · 251	141	140

Frigatebird	**Gadwall**	**Gallinule**	**Gannet**	**Gnatcatcher**
Magnificent		Purple	Northern	Blue-gray
38 · 216	55 · 224	82 · 233	35 · 216	162 · 252

Godwit	**Goldeneye**	**Goldfinch**	**Goose**	**Goose**
Marbled	Common	American	Canada	Snow
94 · 235	65 · 226	212 · 271	52 · 222	52 · 222

Grackle	**Grackle**	**Grebe**	**Grebe**	**Grosbeak**
Boat-tailed	Common	Horned	Pied-billed	Blue
207 · 272	207 · 272	30 · 214	30 · 214	202 · 270

Grosbeak Evening	**Grosbeak** Rose-breasted	**Gull** Bonaparte's	**Gull** Great Black-backed	**Gull** Herring
213 270	201 270	105 240	107 240	106 240

Gull Laughing	**Gull** Lesser Black-backed	**Gull** Ring-billed	**Harrier** Northern	**Hawk** Broad-winged
104 240	106 240	105 240	71 227	73 230

Hawk Cooper's	**Hawk** Red-shouldered	**Hawk** Red-tailed	**Hawk** Sharp-shinned	**Hawk** Short-tailed
72 229	72 230	74 230	71 229	73 230

Heron Black-crowned Night-	**Heron** Great Blue	**Heron** Green	**Heron** Little Blue	**Heron** Tricolored
45 218	40 219	44 220	42 220	42 220

Heron Yellow-crowned Night-	**Hummingbird** Ruby-throated	**Hummingbird** Rufous	**Ibis** Glossy	**Ibis** White
46 218	132 248	132	47 221	46 221

Jaeger	Jaeger	Jaeger	Jay	Jay
Long-tailed	Parasitic	Pomarine	Blue	Florida Scrub-
104 239	103 239	103 239	149 254	149 254

Junco	Kestrel	Killdeer	Kingbird	Kingbird
Dark-eyed	American		Eastern	Gray
200 268	75 228	88 234	144 251	145 251

Kingbird	Kingfisher	Kinglet	Kinglet	Kite
Western	Belted	Golden-crowned	Ruby-crowned	Mississippi
144 251	133 248	161 252	161 252	69 229

Kite	Kite	Kite	Knot	Limpkin
Snail	Swallow-tailed	White-tailed	Red	
69 229	68 229	68	95 237	83 231

Longspur	Loon	Loon	Macaw	Mallard
Lapland	Common	Red-throated	Chestnut-fronted	
200	29 214	29	122 245	57 223

Martin	Meadowlark	Merganser	Merganser	Merlin
Purple	Eastern	Hooded	Red-breasted	
151	255	205	272	65	225	66	225	76	228

Mockingbird	Moorhen	Myna	Nighthawk	Nighthawk
Northern	Common	Common	Antillean	Common
166	257	82	233	168		130	248	129	248

Noddy	Noddy	Nuthatch	Nuthatch	Nuthatch
Black	Brown	Brown-headed	Red-breasted	White-breasted
113	242	113	242	157	256	156	256	156	256

Oriole	Oriole	Oriole	Osprey	Ovenbird
Baltimore	Orchard	Spot-breasted		
210	266	209	266	210	266	67	228	183	265

Owl	Owl	Owl	Owl	Owl
Barn	Barred	Burrowing	Eastern Screech-	Great Horned
126	247	128	247	128	247	127	247	127	247

Oystercatcher	Parakeet	Parakeet	Parakeet	Parakeet
American	Black-hooded	Blue-crowned	Mitred	Monk
89 · 233	120 · 245	121 · 245	122 · 245	120 · 244

Parakeet	Parakeet	Parakeet	Parrot	Parula
Red-masked	Rose-ringed	White-winged	Red-crowned	Northern
121 · 245	119 · 244	123 · 244	123 · 244	172 · 261

Pelican	Pelican	Petrel	Petrel	Pewee
American White	Brown	Black-capped	Wilson's Storm-	Eastern Wood-
36 · 214	36 · 214	31	33 · 215	140 · 251

Phalarope	Phoebe	Pigeon	Pigeon	Pintail
Wilson's	Eastern	Rock	White-crowned	Northern
102	142 · 251	114 · 243	115 · 243	59 · 223

Pipit	Plover	Plover	Plover	Plover
American	American Golden-	Black-bellied	Piping	Semipalmated
169 · 252	86 · 234	85 · 234	88 · 234	87 · 234

Plover	Plover	Rail	Rail	Rail
Snowy	Wilson's	Black	Clapper	King
86	234	87	234	79	232	80	232	80	232

Rail	Rail	Redhead	Redstart	Robin
Virginia	Yellow		American	American
81	232	79		61	224	181	264	165	258

Sanderling	Sandpiper	Sandpiper	Sandpiper	Sandpiper
	Least	Pectoral	Purple	Semipalmated
96	238	97	238	98	237	99	237	96	238

Sandpiper	Sandpiper	Sandpiper	Sandpiper	Sandpiper
Solitary	Spotted	Stilt	Upland	Western
91	236	92	236	100		93		97	238

Sandpiper	Sapsucker	Scaup	Scoter	Scoter
White-rumped	Yellow-bellied	Lesser	Black	Surf
98	238	135	249	62	225	63	226	62	226

Scoter	Shearwater	Shearwater	Shearwater	Shoveler
White-winged	Audubon's	Cory's	Greater	Northern
63 | 226	32 | 215	31 | 215	32 | 215	59 | 224

Shrike	Siskin	Skimmer	Skua	Snipe
Loggerhead	Pine	Black	South Polar	Wilson's
146 | 252	212 | 271	114 | 242	102 | 239	101 | 236

Sora	Sparrow	Sparrow	Sparrow	Sparrow
	Bachman's	Chipping	Clay-colored	Field
81 | 232	191 | 268	192 | 268	192	193 | 269

Sparrow	Sparrow	Sparrow	Sparrow	Sparrow
Fox	Grasshopper	Henslow's	House	Lark
197	194 | 267	195 | 267	213 | 264	194

Sparrow	Sparrow	Sparrow	Sparrow	Sparrow
Le Conte's	Lincoln's	Saltmarsh Sharp-tailed	Savannah	Seaside
195	198	196 | 267	194 | 267	196 | 268

Sparrow	Sparrow	Sparrow	Sparrow	Sparrow
Song	Swamp	Vesper	White-crowned	White-throated
197 269	198 269	193 268	199 269	199 269

Spindalis	Spoonbill	Starling	Stilt	Stork
Western	Roseate	European	Black-necked	Wood
190	47 221	168 253	89 233	48 221

Swallow	Swallow	Swallow	Swallow	Swallow
Bank	Barn	Cave	Cliff	Northern Rough-winged
153 255	154 255	154 255	153 255	152 255

Swallow	Swan	Swift	Tanager	Tanager
Tree	Tundra	Chimney	Scarlet	Summer
152 255	53 222	131 248	189 266	189 266

Tanager	Teal	Teal	Tern	Tern
Western	Blue-winged	Green-winged	Black	Bridled
190	58 224	60 223	112 242	111 242

Tern	Tern	Tern	Tern	Tern
Caspian	Common	Forster's	Gull-billed	Least
108 241	110 241	110 241	107 241	111 241

Tern	Tern	Tern	Tern	Thrasher
Roseate	Royal	Sandwich	Sooty	Brown
109 241	108 241	109 241	112 242	167 257

Thrush	Thrush	Thrush	Thrush	Titmouse
Gray-cheeked	Hermit	Swainson's	Wood	Tufted
163 258	164 258	164 258	165 258	155 256

Towhee	Tropicbird	Turkey	Turnstone	Veery
Eastern	White-tailed	Wild	Ruddy	
191 267	33 216	77 231	95 237	163 258

Vireo	Vireo	Vireo	Vireo	Vireo
Black-whiskered	Blue-headed	Red-eyed	White-eyed	Yellow-throated
148 253	147 253	148 253	146 253	147 253

Vulture	**Vulture**	**Warbler**	**Warbler**	**Warbler**
Black	Turkey	Bay-breasted	Black-and-white	Blackburnian
49 227	49 227	179 263	180 260	176 262

Warbler	**Warbler**	**Warbler**	**Warbler**	**Warbler**
Blackpoll	Black-throated Blue	Black-throated Green	Blue-winged	Canada
179 263	175 262	176 262	170 259	187

Warbler	**Warbler**	**Warbler**	**Warbler**	**Warbler**
Cape May	Cerulean	Chestnut-sided	Connecticut	Golden-Winged
174 261	180 259	173 262	185	170 259

Warbler	**Warbler**	**Warbler**	**Warbler**	**Warbler**
Hooded	Kentucky	Magnolia	Mourning	Nashville
186 264	184 259	174 261	185	172 259

Warbler	**Warbler**	**Warbler**	**Warbler**	**Warbler**
Orange-crowned	Palm	Pine	Prairie	Prothonotary
171 260	178 263	177 263	178 263	181 260

Warbler	Warbler	Warbler	Warbler	Warbler
Swainson's	Tennessee	Wilson's	Worm-eating	Yellow
182 260	171 260	187 264	182 260	173 261

Warbler	Warbler	Waterthrush	Waterthrush	Waxwing
Yellow-rumped	Yellow-throated	Louisiana	Northern	Cedar
175 261	177 262	184 265	183 265	169 252

Whimbrel	Whip-poor-will	Wigeon	Willet	Woodcock
		American		American
93 235	131 248	55 225	92 236	101 236

Woodpecker	Woodpecker	Woodpecker	Woodpecker	Woodpecker
Downy	Hairy	Ivory-billed	Pileated	Red-bellied
136 249	136 249	139 250	138 250	134 250

Woodpecker	Woodpecker	Wren	Wren	Wren
Red-cockaded	Red-headed	Bewick's	Carolina	House
137 249	134 249	158 257	158 257	159 257

Wren	**Wren**	**Wren**	**Yellowlegs**	**Yellowlegs**
Marsh	Sedge	Winter	Greater	Lesser
160 · 257	159 · 257	159 · 257	90 · 235	91 · 235

Yellowthroat
Common
186 · 265

Here are some other books from Pineapple Press on related topics. For a complete catalog, visit our website at www.pineapplepress.com. Or write to Pineapple Press, P.O. Box 3889, Sarasota, Florida 34230-3889, or call (800) 746-3275.

Priceless Florida by Ellie Whitney, Bruce Means, and Anne Rudloe. An extensive guide (432 pages, 800 color photos) to the incomparable ecological riches of this unique region, presented in a way that will appeal to young and old, laypersons and scientists. Complete with maps, charts, species lists. (hb & pb)

Common Coastal Birds of Florida and the Caribbean by David W. Nellis. This comprehensive guide reveals 72 of the most common birds found along the coasts of Florida and the islands to the south. Includes information on each bird's nesting, feeding, mating, and migrating habits, as well as over 250 color photos that show many features of these birds that have never before been so fully illustrated. (hb & pb)

The Everglades: River of Grass, 60th Anniversary Edition by Marjory Stoneman Douglas. This is the treasured classic of nature writing that captured attention all over the world and launched the fight to save the Everglades. This Anniversary Edition includes an update by Michael Grunwald, author of *The Swamp.* (hb)

Exploring Wild South Florida, 4th Edition by Susan D. Jewell. This copious guide to South Florida's natural areas covers Broward, Hendry, Lee, and Palm Beach, Dade, Collier, and Monroe counties. This updated edition has more than 20 new locations for hikers, paddlers, bicyclists, wildlife watchers, and campers. (pb)

Florida's Living Beaches by Blair and Dawn Witherington. Comprehensive accounts of over 800 species, with photos for each, found on 700 miles of Florida's sandy beaches. Covers plants, animals, minerals, and manmade objects—all part of our living beaches. (pb)

The Trees of Florida 2nd Edition, The Shrubs and Woody Vines of Florida, and *The Ferns of Florida,* by Gil Nelson. Comprehensive guides to Florida's amazing variety of plant life. These books serve as both references and field guides. (hb & pb)

Best Backroads of Florida, Volumes 1–3, by Douglas Waitley. For vacationers and residents who want to catch a glimpse of the Florida of yesteryear, these books offer single-day backroads tours on Florida's little-traveled byways. Get out of the car to enjoy beautiful picnic areas, lake and river cruises, airboat rides, snorkeling and scuba diving, and biking and hiking through the beauty of Florida's land. Volume 1: The Heartland (central Florida); Volume 2: Coasts, Glades, and Groves (south Florida); Volume 3: Beaches and Hills (north Florida). (pb)